Constructive Engagement?

Chester Crocker & American Policy
in South Africa, Namibia & Angola
1981–8

D1425198

Constructive Engagement?

Chester Crocker & American Policy
in South Africa, Namibia & Angola
1981–8

J. E. DAVIES

James Currey
OXFORD

Jacana Media
JOHANNESBURG

Ohio University Press
ATHENS

James Currey Ltd
73 Botley Road
Oxford OX2 0BS
www.jamescurrey.co.uk

Jacana Media
10 Orange Street
Auckland Park
2092, South Africa
www.jacana.co.za

Ohio University Press
19 Circle Drive
The Ridges
Athens, Ohio 45701
www.ohio.edu/oupress

Copyright © J. E. Davies 2007
First published 2007

1 2 3 4 5 11 10 09 08 07

British Library Cataloguing in Publication Data
Davies, J. E.
    Constructive Engagement? : Chester Crocker & American
    policy in South Africa, Namibia & Angola, 1981-8
    1. Crocker, Chester A. 2. United States - Foreign relations
    - 1981-1989 3. United States - relations - Angola 5. South
    Africa - Foreign relations - United States 6. South Africa
    - Foreign relations - 1978-1989 7. South Africa - Relations
    - Angola 8. Angola - Relations - United States 9. Angola -
    Relations - South Africa 10. Angola - History - Civil War,
    1975-2002
    I. Title
    327.7'3'068'09048

ISBN 978-1-84701-304-0 (James Currey paper)
ISBN 978-1-84701-305-7 (James Currey cloth)
ISBN 978-1-77009-376-8 (Jacana paper)
ISBN-10 0-8214-1781-9 (Ohio University Press cloth)
ISBN-13 978-0-8214-1781-2 (Ohio University Press cloth)
ISBN-10 0-8214-1782-7 (Ohio University Press paper)
ISBN-13 978-0-8214-1782-9 (Ohio University Press paper)

Library of Congress Cataloging-in-Publication Data
available on request

Typeset in 10/11.5pt Plantin by Long House, Cumbria
Printed and bound in Malaysia

Contents

Acknowledgements

I would like to thank Professor Jack Spence of King's College, London and Professor John Baylis of the Department of Politics and International Relations at the University of Wales Swansea for their help and support. I would also like to thank Alistair Murray, Robert Bideleux and the late Graham Evans.

I would also like to take this opportunity to thank Chester Crocker, Herman Cohen and Donald Rothchild for allowing me the time to discuss the issues of this book with them, and Jeroboam Shaanika of the Namibian High Commission in London for his useful correspondence. I am also very grateful for the financial assistance of the Gareth Jones Memorial Scholarship. I would like to express my gratitude for the assistance of the staff at the Ronald Reagan Presidential Library in California, the staff of the Library of Congress in Washington, DC and the staff at the National Archives in Maryland. Many thanks also go to the librarians at the Oxford Brooks Library and the School of Oriental and African Studies in London. On a personal note, I would like to thank Rhodri, my parents and Nest and John for all their encouragement and support.

List of Acronyms

AALC	African-American Labor Center	HNP	Herstigte Nasionale Party
ANC	African National Congress	IAEA	International Atomic Energy Agency
AWB	Afrikaner Weerstandbeweging	ICJ	International Court of Justice
CAAA	Comprehensive Anti-Apartheid Act	ILSA	Iran Libya Sanctions Act
CIA	Central Intelligence Agency	IMF	International Monetary Fund
CONSTAS	Constellation of States	JEM	Justice and Equality Movement
COSATU	Congress of South African Trade Unions	JMC	Joint Monitoring Commission
CP	Conservative Party	MPLA	Movimento Popular de Libertação de Angola
CSR	Corporate Social Responsibility		
CTW	Cuban Troop Withdrawal	NACTU	National Council of Trade Unions
DTA	Democratic Turnhalle Alliance	NGO	Non-Governmental Organization
EC	European Community	NP	National Party
		NSC	National Security Council
EU	European Union		
EPG	Eminent Persons Group	NSDD	National Security Decision Directive
FCO	Foreign and Commonwealth Office	NSSD	National Security Study Directive
		NSSM	National Security Study Memorandum
FDI	Foreign Direct Investment	OAU	Organization of African Unity
FLS	Front Line States		
FNLA	Frente Nacional de Libertação de Angola	OPC	Ovamboland People's Congress
FSAM	Free South Africa Movement	OPEC	Organization of Petroleum Exporting Countries
GATT	General Agreement on Tariffs and Trade	OPIC	Overseas Private Investment Corporation
GNP	Gross National Product		

OPO	Ovamboland People's Organization	SRI	Socially Responsible Investment
PAC	Pan-African Congress	SWAPO	South West Africa People's Organization
PFP	Progressive Federal Party	SWAPOL	South West Africa Police
SAAF	South African Air Force	UDF	United Democratic Front
SADC	Southern African Development Community	UN	United Nations
		UNITA	União Nacional de Independencia Total de Angola
SADCC	Southern African Development Co-ordination Conference	UNSCR	United Nations Security Council Resolution
SADF	South African Defence Force	UNTAG	United Nations Transition Assistance Group
SAG	South African Government	UPA	União das Populacoes de Angola
SASOL	South African Oil and Gas Corporation	US	United States
SAWG	Special Working Group on South and Southern Africa	USAID	United States Agency for International Development
SLM/A	Sudanese Liberation Movement/Army		
SPLA	Sudan People's Liberation Army	WTO	World Trade Organization

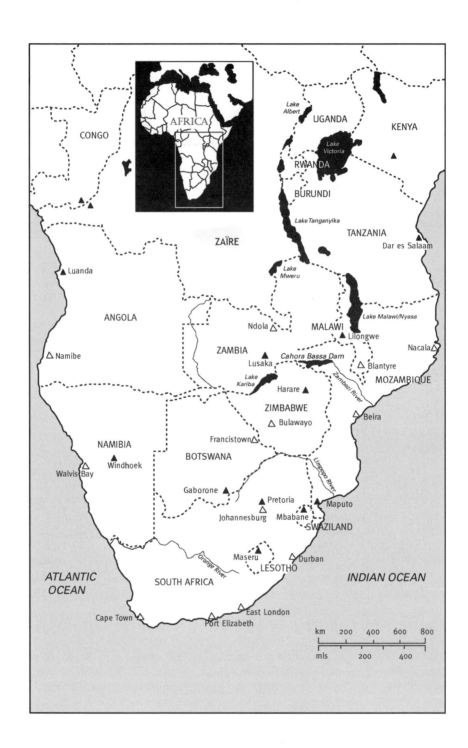

Southern Africa 1986

Introduction

The notion of engagement underlies the history of diplomacy – and as such represents the most important tool in a foreign policy practitioner's armoury. Today, improved communications are allowing the citizens of democratic nations to see the real nature of the states with which their governments necessarily engage, including those with dire records concerning the human rights of their own citizens. The idea of 'constructive engagement' is advanced by governments as a method whereby pressure can be brought to bear on these countries to improve their record on human rights, while diplomatic and economic contacts can be maintained. To determine what this concept entails, and how likely it is that such an approach can achieve positive outcomes, this book offers a critical evaluation of one of the best-known examples of constructive engagement – the Reagan administration's engagement of South Africa from 1981 to 1988.

Dr Chester Crocker was appointed as Reagan's Assistant Secretary of State for African Affairs in 1981. Before his appointment, he had published 'South Africa: Strategy for Change',[1] an article in which he outlined his favoured policy of 'constructive engagement' towards the governments of the southern African region – and Pretoria in particular. Crocker maintained that unvarying hostile rhetoric levelled at the apartheid regime in South Africa only served to increase Pretoria's mistrust and dislike of Washington. Instead of increasing America's influence over Pretoria's decisions, he asserted, this approach merely hardened Pretoria's intransigence and made the South African government more hostile towards the idea of a gradual dismantling of the apartheid regime. This, he believed, is what had happened during the Carter administration from 1976 to 1980. Constructive engagement would involve an open dialogue with Pretoria, together with a reduction of counterproductive punitive measures such as certain export restrictions. In this way, Washington could maintain a friendly relationship with the South African government – which was important for American geostrategic and economic/trading interests – while gaining the confidence of Pretoria and thus enabling Washington to influence South Africa towards a gradual change away from apartheid.

As well as his intention to address the apartheid situation within South

Constructive Engagement?

Africa, Crocker also stressed the equally important *regional* dimension of his policy. His particular focus was on the issues facing neighbouring Namibia (at that time illegally occupied by South Africa) and the civil war (with the presence of Cuban troops) in Angola. He began by outlining his proposals towards the region, couched in the terms of constructive engagement. In what became known as his 'linkage' strategy, Crocker proposed a formal link between the granting of Namibian independence, under United Nations Security Council Resolution 435 (1978), and the total withdrawal of Cuban troops from Angola. He presented his constructive engagement policy as an approach that encompassed and benefited both the regional issues of Cuban troop withdrawal and Namibian independence, and the difficulties inherent in South Africa's internal situation.

This book aims to determine how successful Crocker's constructive engagement policy was in South Africa, Namibia and Angola between 1981 and 1988. There are four key questions which the following chapters will address: What was the conceptual basis of Crocker's policy? What were his implicit and explicit aims – both within South Africa and in regard to the situations in Namibia and Angola? What was the impact of the implementation struggles on constructive engagement? The analysis involved in these first three questions will lay the basis for the discussion of the fourth question: What were the results of Crocker's policies – as measured against his aims? Finally, the conclusions reached by this critical evaluation of Crocker's policy will be examined, to determine what they have to tell us about the current applications of 'constructive engagement' as a tool of foreign policy.

The first of these subsidiary questions involves understanding the reasoning behind Crocker's policy – what were its conceptual underpinnings? Constructive engagement must be understood in the context of the East–West struggle and the emerging influence of the anti-communist Reagan Doctrine in United States' foreign policy. The views of President Reagan himself reflected an era of reignited Cold War tension – particularly during Reagan's first term in office. Crocker struggled to reconcile both regionalist and globalist perspectives in his policy, and this had an important impact on its development. The initial task of this work is to identify this conceptual base, and to evaluate the results of these competing regionalist and globalist agendas.

The next question asks – just what was it that Crocker hoped to achieve? This will involve distinguishing between his *explicit* and *implicit* goals. An important source is Crocker's own 'South Africa: Strategy for Change' article, in which he set out the aims of constructive engagement before he had taken office. Within this article, he focused mainly on South Africa's internal situation and the dilemma that Pretoria's apartheid policies were causing for Washington's policy makers. Constructive engagement was presented as an approach which could help to influence Pretoria away from the system of apartheid. He also stated that he wanted this constructive engagement approach to achieve a situation whereby the US could continue its (profitable) relationship with South Africa 'without constraint, embarrassment or political damage'.[2] But had Crocker determined what priority was accorded to this aim in relation to the other stated aim of dismantling apartheid? If Pretoria was to prove intransigent, would pressure against apartheid be maintained, despite the risk that this could pose to the preservation of a positive US–South Africa relationship? This work will discuss whether an implicit agenda placed the emphasis on the acceptable *appearance* of these actions rather than, as Crocker claimed, the *substance* of actually helping to bring apartheid to an end. This question of a potential implicit agenda within constructive engagement also extends to his regional policy – and his involvement in the Namibian/ Angolan settlement. This will involve determining what Crocker's regional agenda was – and unravelling the relationships between his motives there.

The third question involves an evaluation of the implementation of constructive engagement. Regardless of the conceptual underpinnings of his policy, his implicit agendas and explicit goals, Crocker also faced a number of factors during the implementation of his policy that altered the course of constructive engagement – often in spite of his own aims. The question of implementation will involve an investigation of how direct the links were between his policies and America's actions regarding South Africa. This includes consideration of the various factors that either had a strong influence on his formulation of policy, or simply served to undermine what he set out to do. These factors will be assessed to determine the extent to which they impacted upon the development and implementation of constructive engagement – and the ways in which they affected the final outcomes.

These questions are designed to provide the basis for the fourth and key question – the assessment of the results of constructive engagement. This will involve a discussion of what Crocker and his policy contributed to the situation inside South Africa and will assess how far this policy went in addressing the interests of both the white government in South Africa and the black opposition. It will also discuss the extent to which the constructive engagement approach succeeded in influencing the actions of Pretoria.

Yet this work must go a stage further in its evaluation of results. The second key question posed the possibility of an implicit agenda behind Crocker's aims. An important task, therefore, will be to determine if the dismantling of apartheid really was his primary aim within South Africa, or whether a Cold War agenda undermined this aim. This analysis takes the present work beyond an evaluation of constructive engagement within South Africa and investigates its efficacy as an exercise in US strategy. This study also questions Crocker's implicit agenda in the regional context, and evaluates how successful his policies were in achieving his regional aims, particularly a reduction of Soviet influence in the region. The concluding chapter carries these findings on to a current context and asks – what is there to be learnt from Crocker's experience in southern Africa? How do these lessons impact upon current examples of constructive engagement?

In the process of addressing the questions identified above, a number of themes emerge. The discussion of Crocker's agenda raises the theme of constructive engagement as an exercise in *realpolitik*. Although constructive engagement was presented as a policy designed to address regional, as well as global, goals, one can question the notion that constructive engagement ever went beyond a strategy of the pursuit of national interest. Clearly, national interest was the guiding principle of constructive engagement – as it is in all foreign policy. What this theme highlights, however, is the extent to which constructive engagement went beyond this pursuit of *realpolitik* and national interest by addressing the interests of, and issues raised by, other governments and actors in the region.

The notion of internal and external forces impacting upon the formulation and implementation of policy, as discussed in the third question on policy implementation, results in two further themes that occur throughout this work. The theme of bureaucratic infighting becomes a question of just how much control any foreign policy practitioner actually has over the development and results of his own policy. Crocker was forced to fight tenaciously within the administration to maintain his hold over the implementation of his own policy. In fact, he was not always successful – the discussion regarding American funding of the Angolan resistance group UNITA in Chapter 9 provides the clearest example of this.

The final theme concerns the influence of commercial and business interests on the aims of foreign policy, and has a very real relevance for policy makers today. Economic interests remain a critical factor in the determination of foreign policy, particularly as the international economy becomes ever more interdependent and the performances of national economies are increasingly influenced by decisions taken by other governments and multinational corporations. Throughout this study, one sees the way in which business decisions can undermine what a government is trying to achieve. This is apparent in Crocker's attempts to maintain strong and constructive business links with South Africa's struggling economy, whilst commercial pressures were forcing companies to withdraw. On the other hand, this commercial and business influence, independent of government guidance or control, was also apparent in the conflicting situation inside Angola. American companies maintained their profitable links with the MPLA regime *despite* opposition from the US government. In South Africa, too, the business community was instrumental in generating pressure for change, because Pretoria's apartheid policies did not suit their commercial interests. The significance of this theme, therefore, is that business activity in southern Africa crossed national boundaries, and crossed the lines of national interests as defined by the governments involved. By remaining in Angola, and withdrawing from South Africa, American business was to prove a major obstacle for Crocker in the implementation of his constructive engagement policy.

The Historical Context

America and the Cold War

Throughout this work, one cannot underestimate the overarching significance of one particular issue in American foreign policy – the Cold War.[3] While both superpowers fought hard to gain and preserve influence in the newly decolonising Third World, neither power found this task an easy one. The strong American tradition of anti-imperialism was called into question as anti-communism became the prevailing mantra in US foreign policy circles. If the status quo was to be preserved, or a brutal regime to be protected, in order to prevent the spread of communism, then the end was seen to justify the means. Bruce Jentleson identifies this as the 'ABC' approach to foreign relations – Anything But Communism. The more belligerent the United States became regarding this policy, the more it was reflected in myopic foreign policy decisions. The examples of the CIA helping to train the Shah's 'SAVAK' (Secret Police) in Iran – a 'hated instrument of domestic repression' – and the US support of dictatorships such as Emperor Bao Dai in Vietnam and the Samozas in Nicaragua serve to illustrate this 'ABC' approach, supporting regimes with no virtue other than their anti-communism. The fact that America was attempting to promote Western-style democracy and capitalism also caused it difficulty in winning allies. Recently independent states, newly liberated from decades of Western imperialism, were inclined to reject anything that seemed to turn back the clock on their hard-won independence. The Soviets soon sought to capitalize on this implicit – and often explicit – anti-Western perspective. Yet engaging with the Third World caused the Soviets many problems of their own.

It is hard to quantify what the Soviets actually achieved from their Third World adventurism. The example of their experiences in both Egypt and India, where many years of Soviet support did not prevent criticism of Soviet action, or persecution of domestic communists, calls into question what permanent benefits the Soviet Union actually gained. There was also considerable internal debate on how involvement in the Third World should proceed. The question was whether to follow Lenin's approach of support-ing all anti-imperialist movements (regardless of whether or not they were communists) in order to undermine international capitalism, or to follow Stalin in only supporting proven communists. Khrushchev followed firmly in the path of Lenin, exploiting anti-imperialism and becoming increasingly involved in Third World issues. Yet Khrushchev had to remain careful to avoid the accusation that he was abandoning the socialist struggle – a very potent accusation during the Sino-Soviet split in the late 1950s.

Both superpowers discovered the limits of their influence in their Third World adventurism. Even considerable investment of time, money, supplies and training could not guarantee them stable allies. The fact that many of the governments of these newly independent states were themselves very weak also meant that much investment in cultivating a friendship could be undone overnight by a coup or change of government. Both powers were dealing with a multitude of competing agendas in these regions. One of their main obstacles was their insistence on seeing the world in Cold War terms. By viewing these diverse regions almost solely from an East–West perspective, both sides failed to recognize the many domestic and internal aims and beliefs of the very countries they aimed to convert.

The gradual lateral expansion of the Cold War began to take on a momentum of its own, leading to 'indiscriminate global involvement'. Whether protecting liberty and democracy, or capitalism and their own markets, the United States certainly achieved global reach. One commentator described the situation in 1970 thus:

> The United States has over 1 million soldiers in 30 countries, is a member of 4 regional defence alliances and an active participant in a fifth, has mutual defence treaties with 42 nations, is a member of 53 international organizations and provides military and economic aid to nearly 100 nations across the face of the globe.[4]

The extent to which the Cold War affected the foreign policies of the once-isolationist United States was remarkable and, as we shall see when considering their activities in southern Africa, formed a vital and significant context for the foreign policy of successive administrations throughout the second half of the twentieth century.

The formation of Crocker's constructive engagement policy was inextricably linked to Cold War calculations. As was witnessed throughout the developing world, Cold War imperatives sat uncomfortably with a welter of complex regional realities – sometimes attempting to co-opt these regional goals, sometimes 'overlaying' them – so that the regional goals were no longer visible under the blanket of the global East–West conflict. When Crocker was appointed Assistant Secretary of State for African Affairs in 1981 he faced just this dilemma – how to combine the globalist goals of the Reagan administration with the numerous and complex regional realities to be found in the history of the southern African region.

South Africa and apartheid

When Malan's National Party triumphed over Jan Smuts's United Party in 1948, the result was the first exclusively Afrikaner cabinet in South Africa. From this point on, the interests of the Afrikaners assumed priority for the South African government. One of the initial concerns of the new government centred on the fact that the Afrikaners had not yet been able to determine a relationship between themselves and other South Africans – English-speaking whites or blacks. This resulted in the dual goals of severing ties with Britain by becoming a Republic, and the separation of the races through apartheid. In post-war South Africa, there was still a good deal of division over the Republican question. Apartheid, on the other hand, raised few problems within the Afrikaner community and from 1948 the government began to increase its control of the social order in the interests of white domination 'by a monopoly of the constitutional means of change'.[5]

The Prohibition of Mixed Marriages Act 1949 and the Immorality Amendment Act 1950, reaffirming the prohibition of interracial sexual relations, were designed to build upon the belief that the Afrikaner race should be kept 'pure'. This was followed by the Population Registration Act – which resulted in a racially classified national register that Malan viewed as the whole basis of apartheid. The realization of apartheid followed shortly afterwards with the Group Areas Act 1950, which developed the land apportionment principle of the black reserves or 'homelands' across the whole of South Africa, including its urban areas. This is when large-scale resettlement of the races became a reality, and as such the Group Areas Act was described by Malan as the essence of apartheid. The Bantu Education Act of 1953 and the 1959 Promotion of Bantu Self-Government Act were added to the above, forming the six constitutional pillars of apartheid. Prime Minister Verwoerd explained that the ultimate goal of 'self-government' would be to make blacks citizens of their own 'independent' homelands, and therefore legitimize the government's denial of the franchise to blacks, as they would no longer be citizens of South Africa. Verwoerd's plans began to come to fruition in the mid-1960s. In 1963 the Transkei was the first 'Bantustan' (or 'homeland') to receive limited self-government. Washington, under Kennedy and then Johnson, joined the rest of the international community in refusing to recognize the validity of these independent homelands. This stance was maintained under the subsequent administrations in Washington, including Reagan's.

As, diligently, the bricks of apartheid were being laid, life in the Afrikaner community was improving rapidly. Large parastatal companies and investment programmes were being established by the government as a way of ensuring Afrikaner employment. Afrikaners were given precedence in promotions and appointments to public bodies and government contracts were awarded to Afrikaner companies. The pressures caused by this increasing dichotomy between the fortunes of black and white soon began to show. From the early 1940s a more radical mood had begun to develop among the growing opposition groups, led by the African National Congress (ANC).

The ANC had begun as the South African Native National Congress in 1912 and had grown to become the main voice of black opposition to apartheid. The more hardline Robert Sobukwe broke from the ANC in November 1958 and by March 1959 he had established the Pan-African Congress (PAC). This was a more 'Africanist' movement – concerned with black rights and opposed to cooperation across racial lines. The scale of protest began to escalate as both the ANC and the PAC attempted to prove themselves as the most effective black opposition group. On 21 March 1960 the PAC organized a huge demonstration against Pass Laws and 20,000 protesters took to the streets. Although the protest was a peaceful one, the police panicked and shot dead 69 people, injuring a further 180. The repercussions were profound. On the day of the funerals, blacks did not go to work. The outcry from the rest of the world was immediate, followed by large-scale disinvestments and capital flight. On 28 March both the ANC and the PAC were banned and 18,000 people were arrested. A state of emergency was declared and the ensuing 'massive wave of repression silenced black opposition for a generation'.[6] What political activity there was was driven underground and began to develop a more radical outlook in response to the brutal repression it was suffering. By 1961, Nelson Mandela and most of the ANC leadership began to lose hope for peace and in August they chose no longer to restrict themselves to non-violent protest. In November the ANC's armed wing, *Umkhonto we Sizwe* – 'Spear of the Nation' – was established.

Meanwhile, as political control remained tight, developments in the economy began to pull in the opposite direction. The 1960s had witnessed an economic boom, which had exposed South Africa's serious lack of skilled labour. As Oppenheimer, the Chairman of the giant Anglo-American Corporation, explained, 'racial discrimination and free enterprise are basically incompatible and failure to eradicate the one will ultimately result in the destruction of the other'.[7] The end of the 1960s saw South Africa fall victim to a global recession. The whole country suffered as the severe economic recession continued to deepen throughout the late 1970s.

When Nixon became President in 1969, he recognized a strong trend in policy circles towards disengagement, caused largely by events in Vietnam. Although unable to reverse this trend entirely, Nixon did want the US to have a leadership role in the world. His administration undertook a series of reviews of foreign policy in different regions. Nixon's policy towards the southern African region was formalized in National Security Study Memorandum number 39 (1969). This review presented Washington's policy makers with five options in dealing with the region, ranging from closer cooperation with the whites to total disengagement. Nixon chose to follow 'Option 2', which assumed that the whites were there to stay in southern Africa. The best way forward, therefore, would be to communicate with the whites and relax punitive sanctions. The belief was that isolation of South Africa only intensified repression there. However, Pretoria's significance as an ally against communist expansion in the region also played an important part in these policy calculations. Although public opposition to racial policies would continue, political isolation and economic restrictions would be reduced. By 1970 some of the bans on sales of arms to South Africa had been lifted, as had some Eximbank loan restrictions. The problem was that Option 2's stated aim was to create conditions whereby blacks and whites could work together to develop their own solution to South Africa's problems, whilst avoiding a radical upheaval (which would be detrimental to America's economic and strategic interests) and a possible bloodbath. Yet blacks had no channel of communication to make such a solution possible.

Many of Nixon's 'Option 2' decisions appear to provide a clear basis for Crocker's own policy, especially a relaxation of punitive sanctions, and communication with white regimes. When confronted with the idea that his policy was a direct descendant of Nixon's, however, Crocker maintains that the two were different, mainly because they were dealing with a very different regional situation. This was because, until 1974, white governments still ruled in Mozambique, Angola and Zimbabwe, and the Portuguese coup had not yet taken place. It is also important to note that Nixon did not advocate *public* engagement with Pretoria.

It was at this time that a new generation of black opposition began to mobilize in South Africa. This generation had known only Bantu education and had witnessed increasing repression. The simmering tension came to a head on the morning of 16 June 1976. A huge number of young students marched through Soweto to protest at the enforced teaching of Afrikaans in their schools. One policeman opened fire, killing a 13-year-old boy. A riot broke out, followed by four days of running battles. By the end of the week the official death toll was 176, with 1,800 injured. The violence spread to other parts of the country, and continued for many months. Within a year the death toll had reached 575, with 4,000 wounded. Although the killings filled both the white South African and the international communities with profound shock, the student movement itself lacked direction. The momentum began to falter from September onwards as more of the student leaders were arrested, wounded or killed.

The scale of the violence had shaken Afrikaners particularly, making it harder for them to turn a blind eye to the plight of 'their blacks'. The government pledged to improve conditions, for example by providing all of Soweto with electricity, yet the fundamental structure of apartheid remained in place. Meanwhile, the Afrikaner community had developed its own affluent and more open-minded middle class, and the attitudes of some were starting to change. The fear of blacks which had been rife in the job-scarce years of the depression was receding for some members of the classes that felt secure in their own wealth. And waiting in the wings of this political stage was P. W. Botha, a reformer when judged by the standards set by Vorster. Botha's opportunity soon came to pass in the form of the 'Muldergate' scandal of 1978.[8] In 1978, with the resignation of Vorster and his heir-apparent, Connie Mulder, P. W. Botha became Prime Minister of South Africa.

In Washington, the advent of Carter as President in 1977 initially signalled a dramatic change in US African policy. His Secretary of State, Cyrus Vance, made it clear that the new administration would seek to replace the previous 'negative, reactive American policy that seeks only to oppose Soviet or Cuban movement in Africa'. With regard to the apartheid issue, Carter promised 'unequivocal and concrete support for majority rule in South Africa'[9] as part of an overall aim to put the United States more 'in step' with black aspirations at home and abroad. Carter's stance led to a marked improvement in American relations with many black African countries. A number of measures were taken in line with Carter's accommodative stance towards black Africa: nuclear cooperation with South Africa was suspended, unless it agreed to sign the Nuclear Non-Proliferation Treaty; official sports contacts were curtailed; some bank loans and credit facilities were withdrawn; and the voluntary arms embargo was tightened. Yet despite this apparently hardline stance towards

Pretoria, links between the two countries did remain and the US continued to oppose mandatory economic sanctions, saying business links could be used to promote change in South Africa.

Concern over Soviet activities in Angola and the Middle East led to a hardening of American attitudes. The shift was also due in large part to changes within the administration. Carter's National Security Adviser, Zbigniew Brzezinski, was most instrumental in bringing about a change in policy direction. His conservative, globalist views were increasingly influential, particularly after the departure of two prominent regionalists – Ambassador to the United Nations Andrew Young and Secretary of State Cyrus Vance – from the administration. In the last two years of his presidency, Carter paid less attention to African issues and African perspectives. Relations between the United States and South Africa continued in this unresolved, largely hostile manner until the appointment of Ronald Reagan as President at the beginning of 1981.

South West Africa/Namibia [10]

During the period of Pretoria's consolidation of apartheid within South Africa, the government had also begun to assert itself in the regional sphere. Particularly vulnerable to this display of power was South Africa's northern neighbour – Namibia. In 1884 a German protectorate was established over the coastal regions of South West Africa (excluding Walvis Bay, annexed by Britain in 1878) and the German settlers claimed the territory as their own. After Germany's defeat in the First World War, it was agreed that South Africa, acting on behalf of Britain, would be responsible for South West Africa under a League of Nations Class C mandate. The mandate came into effect on 1 January 1921. Class C mandates covered the least developed of the colonies and, in view of its geographical proximity, it was agreed that South West Africa could be governed under the laws of the mandatory (South Africa) as an integral part of its territory. The mandate system had been established in Article 22 of the League of Nations Covenant. It specified that, for those countries and peoples being covered by a mandate,

> the well-being and development of such peoples form a sacred trust of civilization ... the tutelage of such peoples should be entrusted to advanced nations ... [but] ... will guarantee freedom of conscience and religion, subject only to the maintenance of public order and morals....[11]

The end of the Second World War saw the League being replaced by the United Nations (UN). Pretoria saw this as an opportunity to put forward its case for the full incorporation of South West Africa into South Africa. On 14 December 1946 the UN General Assembly rejected South Africa's request, and ruled that South West Africa be placed under the UN's newly established International Trusteeship System. South Africa was the only mandatory to refuse to submit its mandate to this system. It refused to accept the UN as a successor to the League and argued that it was an entirely separate organization. Washington had previously enjoyed good relations with South Africa under Smuts's moderate United Party and it refrained from condemning South Africa as it was still 'too early to see how this issue would develop'. Neither did Washington wish to draw attention to its own emerging civil rights dilemmas. However, the State Department did publicly oppose South Africa's plan to incorporate South West Africa. In the 1948 South African election, Smuts's United Party was defeated by Malan's National Party. This further damaged relations with Washington and the rest of the international community. By 1949 the annual reports that South Africa had been required to submit under the League Mandate for South West Africa ceased. In the same year, legislation was passed which decreed that South West Africa was to have six elected representatives in South Africa's House of Assembly and four in the Senate. The *de facto* incorporation had begun.

Faced with South African intransigence, the UN turned to the International Court of Justice (ICJ) to ask what could be done. Its ruling, delivered on 11 July 1950, stated that the League mandate was still in force, but that South Africa had no legal obligation to place the territory under the Trusteeship system. In June 1960, in a move commended by the UN's General Assembly, Liberia and Ethiopia announced they would instigate legal proceedings at the ICJ, accusing South Africa of modifying the terms of the mandate without UN consent. It took until 18 July 1966 for the Court to deliver its eagerly awaited ruling. When the Court announced that, in fact, it had no power to rule on the substance of the case because Liberia and Ethiopia had 'no special right or interest' in bringing the case, the international community's reaction was one of shock. The response from the General Assembly was to terminate South Africa's mandate and decree that South Africa had no other right to administer the territory. The United Nations Council for South West Africa was established to administer the territory. However, South Africa refused to allow its representatives admittance to the territory and, without any form of sanction to support it, the UN's termination of the mandate remained, in effect, an impotent gesture. All that was needed was 'a relaxation of pressure from the outside world for South Africa to extend apartheid to Namibia. The 1966 ICJ ruling signalled that reduction.'[12]

In Washington, the increasingly urgent demands of the Cold War meant that good relations with the anti-communist government in South Africa outweighed the potential drawbacks of associating with the apartheid regime. Southern African concerns remained low on the list of America's priorities. Although Washington remained unhappy with South Africa's occupation of Namibia, it was decided that the global struggle against communism had to take priority over the regional struggles in southern Africa.

By 1970 the UN Security Council accepted the termination of South Africa's mandate and declared that all states should cease to recognize South Africa in Namibia – which meant precluding trade and treaty arrangements. In January 1971 the ICJ was asked once again what the legal implications of this would be. In June 1971 its opinion was delivered: South Africa's occupation of Namibia was illegal and they should withdraw, and UN member states were obliged to refrain from any acts implying otherwise. This change in the ICJ's ruling reflected a shift in the attitudes of the international community, but still, no concrete action was taken to enforce this ruling. It was clear soon after the ICJ's 1971 ruling that the Security Council was reluctant to act. Resolutions passed in December 1974 and January 1976, calling for mandatory sanctions against South Africa, were vetoed on both occasions by the United States, Great Britain and France. During this time South Africa was developing its own 'internal settlement' within Namibia.[13] Washington under Nixon continued follow the 'Option Two' policy in southern Africa during this time. The priority given to dealing with the white governments of the region was maintained, particularly in the face of the relative importance African concerns held when compared with the calculations of the Cold War.

Among the Namibians themselves, these constant examples of the international community's inability or unwillingness to act had a profound effect. In 1958 Namibian migrant workers based in Cape Town founded an organization called the Ovamboland People's Congress (OPC) under Andimba Ja Toivo. Originally campaigning against the conditions of migrant workers, its goals were soon widened to include the whole issue of South Africa in Namibia. On 19 April 1959 the OPC became the Ovamboland People's Organization (OPO) under Sam Nujoma – campaigning both for workers' rights and full independence for Namibia. In June 1960 the organization began to broaden its appeal across Namibia, and became the South West Africa People's Organization (SWAPO). By 1965 the Organization of African Unity (OAU – established in 1963) decided to provide SWAPO with financial assistance. Since 1962 SWAPO had been preparing for an armed struggle and the turning point came with the ICJ's 1966 ruling. This made SWAPO realize that it could not rely on the international community and a short firefight between SWAPO and the South West Africa Police (SWAPOL) on 26 August 1966 signalled that the armed struggle had begun.[14] Between 1973 and 1975 a series of trials of the SWAPO Youth League took place and the number of activists fell as they were either incarcerated or fled. Sabotage activities increased during the 1970s and offices established in Zambia and London helped to organize SWAPO activities. SWAPO also campaigned at the OAU and the UN. In 1976 the UN recognized SWAPO as the 'legitimate representative of Namibia'. Washington remained extremely suspicious of SWAPO – and its Marxist links in particular. This hostile relationship was to continue until independence in 1990.

Meanwhile, during the early months of 1977 five Western nations – Britain, the US, France, West Germany and Canada (all members of the Security Council at the time) – were attempting to facilitate a settlement themselves. Known as the 'Contact Group of Western Nations', they arranged separate negotiations with South Africa and SWAPO. UN Secretary General Waldheim's proposals, based on reports of the negotiations, were accepted by the Security Council in September, and formalized as UN Security Council Resolution 435 (UNSCR 435). From that point

UNSCR 435 formed the basis of UN plans for Namibia. However, the Contact Group suspected South Africa of trying to stall the negotiations. A brutal example was the attack in May 1978 on a Namibian refugee camp in Kassinga, Angola, just as SWAPO was about to agree arrangements with the Contact Group on independence. Yet when, in April 1981, four Security Council resolutions were proposed regarding sanctions and an oil embargo on South Africa, partly in retaliation for its intransigence on the Namibian issue, the resolutions were vetoed by Britain, France and the United States.[15] Despite continued condemnation of South Africa's occupation of Namibia, the Western members of the Security Council still refused to act decisively to persuade South Africa to alter its behaviour. While these developments were taking place in Namibia, an important change was taking place in the region. These power shifts were soon to be inextricably linked to Namibia's own future by events across its northern border in Angola.

Angola – the international dimension

By 1920 the Portuguese had established military control over Angola. The late 1940s saw the beginning of anti-colonial protest there and two nationalist resistance movements were formed in the 1950s. The Movimento Popular de Libertação de Angola (or People's Movement for the Liberation of Angola – MPLA) was established in 1958 and was led from 1962 by Dr Antonio Neto. The União das Populacoes de Angola (UPA) began as a northern Angolan movement, but broadened its scope under its leader Holden Roberto, and began to campaign for the independence of all Angola. The UPA then merged with other small nationalist groups to become the Frente Nacional de Libertação de Angola (or Angolan National Liberation Front – FNLA). Both the MPLA and FNLA were receiving external support from the early 1960s. The Kennedy administration had been funding the UPA and then the FNLA from 1961. Roberto also approached China, from whom he received military aid.[16] An increase in aid and military material from the Soviet Union and Eastern European countries, coupled with an influx of Cuban trainers to establish an MPLA training base in Brazzaville, meant a significant increase in MPLA military ability.

The beginning of the 1970s saw a continued growth of MPLA influence. Whilst still recognizing the FNLA, in 1971 the OAU chose to extend recognition to the MPLA. By 1966 an associate of Roberto's, Jonas Savimbi, had begun to develop his own constituency, based on the notion that: 'Only the Angolan people within the country is capable of freeing itself from foreign domination.'[17] He criticized the opposing liberation movements for their dependence on outside help, explaining that it was vital to avoid a direct or indirect confrontation of the great powers on Angolan soil. It was with these aims that, in March 1966, the União Nacional de Independencia Total de Angola (or National Union for the Total Independence of Angola – UNITA) was born.

By the early 1970s the cost to Portugal of preserving its hold over its African colonies had exceeded 50 per cent of the national budget, and resentment within Portugal itself was rising. The discontent was vented in the form of a coup on 25 April 1974. The new administration, headed by General Spinola, soon made it clear that it favoured the independence of the colonies and, with this, the end of the draining colonial wars. The news of the coup, and forthcoming independence, eventually led to all three nationalist movements signing a ceasefire. At a conference in Kenya in January 1975 they signed the 'Alvor Agreement'. This allowed for a transitional government to be inaugurated on 31 January 1975, to govern until November, when independence would finally be realized. Unfortunately, without a genuine consensus on the agreed rules or an authoritative body to enforce them, the exercise was destined to fail. The nationalist movements, who from their inception had been illegal guerrilla groups, were not accustomed to abiding by legal provisions or agreed rules.[18] The skeleton police force left by the Portuguese was too weak to maintain order. Within days of the inauguration of the transitional government, the MPLA/FNLA conflict had resumed. By mid-August all three movements had resorted to nationwide fighting and levels of international support played a significant role. China and the United States were supporters of both the FNLA and UNITA, while Russian aid and Cuban forces were providing support to the MPLA.

After the coup, even as the Alvor Agreement was being signed, the political solution was already being undermined by outside interference. Kissinger did not want to accept the possibility of a settlement where the MPLA would be included in the Angolan government. In 1975 two CIA-orchestrated offensives took place against the MPLA, but by the end of that year Cuban involvement had already begun to tip the balance in the MPLA's favour. While the American public was still trying to come to terms with events in Vietnam, Washington had committed $32 million in aid and $16 million in arms to the FNLA. The CIA had also trained FNLA troops and hired mercenaries to assist them. There had been no official admission of US complicity in Angola but, in December 1975, reports in the press disclosed that Washington was supplying arms to the FNLA.

That same month Senator Tunney introduced an amendment to the Defense Appropriations Bill eliminating any funds requested for activity involving Angola directly. This was passed by both Houses, as was Senator Clark's amendment to the Security Assistance Bill. This did not ban military activity in Angola completely, but meant that the President would have to request permission from Congress to allow it. The Bill was passed and Ford and Kissinger's hands were effectively tied regarding the issue of involvement in Angola. Military superiority was now increasingly on the side of the MPLA, and international support for the FNLA and UNITA, particularly from other African nations, was waning in the light of revelations that UNITA had been receiving support from South Africa. Yet fierce resistance continued throughout Angola from Savimbi's UNITA. Carter's Angolan policy, too, became a casualty of the Carter administration's shift to the right under Brzezinski (see above). Brzezinski, like Kissinger, saw the MPLA victory as a Soviet gain, and the remaining

Cuban presence in Angola had a symbolic significance for the globalist camp in Washington. It was under this influence that Carter decided not to extend diplomatic recognition to the MPLA government.

There has been much debate regarding the role played by the Soviet Union in the Cuban intervention in Angola, with the Cubans maintaining that their decision to intervene was taken as a sovereign state and not at the behest of Moscow. Cuban and MPLA links go back to initial contact with Che Guevara when he was fighting in the Congo in 1965. In 1966 Neto met Fidel Castro and the ties were strengthened. On 25 March 1975, Zaïrian troops entered Angola to proclaim the FNLA's Holden Roberto as President. (Roberto, incidentally, was the brother-in-law of President Mobutu of Zaïre.) It was also publicly acknowledged that the CIA was funding FNLA and that South Africa was sending arms and instructors to UNITA. By September South African troops had also invaded Angolan territory. In a 1976 speech Castro himself pointed out:

> At that time there wasn't a single Cuban instructor in Angola. The first material aid and the first Cuban instructors reached Angola at the beginning of October, at the request of the MPLA.[19]

The Zaïrians and South Africans, together with UNITA and the FNLA, continued to advance on the MPLA's stronghold in Luanda. The MPLA sent an urgent request to Cuba for troops. On 5 November 1975, Cuba took the 'sovereign decision' to send troops and began to despatch between 10,000 and 20,000 troops to Angola.[20] Marquez states that the Soviets were informed *after* the decision had been taken. The intervention, codenamed 'Operation Carlota', got off to a bad start with many Cuban losses in December. By January, however, the number of Cuban forces had steadily increased and, by March, South African troops had suffered a rout and begun a rapid retreat. By the end of March the South Africans had left Angolan soil.

On 14 March, Castro and Neto agreed a troop withdrawal schedule at Conakry, Guinea. Cuba agreed to a gradual withdrawal, and vowed to keep troops in Angola until the MPLA government felt it could adequately defend itself. In fact, the United States continued to fund UNITA and the South Africans continued to invade Angola, under the pretext of the pursuit of Namibian guerrillas. South Africa began its destabilization campaign in Angola within a week of the MPLA's victory, and between April and July 1976 launched 17 raids into Angola from Namibia. The Cubans had promised to remain while external powers still attempted to undermine the government. At the end of 1976 there were only 1,400 Cubans left in Angola, but by 1979 this number had increased to 19,000 and reached 23,000 by 1981. This was in direct response to the escalating destabilization perpetrated by South Africa.

This brief account of the region's historical background has illustrated the problems that the region was facing when Crocker assumed office in 1981. It was these issues that his policy would have to address, albeit in the context of the pursuit of American interests and under the umbrella of the Cold War. At the beginning of the 1980s, US policy makers were faced with an intransigent South Africa, an occupied Namibia and a situation developing in Angola that appeared to favour the Soviet Union.

Methodology

This book undertakes what is essentially an historical analysis of Crocker's actions, which is broadly sufficient to achieve the objectives listed above. However, this work is also informed by conclusions drawn from foreign policy analysis – particularly the 'bureaucratic politics' approach.[21] This is because the reader should be aware that foreign policy is something other than simply goal-oriented – other factors impact upon it to affect the resulting policy. Also, although accounts of foreign policy attempt to explain foreign policy *decisions*, all too often the analysis stops there. One must proceed to investigate the *implementation* of a policy if one wants to understand foreign policy behaviour. This implementation perspective is not a theory in itself, but it is a necessary development of the bureaucratic politics approach. With regard to the key questions in this book, this approach is important in understanding which goals were formulated by Crocker himself, and which were imposed upon his policy by the competing agendas within the Reagan administration. To what extent were Crocker's aims distorted by Reagan's White House Director of Communications, Patrick Buchanan, or by CIA Director William Casey? To what extent was he undermined by the machinations of Congress? It is argued here that these competing agendas had a significant and negative impact on Crocker's policy – in particular the climactic year of 1986 in which Congressional sanctions were imposed *and* American funding of UNITA was resumed – both decisions going specifically against Crocker's wishes.

Although the arrangement of material within each chapter is largely chronological, a thematic approach is used throughout the book as a whole. This approach was chosen in order to distinguish between Crocker's policies towards the domestic situation inside South Africa itself (Part I) and his regional approach towards the situations in Angola and Namibia (Part II). This was necessary because much of the available literature tends to treat these two policies together, which can detract from separate evaluations of the results of each of the above areas. Within the context of both of these sections, this study will endeavour to address the four key questions that have been raised above. Part III then discusses the conclusions reached.

Part I will focus on Crocker's policy towards South Africa's internal situation. The first chapter explores the conceptual basis and the goals behind Crocker's constructive engagement policy with regard to apartheid in South Africa. It examines the agenda behind the American approach, and it will discuss the possibility of competing 'explicit' and 'implicit' aims behind the policy's formulation. Chapter 2 will discuss the economic aspects of constructive engagement with South Africa and will explore the divisions in Washington with regard to the imposition of economic sanctions against Pretoria. Chapter 3 identifies the remaining debates this policy provoked in Washington, and discusses the obstacles faced in its implementation – from both inside and outside the Reagan administration. A variety of obstacles and inputs helped to shape constructive engagement. This chapter looks at the debates that took place in the United States regarding the role of containment and the Cold War and the strategic importance of South Africa itself. It also explores the public perception of the policy, and investigates rival perspectives in the political sphere. The fourth chapter begins an analysis of the results of this policy inside South Africa. It assesses Pretoria's reaction to the policy, and explores what actions were being taken by Botha's government at this time. It focuses on Pretoria's perception of constructive engagement, what they expected from it and how they eventually interpreted it. Chapter 5 turns to an account of the influences that were attempting to push Botha further down the path of reform. It will discuss the way in which both Washington and Pretoria viewed the strength of the black opposition within South Africa. The actual role played by the various internal opposition groups is also discussed, and their impact assessed. The competing interests of the Afrikaner right wing and the more liberal business community inside South Africa will also be looked at. Both of these factors had a significant impact upon Botha's actions within South Africa and these had to be taken into account as Crocker formulated his approach towards Pretoria. Finally, Crocker's own policy is also put into a wider context by a survey of the actions of the main international institutions and their responses to apartheid. Chapter 6 concludes with an analysis of just how successful constructive engagement was in addressing the interests of the two main groups of actors within South Africa: the South African government and the black opposition. It discusses how flexible constructive engagement was in the light of Pretoria's response to it – and investigates the way Washington perceived the interests and aims of the black opposition parties.

Part II switches the focus of this analysis away from Crocker's policies regarding South Africa's apartheid dilemma and towards its regional policies in Namibia and Angola. Chapter 7 begins by analysing the aims and beliefs behind Crocker's policy towards this regional question, and the development of his 'linkage' strategy. It will involve a discussion of American interests in the region and an assessment of the beliefs and aims that formed the basis of the linkage strategy. Chapter 8 analyses what Washington hoped linkage could achieve for its main allies in the region – South Africa and UNITA. This chapter also discusses the opinions of these actors regarding the linkage strategy. Chapter 9 addresses two issues that had a major impact on the implementation of Crocker's policy: South African destabilization in the region, and the Reagan administration's decision to resume funding UNITA. It discusses the way in which both of these factors were outside Crocker's control – and assesses the way they affected the development and implementation of his policy. Chapter 10 assesses the final settlement and discusses which factors were significant in its eventual achievement. This is vital in order to evaluate the role played by Crocker's own policy in the final solution of the Namibia/Angola question. Chapter 11 avoids a Washington-centric analysis by assessing the results of Crocker's linkage policy for the regional and international actors other than South Africa and the United States.

Part III discusses the conclusions reached in this book. Chapter 12 brings these threads together and provides an overall evaluation of the four key questions as identified in the Introduction. Its main focus will be on the last question, which addresses the overarching aim of the book: a critical evaluation of Crocker's strategy of constructive engagement towards South Africa, Namibia and Angola. Chapter 13 relates the conclusions of this study to current events. This last chapter will compare the engagement policies of today with the actions of the US in the 1980s. The successes and pitfalls of that experience are just as relevant now, as governments attempt to reconcile their global goals and interests with concern for human rights abuses around the world.

Notes

1   Crocker, Chester, 'South Africa: Strategy for Change', *Foreign Affairs*, Vol. 59, No. 2 (Winter 1980–1).
2   *Ibid.*, p. 324.
3   This study only looks at the specific aspect of American foreign policy in the Third World in the context of the Cold War, although clearly the subject itself is far wider than this, guiding much of international politics since the end of the Second World War. For a further discussion of developments in the Cold War, see Kennedy, Paul, *The Rise and Fall of the Great Powers: Economic Change and Military Conflict from 1500 to 2000*, London: Fontana Press, 1989; McNamara, Robert S., *In Retrospect: The Tragedy and Lessons of Vietnam*, New York: Times Books, 1995; Melanson, Richard A., *American Foreign Policy Since the Vietnam War: The Search for Consensus from Nixon to Clinton*, New York and London: M. E. Sharpe Inc., 1996; Ambrose, Stephen E., *Rise to Globalism: American Foreign Policy Since 1938*, seventh edition, New York and Harmondsworth: Penguin Books Ltd, 1993; Bell, Coral, *The Reagan Paradox: US Foreign Policy in the 1980s*, Piscataway, NJ: Rutgers University Press, 1989; Calvocoressi, Peter, *World Politics 1945–2000*, eighth edition, Harlow: Pearson Education Ltd, 2001; Crockatt, Richard, *The Fifty Years War*, London and New York: Routledge, 1995; Jentleson, Bruce W., *American Foreign Policy: The Dynamics of Choice in the Twenty-First Century*, New York and London: W. W. Norton and Company, 2000.
4   Kennedy, *The Rise and Fall of the Great Powers*, p. 502.
5   Lemon, Anthony, *Apartheid in Transition*, Aldershot: Gower Publishing Company Ltd., 1987, p. 49.
6   Attwell, Michael, *South Africa: Background to the Crisis*, London: Sidgwick and Jackson Ltd., 1986, p. 96.
7   As quoted in Meredith, Martin *In the Name of Apartheid: South Africa in the Post War Period*, New York: Harper and Row Publishers Inc., 1988, p. 166.
8   The misuse of public funds by Connie Mulder's Department of Information to promote South Africa's image abroad was covered up by Mulder himself. He had been seen in South Africa as Vorster's heir-apparent. Vorster was then also implicated in the cover-up operation and they both had to resign. See Leach, Graham, *South Africa*, London: Methuen/Mandarin, second edition, 1989, pp. 39, 97 for further details.
9   As quoted in Barber, James and John Barratt, *South Africa's Foreign Policy: The Search for Status and Security 1945–1988*, Cambridge: Cambridge University Press, 1990, p. 231.
10 A note on nomenclature. On 12 June 1968 the UN General Assembly legitimated the

new name of 'Namibia' by virtue of its resolution 2372, 'in accordance with the desires of the people, and thus enshrined the name in international law'. International Defence and Aid Fund for Southern Africa, *Namibia: The Facts*, London: IDAF, 1980, p. 5; and Richard Dale, 'Melding War and Politics in Namibia: South Africa's Counterinsurgency Campaign, 1966–1989', *Armed Forces and Society*, Vol. 20, No. 1 (Fall 1993), p. 9. This book will follow this convention, as far as is practicable, by referring to Namibia as 'South West Africa' prior to this date.

11 As quoted in O'Callaghan, Marion, *Namibia: The Effects of Apartheid on Culture and Education*, Paris: UNESCO Press, 1977, p. 23.

12 Vigne, Randolph, *A Dwelling Place of Our Own*, London: International Defence and Aid Fund, revised edition, 1975, p. 33.

13 By 1974 South Africa had announced that it would begin constitutional talks inside Namibia. The 'Turnhalle Talks' (named after the German word for gymnasium, here describing the everyday use of the building where the talks took place) began in September 1975, with the majority of the participants being nominated by South Africa. Continued support of the black delegates was insured by a generous package of pay and hotel allowances. By March 1977 the Turnhalle had agreed upon its 'Final Concept' – a three tier administration structure with representatives at the local, ethnic and national level, yet with Pretoria retaining the final say on important areas of policy including defence, finance, foreign policy and internal security. SWAPO denounced the whole process as a farce, and the Turnhalle proposals received no support from the international community. See Katjavivi, Peter H., *A History of Resistance in Namibia*, Paris: UNESCO Press and London: James Currey, 1988, pp. 97–8.

14 See Dale, 'Melding War and Politics in Namibia', p. 10 and Katjavivi, *A History of Resistance in Namibia*, p. 59.

15 Katjavivi, *A History of Resistance*, p. 124. The reluctance of the West was the result of a number of factors. Vested interests, including access to the Cape trading route and strategic minerals (see Chapter 3) and heavy financial investment, were important considerations for the West when planning action. Also, African issues in general remained a low priority for the superpowers. Another important factor was that South Africa was viewed by the US as an important ally against communism in the region.

16 Wright, George, *The Destruction of a Nation: US Policy Toward Angola Since 1945*, London and Chicago: Pluto Press, 1997 p. 9.

17 Ronald Reagan Library, CA. White House Staff and Office Files: Cohen, Herman J., Files 1987-8. African Affairs Directorate, NSC, Box No. 92295, Copy of letter from Jonas Savimbi to Former Missionaries, 29 September 1965.

18 Henderson, Lawrence W., *Angola: Five Centuries of Conflict*, Ithaca and London: Cornell University Press, 1979, p. 246.

19 Speech by Fidel Castro, 1976, reprinted in Deutschmann, David (ed.), *Angola and Namibia: Changing the History of Africa*, Melbourne: Ocean Press, 1989, p. 70.

20 Taber, Michael (ed.), *Fidel Castro Speeches: Cuba's Internationalist Foreign Policy 1975–1980*, New York: Pathfinder Press, 1981.

21 See Clarke, Michael and Brian White (eds), *Understanding Foreign Policy: The Foreign Policy Systems Approach*, Aldershot and Brookfield: Edward Elgar Publishing Ltd., 1989, especially Steve Smith, 'Perspectives on the Foreign Policy System: Bureaucratic Politics Approaches', pp. 109–134 and Michael Clarke and Steve Smith, 'Perspectives on the Foreign Policy System: Implementation Approaches'. See also Allison, G., 'Conceptual Models and the Cuban Missile Crisis', *American Political Science Review*, No. 63 (1969), pp. 689–718; and Allison, G., *Essence of Decision*, Boston: Little, Brown and Company, 1971.

I

Constructive Engagement
& South Africa

1
The Aims
of Constructive Engagement

By the end of his tenure in 1988, Chester Crocker had become the longest-serving Assistant Secretary of State for African Affairs since the department's creation in 1958, setting 'a precedent for influence and survival in office'.[1] He had set out his stall for the post by publishing an article in *Foreign Affairs* in the winter of 1980. This 'academic essay cum job application'[2] pointed out just what he thought was wrong with US African policy – and set out a new way of thinking to deal with his fundamental task: finding a way of pursuing American national interests whilst addressing specific regional issues. Crocker criticized the Carter administration for its inconsistency and policy oscillations. He also believed that Carter's harsh rhetoric had driven the South African government away from a possible sphere of influence that the US could have utilized to bring about change in the region. Crocker believed he could 'combine hard-headed realism (you cannot influence events unless you take part in them) and a sense of mission in which Western values and interests were on trial'.[3]

Crocker's attempt at a balanced approach meant that he faced opposition from critics on both the left and the right. From the right, he had to face the ideology of South Africa as a bastion against communism that should be brought into America's strategic embrace. He was not helped by the fact that the President himself was sympathetic towards this view. Senator Jesse Helms even went as far as delaying Crocker's appointment by six months, afraid that, as a regional specialist, Crocker could lose sight of global priorities and become too sympathetic towards black Africa – and black South Africans. Yet critics on the left saw his desire to 'engage' with the white South African government as an implicit acceptance of apartheid. 'This vulnerability to both left and right meant Mr Crocker embarked on his new strategy with a weak domestic base.'[4]

The Conceptual Underpinnings
of Constructive Engagement

There is an important caveat to bear in mind when assessing the role of US influence in southern and South Africa. The Director of the Office of Public Diplomacy for South Africa explained: 'Many Americans, and many South Africans, believe that US power to effect change in southern

Africa is virtually limitless. This misperception is not only naïve, it is dangerous.'[5] The issue of how successfully the US husbanded its limited influence towards South Africa is discussed in Chapter 6, but it is important to make the point here that, when looking at the conceptual basis upon which constructive engagement was founded, the limited degree of influence US policy makers saw themselves as possessing was a significant underlying assumption. As Crocker explained in 1987: 'At the core of our sobering experience [in South Africa] is the realization that there is a severe limit to what the United States – or any other outside power – can do to bring about change in South Africa.'[6] As one looks at the theories and beliefs upon which Crocker initially developed his strategy of constructive engagement, it is important to bear in mind the wider conflicting views behind American foreign policy itself. Was America able to dictate its will to others, or was it unable to mobilize its influence in an international system constrained by mores and rules of national sovereignty? Was America going to follow some Republicans down the path of isolationism, or was it going to fulfil its unique mission to lead the free world and spread the values of liberty and democracy throughout its sphere of influence? Although these questions were asked by political commentators and practitioners alike, Crocker was appointed by a President who had a clear idea of what the answers *should* be.

The Reagan Doctrine

Reagan came to power in 1981 with the firm belief that the United States had lost influence throughout the world through its own weakness and unwillingness to stand up for what it believed in. The term 'Vietnam Syndrome' was coined to refer to a retreat into isolationism and reluctance to get involved in external conflicts after the disastrous involvement in Vietnam. But Reagan and his right-wing allies stood firm in their globalist views – seeing everything in the zero-sum terms of the Cold War. Reagan's policy was articulated as 'The Reagan Doctrine',[7] which was spelled out in an internal White House memorandum: 'Our policy aims to help resistance forces win the freedom and independence that Communist tyranny denies them.'[8] This aid was then justified in both moral and strategic terms – morally, because human rights abuses are an integral part of Marxist-Leninist dictatorships, and strategically, because these regimes threaten American security and the security of American allies and friends. So the basic assumptions behind the Reagan administration's African policy were: first, that African issues became a lower priority, except where they involved East–West rivalry; second, that regional problems were caused not so much by local factors as by an incipient, ubiquitous Soviet threat; third, Reagan was not willing to suffer criticism or hostility from radical African states – African nationalist rhetoric was to be taken at face value; fourth, human rights were moved down the agenda, to be replaced by a commitment to support 'proven friends', with little regard for their human rights record.[9]

This dramatic commitment to the globalists' right-wing foreign policy perspective was a clear reflection of the new President's beliefs. And yet, together with these strong Republican anti-communist credentials, another aspect of the new President was also fast becoming clear – his now notorious 'hands-off' approach. Apart from his interest in Central America, many of the regional bureaux within the State Department were left largely to themselves, and none more so than the Bureau of African Affairs. The low profile of his department meant that Crocker, as the Assistant Secretary of State for African Affairs, could have a significant influence over the course of policy. Barber points out: 'That US policy stopped short of the full globalist position was partly the result of Reagan's choice of Dr Chester Crocker [for this post].'

Crocker – regionalist or globalist?

Crocker brought to the intractable problem of southern Africa a detailed knowledge of the region and a more nuanced view of how American policy should proceed. The *conceptual* basis of his strategy recognized three important factors. The first of these was the belief that US interests were paramount. He explained that 'we do not face a choice between aligning ourselves with black or white since our interests cross racial lines'.[10] In 1989 he confirmed that his regional strategy of constructive engagement had been 'a possible basis for pursuing American interests in southern Africa'. And in an interview he made it clear that 'of course we were guided by our national interest and I'm proud that we were. I would be ashamed if we weren't.'[11] Yet an important question to ask during this period is – how much was national interest guided by Cold War issues?

This leads to the second factor. Crocker made it explicit that he was aware of and sympathetic to *both* globalist *and* regionalist factors – that he could understand and appreciate the significance of both perspectives and aimed to create a balanced policy on a synthesis of both. In his view, 'Neither the globalists – who saw the Soviet hand behind every problem, nor the Africanists – who imagined that slogans like "African solutions for African problems" could ward off Soviet interventionism – had the answer.'[12] He went on to explain: 'The focus of decisions and diplomatic action would be regional, but our choice of whether to compete or not – when the Soviets and the Cubans were busily exploiting and militarising regional conflicts – would have global implications.'[13] Some commentators saw his policy as 'far more nuanced and ambitious than previous Republican policies',[14] which had focused directly on the Cold War implications. He was aiming for a synthesis that could avoid the 'clandestine embrace' of the Nixon administration and Carter's 'polecat treatment'.[15] Crocker himself, when asked directly about his position in the globalist/regionalist debate, says: 'I am both.' However, he continues: 'There is no way that you can explain the mess southern Africa was in without looking at the global situation, without looking at Soviet and global interests.'[16] Before his appointment to the post of Assistant Secretary, he stated: 'The real choice we will face in southern Africa in the 1980s concerns our readiness to compete with our global adversary in the politics of a changing region....'

Regardless of how often he stressed the importance of addressing both globalist and regionalist considerations, his actions ultimately show his policy to be grounded in the globalist perspective.

The third factor was that Crocker was initially genuinely optimistic regarding the possibilities of white-led change in South Africa. To encourage change within South Africa, he thought, a positive and constructive relationship must be built with the white government in Pretoria. In 'Strategy for Change' he warned against focusing only on the goal of a 'full-blown national convention' and pointed out: 'Since South Africa is a sovereign state, only the government itself can call and supervise such an exercise … the West has everything to gain if it succeeds in pressing white-led change in the direction of real power-sharing.' Crocker's beliefs were based on two key assumptions: first, that constructive change could only come about through the whites and, second, that blacks could not gain political rights through violence. Such an approach would lead to chaos and would open the country up to communist influence. Crocker does acknowledge the importance of dialogue with South Africans of all races, but this book examines exactly what balance was struck between communication with Pretoria and communication with black opposition groups. The Reagan administration may well have believed that white-led change was the only possibility for change, but another goal, just as important, was that they did not simply wish for change away *from* apartheid. They wanted change *to* a country that preserved economic stability so that their financial interests were not damaged, and they wanted a South Africa that remained a bastion against communism so that their strategic interests were not damaged.

In 1981 Crocker stated: 'The Botha government had committed itself to a moderate reformist process … the current fluidity does not make meaningful change certain, but it does make it possible.' The White House had their hopes firmly pinned on Pretoria's new reformist strategy as the means of change away from apartheid in South Africa. This fitted in with the US goal of a *gradual* change in South Africa. The possibility of upheaval or revolution was viewed nervously by Washington as providing an open door for Soviet influence. Crocker, therefore, continued to stress the importance of talking to Pretoria throughout, to achieve what he presented as the inevitable process of gradual change. Constructive engagement would focus on the *process* of change, and would avoid focusing on the end result of dismantling apartheid, as this would keep the West immobilized by a distant objective. Crocker also accused both liberals and conservatives of enjoying being seen publicly telling foreigners what to do, rather than actually persuading them to do it. Incremental steps towards reform must be supported rather than, as Secretary of State George Shultz warned, 'cheer[ing] on, from the sidelines, a race war in southern Africa'.[17]

A question of ethics
An issue like apartheid seems unable to escape the questions of morality and ethics in foreign policy. For American campaigners, apartheid

represented 'the antithesis of what are commonly referred to as American ideals'.[18] The Declaration of Independence provided an articulation of those beliefs when it stated 'all men are created equal, that they are endowed by their Creator with certain inalienable rights, that among these are life, liberty and the pursuit of happiness'. Charles Freeman, Crocker's Deputy Assistant Secretary of State for African Affairs, asserted that for Africans and Americans alike, apartheid was, first and foremost, a moral issue. And yet, as Crocker often pointed out, indignation is not a foreign policy. One cannot simply select proposals according to how good they make us feel. In testimony to a Congressional committee Crocker spelt out his views on the role of morality:

> The policy that this Administration had pursued combines America's strong opposition to apartheid with a sense of conviction that we should be involved for reasons both ideological and humanitarian, both strategic and moral, in helping to bring about change in South Africa.

But how does one combine what are often two opposing elements in one policy? Is it possible to pursue strategic and moral aims simultaneously? The best illustration of the intractability of such a problem in this region was given by the United States' Ambassador to South Africa, Herman Nickel, as he introduced Senator Kennedy at a meeting in South Africa:

> And let us be honest enough to acknowledge that the problem is full of moral ambiguities, with the result that no one can claim moral purity. How else can one explain that such implacable opponents of apartheid as Desmond Tutu and Gatsha Buthelezi, as Alan Paton and Donald Woods differ so profoundly?

The role of economics in foreign policy

The often bitter divisions that surfaced in the discussion of the morality of constructive engagement were just as apparent when discussing economic engagement with South Africa. Crocker was adamantly against the idea of increasing sanctions as a method of ending apartheid. Some sanctions already in place, primarily the arms embargo, were maintained. However, before the government had to alter its stance in public after the Comprehensive Anti-Apartheid Act of 1986 (CAAA), Crocker strongly denounced further sanctions in his testimony before Congress:

> All evidence suggests that US influence for change is unlikely to be increased by 'pinpricks' such as restrictions on Kruggerrand sales or on landing rights for South African Airways. Such moves are more likely to become a show of impotence and to erode our influence with those we seek to persuade.[19]

He also warned against the likely results of increased sanctions for the people of South Africa, saying that they could sabotage desperately needed economic opportunity for the black majority while at the same time damaging important US economic interests. The chaos and financial collapse that could ensue would not benefit any of the parties. Rather, Crocker and the Reagan administration believed that strong economic growth would be an important engine of constructive change in South Africa. A further exploration of this view, and the criticisms of it, is undertaken in Chapter 2, but it is important to acknowledge this belief in economic growth as an engine of change as one of the assumptions upon which Crocker claimed constructive engagement was based.

Despite the immense problems attendant on formulating a policy to protect and promote American interests in a region that was fast developing into a political and moral minefield, Chester Crocker assumed this task with an air of quiet confidence and optimism. He had set out many of his fundamental assumptions regarding the region in 'Strategy for Change'. He had a good theoretical and practical knowledge of the region and he had already developed a conceptual basis on which to build a policy. Once appointed, he would need to structure a clear policy with specific aims. He labelled his new approach 'constructive engagement' in the 1980 *Foreign Affairs* article and, once appointed, he began to make the specific aims of constructive engagement known.

The Aims of Constructive Engagement

The explicit aims of constructive engagement

When analysing the aims of constructive engagement, one must take into account a factor that is vital in all foreign policy. At a seminar on southern Africa, chaired by Crocker seven years before his appointment as Assistant Secretary of State for African Affairs, Jack Spence pointed out that unless an objective is clearly defined and it is clear how it can be achieved, influence and intervention have no purpose. But how clearly did the administration define and present its aims in the region? How unified was it behind these aims? Were there implicit aims that were not publicly presented, and that muddied the waters of the policy? Were different justifications and explanations given to different audiences? As Secretary Shultz pointed out: 'The key element of our diplomacy must be clear to the American people, to our allies and to Africans....'[20]

Certainly the administration was united in its public condemnation of apartheid. In Congressional hearings Crocker always made clear:

> our strong moral and political convictions about a system based on legally entrenched racism ... any system that ascribes or denies political rights on this [racial] basis – including the right of citizenship itself – is bound to be ... repugnant.[21]

President Reagan also joined in the public denunciation of apartheid, emphasizing America's concern and grief over the 'human and spiritual cost' of apartheid in South Africa. In fact, virtually every explanation of US policy was prefixed with a similar rejection of apartheid. So how did Crocker, and the other senior figures in the administration, actually spell out how they intended to deal with this problem? How successful were they, and how successful did they *want to be*, in making their aims clear to the diverse actors in this region?

A paper leaked in the early days of Crocker's appointment identified Namibian independence as his primary regional goal. The 'Scope Paper' written for Secretary of State Al Haig prior to his meeting with South African Foreign Minister Botha on 14 May 1981 clearly stated what Crocker's main objectives were in the region, and how he wanted to communicate them to the South Africans:

Objectives:

To tell the South Africans that we are willing with them to open *a new chapter in our relationship* based upon strategic reality and South Africa's position in that reality and the continued explicit commitment of P. W. Botha's government to domestic change.

To make clear to the South Africans that we see the continuation of *the Namibia problem as a primary obstacle* to the development of that new relationship and that we are willing to work with them toward an internationally acceptable settlement which will not harm their interests. [Emphasis in original.] [22]

A comprehensive categorization of US interests in the region can be found in a Special Report by the editors of the New York-based 'Foreign Policy Association' entitled *South Africa and the United States*. This report categorized US interests into four broad areas. Firstly, human rights were identified as being important to US interests in the region, because of the way in which the system of apartheid went against the democratic values of the United States. The second area was that of economic interests. In 1985 the United States had $15 billion worth of investment in South Africa, including securities, bank loans and direct investments. Trade between the two countries stood at $4.8 billion in 1984, but this notably included the import of certain minerals that were of vital strategic importance to the US (see the strategic debates in Chapter 3). Political interests accounted for the third category, with the report pointing out that stability throughout this region was important to the US. Chances of achieving this stability and improving American relations with other countries of the region were materially lessened by South Africa's refusal to grant Namibian independence, despite its occupation being condemned by the UN. The fourth and final category of US interests was strategic concerns. The United States sought to curb communist interests in the region and feared that the poverty, unrest and dislocation caused by the system of apartheid could provide the type of revolutionary conditions that the Soviet Union and its allies could exploit. Working to end apartheid and promote peace in the region would, the administration insisted, serve both America's ideals and its interests.

Just *how* the US planned to go about combating apartheid was summed up by Kenneth Dam (Deputy Secretary of State) in his testimony before a Senate hearing. His testimony is quoted here at some length, as it is useful in covering the significant points succinctly:

The policy of this Administration has been to foment change away from apartheid: by unambiguous public statements condemning apartheid's evils; by reinforcing these views with quiet diplomacy; by working with elements within South Africa that share a vision of peace and equality; by encouraging laudable fair employment practices of US companies; and by involving ourselves as a government in financing programmes – some $30 million in three years – to give South African blacks better training and educational opportunities.[23]

The focus of the policy within South Africa was on encouraging a gradual change away from apartheid. Any revolutionary upheaval, even in the unlikely case that such an action did manage to undermine the apartheid system, would be against US interests. Trading could be disrupted, the stability of the whole region undermined, and the conditions for the encroachment of Soviet influence would be worryingly apparent. Crocker appeared to give mixed messages on this approach to gradual change. He maintained that the US had little power to actually coerce South Africa to reform, which is why persuasion was the best route for the US to take. Yet he also made it clear that if the option *had* been open to coerce South Africa away from apartheid, he would not have taken it. Washington's primary goal was:

> the emergence in South Africa of a society with which the United States can pursue its varied interests in a full and friendly relationship, without constraint, embarrassment or political damage. [The American government should] … foster and support such change, recognizing the need to minimize the damage to our interests in the process.[24]

Crocker warned against scenarios of instigating revolutionary violence and all the bloodshed and risks of external intervention that would ensue. The human cost of a violent revolution is self-evident. What did cause criticism, however, was that his focus on a gradual transition towards a South African society more amenable to American interests seemed to lack any sense of urgency with regard to the plight of the blacks in South Africa. UN Representative Okun stated before the Security Council in 1986: 'there are no hidden agendas on our part. We want apartheid to disappear from the face of the Earth, peacefully, but quickly – I repeat, quickly.'[25] Crocker never properly made it explicit that he appreciated this need.

The implicit aims of constructive engagement in South Africa
Namibian independence and the dismantling of apartheid both featured heavily in public statements made by the administration regarding its aims in the region. Yet many private documents indicate that, in reality, these aims were superseded by the main goal of reducing Soviet influence in the region – a goal that was not openly acknowledged as the highest priority for the US in the region. There are a number of other areas in the formulation of this policy that point to motivations other than those made explicit by Crocker. The extent to which US and South African strategic interests coincided, and the extent to which the US viewed South Africa as a vital ally in the region, were aspects of the constructive engagement policy that were never made fully explicit. By some members of the administration, apartheid was viewed simply as an awkward obstacle in the

way of the open pursuit of United States interests in the context of its friendly relationship with South Africa.

In a secret memorandum to the President, Al Haig was pleased to report on the administration's successful meetings with South African Foreign Minister 'Pik' Botha (including a meeting with President Reagan himself). Haig explained:

> I believe we accomplished our major objective – *to establish a new relationship with South Africa based on a realistic appraisal of our mutual interests in the Southern African region*.... They know that we are determined to roll back Soviet influence throughout the world and in their region.[26] [Original emphasis.]

As Michael Clough later pointed out: 'In 1981, constructive engagement was perceived, correctly, as laying groundwork for limited strategic United States/South African co-operation.'[27] Explicit explanations of constructive engagement present it as being the best strategy to urge South Africa away from apartheid and regional unrest peacefully. This confidential communication within the government, however, seems to point towards constructive engagement as being a strategy to enable the US to pursue its strategic interests in the region in concert with its regional 'deputy sheriff' – South Africa. Constructive engagement was not heedless of apartheid, but it seemed to view this system more in terms of its potential to cause embarrassment than as an intrinsic moral abhorrence, despite public statements to the contrary.

In Crocker's 'Scope Paper'[28] Haig is advised to make it clear to Pik Botha that the US envisages the possibility of:

> a *new era of cooperation, stability and security in the region. We also share their view that the chief threat to the realization of this hope is the presence and influence in the region of the Soviet Union and its allies.* [Original emphasis.]

Many regional actors would have pointed to apartheid itself as the chief destabilizing threat, but nowhere in the Scope Paper is this possibility addressed. Although apartheid is criticized, its treatment does not match the urgency and disgust so apparent in many of Crocker's, and Reagan's, public statements. A focus on national interest in the region by the US government is neither surprising nor open to serious criticism. Indeed, this focus is the primary aim of any government engagement. What is interesting to note, however, is the dichotomy between the aims made explicit to the American public and regional actors and the implicit aims discussed within the administration. Were the 'explicit' aims a smokescreen to cover the fact that constructive engagement was *only* a *realpolitik* policy of national interest, or were they genuine elements to be taken into consideration when evaluating the policy?

Implicit aims regarding the internal settlement in South Africa

Crocker often stated that the US was not offering blueprints in South Africa, nor did it want to. It was not the purpose of Washington to impose US-style institutions. In various interviews, representatives of the administration were questioned on their support for the principle of 'one man one vote' in South Africa. The standard response was to point out that the specific formula was for the South Africans themselves to negotiate. Unfortunately, just how the banned, imprisoned and repressed black majority were to make their views known on this issue was not made clear. But Washington did assert that aiming to create a certain type of result in South Africa was not its goal. 'We do not aim to impose ourselves, our solutions, or our favorites in South Africa; such an intrusion would be unwarranted and unwise for any outside party.'[29] Yet neither liberal critics in the US nor white South Africans were convinced by this position. Despite their opposing perspectives, both groups believed that the American intention in South Africa was an internal settlement that would establish a society fully conducive to American interests. 'The policy of constructive engagement was ... never intended to be a policy of friend-ship,' maintained a paper published by the South African Human Sciences Research Council. 'It is rather based on a carrot-and-stick approach intended to further American self-interest by promoting "significant" internal change in South Africa.'[30] Those on the opposite side of the fence, who never believed the US should enter into a friendship with South Africa, nevertheless agreed on the underlying point, that US insistence on gradual and moderate change was in order to support US interests, rather than to aid either Pretoria or its critics. This camp maintained that:

> constructive engagement's short term objectives of promoting evolutionary changes in South Africa and increasing US influence over South Africa [were] in order to ensure its long-term objectives for the firm establishment of a pro-Western, pro-capitalist South Africa as a full and open member of the Western military community and as the region's dominant economic and military power.[31]

Indeed, certain statements later in the Reagan administration's second term seem to belie the initial insistence on not imposing 'ourselves, or our solutions'. As Secretary Shultz explained in September 1984 'working with our allies, we will continue to assert a Western vision of what we favour as the outcome in South Africa'.[32] In a secret memorandum of May 1987, among the aims of the US in southern Africa, it is stipulated that the US seeks:

- Avoidance and prevention of a scenario in South Africa of revolutionary violence and expanded Soviet influence through exploitation of internal and regional conflict.
- Broadened participation in and acceptance by all South Africans of a strong market-based economic system in South Africa.[33]

Reagan's transition team, Al Haig in particular, was also very clear about the need for resource and mineral access and that they needed this on their own terms. The Reagan administration did have a clear view of how they wanted the apartheid question to be answered. In private, the race question was sidelined by the priority that, whatever solution was achieved in South Africa, it had to be a stable country that was open to US capitalism, and closed to Soviet communism.

Implicit regional aims

Crocker made it clear that he believed that internal change in South Africa and improved regional relations were directly linked, and that therefore constructive engagement had to be both a bilateral and a regional policy. His emphasis on this aspect of policy, however, only really surfaced after the South African uprisings in 1985 and the subsequent public outcry about just what constructive engagement was doing to help to bring about the end of apartheid. Before this, the explicit focus of his regional goals had been the situations in Angola and Namibia. The potential impact of a regional strategy upon South Africa's internal situation had not been mentioned. He explained in 1985 that elimination of apartheid in South Africa and reduction of regional violence and instability were two 'mutually dependent' goals:

> External conditions have a direct bearing on the situation within South Africa; a white Government that does not feel besieged from outside its own borders will be better able to take steps to reform its own society. Conversely, internal conflict in South Africa can spill over borders, increase tensions and compel its neighbours to divert scarce resources away from pressing economic development needs.[34]

In a Congressional hearing of May that same year, he went on to explain that 'as long as the South African leadership finds itself distracted by reacting to violent threats across frontiers … it is unlikely that you are going to see the kind of willingness to take risks for change domestically'. Crocker was also concerned that this regional instability would allow communist influence to take a firmer hold in the region. Yet there was room for optimism. He saw a window of opportunity in the region because most of the region's governments were in 'pragmatic hands'. Stability in the region, and particularly a satisfactory settlement of both the Angolan and Namibian conflicts, could help significantly to limit opportunities for Soviet adventurism. He presented all these factors in the light of a long-term strategy in the region that would result in justice throughout the region, including South Africa. The aims in terms of America's own national interest remained more implicit, particularly the fact that a stable region conducive to American interests was a higher priority than the goal of ending apartheid.

Much criticism at the time focused on the impression given by Crocker that South African security concerns must be seen as the key issue, and that cross-border violence was at least as much the fault of the Frontline States as of South Africa itself. During a Congressional hearing in which he accused the regional states of 'distracting' South Africa away from reform, one exasperated Senator remarked 'is it not precisely the current activities of the South African Government that are so abhorrent to its neighbors … that causes external pressure from the neighbors of South Africa?'[35] What Crocker allowed to remain largely implicit was the way in which this sequencing was more vital for US interests, particularly Cold War considerations, than for the ending of apartheid, which seemed to be the root cause of much of the instability in the region.

Implementation of the Constructive Engagement Policy

This chapter has discussed the conceptual basis and the explicit and implicit aims of Washington's constructive engagement with Pretoria. But did the US government's actions actually alter as a result of this policy? When addressing the issue of actions taken with regard to South Africa, Crocker characterized the debate as '…spanning a spectrum that runs, at one end, from those who believe primarily in the power of persuasion and the efficacy of diplomacy, to those at the other end, who champion a policy of punishment and isolation'.[36] He did acknowledge that most participants advocated a mixture of these measures. But what mixture did constructive engagement entail? It was initially asserted that an important tool of US policy was publicly expressed encouragement and support of positive steps. Crocker was adamant that showing support for the gradual reform and evolutionary change that he deemed to be taking place in South Africa was a vital element in the process of constructive change. When asked how constructive engagement was being implemented, this continued encouragement was one of the main factors that he consistently identified. Unfortunately, the rest of his explanation of how his policy should be implemented often appeared rather vague. He explained to a House committee in March 1986 that what the government sought to do was to create conditions to draw the people of goodwill together, and to encourage the government to repeal all apartheid laws. In a hearing at the US Senate in 1985, Crocker was asked directly by Senator Trible what *specific* steps he advocated. Again the answer was vague. He mentioned programmes aiding black advancement, but other than that explained that 'there are, no doubt, many areas in which we could do more.'[37] Yet to say this was a modest beginning after Reagan had already been in office for a whole term seems somewhat inadequate. When asked for specific examples of constructive engagement in action, both Crocker and Shultz would point to the 'action' of 'encouraging' the South African government towards change. The only other concrete action they illustrated was the aid programme to South Africa. It is true that the main focus of constructive engagement was communication and dialogue with South Africa, but four years into the policy this had not yet materialized as demonstrable achievements in, or agreements with, Pretoria.

With regard to the aid programmes undertaken, it is certainly true that the US government was instrumental in financing a range of black empowerment programmes. Crocker does, however, acknowledge that the credit is due to Congress rather than the strategy of constructive engagement. These 'black empowerment initiatives' had actually come from various religious and business groups in the 1970s. The move towards government endorsement began in 1980 when the Democratic Chairman of the House of Representatives, Stephen Solarz, organized bipartisan support of a two-year scholarship programme for black South Africans. The funding was massively increased from an initial $40,000 in 1981 to a remarkable $25 million in 1988. Nevertheless, the Reagan administration saw this aid as a 'politically acceptable alternative' to sanctions, and the major funding increases (in 1983, 1985 and 1986) all occurred during heightened Congressional pressure for sanctions.[38]

Another project, also cited by Crocker when outlining the achievements of his policy, was the Code of Conduct known as the Sullivan Principles. This was a scheme to ensure that American employers in South Africa avoided discrimination and improved black living conditions and work opportunities. (It is looked at in greater depth in the section on disinvestment/sanctions in Chapter 2.) It was actually the initiative of the Reverend Leon Sullivan, a respected black director of General Motors, who proposed the scheme in March 1977. This scheme certainly did encourage large investments in black welfare initiatives and provided considerable benefits to black workers and their families in South Africa, whilst simultaneously salving the consciences and improving the public relations of those firms who continued to work in South Africa under apartheid. Although the scheme received government encouragement, it seems dubious to claim it as a benefit of constructive engagement, when, like the educational aid programmes, it was not actually a product of this policy, and particularly as the Reagan administration repeatedly refused calls from Congress and elsewhere to make the Principles mandatory for all US firms operating in South Africa.

Implementation – Washington moves towards Pretoria

When the administration was questioned on specific actions taken under the auspices of constructive engagement, little emphasis was placed on the specific changes that were made in many spheres to alter the US/South African relationship towards a more friendly and open dialogue. As early as May 1981, in a secret memorandum to the President, Al Haig stated 'we have publicly endorsed a stance of "constructive engagement" toward the Republic'.[39] Yet this new stance had already become apparent through the actions of the new administration. Initially, the tone of the new policy was ambiguous, due to an event that took place in March 1981. Jeane Kirkpatrick, the US Ambassador to the United Nations, agreed to meet a group of four of South Africa's highest-ranking intelligence officers in Washington, DC in March 1981. The group included the Head of South Africa's Military Intelligence – General van der Westhuizen – and had also visited the Pentagon and met with members of the National Security Council. After initially (and truthfully) denying all knowledge of these visits, the State Department was then forced to acknowledge that they had, in fact, taken place. The Department went on to explain that the officers had not identified their rank when applying for visas. Had this been known, the visa applications would not have been accepted. The visas were revoked, but the State Department was left furious at this evidence that parties – in both Pretoria and Washington – were prepared to by-pass the official diplomatic channel between Washington and Pretoria which Crocker's Africa Bureau was trying to establish. This incident certainly marred the thawing of relations. It was not long, however, before more concrete friendly overtures began, this time fully supported by the State Department.

On 30 June 1981 new guidelines were issued to allow the sale of certain medical supplies to the South African military on a case-by-case basis. On 14 July, the State Department agreed to issue visas to the South African rugby team. The team included some members of the South African armed forces, which meant that there could be a possible violation of the UN arms embargo.[40] That same summer, South African military officers began training with the US Coastguard, the administration began moves to re-establish its military attaché link with South Africa, and South African nuclear experts visited a plant in Ohio dealing in uranium purification.

Initial signs on economic cooperation were also good for Pretoria. In 1982, South Africa had requested a desperately needed $1.1 billion loan from the International Monetary Fund (IMF). On 22 October the General Assembly voted to ask the IMF to reject the loan: 121 countries agreed to this measure, with 23 abstentions. Only Britain, West Germany and the United States voted against it. On 3 November the IMF approved the loan because, with 20 per cent of the vote, the US was able to override international opposition. At the same time, US bank lending to South Africa dramatically increased by 246 per cent between 1981 and 1983, the highpoint being $4.6 billion in 1983.[41] The first few years of the Reagan administration also demonstrated a far more relaxed attitude towards other areas of export restriction.

> In 1978, Carter's State Department Office of Armaments Control had author-ized licences for goods worth $4.6 million destined for the Republic; by 1979 this figure had fallen to just $25,000. In 1980, no licences were issued at all. By contrast, in the first three years of the Reagan Administration, goods to the value of $28.3 million were licensed for export to South Africa in this category.[42]

The few interested parties in the United States who followed events in South Africa at this time began to question some of the sales, particularly computer exports sold to government agencies that directly administered apartheid.[43] The Democratic Head of the House Subcommittee on African Affairs – Howard Wolpe – called the shift in export licensing a 'tragic mistake' and said it was evidence of a further 'tilt' towards South Africa.

The most public forum for this new-found support was in the United Nations. One of the earliest indications of this support was the fact that the US abstained on a 1981 General Assembly Resolution that expressed solidarity with the women and children who had suffered under apartheid (UN General Assembly Resolution 36/172K 17 December 1981). The support continued when the United States was the only country to vote against a 1982 General Assembly Resolution dealing with apartheid in sport (UN General Assembly Resolution 37/69G 9 December 1982). There was also criticism of another of the early signals of friendship sent to Pretoria. In 1977 the Carter administration had cut the representation of military attachés to South Africa in protest at the South African crackdown in the wake of the uprisings of Soweto in 1976. Reagan returned the representation of South African attachés in the US to its former level and sent American attachés to South Africa. At a later Congressional Hearing, Wolpe stated that such military cooperation 'directly undermines American interests both in Southern Africa and throughout the African continent'.[44]

Although Crocker presents his policy as a synthesis of globalist/realist and regionalist considerations, this chapter has argued that *realpolitik* was its guiding principle. Both the Cold War and the Reagan Doctrine proved significant in this context – moving the policy away from Crocker's Africanist leanings and towards a policy based firmly on the strategic considerations of America's anti-communism. These beliefs were also, in part, behind his insistence on the importance of gradual, white-led change in South Africa. Washington did not trust the African National Congress (ANC) and its links with Moscow. Crocker's insistence on this gradual change drew deep antagonism from the black opposition within South Africa. He sidelined the urgency of the blacks' predicament in favour of the aim of an emerging society that would be unfailingly sympathetic to American interests. The importance of Pretoria as an anti-communist and economic ally clearly outweighed the administration's displeasure at apartheid: South Africa's system was more of a political embarrassment than an intrinsically moral concern.

Notes

1 Baker, Pauline H. *The United States and South Africa: The Reagan Years. Update South Africa: Time Running Out*, New York: Ford Foundation and Foreign Policy Association, 1989, p. 8.

2 Finnegan, William, 'Coming Apart over Apartheid: The Story Behind the Republicans' Split on South Africa', *Mother Jones* (San Francisco) April–May 1986, p. 42.

3 Barber, James, 'Review – *High Noon in Southern Africa: Making Peace in a Rough Neighborhood*, Chester Crocker', *International Affairs (RIIA)*, Vol. 70, No. 1 (1994), p. 182.

4 *The Economist*, 'America and South Africa', 30 March 1986, p. 18.

5 Holladay, J. Douglas, 'Using Our Leverage', *Africa Report*, March–April 1986, p. 30.

6 Crocker, Chester, 'A Democratic Future: The Challenge for South Africans', *Current Policy*, No. 1009 (1 October 1987), US Department of State Bureau of Public Affairs, Washington, DC.

7 The Reagan Doctrine did not begin as an official 'Doctrine'. Rather, it emerged from the writings of right-wing Republican supporters and think tanks. The phrase was popularized by Charles Krauthammer of *New Republic* and *Time* magazines in 1985. The essence of this approach was the active destabilization of target states held to be pro-Soviet in order to halt the perceived expansion of Soviet power during the so-called 'decade of neglect' in the 1970s. Confrontation was built up through Reagan's rhetoric, rearmament and selective intervention in the Third World. See Evans Graham and Jeffrey Newnham, *The Penguin Dictionary of International Relations*, Harmondsworth: Penguin Books Ltd and New York: Penguin Putnam Inc. 1998, p. 464.

8 Ronald Reagan Library, CA. WHORM Subject Files: 'South Africa, US Policy Towards' File FG 011 – 390429 Memorandum – By: The White House Subject: The Reagan Doctrine 4 October' 86. The memo says that Reagan did not think 'Doctrine' was the right word to use as it implied too much rigidity.

9 Adapted from Rothchild, Donald and John Ravenhill, 'Subordinating African Issues to Global Logic: Reagan Confronts Political Complexity', in K. A. Oye, R. J. Lieber and D. Rothchild (eds), *Eagle Resurgent? The Reagan Era in American Foreign Policy*, Boston, Toronto: Little, Brown and Company, 1987, p. 424.

10 Crocker, Chester, 'South Africa: Strategy for Change', *Foreign Affairs*, Vol. 59, No. 2 (Winter 1980–1), p. 345. Crocker was also very clear on the fact that US aid should only go to countries which supported the US, and whose attitudes were in line with the US on issues of importance. See, for example, Crocker, Chester and William H. Lewis, 'Missing Opportunities in Africa', *Foreign Policy*, No. 35 (Summer 1979), p. 159.

11 Personal interview with Dr Chester Crocker, 19 June 2001, Washington, DC.

12 Crocker, Chester, *High Noon in Southern Africa: Making Peace in a Rough Neighborhood*, New York and London: W.W. Norton and Company, 1992, p. 28.

13 Crocker, Chester, 'Southern Africa: Eight Years Later', *Foreign Affairs*, Vol. 68, No. 4 (1989) p. 145. See also Crocker, 'Strategy for Change', p. 345, in which Crocker states: 'The choice has global implications, but the immediate decisions are, more often than not, regional ones.'

14 Baker, *The United States and South Africa*, p. 8.

15 Crocker, 'Strategy for Change', p. 346.

16 Personal interview with Dr Chester Crocker, 19 June 2001, Washington, DC.

17 Ronald Reagan Library, CA. White House Staff and Office Files: Chumachenko, Katherine: File number OA 19268, George Shultz, 15 February 1984, in US Department of State Bureau of Public Affairs: Public Information Series – April 1985.

18 Thomas, A. M. *The American Predicament: Apartheid and United States Foreign Policy*, Aldershot and Brookfield: Ashgate Publishing Ltd., 1997, p. 1.

19 *United States Policy on South Africa* Hearing before the Subcommittee on African Affairs of the Committee on Foreign Relations United States Senate, 26 September 1984, p. 12.

20 ARC Identifier: 54794, *Secretary Shultz's Speech on South Africa, 1987*. Creator: United States Information Agency (1982–) (Most Recent). Item from Record Group 306: Records of the USIA 1900–1988. Series: Motion Picture Films 1944-1999. NAIL Locator: 306.9758 Motion Picture, Sound and Video Recordings, LICON, National Archives at College Park, Maryland USA.

21 *United States Policy on South Africa* Congressional Hearings, 26 September 1984, p. 12.

22 Crocker's 'Scope Paper' for Secretary of State Alexander Haig in preparation for Haig's meeting with Pik Botha on 14 May 1981. Reproduced in Baker, *The United States and South Africa*, Appendix A.

23 Testimony of Kenneth Dam, *United States Policy toward South Africa* Hearings before the Committee on Foreign Relations, United States Senate, 24 April, 2 May, and 22 May 1985, p. 62.

24 Crocker, 'Strategy For Change', p. 324.

25 'Explanation of US Abstention on UN Security Council Resolution 581', Statement by the Representative (Okun) before the UN Security Council, 13 February 1986. Source: US Mission to the UN, Press Release USUN 11-(86).

26 Ronald Reagan Library, CA. White House Staff and Office Files: Cohen, Herman J., Files 1987–8. African Affairs Directorate, NSC, Boxes 91875 and 91876. Secret Memorandum – From: Secretary of State Alexander Haig. To: The President, 20 May 1981. Subject: Summing up of Pik Botha Visit. Declassified 21 January 1999.

27 Clough, Michael, 'Beyond Constructive Engagement', *Foreign Policy*, No. 61 (Winter 1985–6), p. 12.

28 Crocker's 'Scope Paper'.

29 See especially *Developments in South Africa: United States Policy Responses*, Hearing before the Subcommittee on Africa of the Committee on Foreign Affairs, House of Representatives, 12 March 1986, p. 102 for Crocker's repeated refusal to be pinned down on this issue.

30 Kapp, P. H. and G. C. Oliver, *United States–South African Relations: Past, Present and Future*, Human Sciences Research Council Publication Series, No. 87, Cape Town: Tafelberg Publishers Ltd., 1987, p. 23.

31 Irogbe, Kema, *The Roots of United States Foreign Policy Toward Apartheid South Africa, 1969–1985*, Lewiston, Queenstown and Lampeter: Edwin Mellen Press, 1997, p. 96.

32 *United States Policy on South Africa* Congressional Hearings, 26 September 1984.

33 Ronald Reagan Library, CA. White House Staff and Office Files: Cohen, Herman J., Files 1987-8. African Affairs Directorate, NSC, Box No. 92295, National Security Study Decision Directive, Background 'United States Objectives in Southern Africa', April/May 1987.

34 *America*, Vol. 153, No. 3 (3–10 August 1985), published by the Jesuits of the United States and Canada, New York: America Press Inc., p. 49.

35 Senator Evans, in *United States Policy on South Africa* Congressional Hearings, 24 April, 2 May, and 22 May 1985, p. 142.

36 Crocker, 'A Democratic Future: The Challenge for South Africans', p. 1.

37 *United States Policy on South Africa* Congressional Hearings, 24 April, 2 May, and 22 May 1985, p. 129.

38 Baker, *The United States and South Africa*, p. 23.

39 Ronald Reagan Library, CA. White House Staff and Office Files: Cohen, Herman J., Files 1987-8. African Affairs Directorate, NSC, Boxes 91875 and 91876, Secret Memorandum – From: Secretary of State Alexander Haig. To: The President 20 May 1981. Subject: Summing up of Pik Botha Visit. Declassified 21 January 1999.

40 Irogbe, *Roots of US Foreign Policy*, p. 95.

41 *Ibid.*, p. 129.

42 Thompson, Alex, *Incomplete Engagement: United States Foreign Policy towards the Republic of South Africa 1981–1988*, Aldershot and Brookfield: Avebury, 1996, p. 125.

43 A furore was caused by the sale of 2,500 shock batons to the South African Police, but it does seem plausible to accept the administration's explanation of this as an 'honest mistake', as they never tried to justify the sale and would have been well aware of the political cost of such a decision.

44 *Developments in South Africa: United States Policy Responses*, Congressional Hearings, 12 March 1986, p. 112.

2
Resisting Sanctions:
Constructive Economic Engagement?

The implementation of the policy of constructive engagement sparked a major struggle for control inside Washington. The most high-profile of the policy debates was the issue of economic engagement versus sanctions. This debate had a very significant impact on the development of constructive engagement. It can be argued that this issue succeeded in derailing constructive engagement altogether.

Although South Africa's trade traditionally had overwhelmingly been directed at Britain, as political ties weakened, so did the trade link. Once South Africa left the Commonwealth in 1961, her economic relations began to diversify rapidly, and her economic ties to America, in particular, began to increase. This growth in trade was criticized by Randall Robinson, the Executive Director of TransAfrica,[1] in a 1985 Senate Hearing. He pointed out that in 1950 the US had about $125 million invested in South Africa. The direct investment figure in 1985 stood at over $2.5 billion. If indirect investment and loans were also included, this figure would rise to $4.6 billion. During this same period, conditions in South Africa had worsened, particularly since apartheid was codified into law in 1948.[2]

The benefits of economic involvement in South Africa, despite the internal situation, have always played an important part in policy calculations. In a confidential memorandum from Fred Wettering of the National Security Council (NSC) to Bill Clark (NSC) in April 1983, there was a discussion about the transfer of two Department of Commerce field positions from Europe to South Africa and the Cameroon:

> This will take advantage of improved trade circumstances in these two African countries. [There is a] rising level of US trade coupled with increased trade opportunities for US investment in South Africa ... the indication of increasing US commercial interest in South Africa will displease liberal quarters but reflects both reality and opportunity.[3]

The American public, at this stage, was largely ignorant of or uninterested in events in South Africa. The government knew that employment and living standards at home were far more important to its domestic audience – particularly at election time. The testimony of James B. Kelly – Department of Commerce – to a House Subcommittee in 1985 stated: 'Our exports to South Africa in 1984 were $2.3 billion or 1.1 per cent of our total exports. South Africa was our twenty-third largest export market.'[4] Although he did not have exact figures, he estimated that $2.3 billion in exports generally translated into over 60,000 jobs in the United States.

Arguments against sanctions

This question of economic involvement with South Africa was of great importance to Crocker's policy of constructive engagement. The most significant practical manifestation of his policy was an improved political relationship with Pretoria, and one of the clearest results of this would be an improved and open trading relationship. Crocker's left-wing opponents were championing a policy of isolating South Africa through wide-ranging mandatory sanctions – the opposite of what constructive engagement was trying to achieve. Crocker was determined not to lose control of his policy to the liberals and was adamant in his resistance to sanctions. Although Crocker himself said that sanctions were not the opposite of constructive engagement, the fact was that further sanctions would undermine a policy that was based on fostering closer ties and improving communication with Pretoria. Even beyond the political debate, there were questions from those outside the administration on the efficacy of sanctions as a political tool. In testimony to the House Committee on Foreign Affairs in 1982, Charles Burton Marshall, Head of the System Planning Corporation and previously an academic and policy planner at the State Department, stated:

> [I]f you aspire to get direction over general affairs in some other country, then start out by fastening jurisdiction upon it – attacking, invading, conquering and occupying the country and then keeping it in charge. If you are not willing to do all those things, then reconcile to being frustrated … do not humour yourself with the idea of using commercial manipulations as a bloodless substitute for bloody conquest.[5]

When looking at South Africa in particular, a further argument against sanctions was put forward, this time by Professor Lewis Gann, a Senior Fellow of the Hoover Institute of Stanford University:

> We seem to assume in this country that South Africa is still what it was 60 years ago, a neo-colonial dependency. But South Africa today, in fact, generates the bulk of its capital at home … we are not likely to bring it to its knees by boycotts and such like measures. Even if we could do so, we would have to crush the economies of South Africa's neighbouring black countries.[6]

Crocker's deputy, Charles Freeman, went on to point out that South Africa's economy was particularly well insulated against international sanctions: 'Three fifths of the country's exports are gold and other minerals and metals that cannot be readily obtained from other sources outside the Soviet bloc and which are essential to modern industry in the West.'[7] Another fifth were products like coal, which are widely traded and could find loopholes under sanctions. The damage done in increased unemployment and reduced health, housing and education spending would all be felt far more by the impoverished South African blacks. As Ambassador Herman Nickel explained 'in applied morality one had to consider the likely *results* of a policy. Good intentions, as we all know, pave the way to hell.'[8]

A related argument proved an important underpinning of constructive engagement. Crocker asserted that he was of the belief that damaging South Africa's economy through the use of sanctions and disinvestment was not conducive to change in South Africa, and was certainly not in America's best interests. In 'Strategy for Change' he had stated that engagement in South Africa's economy could be constructive for the majority. He argued that constructive engagement ruled out pinprick measures that would only erode the American position in South African and world markets. *Growth*, not isolation, would undermine apartheid. One of the most respected advocates of this theory was the South African industrialist Harry Oppenheimer, who had been Chairman of the huge Anglo-American Corporation. He spelled out his growth hypothesis in a speech to the US Foreign Policy Association (FPA) in October 1984. An FPA report summarizes his points:

> South Africa's economic growth is not possible without bringing an ever increasing number of African laborers into the workforce and teaching them greater and greater skills. The result ... will be an African labor force, first, integrated economically, then socially, and finally, politically into the South African system.[9]

Another significant element of growth would be the increased purchasing power of blacks. It could also be argued that the success of the black consumer boycotts stemmed from the fact that blacks had capital to withhold. Advocates of continued economic engagement could therefore point, not only to the importance of American interests, but also to the interests of the South African blacks, the very people sanctions supporters said they wanted to help.

The Sullivan principles

There was also another factor which the Reagan administration often cited in defence of US involvement. This was the Sullivan Code of Conduct as practised by a large percentage of US firms operating within South Africa. In the 1960s and 1970s the large US firms had been happy to move into South Africa, exploiting the cheap labour and not particularly concerned about the apartheid system that created it. When the Chief Executive of Ford South Africa was asked if he had any black South African friends, he answered: 'No, I don't mix with them here, and if I ever went back to the States, I wouldn't mix with them there either.' When James Harris, of International Harvester, was asked about his views on the bantustan system, he said: 'I agree with it one hundred per cent ... I don't want hundreds of Africans running around in front of my house.'[10] However, the growing anti-apartheid campaign, already vociferous in the United Kingdom, was beginning to make its voice heard in the US. The big firms, at least in public, began to denounce the 'repugnant' apartheid system. What they did not wish to do, however, was follow up these words with the action of disinvestment. In order to pre-empt the calls for such action, companies began focusing on making their activities in South Africa more socially responsible. The device of a Code of Conduct had its roots in Britain. In 1974 a House of Commons Subcommittee established a Code of Practice for British firms operating in South Africa. This Code provided the basis for the European Community-wide Code of Conduct established in 1977.

This Code focused on trade union rights and equal pay for equal work. The implementation of the Code itself was badly disorganized, with Britain being the only government to submit the required annual report every year.

In March 1977 Reverend Leon Sullivan, a black board member of General Motors, proposed a voluntary Code of Conduct for the US. These 'Sullivan Principles' were similar to the EC Code, but focused more on desegregation than trade unions. The government supported the Code, but had no direct involvement in it. By 1979, 135 firms had adopted and were applying the Code, with varying degrees of conviction.[11] By the mid-1980s this number remained at around 140 out of 250 US companies in South Africa, although these 140 employed over 71 per cent of the workforce employed by American companies. The six core principles of the Sullivan Code were:

1. Non-segregation of races in all work, eating and locker room facilities;
2. Equal and fair employment practices for all employees;
3. Equal pay for equal or comparable work for the same period of time;
4. Training programmes to prepare blacks, coloureds and Asians for management and supervisory positions;
5. An increase in the number of blacks in management and supervisory positions;
6. Improvement of the quality of employees' lives outside work in areas of housing, transportation, schooling, health and recreational facilities.

At the end of 1984 the Code was expanded to include:

• Companies to influence other companies to follow equal rights path;
• Companies must support the rights of black workers to seek jobs wherever they exist;
• Companies must support the rights of black businesses to operate in urban areas;
• Companies must support the rescinding of all apartheid laws.

The companies involved did make a difference to the lives of their employees. Although they had to be careful about their non-racial positions with regard to South African law, many found ways to circumvent it. Ford, for example, was aware of job reservation legislation, yet simply appointed blacks to higher posts. No action was taken and the laws eventually lost significance there. Assistance programmes were also making a difference. By July 1984, approximately $78 million had been spent on schools, housing and other social programmes.[12] And yet, fundamental change was slow in coming – too slow, in fact, for Reverend Sullivan himself. In a dramatic article published in 1985, Sullivan declared:

> I believe the Sullivan Principles, along with other forces, should have 24 more months to work in South Africa, but if statutory apartheid is not ended by that time, there should be a total United States economic embargo against South Africa and the withdrawal of all US companies – to be followed, I hope, by the withdrawal of companies from other countries.[13]

Something needed to be done, he explained, to speed up the far too gradual movement toward fundamental reform. Although he acknowledged that the principles had provided a good deal of benefit and progress, things were simply not moving quickly enough, nor was there any indication that they were about to do so. Sullivan went further: 'It is ... my hope that the President of the United States will set aside "constructive engagement" and use "direct diplomacy" with the South African government, calling in the strongest of terms for the abolition of apartheid.'[14] Reverend Sullivan was as good as his word: in June 1987 he called publicly for US companies to abandon South Africa and sever diplomatic ties with Pretoria. Despite his stand, however, many companies remained in South Africa and continued to extol the virtues of the Sullivan Principles. The companies themselves said that a good deal of suffering would be caused if they pulled out, taking their equal employment practices and community schemes with them. Their presence in South Africa was made increasingly difficult, however, by the expanding sanctions lobby, which did not subscribe to the theory of Oppenheimer, Crocker and others that economic growth would force domestic change in South Africa.

Arguments for sanctions

Opponents of sanctions suggested that progress towards economic equality would result from the exhaustion of labour surpluses in the 'traditional' economy. The implication was that this would increase black bargaining power and that economic growth would therefore result in political reform. Greenberg explained, however, that the inequalities between Africans and Europeans in South Africa had not been helped despite considerable capitalist development in the economy. He also pointed to the available labour surpluses in a country where unemployment estimates varied between one tenth and one quarter of the labour force.[15] Christian Potholm also questioned the idea that a shortage of skilled European labour would force a change in apartheid policies. He argued that the system could even have been reinforced by coincidence between greater non-white economic integration and the totally segregated political sector. The limits on black trade unions and political parties would prevent them from translating their economic strength to political strength and the separate racial political units (bantustans) would serve to channel pressure away from the national centre.[16] A statement by Greenberg, quoted in the Senate by Edward Kennedy, sums up this position: 'This easy association between economic growth and political reform lacks an historic foundation in South Africa; more than a century of industrial development had been accompanied by more, not less, racial discrimination.'[17] Critics also objected to the fact that continued economic engagement represented an indirect form of political assistance by reflecting confidence in the South African system. Economic engagement certainly was viewed as helpful in Pretoria. Clark Else, the Director of the American Chamber of Commerce in South Africa, expressed his approval of the new 'constructive engagement' strategy, saying, in reference to the business opportunities within the Republic: 'Things certainly have improved under the Reagan Administration.'[18] With South Africa approximately $25 billion in debt to the European banks, real fear was developing that the banks could call in these debts, and the pressure on Pretoria was beginning to mount. Advocates of sanctions argued that they would raise the cost of apartheid and embarrass the white government, while encouraging black resistance. Also, although Crocker strongly argued that sanctions would seriously damage the economies of the Frontline States, these same states pointed out that the destabilization being wrought by the apartheid state was causing them even more damage and expense than sanctions would.

The US disinvestment campaign gathers momentum

In the early part of the decade, the sanctions debate was largely confined to academics, politicians and specialist interest groups such as TransAfrica. However, events in South Africa were to cause a dramatic shift, both in public awareness and public opinion, and the heightened profile of the debate meant that the protagonists had to fight their respective corners with increasing vigour. In 1984 Pretoria unveiled its new constitution. This involved a tricameral parliament which afforded limited rights of representation to both Asian and coloured citizens. No provision was made for the black majority. (See Chapter 5 for a more detailed account.) The furious protests that erupted among black South Africans at the end of 1984 met with a massive and brutal police reaction. In February 1985 attempts at forced evictions from the Crossroads squatter camp community resulted in 18 dead and 250 injured. As international opinion began to raise its voice against these actions, worse was to come. On 21 March 1985, the twenty-fifth anniversary of the Sharpeville massacre, police shot into a funeral procession in Langa, Eastern Cape. Thirty-eight people were killed. A wave of protests and uprising spread rapidly throughout the country.

The vivid images served to rally international opinion. Within the US a dramatic shift was witnessed as the horror of the South African situation finally entered the consciousness of the American public. The turmoil in South Africa was shown in almost daily reports from September 1984, when the protests began, to November 1985, when the South African government banned the television cameras. From 21 November 1984, high-profile members of the coalition Free South Africa Movement (FSAM) were arrested during protests in front of the South African embassy. These included Randall Robinson (the founder of TransAfrica), and Congressmen such as Senator Lowell Weicker (Republican, Connecticut), reportedly the first senator in US history to be arrested for an act of civil disobedience while in office.[19]

In many ways, 1984 was a turning point for the profile of South African issues in America. Bishop Tutu received the Nobel Peace Prize, and the black Presidential candidate Jesse Jackson made sure that the issue was kept high on the election campaign agenda. Businesses began to worry as shareholders raised the issue of disinvestment from South Africa and boycotts of companies operating in South Africa were organized. Calls began both for disinvestment – the sale by American companies of subsidiaries doing business in South Africa – and for divestiture – the sale by colleges and other institutions and shareholders of their stock in companies doing business with South Africa. Such actions had begun in February 1981 when Harvard University announced that they had sold approximately $51 million in long-term bonds issued by Citicorp, because that company's banking subsidiary, Citibank, had participated in the direct loan to the South African government in 1980. In the summer of 1983 the seniors at Yale voted to keep investments from a special class fund out of companies that did business with South Africa. By 1984, this 'hassle factor' began to cause real problems for business. As one executive explained, business with South Africa resulted in about 2 per cent of his company's profits, yet managing investments in South Africa took up about 10 per cent of the Board's time. One of the most disconcerting aspects of this activity for the administration was the idea that the government could lose control of its own South Africa policy. Some businesses were beginning to pull out, undermining the strategy of constructive engagement which stated that to influence South Africa, the US must remain involved. Certain state and local governments were also planning their own disinvestment campaigns (see Chapter 3). Although Crocker could, and did, question the constitutional validity of these state actions, he was soon to face opposition from an even stronger force, one that also enjoyed constitutional backing in its fight for control over foreign policy – Congress.

The Executive Order, the Presidential veto and the Comprehensive Anti-Apartheid Act

The Democrats in Congress formed a powerful voice against Crocker's policy. Jesse Jackson stated, during the 1984 Presidential campaign, that: 'a Democratic President will reverse the Reagan Administration's failed policy of "constructive engagement" and strongly and unequivocally oppose the apartheid regime in South Africa'.[20] The difficulties came when the Republicans in Congress were faced with the South African issue. The problem for some of those on the right of the party was that they genuinely hoped for the maintenance of white power in the Republic, believing the white government would best support American strategic and anti-communist interests in the region, but they could not say this openly. The more moderate Republicans found themselves increasingly distanced from those on the right, and they were becoming increasingly impatient with their President's constructive engagement policy. Spurred on by brutal scenes from the township uprisings in 1984, 35 Republican members of Congress sent a letter to South African Ambassador Brand Fourie in Washington. They warned that 'If "constructive engagement" becomes in your view an excuse for maintaining the unacceptable status quo, it will quickly become an approach that can engender no meaningful support among American policy-makers.'[21] This open Republican split was of great significance. As William Finnegan wrote at the time, 'apartheid had divided the right more deeply than any other recent issue'.[22]

Criticism mounted as more and more voices joined in the accusation that constructive engagement was simply not working. The arguments against sanctions that were repeated by Crocker and the anti-disinvestment camp were turned on their head, with the pro-sanctions lobby pointing to the fact that the administration was currently imposing sanctions against the Soviet Union, Cuba, Poland, Iran, Nicaragua and Libya to show their disapproval of those governments. Crocker reacted to the criticism of these double standards by saying, 'Consistency is the hobgoblin of small minds ... we have to look at each case on its merits.'[23] This reply did not go far in satisfying his critics. As the situation in South Africa continued to worsen, public pressure began to increase. The constructive engagement approach was becoming less and less popular the longer it continued without any concrete results. In 1985 a Democrat-controlled House of Representatives passed a new sanctions measure that banned new investment, new loans, computer sales and imports of Krugerrands, and made the Sullivan Principles mandatory for US companies employing more than 25 people in South Africa. The bill had been passed by 295 votes to 127, with 56 Republicans joining the Democrats to vote for the bill. Another worrying fact for Crocker was that a similar Bill[24] was being sponsored by Richard Lugar (Republican – Indiana), Chairman of the Senate Foreign Relations Committee, in the Republican-controlled Senate. In July this Bill was passed by 80 votes to 12. A House–Senate conference committee met to discuss the differences and the weaker Senate version was accepted, with a few changes[25] – as right-wing Republicans would certainly attempt to filibuster any stronger legislation. In August 1985 the report was accepted by the House with a vote of 380 for and 48 against.

The Senate warned the President against trying to veto this legislation as it had considerable bipartisan support. The President had other ideas. He sought to pre-empt the Bill and regain control of US South Africa policy by issuing his own set of sanctions in his Executive Order 12532. The State Department assured the Senate that the Executive Order was essentially the same as the Bill they had been about to pass. There were, however, four significant differences. The Sullivan Principles were no longer mandatory (although export marketing support for companies not adhering to them could be withdrawn), a provision to invoke further sanctions in the event of South Africa refusing to reform was removed, the embargo on Krugerrands was delayed, pending settlement of the dispute on whether it was allowed under GATT obligations,[26] and 'safety equipment' was to be removed from the ban on the transfer of nuclear materials. If the Reagan administration thought this could lay the matter to rest, they had seriously miscalculated. A disastrous pro-South Africa speech delivered by President Reagan on 22 July 1986 (see Chapter 3) badly misjudged the mood of the nation – and Congress. Congress was swift to act and House Resolution (HR) 4868, sponsored by Representative Gray, was reintroduced. Although the Senate was not behind a total economic embargo against South Africa, it again approved a similar Bill, again sponsored by Lugar, by 84 votes to 14.[27] As well as responding to their own views on the issue, the Senators and Representatives were aware that a large section of public opinion (i.e. their constituents) had abandoned Crocker's constructive engagement policy. Reagan had written individually to a number of Senators urging them not to vote for the Bill – knowing that if it was passed he would veto it, and this would be treading dangerous ground.[28] And this is just what happened. His veto was overridden by 313 votes to 83 in the House of Representatives and by 78 to 21 in the Senate. In October 1986 the Comprehensive Anti-Apartheid Act (CAAA) was passed into law, representing one of the worst foreign policy defeats the Reagan administration would experience.

Businesses desert South Africa

As well as this dramatic defeat in the political sphere, factors that were independent of Crocker's constructive engagement policy were also at work in determining levels of US economic involvement with South Africa. States were using their (questionable) constitutional powers to force companies to divest (see below); individuals were boycotting both South African produce and companies with involvement in South Africa. The passing of the CAAA by Congress over the President's veto was clear evidence that, for the time being, America's South Africa policy had been wrested from Crocker's grasp. And there was another factor that could not be asked to comply with the policy line – market forces. From the 1960s to the mid-1970s, investment in South Africa was seen as lucrative and low-risk. Returns on investments from 1960 to 1974 were between 16.3 and 20.6 per cent, a healthy figure when compared with the world average return of between 10 and 11.4 per cent.[29] But by the middle of the 1970s, these profit margins began to fall and 'it was reported in July 1982 that, less than 2 years after attaining one of the highest economic growth rates in the world, South Africa was suffering from its deepest recession since the 1930s'.[30] The resulting fall in profits, combined with the public relations headache which South Africa represented, was enough to force many companies to rethink the value of their South African exposure. The situation accelerated in 1985, with giants such as Coca Cola, Kodak, General Motors and IBM all announcing their departure. Between 1984 and 1989 over half the firms with direct investment in South Africa withdrew. Of the 284 American firms operating in South Africa in December 1984, only 136 remained in July 1988. With loan repayments due and no new lending to replace them, South Africa's total loss of capital from all sources between 1984 and 1987 reached $10 billion. This lack of capital damaged the prospects of economic growth. Pretoria was seriously concerned. In May 1986 Pik Botha declared that 'South Africa's first priority is to stop boycotts imposed against it by Western trading partners.'[31] The fact that simply supporting sanctions in South Africa became a criminal offence clearly indicated the seriousness of the situation in the eyes of Pretoria.

Disinvestment and black South Africa

But what of the black South Africans in this debate? Charles Freeman pointed out that if blacks really wanted US sanctions and disinvestment, 'all they have to do is go on strike to force companies out'.[32] Sal Marzullo, of Mobil Oil – and a leading figure in the application of the Sullivan Principles – explained that many blacks understood the constructive role played by US business and that their voices should be heard. It is difficult to say where blacks stood on this issue. Respected black leaders such as Mandela and Tutu campaigned for disinvestment, whereas many church groups and homeland leaders, including the Zulu leader Gatsha Buthelezi, opposed such measures. Many South African surveys were taken which indicated, on the whole, that roughly 70 per cent of the black population favoured continued investment from the West.[33] However, these surveys tended only to allow an opinion either for or against sanctions and disinvestment. A larger study in September 1985 gave a third option – that foreign firms could invest only if they were actively pressuring Pretoria to end apartheid. This option was supported by 49 per cent of respondents, with 24 per cent still behind total disinvestment and 26 per cent encouraging all investment. In this scenario, 73 per cent favoured disinvestment when companies were not working to end apartheid.[34] Meanwhile, the role of blacks in the economy was of increasing importance. They were producing 50 per cent of the gross national product (GNP). Trade unions were also gaining in stature, with a membership that grew from between 50,000 and 70,000 in 1977 to 670,000 in 1983.[35] Significantly, even the Council of Unions voted for a resolution for disinvestment, stating: 'The national executive committee therefore concludes that any investment in South Africa is therefore an investment in apartheid. There should be no new investment in South Africa while apartheid still exists.'[36] The African National Congress (ANC), South Africa's oldest black political movement, also campaigned for a programme of complete international isolation of South Africa. The more moderate United Democratic Front, an umbrella organization of many anti-apartheid groups, pointed out that an important fact had been missed in many of the discussions regarding black opinions on international sanctions: simply to call for disinvestment and sanctions in South Africa was a criminal offence in that country. Discussions of this topic should be aware of this fact. Crocker maintained that sanctions could not be seen as the alternative to constructive engagement, as sanctions themselves were not a policy – only an instrument of policy. The opponents of constructive engagement saw the matter differently, believing that only by causing Pretoria real economic pain through mandatory international sanctions would the South African government be shaken from its obdurate stance on apartheid.

Constructive economic engagement?

The Reagan administration's control of foreign policy, and particularly its South Africa policy, underwent many challenges from forces with a measure of economic power. These ranged from major political and constitutional challenges from Congress and local state governments, to the unstoppable influence of market forces, and to the group and individual decisions made by universities and private citizens to boycott South Africa themselves. To what extent did this sanctions debate damage the policy of constructive engagement itself and to what extent was the debate over constructive engagement 'laid to rest' by the passing of the CAAA in October 1986? Crocker himself stood firm, still refusing fully to endorse the sanctions that had been forced upon him. He still pointed out that imposing sanctions did not represent a policy. Once they were imposed – then what? In October 1987, the year after Congress had imposed sanctions, he explained that the CAAA had failed because 'no meaningful reform has taken place since October 1986'.[37] (He continued to maintain, however, that constructive engagement was still in place during this time – so which policy was to blame?) The mid-1980s was a time of confusion within the administration itself, and this was reflected in the policy. In a secret memorandum from Herman Cohen to Frank Carlucci of the National Security Council prior to his meeting with Ambassador Perkins, Cohen asks, even at this late stage in 1987: 'Let's be frank about sanctions. Are they really making the whites more intransigent and causing harm to the blacks, or are they making the whites think more about reform?'[38] That he was asking this question at this stage calls into question the sincerity of the administration's vehement arguments against the notion of sanctions having a positive effect. Even Crocker said later: 'We are not against sanctions. We just want to get sanctions right.'[39] The right of the party had no illusions as to what the reasoning behind sanctions should be. In a memorandum to Patrick Buchanan (Director of Communications at the White House), Mona Charen (Associate Director of the Office of Public Liaison) stated:

> We lose ground every time an Administration official explains our opposition to sanctions on the grounds that it will hurt the very people we are trying to help. It's garbage. The left knows it and so do we. No wonder we sound half-hearted.[40]

Charen made clear what at least one faction of the administration saw as the main priority:

> We don't like apartheid but we're just afraid to be too hard on South Africa if the likely outcome will be communism. Everyone will be permanently worse off then.... Let's say it plainly. We have nothing to be ashamed of. The American people understand opposition to communism. They have no idea that that's what we're worried about because we haven't told them yet.

So did constructive engagement actually survive the onslaught from left and right in the sanctions debate? In a background memorandum prepared for Robert McFarlane (Assistant to the President for National Security Affairs, NSC) prior to Congressional briefings in 1985, the warning seems clear: 'Measures which call for penalizing US firms which are involved in South Africa undercut a very important aspect of the constructive engagement philosophy on which our policy is based.'[41] Constructive engagement was derailed, at least temporarily, by the implementation of the CAAA, but this Act was not the only reason. One of the biggest obstacles was that of market behaviour. Once Chase Manhattan Bank refused to roll over a very significant loan, South Africa saw the closing down of the capital markets. This worried them more than the threat of sanctions. As Crocker explained: 'Capital goes where there is confidence, and both were rapidly leaving South Africa.' He went on to say that this was useful, because the administration could then point out to South Africa that this was 'the inevitable result of your own stupidity'.[42]

To describe this withdrawal as useful seemed like an odd conclusion from a man who had always stressed the value of US corporate presence in South Africa, and who believed it was an important aspect of his own policy. During an interview with the author on the importance of American companies and economic growth in South Africa, he explained that, on a micro level, the removal of US business had a negative effect, because US companies had played such an important part in supporting black welfare programmes. 'But on the macro level it was useful for sending an important signal.'[43] This point was not previously acknowledged in Crocker's arguments against sanctions. He was forced to put a brave face on the fact that the withdrawal of business did indeed fundamentally undermine the foundations of constructive engagement, regardless of the benefits he now seems to identify. The policy of constructive engagement, founded on the concept of maintaining an open relationship with Pretoria in order to influence it away from apartheid, could not suddenly claim that American disinvestment was a useful and compatible part of this approach.

Notes

1   This was the black American foreign policy lobby for Africa and the Caribbean.
2   *United States Policy toward South Africa* Hearings before the Committee on Foreign Relations, United States Senate, 24 April, 2 May and 22 May 1985, p. 188.
3   Ronald Reagan Library, CA. Executive Secretariat, NSC: Records Boxes 91340 and 91343 Memorandum – From: Fred Wettering (NSC). To: Bill Clark (NSC). Subject: Transfer of Commerce Positions 7 April 1983.
4   'Statement of James B. Kelly – Department of Commerce' before the Subcommittee on Africa of the Committee on Foreign Affairs, House of Representatives, 17 April 1985.
5   *Controls on Exports to South Africa* Hearings before the Subcommittee on International Economic Policy and Trade, and the Subcommittee on Africa of the Committee of Foreign Affairs, House of Representatives, 97th Congress, Second Session, 2 December 1982 and 9 February 1983, pp. 88–9.
6   *Developments in South Africa: United States Policy Responses* Hearing before the Subcommittee on Africa of the Committee on Foreign Affairs, House of Representatives, 99th Congress, Second Session, 12 March 1986, p. 35.
7   Freeman, Charles W., 'South Africa: What Are America's Options?', *Current Policy*, No. 1033 (9 December 1987), US Department of State, Bureau of Public Affairs, Washington, DC.
8   Bloom, Jack Brian, *Black South Africa and the Disinvestment Dilemma*, Johannesburg: Jonathan Ball Publishers, 1986, p. 35.

9 Hoepli, Nancy L., *South Africa and the United States*, New York: Foreign Policy Association, 1985, p. 6.

10 As quoted in Thompson, Alex, *Incomplete Engagement: United States Foreign Policy Towards the Republic of South Africa 1981–1988*, Aldershot and Brookfield: Avebury, 1996, p. 74.

11 Grundy, Kenneth W. *South Africa: Domestic Crisis and Global Challenge*, Boulder, San Francisco, Oxford: Westview Press, 1991, pp. 61–3.

12 Bloom, *Black South Africa and the Disinvestment Dilemma*, p. 37.

13 Ronald Reagan Library, CA. White House Staff and Office Files: Cohen, Herman J., Files 1987–8. African Affairs Directorate, NSC, Boxes 91875 and 91876, Sullivan, Leon, 'Give the Sullivan Principles Two More Years', 1985 (article – no reference given).

14 *Ibid.*

15 For further details see Greenberg, Stanley B. 'Economic Growth and Political Change: The South African Case', *Journal of Modern African Studies*, Vol. 19, No. 4 (1981), especially pp. 672–701.

16 Potholm, Christian P. 'After Many a Summer? The Possibilities of Political Change in South Africa', review article, *World Politics*, Vol. 24, No. 4 (July 1972), pp. 618–19.

17 Quoted by Edward Kennedy in testimony before the *United States Policy toward South Africa* Congressional Hearings, 24 April, 2 May and 22 May 1985, p. 12.

18 Kline, Benjamin, *Profit, Principle and Apartheid 1948–1994: The Conflict of Economic and Moral Issues in United States–South African Relations*, Studies in African Economic and Social Development, Volume 10, Lewiston, Queenstown, Lampeter: Edwin Mellen Press, 1997, p. 128.

19 Baker, Pauline H., *The United States and South Africa: The Reagan Years. Update South Africa: Time Running Out*, Ford Foundation and Foreign Policy Association: 1989, p. 29.

20 *Congressional Quarterly Weekly Report*, 1984 42 (49) 1779.

21 See Ronald Reagan Library, CA. WHORM Subject Files: 'South Africa, U.S. Policy Towards' File Numbers FG001-FG013; PR003-PR007-02 Letter – From: House of Representatives To: Bernardus G. Fourie, South African Ambassador to the United States Subject: S.A. View of Constructive Engagement 12 April 1984 for full list of signatories.

22 As quoted in Baker, *The United States and South Africa*, p. 36.

23 ARC Identifier: 59701, *Role of the US in Southern Africa – Crocker, 1985*. Creator: United States Information Agency (1982–) (Most Recent). Broadcast 26 June 1985. Item from Record Group 306: Records of the USIA 1900–1988. Video Recordings from the 'Worldnet Today' Program Series, National Audovisual Information Locator (NAIL): 306-WNET-128, Motion Picture, Sound and Video Recordings LICON (life cycle control unit), National Archives at College Park, Maryland USA.

24 Differences were that this Bill originally stated that the sanctions would only be passed if there was no improvement in the South African situation within two years, and that it did not impose a ban on new investment in South Africa.

25 The House of Representatives insisted, for example, that a Krugerrand ban be included.

26 For details of this dispute see, for example, *United States Policy toward South Africa* Congressional Hearings, pp. 65–6.

27 For the full text of the Comprehensive Anti-Apartheid Act 1986 (HR4868), see Baker, *The United States and South Africa*, Appendix D, p. 138.

28 Records remain of the many personal telephone calls Reagan made to Republican Senators in order to prevent the veto. The transcripts of the calls (dated 1 October 1986) show that Reagan himself explained to the Senators: 'I believe the veto vote now is one that should turn on whether the Senate is going to risk undermining the President's pre-eminent position as the chief executive responsible for the conduct of foreign affairs – just prior to meeting the Head of State of the world's other super power [referring to his meeting with Gorbachev that same month – October 1986]'. Ronald Reagan Library, CA. WHORM Subject Files: 'South Africa, US Policy Towards', File Number PR007-02.

29 Grundy, *South Africa Domestic Crisis and Global Challenge*, p. 56.

30 Kline, *Profit, Principle and Apartheid*, p. 126.

31 *South African Digest*, 9 May 1986.

32   Freeman, 'South Africa: What are America's Options?'

33   See Bloom, *Black South Africa and the Disinvestment Dilemma*, pp. 62–4, for accounts of and results from a number of these surveys.

34   Grundy, *South Africa Domestic Crisis and Global Challenge*, pp. 58–9.

35   Hoepli, *South Africa and the US*, pp. 7–8. See also Christopher Coker, 'Collective Bargaining as an Internal Sanction: the Role of US Corporations in South Africa', *Journal of Modern African Studies*, Vol. 19, No. 4 (1981), pp. 647–65 for a further discussion of the role and influence of the South African trade union movement.

36   As quoted in the testimony of T. Donahue, *United States Policy toward South Africa* Congressional Hearings, p. 285.

37   Crocker, Chester, 'A Democratic Future: The Challenge for South Africans', *Current Policy*, No. 1009 (1 October 1987), p. 2, US Department of State Bureau of Public Affairs, Washington, DC.

38   Ronald Reagan Library, CA. White House Staff and Office Files: Cohen, Herman J., Files 1987–8. African Affairs Directorate, NSC. Boxes 91875 and 91876. Secret Memorandum. – From: Herman J. Cohen (NSC). To: Frank C. Carlucci (National Security Adviser), 1 June 1987. Subject: Meeting with Ambassador Edward Perkins, 2 June 1987. Declassified 7 June 1999.

39   ARC Identifier: 59926 *Current Situation in South Africa – Crocker 1987.*

40   Ronald Reagan Library, CA. WHORM Subject Files: Veto and Override of H.R. 4868. File number CO141 – 437840. Memorandum – From: Mona Charen (White House). To: Patrick Buchanan (White House), 29 July 1985. Subject: Framing the Argument on S. Africa.

41   Ronald Reagan Library, CA. White House Staff and Office Files: Cohen, Herman J., Files 1987–8. African Affairs Directorate, NSC. Box No. 92241. Background Report – For: Robert McFarlane. Subject: Congressional Briefings arranged for 21 May 1985 and 23 May 1985.

42   Personal interview with Dr Chester Crocker, 19 June 2001, Washington, DC.

43   *Ibid.*

3
Further Debates in Washington

The 'Cold War' Debate – Regionalists versus Globalists

The struggle over the South African policy was not just between the Executive and Congress, but also involved corporate influence, public opinion and even battles between members of the Executive itself. Many factors, inputs and obstacles were responsible for shaping the eventual outcomes of the constructive engagement policy and these discussions and disagreements tended to coalesce around certain issue areas. Although the debate over sanctions and disinvestment was the most high profile attack on Crocker's policy, it was by no means the only issue to divide Washington.

Constructive engagement – Cold War realpolitik in disguise?

It seems possible that constructive engagement never actually went beyond a *realpolitik* pursuit of global national interest. Yes, apartheid was addressed by the policy, but was this only done because it was unavoidable? Was there ever any genuine belief that the removal of apartheid should have been a top priority in the region? Or if the issue had gone unnoticed by the wider public, like Mobutu's human rights abuses in Zaïre for example, would America simply have continued to support whichever group was most conducive to its interests in South Africa, as prescribed by the Reagan Doctrine?

President Carter was criticized initially for being too 'regionalist', overlooking – his critics said – the vital overarching 'globalist' imperatives of the spread of communism and the global balance of power. Reagan was determined to use his administration to reverse this trend. The pervading view of the Cold War in both the United States and the USSR was as a zero-sum game – a gain by one side would necessarily be a loss for the other, regardless of whether 'vital' interests were involved. 'Symmetrical containment was viewed as of the greatest importance, wherever the Soviets or their proxies were gaining ground.'[1] Reagan believed that America had lost much influence and credibility through the legacy of the 'Vietnam Syndrome' – the trend in thinking in US foreign policy circles that the debacle in Vietnam had been caused by American overstretch, and that in future America would benefit from a policy of isolationism. He was remarkable in his ability to reverse this phenomenon in the American psyche, invoking a new sense of national pride and insisting that the US must stand up against its global foe. In some instances, the Reagan Doctrine advocated supporting 'freedom fighters' that were resisting communist or socialist governments. In others, the prescription was to support and befriend autocratic regimes that, despite their own disregard for democracy, nevertheless provided a bastion against the spread of communism in their own region. Those regimes under attack from national liberation movements with real or perceived communist leanings were especially worthy of US support. The problem with this Doctrine was that the Reagan administration often mis-interpreted African nationalist socialism for Eastern Bloc communism. Also, while the Soviet Union and the spread of communism were identified as the main destabilizing factors in the region, factors such as poverty and racism, which were clearly undermining societies, were often overlooked. As Reagan himself told the *New York Times* in June 1981: 'The Soviet Union underlies all the unrest that is going on. If they weren't engaged in this game of dominoes, there wouldn't be any hotspots in the world.'[2]

Crocker also supported the view that Soviet adventurism was an important challenge to US vital interests. When questioned on the idea of supporting regimes led by 'pliable autocrats', he defended the policy: 'No responsible American official should apologize or will apologize for being concerned about the Soviet Union.'[3] He went on to explain that the US had a global responsibility for insuring the fabric of international stability, and said that to ignore the Soviet threat was to bury one's head in the sand. This fear was reflected in his strategy of constructive engagement. As he pointed out in a 1986 interview on southern Africa: 'What foreign power will fill the vacuum if its ties with the West are broken?'[4] Partly in response to this fear of Soviet encroachment in the area, he argued that South Africa was the ablest ally of the US in the region. In fact, the Soviets proved to be little more than opportunists in southern Africa (see below), although many in the Reagan administration viewed them as having a far more sinister 'grand strategy'. When asked, in an interview with the author, if his perspective was globalist or regionalist, Crocker answered 'both'. Baker asserts that Crocker's policy was more 'nuanced' than many of the ultra-globalist statements emanating from the White House. He did not accept the vision of the 'total onslaught' as espoused by Pretoria, and was aware that some African governments, using Marxism for their own purposes, were not necessarily puppets of Moscow. But Crocker had to acknowledge the strong anti-communist beliefs of Reagan and Haig when formulating policy. In fact Crocker can, and often did, come across as just as firm a believer in the globalist perspective. He explained that: 'the cardinal principle of this administration, we are, in our bones, realists ... so we do believe what takes place in Africa has global consequences'.[5] The statement he made in 1981, reiterated at the end of his term in 1989, made his beliefs clear:

The real choice we will face in southern Africa in the 1980s concerns our readiness to compete with our global adversary in the politics of a changing region.... There can be no presumed communist right to exploit and militarise regional tensions, particularly in this region where important Western economic, resource and strategic interests are exposed.[6]

Republican opposition to the ANC

The globalist perspective shared by many in the Reagan administration and the Republican group in Congress resulted in a real suspicion of the ANC and its Soviet links – to the extent that some viewed the ANC as posing far more of a risk to US interests than the apartheid policies of Pretoria. In a House of Representatives hearing, Republican Congressman Burton noted that

> Some 19 of the 30 members of the executive committee of the African National Congress are known communists, and we believe as many as 25 ... this committee would not support an organization allied with Nazis or fascists, and I do not think we should lend legitimacy to a group allied with people who are equally anti-democratic and anti-American.[7]

An earlier hearing before the subcommittee on Security and Terrorism, held in March 1982, also pointed out that the original aims of both the ANC and SWAPO in Namibia had been subverted and that now they were both believed to be 'Soviet-sponsored terrorist organizations'.[8] President Reagan made clear his administration's views when he publicly referred to 'the Soviet guerrillas' of the African National Congress and stated that 'the South African government is under no obligation to negotiate the future of the country with any organization that proclaims a goal of creating a communist state and uses terrorist tactics and violence to achieve it'.[9]

Crocker shared the administration's hostile view of the ANC, confirming that they were backed and trained by 'Eastern bloc countries' and warning that 'to say that if we do not do X, Y and Z, they [the ANC] will run to Moscow, implies that they have not done so already ... there are very strong ties between that movement and Moscow ... it is obviously a competitive situation. We have got to compete.'[10] An explanation of these links was given by the then Bishop Desmond Tutu in 1981 to the House of Representatives subcommittee on Africa:

> blacks deplore communism as being atheistic and materialistic. But they would regard the Russians as their saviours, were they to come to South Africa, because anything in their view would be better than apartheid, for the enemy of my enemy is my friend ... after all, the West was not too finicky in accepting the Russians as allies against Nazism.[11]

Unfortunately for the ANC, there was a further factor in South Africa's situation that made Washington even more determined to protect it from any risk of communist influence, but which served to remove the focus still further from the local realities of importance to the majority of the South African people. The region as a whole had a significant strategic value, and it was seen as a vital interest that the resources of value to the United States must be defended from the Soviet Union.

Table 3.1 South Africa – Source of Strategic Minerals

Mineral	US import dependence %	% Supplied by South Africa	% SA share of world reserves	Other Suppliers
Chromium	100	48	46	USSR
Ferrochromium	70	44	50	Zimbabwe
Industrial diamonds	100	67	7	Zaïre
Gold	21	13	54	Canada
Fluorspar	83	29	29	Mexico
Ilmenite	75	7	15	Australia
Manganese	99	33	71	Gabon
Ferromanganese	75	43	15	France
Platinum	84	67	81	USSR
Vanadium	52	54	47	Canada
Uranium	30	24	14	Canada

Source: Prepared by Office of Africa, ITA, US Department of Commerce, 1985.

Strategic mineral access

Southern Africa, and South Africa in particular, has been called the 'Persian Gulf of minerals', because it has such large reserves of a number of important minerals (see Table 3.1). The West was reliant upon these reserves for supplies of many minerals of strategic importance and the US was particularly dependent upon South Africa for reserves of chromium, manganese, vanadium and platinum group metals. During the 1980s, South Africa possessed 66.4 per cent of the world's reserves of chromium. This mineral is vital for the US in the manufacture of automobile and computer components. It is also used in the production of stainless steel and in chemical industries. It was also significant because the US lacked domestic reserves of its own. There is no substitute for manganese in the manufacture of wrought steel – and the platinum group metals, of which South Africa had about 73.2 per cent of the world's reserves, have unique properties that make them vital in many industrial applications.[12]

With regard to mineral access, the American government viewed this as a very significant issue.[13] Haig stated that if this critical resource area became aligned with Moscow, 'the USSR could control as much as 90 per cent of several key minerals for which no substitutes have been developed and the loss of which could bring the severest consequences to the existing economic and security framework of the free world'.[14] The importance of these minerals led some conservatives to claim that the US would be better off supporting the white government in Pretoria, assuming that a black government would threaten supply. (This was not the case elsewhere in Africa, however, where, even if they had wanted to, few governments could afford to withhold these exports and sacrifice their resultant earnings.)

Representative James Santini, Chairman of the House Mines and Mining subcommittee, undertook a fact-finding mission to southern Africa in 1980. His report stated that 'no issue facing the US in the future posed as much risk and danger as the dependence on foreign sources for strategic and critical minerals'.[15] The combination of South Africa's overall production, the West's dependence on these reserves, and the strong position of the Soviet Union and its allies as the primary alternative suppliers all combined to strengthen South Africa's standing and importance to America.

The importance of the Cape route

Another strategic consideration in the American policy towards South Africa was its geographic importance. In testimony to Congress in 1980, Crocker had stated: 'To me there is no debate, that the security of the Cape Route is by far the most important Western interest in the African region.'[16] In 1979 the US was the world's largest oil producer (about 10.3 million barrels a day) but it was also the largest consumer (about 19 million barrels a day). Every month about 2,300 ships, including 600 oil tankers, used the Cape route, making it the main access route to the West for oil tankers coming from the Persian Gulf. The Suez Canal was too narrow for Ultra Large Crude Carriers (ULCC), levied higher tolls and was unreliable due to the instability of the region. The canal was closed in 1956, 1967 and 1973 due to the Arab–Israeli wars.[17] Approximately 65 per cent of Western Europe's oil imports were transported via the Cape route. South Africa was also the only country on the east African coast with the necessary economic infrastructure, military potential, ports, airports and dry docks to support Western defence efforts in that area. These factors were enough to convince many in the Reagan administration that protection of this route, and prevention of its falling into the hands of communists, was vital enough to warrant the support of the pro-West government in Pretoria. Crocker himself stated: 'It is clearly more than a convenience that South Africa's excellent port and air facilities should not be in the hands of a potential adversary (or be made available to such an adversary...).'[18]

These considerations played a vital role in Washington's Cold War debate. Yet, as far as the Soviet Union was concerned, most evidence points to the fact that the Soviets never had a 'grand design' in Africa. Africa was low on its list of priorities, just as it was for America. The Soviets followed a line of opportunism in Africa, and ironically it was America and South Africa that provided many of these opportunities simply by not being receptive to the voices and needs of black Africa. As Graham Evans explains:

> There was certainly no evidence, beyond that alleged by Pretoria, of a communist 'grand design' for control of southern Africa. In fact, the biggest Eastern bloc presence in southern Africa throughout the Cold War period – 50,000 Cuban troops in Angola – was paid for not by the USSR, but by Angola from hard dollar currency earned from petroleum exports to the USA.[19]

Donald Rothchild pointed out that 'Even as Soviet leaders were becoming more flexible – ideology was triumphing over pragmatism in the West.'[20] Liberal critics argued that the Soviet Union had not created the racism in South Africa, and that it was this racism that was the greater danger to Western interests. This was because, as apartheid continued, South African liberation movements became increasingly radical. By misinterpreting African nationalism and anti-colonialism as communism, the United States was missing opportunities for influence in the region. Another criticism levelled at the American Cold War policy in the region was that it led to serious inconsistencies in policy. TransAfrica's Executive Director, Randall Robinson, pointed out: 'Whereas the US pressures other industrialized Western countries to cooperate on Polish and Soviet sanctions, it laments how unenforceable and untenable sanctions are in the case of South Africa.'[21] The inconsistencies and misinterpretations inherent in the Reagan administration's view of communism in Africa were, therefore, actually proving counterproductive in that administration's attempts to increase its own influence in the region.

Public Opinion & Constructive Engagement: The Debate Reaches the American Public

Opposition to Pretoria grows

The economic, political and strategic debates outlined above were often of too technical a nature to be explored or understood fully by the wider public. What the public had begun to question, however, was the policy of constructive engagement itself. The public debate on constructive engagement is of vital relevance to one of the key questions of this book. The introduction asserted that it was important to differentiate between Crocker's implicit and explicit aims in his policy towards South Africa. It is argued here that one of his key implicit aims was to develop a *publicly acceptable* face for his policy of close relations with the apartheid regime. This section explores to what extent he was successful in achieving this goal.

A telling 1979 poll recorded that only 18 per cent of the American public had heard of apartheid.[22] This ignorance meant that the debate was largely confined to specialist groups – business interests, on one hand, and specific anti-apartheid groups on the other. Many of the initial anti-apartheid groups were church-based, with the Protestant Episcopal Church filing the first shareholder resolution in 1971, calling on a US corporation (General Motors) to cease its activities in South Africa. Another locus of anti-apartheid action was on the college campuses. Both students and staff began to question the investment policies of their universities' huge endowment funds, objecting to the idea that some funds were invested in South Africa. The scale of these investments can be illustrated by Harvard's decision, in 1981, to divest its $51 million worth of Citicorp bonds and certificates because the bank was involved in large-scale lending to South Africa.

Another section of domestic opinion was also calling for change in the US policy towards South Africa. This was the black American population. In 1977, the Congressional Black Caucus formed an African-American foreign policy lobby group, TransAfrica. This lobby was strongly of the opinion that the way to deal with Pretoria was radically to increase the pressure on it from outside. 'TransAfrica was actively trying to change the constructive engagement policy of the Reagan Administration.'[23] This conflict of opinion meant that relations between TransAfrica and the Reagan administration were hostile. This situation worsened very early on in the relationship when six documents were leaked to the lobby group – four prepared by the State Department and two by the South African government. They reflected the Reagan administration's intention to establish close relations with Pretoria. TransAfrica published the documents in a special edition of the *TransAfrica News Report* in August 1981.[24] Because of this, the group's Executive Director Randall Robinson had no formal meetings with any Reagan administration official during Reagan's two terms in office. Where TransAfrica did have success, however, was in encouraging grassroots disinvestment campaigns, with the American public beginning to object to companies that invested in or traded with South Africa. This in turn led to actions by state and local legislatures. Before the advent of the Reagan administration, only two states and five municipal governments had placed restrictive measures on their dealings with firms operating in South Africa. Between 1985 and 1988, 16 states and 56 municipal governments divested their public funds of investments in companies that did business with South Africa. The other state tactic of 'selective purchasing' (deliberately and openly discriminating against companies dealing with South Africa when holding the tenders for the huge, and lucrative, state purchasing contracts) hit companies more directly than disinvestment. Three states and 28 cities introduced this legislation in the 1985–8 period. One of the most significant aspects of these actions was the way in which states could pre-empt and circumvent the foreign policy of the Executive. In a telephone call from Shultz to Attorney General Meese, Shultz pointed out that these state and local actions: 'continue to be a major force behind the growing exodus of US firms from South Africa'. Shultz's irritation at the undermining of his constitutional position was clear: 'These movements frustrate the achievement of important foreign policy objectives ... these matters are reserved to the federal government under the constitution.'[25] The anti-apartheid movement was gaining ground, but slowly. In 1984, however, events in South Africa were radically to alter the equation on the ground in the United States.

1984 – the South African uprisings

In 1984 the South African government implemented its new constitution, including provisions for a tricameral parliament which excluded the South African black population. In the next two days, 33 people were shot dead by the South African Police as protests against the constitution began to spread. 'By Autumn of 1985, South Africa was experiencing a low-intensity civil war.'[26] The uprisings and unrest continued until 1987, by which time around three thousand South Africans had been killed and thirty thousand detained. The pictures of black demonstrators, many unarmed, being beaten and shot for demanding a voice were beamed nightly into the sitting rooms of the American public. The immediate result was that the anti-apartheid movement began to gather pace. One focus was the greatly increased activity from the student, church and local government disinvestment campaigns. On 21 November 1984 Robinson staged a peaceful sit-in at the South African Embassy in Washington, DC, together with Congressman Walter Fauntroy (Democrat – District of Columbia) and Mary Frances Berry of the US Civil Rights Commission. The action led to Robinson's arrest, and it caught the imagination of the anti-apartheid activists who created the umbrella Free South Africa Movement. The action was repeated at the South African Embassy and Consulates throughout the United States. Its profile was heightened by the fact that 18 prominent members of Congress were arrested taking part. These arrests, in turn, highlighted the increasingly vociferous disinvestment movement. The *Financial Times* stated that

> The reality is the unexpected emergence of the banking system as a conduit for the US public's attitudes towards the situation in South Africa. It has allowed shareholders, depositors and the public directly to impose an economic sanction without having to persuade their government to do so.[27]

This impact was all the more remarkable because, on the whole, the disinvestment campaign did not have the backing of the US public in general. A Harris poll published in *Business Week* in February 1985 showed that, of 1,254 Americans questioned, 68 per cent agreed to the question, 'Should the US press the South African government to give blacks more freedom and participation in government?' 21 per cent of Americans were opposed. When the question turned to economic sanctions, however:

> 51 per cent disagreed that new bank loans should be barred; 54 per cent rejected blocking all new business investment; 66 per cent rejected the option of ending all trade with South Africa; and 76 per cent were against forcing US business to close down all existing South African operations.[28]

Yet, despite these reservations, the anti-apartheid movement itself was a good media subject – and 'Apartheid was an issue with an appealing moral clarity, and sanctions and disinvestment offered tangible ways for Americans to express their feelings about officially sanctioned racism.'[29] As far as media coverage was concerned, the anti-apartheid movement also had a 'secret weapon' in the person of Bishop Desmond Tutu. Not affiliated to any political party, Tutu came across as a charismatic and sincere Christian whose incisive comments were well suited to the American media. His positive reception did not extend as far as the Reagan administration, however – particularly when some of Tutu's 'incisive' comments included labelling constructive engagement as 'immoral, evil and totally unChristian'.[30] Indeed, a rather ill-tempered confidential memorandum from Ambassador Herman Nickel complained about the way in which Tutu played the US media 'like a violin'.[31] The impact of unfavourable public opinion, particularly after 1984, made itself felt in the implementation of the constructive engagement policy. Crocker complained about the way in which this public debate over his own policy had been blown vastly out of proportion and explained to the public that: 'The only real alternative to constructive engagement – [is to tell South Africa to] stew in your own juice and sort out your own problems.'[32]

The Public Diplomacy Program

The main problem was not with the policy itself, Crocker maintained, but with the way in which the American public had misunderstood its goals. All that was needed was for these goals to be properly explained. Due to this reasoning it was decided in September 1985, after Reagan's Executive Order had been issued, that an *ad hoc* working group on South Africa would be established to focus on the way in which the engagement policy was being presented to the American public. Its remit did not include focusing on the substance of that policy. By 1986 the formal 'Working Group on South and Southern Africa' was well established, with its *raison d'être* being the public defence of the constructive engagement policy. Indeed, more staff were actually employed in the Working Group than were employed by the State Department's own southern Africa desk at this time.[33] In fact, the confidential National Security Study Decision Directive (NSDD) 187, dated 7 September 1985, focused a great deal on: 'the necessity of re-emphasiz[ing] the broad objectives of US political strategy toward South Africa'.[34] The directive, although entitled 'United States Policy toward South Africa', actually spent two of its three pages focusing not on this policy, but on public and Congressional criticism of it. Yet what all this emphasis on the Public Diplomacy Program failed to recognize was that the main problem was not that the policy was misunderstood, but rather that, for such a policy as constructive engagement, visible successes were vital in order for it not to be dismissed as appeasement of Pretoria. As *The Economist* explained: 'The policy of constructive engagement required some emphatic success if it was not to be seen as a mere dodging of the apartheid issue.'[35]

But the fact remained that, although there was a dramatic rise of awareness amongst the interested parties of US public opinion, the size of these interested parties remained small. In a notoriously isolationist public, Africa was usually at the bottom of the list of priorities. In a 1985 CBS poll, reported in the *New York Times*, three per cent of its respondents approved of apartheid, but 58 per cent had chosen not to make a response on the basis that they knew too little to offer an opinion.[36] The debate over apartheid, sanctions and constructive engagement was kept alive within the political elite, where it became a threat to the survival of Crocker's policy. The real battle for the South Africa policy was fought within the political arena.

Crocker Faces Political Opposition

Crocker versus Congress

By far the most public of the political confrontations was between the administration and Congress. The fact was that, behind the dramatic events surrounding the passing of the CAAA in 1986 and the override of the Presidential veto, the relationship between the Reagan administration and Congress was increasingly acrimonious. In the first few years of the Reagan administration, Congressional interest in African issues was limited to a small number of interested parties. The leading figure in the right-wing Congressional opposition to Crocker's southern Africa policy was Senator Jesse Helms. His staunchly held right-wing globalist beliefs clashed with Crocker's more balanced attitudes, and Helms even went as far as obstructing the confirmation hearings on Reagan's nomination of Crocker for the post of Assistant Secretary for African Affairs. Throughout Reagan's first term, the main preoccupation of the Senate was anti-communism. Constructive engagement was often attacked for not sufficiently addressing globalist considerations.

The Republican Party had to deal with a serious split in its own ranks over this issue. Meanwhile, relations between the White House, the State Department and Congress were, at times, becoming 'really nasty'.[37] While discussing the increasing repression in South Africa in 1985, and the growing criticism of his constructive engagement policy, Senator Sarbanes told Crocker: 'All of this is happening around you, and yet I do not sense that you're coming to grips with it. You yourself should be questioning your own policy in view of this, and searching for some way to address the situation.' Crocker's response was to state that: 'I think that there is a tendency ... that the South African question today in this country has become for some the moral equivalent of a free lunch....' Senator Sarbanes, in turn, called this 'an unfair put down of a lot of people who I think have a very real and genuine concern'.[38] Mr George Crockatt, (Democrat Representative for Michigan and member of the Congressional Black Caucus) while referring to constructive engagement as a 'dismal failure' pointed out that just before Crocker's 1981 speech in Hawaii outlining his policy, the House Subcommittee on Africa had been to South Africa, visiting Crossroads and Soweto, meeting with a lot of blacks 'with whom the State Department has no contact', and meeting with Foreign Minister Botha and the Constitution Commission. 'We were in a position to ... give you some valuable information before you formulated the policy ... but I do not think anyone on this subcommittee was consulted.'[39] Chairman Wolpe also pointed out that his requests (as many as eight or nine) to meet the Secretary of State following his own visits to southern Africa had all been refused.

Congress managed to inflict very real damage on Crocker's policy when it forced Reagan to issue his Executive Order as a pre-emptive strike against sanctions, and then managed to undermine constructive engagement by passing the CAAA. The overriding of the Presidential veto also demonstrated just how bad relations between the White House and Congress had become. The President made many personal telephone calls to Senators to persuade them not to vote for the override. Republican activists were contacted and instructed to write to their Senators to call on them to vote against the veto override. As a confidential memorandum from Patrick Buchanan points out:

What we are playing with here is the credibility of the President. Let me urge, again, that we hold off any sanctions whatsoever, until we are forced to yield up, grudgingly, inch by inch if necessary, at the midnight hour. (Ronald Reagan, after all, has trashed sanctions up and down).[40]

The override of the Presidential veto was the first on a foreign policy matter since the 1973 War Powers Act. When the result of the vote was announced in the Senate, it was met with complete silence. The Senate was aware that this was an historic rebuff to the Chief Executive.[41]

The low priority and widespread ignorance on southern African issues amongst both the US government and the US public meant that, for the first few years at least, Crocker had been given a free rein when developing and implementing US South Africa policy. The White House remained preoccupied with the Cold War, and as long as Crocker could persuade the White House that he had these issues uppermost in his mind 'he could essentially do what he wanted'.[42] Crocker's acknowledgement of Cold War issues angered the left while his stated aim of building a centrist consensus on South Africa led the right to believe he was underestimating the value of the anti-communist white regime in Pretoria. The hostility between the Africa bureau of the State Department and Congress was by no means unusual. As a political appointee, Crocker was part of the Reagan administration, and conflict between Congress and the executive is a regular feature of US politics. Congress was not, however, Crocker's only enemy. Many of his difficulties emanated from a lot closer to home – the rival departments and Office of the White House that comprised the executive itself.

Crocker and Reagan – 'the great communicator'

Africa had never been prominent on the US foreign affairs agenda, and this certainly continued to be the case under Reagan. When the sanctions debate catapulted this region onto the national agenda, however, Reagan's casual remarks on the situation there became more frequent – much to the chagrin of the State Department. The State Department had an idea of what it was up against very early in Reagan's first term. In an interview in March 1981, Reagan posed the question: 'Can we abandon a country that has stood by us in every war we've ever fought, a country that strategically is essential to the free world in its production of minerals we all must have and so forth?'[43] Reagan seemed ignorant of the fact that the current ruling party of South Africa – the National Party – had not been in power in South Africa during the Second World War, had in fact been sympathetic to Nazi Germany and had opposed joining the Allies. The message of the State Department was often confused by statements emanating from the White House, and its members were frequently embarrassed, having to square the President's comments with its own enunciation of policy. The clearest example of this was a speech given by Reagan on 22 July 1986. There had been a good deal of inter-departmental rivalry when the State Department presented its draft speech on South Africa for the President, only to have it rejected by the White House's Director of Communications, Pat Buchanan. He wrote a speech that was a far clearer reflection of the right-wing globalist views he and the President shared. The President chose to deliver this speech, despite strong protests from Shultz. This speech went against the public mood by dwelling primarily on reforms undertaken by President Botha, at a time when repression and violence were spiralling in South Africa. Reagan explained: 'Segregation is being set aside. Social apartheid laws ... are being struck down ... only in South Africa have the real incomes of blacks risen very substantially....' The speech also featured 'free world' rhetoric: 'Indeed, it's hard to think of a single country in the Soviet bloc, or many in the United Nations, where political critics have the same freedom to be heard, as do outspoken critics of the South African government.' In what appears to be a remarkably insensitive comment, at a time when the US media was covering stories of unarmed protesters being shot by the South African Police, Reagan also stated: 'In defending their society and people the South African government have a right and a responsibility to maintain order in the face of terrorists.'[44]

Interestingly, in this oft-quoted and transcribed speech, there is another error that had been overlooked – and is even corrected in the transcripts. Watching a videotape of the speech itself, it is clear that in the first three references Reagan makes to South Africa, he in fact refers to 'South *America*'. Although this reverts to 'South Africa' on all available transcripts, it could be argued that this was a demonstration of where Reagan's priorities continued to lie. Reaction to the speech was dramatic. The headline in the *New York Times* the next day was 'The Speech that Launched A Thousand Critics' and the Washington-based British journalist Simon Barber wrote: 'Indeed, it seemed deliberately calculated to provoke the worst possible responses from all sides: it gave Pretoria comfort, black South Africa reason to despair, and Congress no choice.'[45] The main problem, Thompson suggested, was that Reagan 'simply failed to convey any sense of understanding or sympathy for what the black South African population was suffering'.[46] A *New York Times* editorial spoke for the views of many when it accused Reagan of being deaf to 'one of the great moral issues of our time'.[47]

A direct result of Reagan's unguarded comments was the immense amount of work they created for the State Department. Each comment had to be 'explained' or 'clarified' in an attempt to make it fit with the rest of the US South Africa policy. Indeed, Shultz actually found himself testifying at the Senate Foreign Relations Committee the day after Reagan's speech. Shultz's testimony, far more pessimistic in tone than his President's, demonstrated the gulf between two apparently different policies.[48] The worst aspect of all this for Crocker was the difficulty it caused him when he was already fighting a losing battle with the left in Congress for control of the policy towards South Africa. As he was later to explain: '[Reagan] had just won a huge [election] victory, so they wanted to get on to him and this was his weak spot. It was easy to go after Reagan on the race issue because on this, he was just not a good communicator.'[49] In his own account of the period, he explained: 'The President tended to discredit his case by sounding so much like the government from which he was so reluctant to distance himself.'[50] Crocker was by no means the only member of the government to be upset by Reagan's handling of this issue. Ambassador Nickel described it as 'one of the "Great Communicator's" most painful failures'. The Republican Senator Lugar summed up what much of Congress felt: 'I would not have persisted in opposing the President if after all these conversations, debates and statements I had developed reasonable confidence in his comprehension of what the South African situation was all about.'[51]

The fact was that Crocker was having enough trouble attempting to present an unambiguous picture of an ambiguous policy both to Pretoria and the US public. Despite Reagan's own lack of interest in or understanding of this region, comments made by him carried a lot of weight. What compounded this situation was that, despite his occasional comments on this policy area, Reagan failed completely to assert his authority over this divisive issue. His laissez-faire management style[52] was entirely unsuited to dealing with the development of a policy that badly needed a consensus behind it. The result was that the constructive engagement policy – under attack from both the left and the right in Congress, among the American public, within South Africa and in the White House itself, was left vulnerable to yet more attacks from yet more enemies – and these were the rival departments within the administration itself.

Bureaucratic politics and interdepartmental conflict – the struggle for control

While Crocker was facing strong criticism from members of Congress regarding his failure to meet, discuss and possibly compromise with them, he was being pulled in just the opposite direction by the White House. A memorandum from Phil Nicolaides (White House Office and Deputy Director of Voice of America) to Patrick Buchanan (Assistant to the President and Director of Communications – White House Office) refers to the fact that Crocker and Senator Lugar had met the day before to work out terms of a 'compromise sanctions bill'. The memorandum goes on to berate Crocker's actions:

> I'm sure I don't need to go through my standard lecture about how this sort of behaviour, born of the Minority Party Syndrome (we cannot seem to shake it even when we are in the majority [in the Senate]!), sends just the wrong signal of weakness to the foes of the President's foreign policy.[53]

Again, in August 1986, while members of the NSC and the Office of the White House were working desperately to persuade senators to uphold the President's veto on HR 4868, Nicolaides told Buchanan that what was needed was a Department of Commerce report on how the sanctions measures would hurt US jobs. The need to source this report from Commerce was reiterated because: 'The Boer Bashers at State are not going to want such a report, so don't expect it from them.'[54]

As the South African issue moved up the political agenda, the suspicions of the White House and NSC staff members towards Crocker and the State Department grew. Just as Crocker was facing the body blow of the CAAA from the anti-apartheid movement on the left, on the right the White House was becoming increasingly frustrated that he was refusing to toe the President's line. In a memorandum discussing a shift in —policy emphasis to constitutional reform in South Africa and away from calling for the release of Mandela and the unbanning of the ANC, Nicolaides said of the latter approach:

> This remains the agenda of the State Department as is evident from their instructions to someone charged with preparing a draft for a Shultz speech on South Africa to be delivered in October. He was told to 'follow the lines of the speech that State originally prepared for the President'. (Not the President's July 22 speech, mind you, but the speech the President rejected!)[55]

Another example of State Department caution regarding the President's view of policy is a cable from the US Ambassador to Lesotho on 30 July 1986, stating that General Lekhana, Head of the Government of Lesotho, had publicly expressed wholehearted agreement with Reagan's policy as outlined in his 22 July speech. The Ambassador requested permission from the State Department to release publicly the General's pro-Reagan statement, but this permission was immediately denied. As an NSC memorandum on this states: 'He was told that while Buchanan and Ringdahl had been responsible for the policy outlined in the speech, that policy had been overwhelmed by opposition and was currently under review.' The memorandum ends with a comment that shows how fragmented the Executive's consensus had become:

> The US Ambassador to Lesotho is very unhappy that he, although appointed by the President, is under orders from the State Department not to report information favourable to the President's personally enunciated policy. He wonders if the President is aware of this situation.[56]

This departmental hostility was intense within the administration, with Reagan's lack of management ability increasing Crocker's vulnerability, as he explained:

> There was no discipline, no system and apparently no means of keeping unauthorized personnel away from the vital machinery of decision-making. Every major element of our Southern African policies – policies Shultz had obtained presidential approval for – was the object of one form of sabotage or another in the NSC, the domestic White House, the CIA or Defense Department.[57]

William Casey, Director of the Central Intelligence Agency (CIA), was often in the forefront of attempts to sabotage Crocker's agenda. As Crocker explained: 'There was a *very* conflictual situation in Washington.' When asked if he thought Casey deliberately undermined him, Crocker replied: 'He tried to. But I beat him.'[58] For example, Casey informed P. W. Botha that, on Crocker's forthcoming visit to Pretoria, a long-awaited offer of an invitation to Washington would be made. The State Department had already decided against this, but, by sowing this seed, Casey had wrong-footed Crocker before he even arrived in South Africa.

Constructive engagement was by no means unique in depending for its successful implementation on factors outside its framers' control. Crocker's miscalculation was to refuse to reevaluate or significantly modify the policy when, in the mid-1980s, a lack of results turned many key supporters against it. And Shultz's urgent warnings in 1983, in retrospect, take on the air of a self-fulfilling prophecy: 'We simply cannot afford Southern Africa to become a divisive domestic issue – tearing our country apart, rendering our actions haphazard and impotent.'[59] As Crocker himself points out when looking back at this period: 'By the end of 1986 we sorely missed that ephemeral "centrist consensus" and had lost the chance to rebuild it.'[60] Somewhere along the line the original aims (at least the original explicit aims) of constructive engagement had disappeared from view. While the State Department struggled to keep a domestic consensus together behind constructive engagement, the original target of the policy – the South Africans – were watching the confusion from the sidelines. As J. Edward Fox (Assistant Secretary of State for Legislative and Intergovernmental Affairs) somewhat implausibly wrote to Congressman Wolpe: 'it is important that we not convey to South Africans or others the *false* impression of American division and partisan wrangling'[61] [my emphasis]. This is, however, what the US had succeeded in doing – or rather, it had *failed* to prevent conveying a very *real* impression of division and wrangling.

Notes

1   Nicol, Davidson 'United States Foreign Policy in Southern Africa: Third World Perspectives', *Journal of Modern African Studies*, Vol. 24, No. 4 (1983), p. 601.

2   As quoted in Kapp, P. H. and G. C. Oliver, *United States–South African Relations: Past, Present and Future*, Human Sciences Research Council Publication Series No. 87, Cape Town: Tafelberg Publishers, 1987, p. 77.

3   ARC Identifier: 59701. *Role of the U.S. in Southern Africa – Crocker, 1985*. Creator: United States Information Agency (1982–) (Most Recent). Broadcast 26 June 1985. Item from Record Group 306: Records of the USIA 1900–1988. Video Recordings from the 'Worldnet Today' Program Series, NAIL Locator: 306-WNET-128 Motion Picture, Sound and Video Recordings LICON (life cycle control unit), National Archives at College Park, Maryland USA.

4   ARC Identifier: 54679, *President Reagan's South Africa Policy Speech, 1986*. Creator: United States Information Agency (1982–) (Most Recent). Item from Record Group 306: Records of the USIA 1900–1988. Series: Motion Picture Films 1944–1999. NAIL Locator: 306.9633, Motion Picture, Sound and Video Recordings LICON, National Archives at College Park, Maryland USA.

5   ARC Identifier: 54305 *Challenges to United States Foreign Policy: Chester Crocker Responds, 1983*. Creator: United States Information Agency (1982–) (Most Recent). Item from Record Group 306: Records of the USIA 1900–1988. Series: Motion Picture Films 1944–1999. NAIL Locator: 306.9172, Motion Picture, Sound and Video Recordings LICON, National Archives at College Park, Maryland USA. For a good illustration of Crocker's globalist position, see in full his 'Scope Paper' for Secretary of State Alexander Haig in preparation for Haig's meeting with Pik Botha on 14 May 1981. Reproduced in Pauline H. Baker, *The United States and South Africa: The Reagan Years. Update South Africa: Time Running Out*, Ford Foundation and Foreign Policy Association: 1989,

Appendix A.

6   Crocker, Chester, 'South Africa: Strategy for Change', *Foreign Affairs*, Vol. 59, No. 2 (Winter 1980–1), pp. 345–6.

7   *Legislation Urging the South African Government to Engage in Meaningful Negotiations with That Country's Black Majority* Hearing and Markup on House Resolution 373 before the Subcommittee on Africa of the Committee of Foreign Affairs, House of Representatives, 24 June and 6 August 1986, p. 5 and p. 15.

8   *The Role of the Soviet Union, Cuba and East Germany in Fomenting Terrorism in Southern Africa* Hearings before the Subcommittee on Security and Terrorism of the Committee on the Judiciary, United States Senate, 22 March 1982.

9   Reagan, Ronald, 'Ending Apartheid in South Africa', address by President Reagan to The World Affairs Council and the Foreign Policy Association, US Department of State, Bureau of Public Affairs, Washington, DC, *Current Policy*, No. 853 (22 July 1986).

10   *Developments in South Africa: United States Policy Responses*, Hearing before the Subcommittee on Africa of the Committee on Foreign Affairs, House of Representatives, 12 March 1986, p. 111.

11   Quoted by Wolpe in *The Current Crisis in South Africa* Hearing before the Subcommittee on Africa of the Committee on Foreign Affairs, House of Representatives, 4 December 1984, p. 6.

12   Thomas, A. M., *The American Predicament: Apartheid and United States Foreign Policy*, Aldershot and Brookfield: Ashgate Publishing Ltd., 1997, pp. 21–3.

13   See, for example, *United States Minerals Supply and South Africa: Issues and Options* Oversight Hearing before the Subcommittee on Mining and Natural Resources of the Committee on Interior and Insular Affairs, House of Representatives, 100th Congress First Session, 10 December 1987, where the main focus of a heated debate was the urgent necessity of securing alternative supplies and stockpiles of minerals in the light of the possibility of the South African government being overthrown, and mineral access falling under communist influence and control.

14   Kapp and Oliver, *United States–South African Relations*, p. 82. See also *US Policy Toward Southern Africa: Focus on Namibia, Angola and South Africa* Hearing and Markup before the Subcommittee on Africa of the Committee on Foreign Affairs, House of Representatives, 97th Congress, First Session on House Resolution 214; Con. Resolution 183, 16 September 1981.

15   Thomas, *The American Predicament*, p. 24. These findings should be treated with a certain amount of caution. One's role can sometimes affect one's perceptions – 'Where you stand depends on where you sit!'

16   Quoted in Thompson, Alex, *Incomplete Engagement: United States Foreign Policy Towards the Republic of South Africa 1981–1988*, Aldershot and Brookfield: Avebury, 1996, p. 123.

17   See Thomas, *The American Predicament*, p. 26.

18   As quoted in *ibid.*, p. 79.

19   Evans, Graham 'The Great Simplifier: The Cold War and South Africa 1948–1994', in Alan Dobson (ed.), *Deconstructing and Reconstructing the Cold War*, Aldershot: Ashgate Publishing Ltd., 1999, p. 145.

20   Rothchild, Donald, Preface to Kenneth Mokoena (ed.) *South Africa and the United States: The Declassified History*, a National Security Archive documents reader, New York: The New Press, 1993, p. xii.

21   *Controls on Exports to South Africa* Hearings before the Subcommittees on International Economic Policy and Trade, and on Africa, of the Committee of Foreign Affairs, House of Representatives, 97th Congress, Second Session, 2 December 1982 and 9 February 1983, p. 90.

22   See Thompson, *Incomplete Engagement*, p. 92, for further poll results.

23   Baker, *The United States and South Africa*.

24 The documents were:

Memorandum of Conversation between Assistant Secretary of State Crocker, Pik Botha (South African Foreign Minister) and Magnus Malan (South African Defence Minister), Pretoria, 15–16 April, 1981.

State Department Overview of US policy toward southern Africa, 31 May 1981.

Memorandum from Paul Hare, Director of State Department's Southern African Affairs Office, to Crocker on Contact Group Meeting of 13 May 1981.

Crocker's 'Scope Paper' for Secretary of State Alexander Haig in preparation for Haig's meeting with Pik Botha on 14 May 1981.

South Africa's list of US interests in southern Africa, May 1981.

South African memorandum on US–South African nuclear relations, 14 May 1981.

Reproduced in Baker, *The United States and South Africa*, Appendix A.

25 See Ronald Reagan Library, CA. White House Staff and Office Files: Dewhirst, Mary, File Number OA 17788, Memorandum – From: Office of Management and Budget. To: The President – Subject: Discussion/Background Paper on South Africa 25 September 1986. For a full list of the states and municipal governments involved, see Hoepli, Nancy L., *South Africa and the United States*, New York: Foreign Policy Association, 1985, p. 11.

26 Thompson, *Incomplete Engagement*, 1996, p. 190.

27 Kline, Benjamin, *Profit, Principle and Apartheid 1948–1994: The Conflict of Economic and Moral Issues in United States–South African Relations*, Studies in African Economic and Social Development, Vol. 10, Lewiston, Queenstown and Lampeter: Edwin Mellen Press, 1997, p. 144.

28 *Business Week*/Harris Poll, 'Fight Apartheid, but Don't Shut up Shop' in *Business Week*, 11 February 1985.

29 Baker, *The United States and South Africa*, p. 34; see also Kline, *Profit, Principle and Apartheid*, p. 142.

30 *The Current Crisis in South Africa* Hearing, 4 December 1984.

31 Mokoena, *South Africa and the United States: The Declassified History*, p. 51.

32 ARC Identifier: 59701 *Role of the US in Southern Africa – Crocker, 1985*.

33 Thompson, *Incomplete Engagement*, p. 255.

34 Ronald Reagan Library, CA. White House Staff and Office Files: Cohen, Herman J., Files 1987–8. African Affairs Directorate, NSC. Box No. 92295. Secret Report – By: The White House. Subject: National Security Study Decision Directive Number 187, 7 September 1985. Declassified 16 March 1998, p. 1.

35 *The Economist*, 'America and South Africa', 30 March 1985, pp.17–34. On 27 April 1987, the National Security Council requested update information from the Public Diplomacy Working Groups. The State Department replied: 'The US objectives in South Africa have not changed but political dynamics in that country plus an altered public affairs environment in the US argue for a more refined approach....' The report continues: 'In South Africa the situation has deteriorated in recent months … meanwhile the US Congress, following passage of the CAAA … has taken up new concerns … the US public has also tended to focus on other issues. Barring some new atrocity by the South Africans, American media and political focus will be on issues other than South Africa in the coming months.' Ronald Reagan Library, CA. WHORM Subject Files: 'South Africa, US Policy Towards', File Number FG011– 497549.

36 'Most Americans in CBS Poll Know Little about Aparthied', *New York Times*, 1 September 1985, p. 17.

37 Thompson, *Incomplete Engagement*, p. 306.

38 *United States Policy toward South Africa United States Policy toward South Africa* Hearings before the Committee on Foreign Relations, United States Senate, 24 April, 2 May and 22 May 1985, pp.148–9. See also *The Current Crisis in South Africa* Hearing, 4 December 1984, p. 1, where Chairman Wolpe says that constructive engagement has 'merely made matters worse'.

39 Crocker Testimony to *Developments in South Africa: United States Policy Responses* Congressional Hearings, 12 March 1986, p. 106.

40 Ronald Reagan Library, CA. Executive Secretariat, NSC: Records Boxes 91340 and 91343, Confidential Memorandum – From: Pat Buchanan. To: Donald Regan and John Poindexter (White House). Subject: Possible Botha/Reagan Meeting, 22 August 1986.

41 See Thompson, *Incomplete Engagement*, p. 226

42 Kyvig, David E. (ed.), *Reagan and the World*, New York: Praeger Publisher, 1990, pp. 16–17. Kyvig goes on to say 'Crocker had [Africa] all to himself and ignored the State Department, just as Kissinger did': p. 17.

43 Reagan's interview with Walter Cronkite, 3 March 1981.

44 ARC Identifier: 54679, *President Reagan's South Africa Policy Speech, 22 July 1986*. Creator: United States Information Agency (1982–) (Most Recent). Item from Record Group 306: Records of the USIA 1900–1988. Series: Motion Picture Films 1944–1999. NAIL Locator: 306.9633 Motion Picture, Sound and Video Recordings LICON, National Archives at College Park, Maryland USA.

45 Baker, *The United States and South Africa*, p. 44.

46 Thompson, *Incomplete Engagement*, p. 292.

47 'What New South Africa Policy?' Editorial, *New York Times*, 23 July 1986, p. A22.

48 Shultz testimony to US Senate, 'Situation in South Africa', 1986, in *American Foreign Policy: Current Documents Annual*, Vol. 1986, Washington, DC., GPO, pp. 76–88.

49 Personal interview with Dr Chester Crocker, 19 June 2001, Washington, DC.

50 Crocker, Chester, *High Noon in Southern Africa: Making Peace in a Rough Neighborhood*, New York and London: W.W. Norton and Company, 1992, p. 319.

51 Lugar, Richard, *Letters to the Next President*, New York: Simon and Schuster, 1988, p. 238.

52 Reagan himself joked about his 'hands-off' approach to the Presidency, on one occasion joking 'the right hand doesn't know what the far right hand is doing!'

53 Ronald Reagan Library, CA. Executive Secretariat, NSC: Records Boxes 91340 and 91343 Memorandum - From: Phil Nicolaides to Patrick Buchanan, 27 June 1986, 'Re: Lugar–Crocker Sanctions Bill Parley'.

54 Ronald Reagan Library, CA. Executive Secretariat, NSC: Records Boxes 91340 and 91343 Memorandum – From: Phil Nicolaides to Pat Buchanan [No Subject] 18 August 1986. See also Peter J. Schraeder, *United States Foreign Policy toward Africa: Incrementalism, Crisis and Change*, Cambridge: Cambridge University Press, 1994, pp. 220–6 for further discussion of rivalry between departments and within the African Bureau of the State Department itself.

55 Ronald Reagan Library, CA. WHORM Subject Files: Veto and Override of HR 4868 File number CO141 – 437008 Memorandum – From: Phil Nicolaides (White House). To: P Buchanan (White House), 25 August 1986. Subject: Congressional Suggestions Re: SA Policy.

56 Ronald Reagan Library, CA. WHORM Subject Files: Veto and Override of HR 4868 File number CO141 – 437995 Memorandum – From: Maseru, Ambassador to Lesotho. Subject: The View From the State Department 30 July 1986.

57 Crocker, *High Noon in Southern Africa*, p. 330.

58 Personal interview with Dr Chester Crocker, 19 June 2001, Washington, DC.

59 *Controls on Exports to South Africa* Congressional Hearings 2 December 1982 and 9 February 1983, p. 56.

60 Crocker, Chester, 'Southern Africa: Eight Years Later', *Foreign Affairs*, Vol. 68, No. 4 (1989) p. 147.

61 Ronald Reagan Library, CA. WHORM Subject Files: 'South Africa, US Policy Towards' File Numbers FG001–FG013; PR003-PR007-02 Letter – From: J. Edward Fox (Asst Secretary Legislative and Intergovernmental Affairs). To: Howard Wolpe (Chairman of House Foreign Affairs Committee), October 1987.

4
Pretoria's Perspective

South Africa's Perception of Constructive Engagement

Early signals from Washington

Carter's emphasis on human rights in foreign policy had led to a good deal of mistrust between the United States and Pretoria. Crocker strongly criticized Carter for the policies which had created this rift, warning in 1980 that South Africans were so disenchanted with Carter's performance that they now viewed the United States increasingly as an object for manipulation. South African writers also failed to understand why Carter did not focus more on the violations of human rights in most communist countries during what they worried was a 'process of estrangement between the United States and her staunchest supporters.'[1] Yet Pretoria had begun to hope that relations with the West would improve after the election of Margaret Thatcher in Britain in 1979. The reality of a conservative government in America, too, was confirmed by Reagan's electoral victory in 1980 and this boosted a mood of optimism in Pretoria. Here at last was an administration that would not naïvely disregard the importance of South Africa as a vital regional player in the struggle against communism, and would recognize her as a state with Western values that belonged within the Western embrace. South African radio described Reagan's 1980 defeat of Carter as the defeat of 'pseudoliberalism, permissiveness, state intervention, appeasement and anti-patriotism ... Mr Reagan himself has said there should be an alignment between the United States and all countries which oppose Soviet expansion.'[2]

To understand Pretoria's reaction to Washington's policy of constructive engagement, one must first understand Pretoria's perception of its own security fears. The spread of communism was perceived as the most urgent threat. Botha's experience as Defence Minister had had a major impact on the development of his world view. He was convinced that, in strategic and geopolitical terms, the contest between the 'free world' and communism was dominant. Within this 'total onslaught', South Africa was a particular target because of its numerous strategic advantages: location; mineral wealth; strong economy; and developed infrastructure. It also posed a major obstacle to the attempts of the Soviet Union to gain control of Africa – which Pretoria firmly believed was one of the Kremlin's goals. Pretoria also believed that, as a direct military attack would prove too expensive, economic boycotts and psychological propaganda would provide a cheaper alternative. The South African Communist Party (SACP), African National Congress (ANC) and Pan-African Congress (PAC) were all viewed as vehicles for promoting these aims. They were assisted by the OAU, the UN, neighbouring black states and the various Western anti-apartheid groups.[3] This sincere belief in an imminent communist threat was what drove both Pretoria's internal and external security policies – and what governed the regime's relations with other states. It was this belief that resulted in much of the intransigence which Western governments found so baffling – and so frustrating. Nor was this fear of Soviet proxies limited to South Africa's domestic situation. In 1985 Magnus Malan claimed that the Russians were planning to develop a base in Angola from which to operate 'wherever necessary in the sub-continent.... If you look at our massive reserves of strategic minerals, don't you ask yourself whether this mineral treasure house is not the cherry on top of the African cake?'[4] It is little wonder that Pretoria greeted Ronald Reagan's election with optimism and relief.

Initially, at least, Pretoria was not disappointed. Reagan's anti-communist message came across loud and clear, together with his message of support to those standing together with the US in this Cold War battle. Reagan chose to see the world as a dichotomy and, in so doing, he chose to fight the fight that the South Africans wanted. This narrow agenda allowed the South Africans to play the card of 'bastion against communism' to full effect. As well as the common Soviet threat, other interests bound the two countries together. Chapter 3 looked at the various strategic and resource benefits that South Africa could offer Washington, in particular the Cape route and mineral access. The South Africans were adroit in exploiting these strengths, publishing a list of US interests in South Africa in May 1981 which included mineral access, Cape route access and use of port facilities, protection of financial and trade interests, and regional stability.

Crocker made it clear that his new approach towards South Africa would acknowledge Pretoria's importance to the West. In a speech in Honolulu on 29 August 1981, he emphasized the importance of protecting trade and regional stability and maintaining good links with southern Africa. He made it explicitly clear from very early on that he did not view pressure on or isolation of South Africa as a useful policy. Even before his appointment as Assistant Secretary he explained that the needs of American domestic politics meant that disengagement was not an option. He went on to point out: 'We do not want to destabilize South Africa or jeopardize our own strategic and economic interests. The power to coerce South Africa is not in our hands.'[5] These statements were all made in the public arena, so Pretoria's optimism can easily be understood. In private meetings, too, this message of rekindled friendship was reinforced. In Crocker's 'Scope Paper' for Secretary Haig, prior to Haig's May 1981 meeting with Pik Botha, it was agreed that Haig would discuss the fact that 'the possibility may exist for a more positive and reciprocal relationship between [the US and South Africa] based upon shared strategic concerns'.[6] Indeed, Pretoria heard just what it wanted to when Crocker described South Africa as part of the Western experience, and an integral part of the Western economic system. In Pretoria's view, this was a welcome statement. South Africa had been accepted back into its rightful position amongst the Western nations. Yet, after receiving these signals, the South Africans were still not quite satisfied. Haig received a letter from Pretoria, five days after his 24 May meeting, with what Crocker described as a 'set of wish list goals'. He accused the South Africans of 'fantasizing about the meaning of Reagan's election' and described Washington's indignation at this 'Boer cheekiness'.[7]

Judging from the messages coming both from Crocker and Reagan, the South Africans could perhaps be forgiven for overestimating what was being promised. Pretoria's disillusionment did not follow immediately, however, because the American government did make real concessions. While calling for a tone of empathy, Crocker pointed out the need to understand both the Afrikaners' siege mentality and their 'awesome political dilemma'. These positive early words were confirmed by actions. The General Assembly's May 1981 vote on trade sanctions against South Africa resulted in five Western powers abstaining, including the United States. The Reagan administration also began a relaxation of the embargoes already in place from the very beginning of its first term. One of the most controversial aspects of this relaxation was the fact that South African military and police organizations were now able to obtain imports of small computers and word processors, which had previously been denied to them under the arms embargo.[8] These actions were an indication to Pretoria of the possible benefits of the new constructive engagement policy.

But when the South African government turned to America with new found optimism, *whose* message were they receiving? Unlike the dramatic confrontation with Congress in 1985–6 over the Comprehensive Anti-Apartheid Act, the initial undermining of Crocker's policy was instigated by the right wing in the Reagan administration. A number of Reagan's staff were also lobbyists or agents for the South African government.[9] Within Congress, too, Republican Senator Jesse Helms was a vociferous supporter of the South African government. He also had direct links with the South African military. On 27 September 1982 the Director of the Central Intelligence Agency (CIA), William Casey, travelled to South Africa for a meeting with government and military leaders to discuss the regional security situation. 'Some press reports claim that Casey proposed a US-backed *cordon sanitaire* to secure South Africa's borders.'[10] These separate channels were constantly undermining Crocker's earliest attempts to construct a unified policy towards South Africa.

The South Africans themselves were, understandably, all too willing to capitalize on this confusion in Washington. When offered, in effect, a menu of policy options from competing American agencies, they could simply choose to accept as policy whichever they liked best to hear. Crocker described the early actions of the South African government after the March 1981 visit (see Chapter 3) thus: 'Dissatisfied with the line coming from official Washington, Botha dispatched senior military emissaries to go round the diplomatic channel and obtain another definition of US policy.'[11] In the early years of the policy, however, attempts to play on the splits in the administration were less successful because the divisions themselves were far less obvious. During Reagan's first few years, African issues remained at the bottom of the agenda.

Pretoria's Perspective on the Policy of Constructive Engagement

The obstacles to constructive engagement with Pretoria

It would seem that, for Pretoria, constructive engagement could not have come at a better time, and could not have been better suited to their view of their own situation. The South African government's fear of isolation and desire for acceptance was addressed by constructive engagement's vision of a new US–South African relationship. The threat of damaging trade sanctions was ruled out explicitly by Crocker as counterproductive. The legitimacy Pretoria so craved in the West would be granted to them via Washington's regional anti-communist approach. Viewed in this way, it seems difficult to imagine that constructive engagement could fail, at least in its attempt to build a new and positive relationship with Pretoria. But did Pretoria feel that the benefits it offered were sufficient for them to begin to meet the international community half-way with regard to the apartheid issue?

Unfortunately for Crocker, the Afrikaners proved an extremely difficult group with which to engage. In his account of his negotiations with the South Africans, Crocker complained that the 'ethnic insecurity of the nationalist Afrikaner' resulted in an arrogance that excluded all outsiders.[12] The fact that black African states would continue to deal with South Africa, despite their hostile rhetoric, only increased Pretoria's condescension towards them, but South Africa was no more at home in dealing with Western nations. Crocker described the South African attitude as a true pariah *politik*. It would certainly be a challenge to engage this notoriously insular and isolationist tribe, even if some sections of Afrikaner society were anxious to be accepted by the West.

The first major obstacle was Pretoria's intensely hostile reaction to outside interference. In a confidential 1983 cable from the American consulate in Johannesburg, regarding Senator Nancy Kassebaum's meeting with Pik Botha, Botha clearly pointed out that any pressure on Pretoria to move faster towards reform would be counterproductive, because the only alternative (given a white electorate) to the National Party's policy was a right-wing government.[13] P. W. Botha was even less compromising in his stance against interference. Ambassador Herman Nickel recalled his first meeting with P. W. Botha in 1982, when he was warned against the United States 'trying to meddle' in South Africa's affairs. Botha went on to warn against this in the far more public arena of the National Party Natal Congress in 1985, in what became known as his 'Rubicon Speech':

We have never given in to outside demands and we are not going to do so now. South Africa's problems will be solved by South Africans and not by foreigners. We are not going to be deterred from doing what we think best, nor will we be forced into doing what we don't want to do.[14]

Botha's strident message was well received by many Afrikaners, and was reflected in the press. An editorial in *The Citizen* – a South African newspaper known to be sympathetic to the government – responded to a bill proposed by Congressman Walter Fauntroy, which threatened massive US withdrawal if South Africa did not instigate radical changes to apartheid within 18 months: 'Our response to his outrageous demands and threats to a sovereign, free and honourable country: Go to hell.'[15] This was indicative of the collective psyche that Crocker was trying to win over. With such hostility towards interference, one can see the attractions of the constructive engagement approach. An attempt to win Pretoria *should* have been more successful than one simply committed to criticizing or bullying the white government. Yet this leads us to a second obstacle in Pretoria's outlook – trust.

In an early meeting between Crocker and Pik Botha, Botha raised the issue of 'trust' and explained that South Africa had been let down by America before, and was therefore not inclined to trust them again. Botha used examples of the US government failing to support moderate governments in Africa, while aiding those with leftist rhetoric. He also explained that he was suspicious of the US government because of the way in which they abandoned the South African government in Angola in 1975 (see Introduction). The fact that Pretoria ranked communist encroachment as its first security priority, and the fact that they perceived in Angola a possible base from which the Soviet Union could orchestrate such an aim, demonstrates how very seriously this desertion was taken in South African government circles. This incident sparked an ever-increasing detachment from the West and certainly Botha was determined that neither Western threats nor Western persuasion would alter South Africa's security calculations from this time. The experience in Angola told him that, in matters of South African security, Pretoria had to be self-sufficient.

In a meeting with the American Chargé d'Affaires in October 1981, Foreign Minister Pik Botha complained of reports circulating in the South African cabinet about an interview given by Secretary of State Al Haig. The report claimed that Haig said that the Reagan administration was merely keeping a low profile on South Africa in order to achieve a Namibia settlement: 'with the implication that as soon as Namibia is out of the way, "you will get down seriously to giving us hell".'[16] Crocker was aware of this intense distrust. In his account of his last meeting with P. W. Botha on 13 January 1986, he clearly acknowledged 'P. W. didn't trust me.' Botha complained bitterly about being let down by two Republican administrations – Ford in 1975–6 (halting funding to UNITA in Angola – see Introduction) and Reagan now. He accused the Reagan administration of ignoring ANC violence and underestimating the difficulty of Pretoria's position. Crocker described the meeting as 'a chilling encounter'.[17]

What seemed curious to many was that members of the South African government appeared genuinely to be shocked by the growing hostility coming from the West. Yet the fact was that Pretoria remained isolated, to a remarkable degree, from the Western debates about the immorality or sheer impracticality of the apartheid system. Pretoria also seemed unable, or unwilling, to accept the fact that governments had to alter their policies due to the level of domestic pressure against supporting the apartheid regime. Pretoria preferred to dismiss such pressure as 'the stormtroopers of the British left'.[18]

The third obstacle to Pretoria's acceptance of constructive engagement was that they were fighting to set the agenda. We have seen that the problem for Crocker was that disunity in American ranks meant that if the South Africans did not like what they heard, they would simply attempt to bypass regular diplomatic channels to find a definition of policy which suited them. There was a cacophony of voices emanating from Washington. Pretoria continued to attempt to persuade the more conservative of the agencies (the CIA, the Department of Defense and the NSC) to enter into strategic co-operation with South Africa regarding the region, in return for a reduced emphasis on apartheid. All these elements in its approach impacted upon Pretoria's understanding of constructive engagement and, in turn, affected the policy of constructive engagement itself. The policy was dependent on both parties being willing to compromise in the search for common ground. So, bearing in mind the obstacles of manipulation, mistrust and an innate sense of hostility towards interfering outsiders, just how did Pretoria respond to constructive engagement?

The thinking behind Botha's reformist agenda

Although the South African government did begin to instigate reforms under P. W. Botha, the reasoning behind these reforms was badly misinterpreted by the policy makers in Washington. Soon after Botha's appointment in September 1978, foreign governments began to hear more hopeful noises emanating from Pretoria. The new Prime Minister was telling whites that they must 'adapt ... or die' and urged the Afrikaners to learn the lessons of their own history: 'The moment you start oppressing people ... they fight back.'[19] Unfortunately, Botha's message of reform was far more complex than the optimistic vision developing in the eyes of the West. Botha's calls to 'adapt or die', often interpreted by those in the West as heralding the dismantling of apartheid, belied the fact that Botha was just as committed to the preservation of white power as the most hardline of his predecessors. This confusion can be explained by exploring the subtleties of Botha's approach to reform.

Botha undertook a plan of cautious reform and symbolic gestures, such as being the first Prime Minister ever to visit a black township. During his visit to Soweto he stated: 'We are all South Africans.' Yet he did not address the fundamental issue of black political representation. In America this gap was explained by the fact that Botha had to deal with a powerful right wing. In his testimony to Congress in 1982, John Chettle explained that the struggle within the National Party affected 'almost every facet of the national life'.[20] For this reason, Botha felt 'obliged to obfuscate what he was doing' when embarking on his reforms, in order to protect his right flank. Chettle quoted Crocker as he explained:

> Changes in racial policy, when they occur, are typically clothed in legalistic and ideological formulas designed to make them either deniable or invisible – a tendency which only aggravates 'misunderstanding'. It requires an expert in the bizarre politics of Afrikanerdom to interpret what is really going on.

The main thrust of Chettle's analysis was that: 'It could hardly be wondered that, in executing a strategy designed to confuse his opponents and keep them off balance, [Botha] should succeed in confusing everyone else.'

There is an element of truth in this explanation of why Botha's early reforms were so difficult to read. His hold on power was dependent on his awareness of the relative strength of the right wing of the National Party, and on taking measures to control its influence and prevent a backlash. But this was not wholly the reason behind Botha's apparently ambiguous reform programme. Even when his reforms – in the shape of the new constitution – caused the party to split, he still did not back down. The widely held view in Washington was of Botha as a man ready to reform South African politics, prepared to begin a gradual dismantling of apartheid, and held back primarily by the political necessity of placating his party's right wing. Unfortunately, this was not the case. The West's understanding of his statements that whites must 'adapt or die' and that 'apartheid … is dead' actually misinterpreted his goals. Yes, Botha intended reform, but he *never* intended to bring about the end of white rule. This was the major difference between Pretoria's and Washington's realities.

One of the best explanations of Botha's actions is given by Robert Schrire of the University of Cape Town, who identified three areas of interest in the white community that successive governments had sought to protect from 1910 onwards.[21] These were the policies of power, privilege and prejudice. The *policies of power* were designed to ensure that whites retained control of the polity. Power over the legislative process, the bureaucracy and the security apparatus were all vital to this end. The *policies of privilege* encompassed the government's health and housing policies, job reservation and Bantu education and the reservation of prime land for whites. This basically covered those laws and policies that favoured and protected white material interests. Although most of these policies were in place by 1948, the National Party continued to build upon and extend the system. The *policies of prejudice* included laws and policies such as the Mixed Marriage Act, the Immorality Acts, and the Separation of Amenities. These were designed to minimize black/white contact as much as possible. Again, this system was established before the National Party came to power, but the Nationalists extended and codified such rules and gave them an ideological and 'moral' foundation.

Schrire explained that, historically, the 'policies of power' enjoyed the greatest legitimacy in the white community – there was very little dissent concerning the belief that the whites should control the country. The policies of both privilege and prejudice, however, were more controversial within the white community, particularly when they imposed costs on certain sectors. Job reservation, for example, was supported by poor whites, but became unpopular with employers (see Chapter 5 for further discussion). Many affluent, English-speaking whites viewed the 'policies of prejudice' such as the marriage laws as unhelpful and unnecessary. Many Afrikaners, on the other hand, viewed these same laws as vital to the preservation of Afrikaner identity.

Schrire states that the apartheid system remained viable as long as four conditions persisted:

1. the South African economy continued to be dynamic and growth-oriented;
2. black South Africans acquiesced in white rule;
3. the international community was prepared to trade with and invest in South Africa;
4. white South Africans remained broadly united.

It was during Botha's time in office that these four prerequisite conditions began to unravel. Economic failures, the growing internal security problem and increasing international pressure regarding South Africa's race relations meant that although the apartheid state was not yet defeated, it was becoming increasingly beleaguered. Although the necessity of reform became apparent, at no time did the abandonment of white rule feature as part of those reforms. Rather, the reforms were seen as necessary in order to *preserve* white power. The ambiguity of Botha's actions, particularly in his first term, can be explained thus: 'Botha tackled the policies of privilege and prejudice while shoring up the policies of power.'[22] It was the failure to recognize this distinction that meant constructive engagement was destined to fail from the start. Belief that Pretoria was ready to reform was in fact based on truth. The important and misunderstood fact was that this reform *never* intended to include the dismantling of white rule.

Pretoria rejects constructive engagement

What Pretoria knew all along, and the Reagan administration should soon have realized, was that Botha was simply unable and unwilling to deliver the level of reform that constructive engagement needed to vindicate Crocker and his policy back home. In a secret telegram to Secretary of State Shultz in 1986, Crocker described his discussions with Pik Botha regarding a possible visit by P. W. Botha to Washington. Crocker pointed out that substantive reform would be needed before such a meeting could be politically acceptable. Pik Botha explained to Crocker privately: 'We simply cannot meet your price.'[23] In fact, the South Africans seemed to take many of the American policy makers by surprise by the sheer degree of their intransigence. Commentators remarked that Reagan's conciliatoriness to the South African regime assumed it shared Western values of good-faith bargaining. But constructive engagement was ineffective in the face of South African obduracy.[24] Pretoria seemed happy to receive any of the carrots presented to them by Washington in the name of constructive engagement, without actually feeling compelled to reciprocate with any moves of their own. Crocker explained to Haig that the South Africans deeply resented being treated as an embarrassment and were not used to the give and take of pragmatic relations. A series of secret memorandums regarding upcoming meetings with Ambassador Nickel and Crocker demonstrated that this total deadlock had not gone unnoticed in Washington, with NSC members asking themselves: 'whether we should continue to commit our diplomatic prestige where the key player – South Africa – appears to be immune to any US influence or suggestions which rub against its policy aims'.[25]

Botha had always been personally inclined to resist international pressures. After his 'Rubicon' speech had caused such international alarm, and particularly because much of this alarm was felt among the business and banking community, Botha announced what he believed to be a number of significant reform measures. He was furious that these steps on his part met with such little acknowledgement from the West (where many were inclined to see them as too little, too late). This caused him to reach a turning point. He would no longer allow external criticism and threats to influence him or dictate the pace of reform.[26]

A confidential observation of the NSC shows that, rather than simply being stubborn, perhaps Pretoria just had too good an understanding of the implicit agenda of the constructive engagement strategy: 'There is no sign of South African gratitude or even acknowledgement of the Reagan Administration's more friendly attitude towards the Pretoria regime. They assume that our policies are driven by pursuit of our interests, not theirs.'[27] It would seem that the South Africans were astute in their comprehension of what constructive engagement was about. They knew that Washington wished to pursue a relationship with Pretoria for its own benefit, but had to present this relationship in such a way as to avoid criticism for dealing openly with the apartheid regime. Pretoria resented this implication, and saw no need to alter its actions or priorities in order to suit Washington.

Although most liberals (or *verligtes*) in South Africa did acknowledge that constructive engagement was worth preserving, Pretoria, having expected so much, was disappointed with constructive engagement, and furious over the continued imposition of even limited sanctions. As Pauline Baker comments: 'Indeed, South Africa seemed to have become an adversary of the United States rather than the regional ally originally envisioned by the Reagan Administration.'[28] In a private meeting with Senator Kassebaum, Pik Botha responded to her comment about constructive engagement's need to see concrete results in return

> by lamenting the impression created by 'some US Spokesmen, not necessarily members of the government, but members of Congress' that there is a price to be paid by South Africa for constructive engagement. This was causing resentment in South Africa.[29]

It seems remarkable that this statement, made in early 1983 and openly stating that Pretoria was not prepared to play the reciprocal role demanded by constructive engagement, had no apparent impact on the constructive engagement strategy. The *explicit* agenda of constructive engagement was that Pretoria could be influenced away from the apartheid system through establishing a positive and open relationship. This was undermined, however, by the fact that the South African government had stated that it resented the idea that it should make any moves towards reform, just because America criticized and threatened it less. The fact was that Pretoria had never asked for constructive engagement and, although grateful for the limited benefits constructive engagement provided, was not about to alter its policies to suit Washington. Pretoria did, however, welcome the fact that Crocker attempted to rule out one very direct way to attempt to influence policy – the use of sanctions.

Non-cooperation with constructive engagement and the sanctions threat

Although P. W. Botha had been unmoved in the face of constructive engagement, he was just as truculent towards the threat of sanctions. Indeed, he openly declared: 'I'm nobody's jellyfish. If we have to suffer sanctions for the sake of maintaining freedom, justice and order, we will survive. Not only will we survive, we will emerge stronger on the other side.'[30] After a visit to South Africa, Senator Edward Kennedy told Congress that he had 'heard a universal refrain from government ministers, "We do not care what the United States does or says. We will decide for ourselves, and we will proceed at our own pace."'[31] Yet Kennedy pointed out that the 'extreme interest' in the protests within the US, and the disinvestment campaign, showed that most South Africans did care very deeply about what the US thought. Indeed, in May 1986 Pik Botha declared that South Africa's first priority was to stop boycotts imposed against it by Western trading partners. A report by the Foreign Policy Association identified South Africa's 'Achilles heel' as certain high technology and growth sectors. It pointed out that although US investments accounted for only 20 per cent of total foreign investment in South Africa, they made up 70 per cent of investments in the computer sector. As an editorial in the South African newspaper *The Star* pointed out in 1985: 'Some might have felt inclined to pooh-pooh the recent spate of demonstrations [in the US], but no-one dares ignore the flood of anti-investment bills now being processed in Congress.'[32]

The passing of the Comprehensive Anti-Apartheid Act on 2 October 1986 had an important effect on US–South African relations. Crocker maintained that it further reduced US influence (although this presupposes that the US had a significant level of influence beforehand). Botha was furious that sanctions had been imposed. When Crocker attempted to discuss the situation, Botha would not accept that any of the responsibility had been his. Nor did he care that the sanctions had been imposed, not by the State Department, but by a separate branch of government. To Crocker he stated simply: 'Sanctions are your problem.' Relations between Washington and South Africa were put on deep freeze from October 1986 to June 1987.

The early optimism regarding Reagan's election was soon overshadowed by a combination of Afrikaner manipulation of a divided American government, together with traditional Boer intransigence and mistrust of outsiders. Throughout this confusion, the communist threat remained very real to Pretoria. While the West looked on, baffled by Pretoria's tenacious obduracy, Pretoria looked back, equally confused by what they saw as the West's perverse refusal to acknowledge South Africa's vital role in the struggle against communism. The fact that some right-wing elements of the Reagan administration were using this very same argument to attempt to guide America's South African policy did not help Crocker. When describing the conflictual situation in Washington, he now concedes, 'maybe we could have been clearer'.[33] In his book *High Noon in Southern Africa* he describes the situation in Washington by 1985: 'Some people were preparing sanctions packages; some were telling South Africa – don't worry, we'll help you get rid of your communists; some were telling Botha to give a statement of reform ... we probably contributed to his self-destructive behaviour.'[34] As one South African writer rather damningly put it: 'On her part, South Africa realizes that the road to a stable and durable democracy will be very lonely and full of stumbling blocks of the worst kind. If she succeeds at the end, it will be in spite of America.'[35]

Notes

1   Kapp, P. H. and G. C. Oliver, *United States–South African Relations: Past, Present and Future*, Human Sciences Research Council Publication Series, No. 87, Cape Town: Tafelberg Publishers, 1987, p. 76.

2   See Kline, Benjamin, *Profit, Principle and Apartheid 1948–1994: The Conflict of Economic and Moral Issues in United States–South African Relations*, Studies in African Economic and Social Development, Vol. 10, Lewiston, Queenstown and Lampeter: Edwin Mellen Press, 1997, p. 119.

3   Geldenhuys, D., *Some Foreign Policy Implications of South Africa's Total National Strategy*, Special Study, South African Institute for International Affairs, 1981.

4   *The Star*, Johannesburg 27 September 1985.

5   Crocker, Chester, 'A US Policy for the '80s', *Africa Report*, Vol. 26, No. 1 (1981), p. 14.

6   Crocker's 'Scope Paper' for Secretary of State Alexander Haig in preparation for Haig's meeting with Pik Botha on 14 May 1981. Reproduced in Pauline H. Baker, *The United States and South Africa: The Reagan Years. Update South Africa: Time Running Out*, Ford Foundation and Foreign Policy Association: 1989, Appendix A.

7   Personal interview with Dr Chester Crocker, 19 June 2001, Washington, DC.

8   For a useful and comprehensive outline of the early relaxation of the embargoes, see the testimony of Thomas Conrad, American Friends Service Committee, *Controls on Exports to South Africa* Hearings before the Subcommittees on International Economic Policy and Trade, and on Africa, of the Committee of Foreign Affairs, House of Representatives, 2 December 1982 and 9 February 1983 – especially pp. 63–5.

9   For a comprehensive list see Thompson, Alex, *Incomplete Engagement: United States Foreign Policy towards the Republic of South Africa 1981–1988*, Aldershot and Brookfield: Avebury, 1996, p. 68.

10 Mokoena, Kenneth (ed.), *South Africa and the United States: The Declassified History*, a National Security Archive documents reader, New York: The New Press, 1993, p. 31.

11 Crocker, Chester, 'Southern Africa: Eight Years Later', *Foreign Affairs*, Vol. 68, No. 4 (1989), p. 159.

12   Crocker, Chester, *High Noon in Southern Africa: Making Peace in a Rough Neighborhood*, New York and London: W. W. Norton and Company, 1992, p. 111.

13   Ronald Reagan Library, CA. WHORM Subject Files: 'South Africa, US Policy Towards' File Numbers FG001–FG013; PR003-PR007-02 Confidential Cable – From: Nickel – American Consulate Johannesburg. To: White House Situation Room and Secretary of State 10 January 1983. Subject: Senator Kassebaum's Meeting with Pik Botha. Declassified 22 January 1999.

14   Address by State President P. W. Botha at the Opening of the National Party Natal Congress Durban, 15 August 1985 ('The Rubicon Speech'), The South African Consulate General, New York, August 1985. See also Barber, James and J. Barratt, *South Africa's Foreign Policy*, Cambridge: Cambridge University Press, 1990, pp. 321–3 for a further analysis of this speech.

15   *The Citizen* (Johannesburg), February 1985.

16   Ronald Reagan Library, CA. White House Staff and Office Files: Cohen, Herman J., Files 1987–8. African Affairs Directorate, NSC. Boxes 91875 and 91876. Cable from: American Consulate Cape Town. To: Secretary of State Haig. Subject: Situation Listing 10 November 1981.

17   Crocker, *High Noon in Southern Africa*, p. 310–11.

18   Editorial, *Sunday Times*, Johannesburg, 10 June 1984.

19   Meredith, Martin, *In the Name of Apartheid: South Africa in the Post War Period*, New York: Harper and Row, 1988, p. 171.

20   Testimony of John Chettle (Director for North and South America of the South Africa Foundation, a private multiracial foundation supported by private and corporate donations, and representing a wide cross-section of views in white South Africa), *The Role of the Soviet Union, Cuba and East Germany in Fomenting Terrorism in Southern Africa* Hearings before the Subcommittee on Security and Terrorism of the Committee on the Judiciary, United States Senate, 22 March 1982.

21   Schrire, Robert, *Update South Africa: Time Running Out. Adapt or Die: The End of White Politics in South Africa*, London: Hurst & Co., 1991, pp.4–8.

22   *Ibid.*, p. 8.

23   Ronald Reagan Library, CA. White House Staff and Office Files: Cohen, Herman J., Files 1987–8. African Affairs Directorate NSC. Boxes 91875 and 91876. Secret Cable. From: Crocker. To: Poindexter (The White House). Subject: Geneva Meeting with Pik Botha, February 1986. Declassified 26 May 1999.

24   Rothchild, Donald and John Ravenhill, 'Subordinating African Issues to Global Logic: Reagan Confronts Political Complexity', in K. A. Oye, R. J. Lieber and D. Rothchild (eds), *Eagle Resurgent? The Reagan Era in American Foreign Policy*, Boston, Toronto: Little, Brown and Company, 1987, p. 410.

25   Ronald Reagan Library, CA. Executive Secretariat, NSC: Records Boxes 91340 and 91343. Secret Memorandum – From: Phillip Ringdahl. To: Robert McFarlane. Subject: South Africa – Your Meeting with Crocker and Nickel, 7 March 1985. Declassified 7 June 1999.

26   Barber and Barratt, *South Africa's Foreign Policy*, p. 332.

27   Ronald Reagan Library, CA. White House Staff and Office Files: African Affairs Directorate, NSC: Records Boxes 91026 and 91028. Confidential Memorandum – From: Phillip Ringdahl (NSC). To: Robert McFarlane. Subject: South Africa – Meeting with Ambassador Nickel 19 June 1985. Declassified 7 July 1999.

28   Baker, *The United States and South Africa*, p. 5.

29   Ronald Reagan Library, CA. WHORM Subject Files: 'South Africa, US Policy Towards' File Numbers FG001–FG013; PR003-PR007-02. Confidential Cable – From: Nickel – American Consulate Johannesburg. To: White House Situation Room and Secretary of State 10 January 1983. Subject: Senator Kassebaum's Meeting with Pik Botha. Declassified 22 January 1999.

30   As quoted in Kline, *Profit, Principle and Apartheid*, p. 140.

31   *Ibid.*, p. 12.

32   *The Star* (Johannesburg), February 1985.

33   *Ibid.*

34   Crocker, *High Noon in Southern Africa*, pp. 288–9.

35   Gerrit Olivier in Kapp and Oliver, *United States–South African Relations*, p. 165.

5
Competing Agendas within South Africa

The Growth & Consolidation of Black Opposition

Black opposition begins to resurface

The Soweto uprising of 1976 was significant, not only because it precipitated a growing international awareness of the ills of apartheid, but also because it altered the perceptions of black and white *within* South Africa. Soweto began to change the widespread belief in black powerlessness. Although black opposition appeared to have been crushed after Soweto, visible activity began to resume in 1980. In March 1980 the Soweto newspaper *The Post* began a petition demanding Nelson Mandela's release. In 1980 Coloured school students boycotted classes to protest at their inadequate education. Gradually, opposition was beginning to resurface.

The next significant development in the growth of black opposition was the formation of the United Democratic Front (UDF). The UDF was launched at a mass rally in Cape Town in August 1983. At its inception, it was a broad-based coalition of 300 anti-apartheid groups, spurred into action by the forthcoming constitution which was to continue the exclusion of blacks from the government of the country whilst offering concessions to both the Coloured and Indian populations. The UDF assumed the 'Charterist' position of the ANC,[1] which meant that it rejected the homelands and the new constitution, and called for a unified, single state of South Africa. It also welcomed white and multiracial anti-apartheid organizations, unlike the black consciousness movements that had dominated internal resistance outside of the labour movement in the 1970s. By March 1984 it encompassed around 600 anti-apartheid organizations. The UDF resisted becoming a formal political party, preferring to remain a broad 'popular front' umbrella organization. Its links with the ANC were strong, and one of the main reasons it rejected political party status was to avoid competing with the ANC. This grouping of trade unions, religious and sports clubs eventually had an affiliated membership of over 2 million, representing all classes and races. As Meredith explains: 'Only by repudiating violence were its aims distinguishable from the ANC.'[2]

The ANC had gradually been growing in stature, particularly on the international scene. In 1974 the United Nations had granted it observer status. In the same year the Portuguese coup had dramatically altered the face of the region, greatly facilitating the exiled sabotage units of the ANC in their access to South Africa. In 1980 several bombs were planted by the organization, including one which caused considerable damage at the Sasolburg fuel plant near Johannesburg. The ANC also managed to delay the opening of South Africa's first nuclear power station in Koeberg due to reactor damage caused by a series of explosions on 19 December 1982.[3] As the profile of the ANC increased, so did its popularity. In fact, much of the increased support for this organization was as a direct result of actions taken by the Botha government.

The 1983 constitution

Botha's piecemeal reforms had enhanced the ability of the black community to contest the policies of apartheid, whilst simultaneously causing a misplaced optimism to grow both within and outside South Africa. However, the imposition of a new South African constitution in 1983 provoked a new and concerted wave of black opposition. The decision to reform South Africa's constitution had begun under Vorster in 1977. By 1980 a council had been established to advise the government on the new constitution and a constitutional committee was appointed under Dr Denis Worrall, a political scientist. The Worrall Report, published in 1982, had addressed the vast literature available on constitutional options. Although the Report advocated a confederal relationship with the black homeland governments, or 'independent states', it concluded that 'a single political system in South Africa which includes blacks on an unqualified majoritarian or consociational basis could not function as a successful democracy in current or foreseeable circumstances'.[4] The conclusions of the committee were acceptable to the National Party, which had commissioned it. After the Constitution Bill was passed through parliament, a whites-only referendum was held on its proposals in November 1983. Limited measures were taken to gauge the opinions of Indians and Coloureds, who were to have a position in this new arrangement, but blacks were not consulted. Botha's Minister for Transport, Hendrik Schoeman, explained in August 1981: 'In this country four million whites must think and plan for 25 million people. It is a question of the protection of the minority with whom the brain power lies.'[5] The main emphasis of the new constitution was on 'group rights' – meaning that each group could govern itself without being dominated by another. The tricameral parliament would consist of three chambers. The House of Assembly would have 178 members to represent a white population of 4.5 million; the House of Representatives had 85 members to represent a Coloured population of 2.5 million; and the House of Deputies would have 45 members to represent an Indian population of 800,000. Each House had a 'Ministers' Council' for 'Own Affairs', which included welfare, housing, health and education. Legislation for 'General Affairs', which included foreign policy, defence, commerce, and law and order would be discussed in 'Joint Standing Committees' of all three Houses. The new office of Executive President meant that the Head of Government had greatly increased powers and disputes over 'General Affairs' would be resolved by the President's Council. The President himself was to be elected by an electoral college in which the majority white party had control. African Affairs were to remain in the hands of the Executive.

A concerted propaganda campaign, an optimistic view of the constitution as a step towards reform and a belief that it could be a way to protect white interests all combined to give the government a healthy two-thirds majority of support for the proposals in the white referendum. Indians and Coloureds were simply presented with a *fait accompli*. Not until the 1984 election were Indians and Coloureds able to make their views known – with only thirty per cent of Coloureds and twenty per cent of Indians voting. The imposition of this new constitution was responsible both for splitting the Afrikaner community in full public view, and for finally lighting the touch paper which sparked some of the most determined black opposition Pretoria had ever seen.

The 1985 uprisings and the State of Emergency

On 3 September 1984 – the day the new constitution came into effect – many of the townships exploded in violent protests, unrest that was to turn 'into a popular uprising of unprecedented scope, duration and intensity'.[6] Fourteen people died in clashes with the South African Police (SAP). By the end of the following day, another 29 people had been shot dead by the SAP in various township protests within the Vaal Triangle. The unrest soon spread to the Eastern and Western Cape and the townships around Johannesburg. By 1985 many observers were describing the situation as 'civil war' with the black townships reduced to no-go areas for whites – even the police and the army. One of the principal targets of this anger was the Black Local Authority System. This had been the system of government presented to the blacks instead of central representation in the new constitution. As such, these systems represented much of what the black community hated about apartheid. As the authority of these organizations was increasingly undermined, residents began to form their own alternative governing organizations within the townships. Youth organizations, workers and other community members came together to form 'Street Committees' which were effective in organizing rent and consumer boycotts. It did not take long for these protest actions to assume a more violent nature. Blacks who had participated in the system, from councillors to policemen, were seen as legitimate targets due to their role as 'collaborators'. In the first nine months of the insurrection, twelve black councillors were assassinated, while two hundred more had their homes or businesses destroyed.[7] Within a year, virtually all of the black community councils had ceased to function.

Meanwhile, violence was continuing to spread. On the twenty-fifth anniversary of Sharpeville, 21 March 1985, a funeral procession was taking place in Langa, Uitenhage. The procession had not been violent but the SAP, who had not been properly trained for such a situation, and who had been provided with lethal, rather than crowd control equipment, seem simply to have panicked. Twenty unarmed mourners were shot dead. The incident sent a shockwave through South Africa and sparked off a second cycle of violence even more intense and sustained than the first.[8] Protests, boycotts and fighting spread throughout the country. On the anniversary of the Soweto uprisings (16 June), bombs exploded in Durban and Port Elizabeth.

The blacks in the townships had aimed to make themselves ungovernable, but as anarchy and violence increased, some rebels were not only 'ungovernable to the enemy, but ungovernable to their own organizations'.[9] Black-on-black violence spiralled. Black policemen who had been attacked pursued their own vendettas. Many suspected collaborators died at the hands of mob violence. Gruesome scenes of 'necklacing' (filling a tyre with petrol, placing it over the victim's neck and setting it alight) were broadcast through outside media. Local vigilantes took the law into their own hands, and many observers suspected that these vigilantes had the backing of the security forces as a cheap, alternative method of regaining control of the townships. In Natal alone, the township violence left 4,000 dead – mainly youths.

For the government, the situation had become critical. On 20 July 1985 a State of Emergency was declared in 36 magisterial districts of the Vaal Triangle and the Eastern Cape, and was extended to the Western Cape three months later. The emergency regulations gave the police the power to arrest, detain and interrogate without a warrant and meetings were banned. Television and radio coverage of the unrest was not allowed and newspaper coverage was severely curtailed. Louis Le Grange, the Minister for Law and Order, banned:

> all gatherings held where ... any policy principle, or any actions of the government, or any statement, or the application or implementation of any act is approved, defended, attacked, criticized or discussed, or which is in protest against or support or in memory of anything.[10]

As Leonard Thompson concludes: 'The government had resorted to legalized tyranny.'[11] Apart from a short break between 7 March and 12 June 1986, the State of Emergency was renewed annually until 1990.

Although the black opposition could not overthrow the power of the state, neither could the state eliminate opposition completely. The government had lost the initiative, but no other group had the ability to seize it. Crocker had appreciated the limits of black power in 1981 thus: 'the black communities of South Africa do not possess the means for a direct assault on white power, and there is little likelihood that this will change soon. The attitudinal ingredients of a potential revolution may be present, but the physical ones are not.'[12] What he perhaps overlooked, however, was that failure to possess the means to force change did not necessarily preclude the possibility that South Africa's black communities could make governing their country a near impossible task for the apartheid rulers. Constructive engagement had done nothing to prevent the radicalization of the black communities.

The achievements of the black opposition and their impact on Washington

The ANC had gained in stature during the 1980s, both domestically and abroad. By 1985–6 business, student, church and trade union delegations from South Africa were visiting the ANC headquarters in Lusaka. The ANC was perceived by these groups as a 'government in exile'. Even Pretoria's carefully orchestrated series of reforms had not served to alter the ANC's ultimate course, as Oliver Tambo explained: 'We are not fighting and dying in order to have a better system of waste disposal.'[13] The South African press commented that 'the continuing unrest in black townships and external political and financial pressures have done more to better the position of black people than years of useless debating'.[14] Nigel Worden sums up the critical situation in South Africa and the stalemate that the uprisings had created:

> The resistance of the mid-1980s destroyed utterly the 'total strategy' tactics of the Botha government. Tricameralism and African urban councils had been firmly rejected by the demand for 'People's Power'. The campaign to win hearts and minds was in tatters, with thousands in detention without prospect of trial and an occupying army in the townships.[15]

The significance of the scale of the black uprising for Crocker was the influence it had on the attitude of the American public towards South Africa's black opposition and the profound effect it had on his strategy of constructive engagement. The awarding of the Nobel Prize for Peace to Bishop Desmond Tutu on 16 October 1984 had already significantly raised the international profile of black opposition. When reports began to appear nightly on US television of the black unrest, unarmed demonstrators being attacked by South African police, mass public funerals and 'necklace' killings, Congress and the public began to ask what 'constructive engagement' was contributing to the situation. As Alex Thompson pointed out, up to that point the Reagan administration had continued to insist that the focus must remain on 'reform from above' in South Africa. 'It was only after the violence of the mid-1980s that the Reagan administration was persuaded to back the participation of the black opposition in this reform process.'[16] This decision was made all the more urgent as the uprisings were also strengthening the voice of Congress in its call for sanctions. The strength of the black opposition was eventually having a real impact on Crocker's policy. Low-level contacts between the US Government and the ANC began to take place, followed in September 1986 by a meeting between Crocker and the ANC leader-in-exile Oliver Tambo in London. In July of that year the State Department declared that the ANC had 'a legitimate voice in South Africa'.[17] On 24 January 1987 Tambo met with Secretary of State George Shultz in Washington, DC. These moves represented a dramatic shift away from the early, suspicious American view of the ANC as a puppet of Moscow, although the two never developed an easy relationship (see below).

Crocker had argued correctly that the black opposition did not have the power to overthrow the apartheid system. But by creating a stalemate with the rulers of an increasingly ungovernable country, it had managed to plunge South Africa into a crisis which caused an international outcry. It was also immensely significant in forcing Pretoria to realize the enormous cost of clinging to power. By the end of the uprisings, too, ordinary white

South Africans had been forced to acknowledge that the situation of 'their blacks' was not a happy one. And the perception was dawning on some in government circles that it was simply too late to save the situation with brutal repression and superficial reform. Radical change would be needed.

The force of black opposition also had a direct effect on the strategy of constructive engagement. It was a vital factor in garnering the public support that led to the eventual enactment of the Comprehensive Anti-Apartheid Act. It also meant that Crocker began negotiations with the ANC. He had been adamant that sanctions could not help the situation in South Africa. He was also a firm believer in white-led change. Despite the fact that a policy of constructive engagement should have involved dialogue with the government *and* the opposition, his meetings with the ANC were liable to antagonize the government in Pretoria – exactly the opposite outcome to the constructive relationship with Pretoria that was the key to his South African policy.

Business Calls for Reform

By the 1970s, South Africa was facing a dilemma. Between 1948 and 1970, the South African economy was the second fastest growing economy in the world.[18] While the economy was based largely on agriculture and mining, the apartheid system had been very effective in creating wealth for the whites by providing a pool of cheap black labour. Unfortunately for white South Africans, a number of factors were to cause a major change in this balance. The oil crisis caused widespread economic stagnation in the 1970s, which also affected South Africa. A shift in the economic base towards manufacturing also began to highlight South Africa's critical need for skilled labour. White immigration was slowing and the black population was rising. The enforced situation of blacks as unskilled and under-educated labour aggravated the shortage of skilled labour and robbed the economy of potential, and badly needed, consumers. Between 1960 and 1974 South Africa's annual growth rate was averaging a healthy 5.5 per cent, but between 1975 and 1985 this had dropped to 1.9 per cent. Business interests were beginning to realize that the combination of restrictions on black education and movement would only serve to damage economic growth further.

Pretoria was thrown a temporary lifeline when the price of gold soared. Ever since the US had effectively abandoned the gold standard for the dollar and allowed gold to find its own price in 1971, the price of gold had begun to increase. (Gold had been fixed to the dollar at $35 an ounce for 40 years previously.) As economic uncertainty grew, gold seemed to be the safest bet for speculation. In 1972 the price stood at $60 an ounce. By 1974 it had reached $194 an ounce. By 18 January 1980 it had jumped to a record $835 an ounce.[19] This 'mini-boom' created a welcome windfall for the South African economy, but the growth in the money supply also caused inflation – and the boom temporarily masked the incompatibility between apartheid and economic growth.

Botha was aware, however, that the business community was increasingly concerned about this incompatibility. He began his first term as Prime Minister with some intelligent overtures towards this group, bringing businessmen into government committees and seeking their advice. He also held two high-profile conferences with business representatives, which his entire cabinet attended. These became known as the 'Carlton' (1979) and 'Good Hope' (1981) conferences. There had been a long-standing hostility between the predominantly English-speaking corporate business community in South Africa and the mainly rural Afrikaners. After the Carlton conference, one South African newspaper remarked that 'The Anglo-Boer War is finally over.' Botha's new attitude went beyond words and cautious reform began. Crocker links directly the legalizing of the black trade unions to pressure from South African businessmen. He states that 'no single change in the past 25 years did more to empower blacks'.[20] In these early stages, Botha benefited from business support, particularly over the contentious issue of the new constitution.

These initial reforms were gradual and cautious, yet pressure from the business community was also beginning to mount. The lack of skilled labour and the high cost of influx control slowed growth, and the unwieldy and duplicating machinery of the apartheid system also imposed huge taxation costs. Businessmen, whose interests were articulated through organizations such as the Associated Chamber of Commerce and the Federated Chamber of Industries, began to put pressure on the government to develop more growth-friendly policies. Progress was made on the issue of job reservation – partially ended in 1979 and abolished in 1983 (with the exception of blasting certificates in the mining industry, not issued to blacks until 1987). By the mid-1980s Botha finally bowed to pressure and repealed the pass laws in 1986. As Schrire explains: 'While none of these measures can be attributed exclusively to business pressures – many other forces were at work – some of them probably would have been delayed without business intervention.'[21]

Unfortunately, these gradual yet business-friendly reforms were brought to a halt by the domestic crisis which seized South Africa during 1985–7. The township uprisings during this period caused an international outcry. Once foreign banks began to refuse to roll over South Africa's loans (starting with Chase Manhattan on 31 July 1985), the economy began to teeter on the brink of collapse. South Africa owed $4 billion on short-term credit – this was more than two and a half times the total available in its national reserves.[22] The unrest also spurred sanctions from the European Community, the United Nations and the United States, dealing a further severe blow to business confidence in South Africa.

Botha heightened international indignation and further infuriated his own business community with his 'Rubicon' speech, delivered at the opening of the National Party Natal Congress in Durban on 15 August 1985. Certain elements within Pretoria's establishment (including Pik Botha – allegedly to further his reform agenda) had encouraged the belief that Botha was to promise far-reaching reforms in this speech and was to demonstrate some sort of vision regarding how South Africa's apartheid system could be radically overhauled. The speech was a bitter disappointment to many observers. Botha was intransigent, criticizing outside interference and ending any hopes of a peaceful change to majority rule while he was head of government. The international reaction to this speech was dramatic. Further loans were refused, the withdrawal of foreign firms accelerated, and the value of the rand plummeted.

The reaction of the South African business community was furious and swift. A full page advertisement was placed in Johannesburg's *Sunday Times* and signed by 91 leading South African industrialists. It called for the lifting of the State of Emergency, granting of full citizenship to all South Africans, the ending of statutory racial discrimination and the commencement of negotiations with acknowledged black leaders.[23] In September 1985 a group of businessmen, led by Anglo-American Chairman Gavin Relly, met with Oliver Tambo and other ANC members in Zambia. On 9 July 1987 another group of 61 white South Africans, led by ex-PFP leader Frederick van Zyl Slabbert, met with 17 ANC members in Dakar, Senegal for three days of talks. The result was a joint communiqué calling for a negotiated settlement in South Africa. Botha was furious and told the group that no further meetings with the banned ANC would be permitted. The liberals and the ANC met again, however, in West Germany on 26 May 1988. These meetings were in direct opposition to Botha's strategy of isolating these 'militants'.[24] They seemed to be more in tune with the philosophy of constructive engagement than either Botha or Crocker.

By the end of the 1980s the ultimate dilemma between apartheid and economic growth was manifesting itself to many ordinary white South Africans as a real decline in living standards. The incompatibility of apartheid with a modern economy was now being demonstrated beyond doubt. Neglect of black education and training was leaving an increasing proportion of the population unable to contribute to growth through either production or consumption. In some areas of South Africa, 50 per cent of the under-25 black population available for work were unemployed. The unwieldy apartheid infrastructure was itself an extravagance and the cost of keeping such a system in place against mounting internal opposition was reflected in the fact that in 1960 the government's defence spending totalled 7 per cent of its total budget. By 1980 this had reached 16 per cent, much of it spent on internal security.[25]

When Crocker's successor, Herman Cohen, was questioned on the extent to which business pressure helped to hasten the end of apartheid, he explained that it was indeed useful. The older generation of South Africans had grown up with a theological attachment to apartheid, they were 'caught up in the emotion of apartheid'. They also had little understanding of modern global economics. When the new generation took charge under F. W. de Klerk, they could perform a cold analysis of the apartheid system.[26] They understood that a modern economy could not thrive when over 80 per cent of its population could not contribute to this growth. South Africa's business community, spurred on by the desire for profits, played an important role. By uniting with the black opposition and white *verligtes*, they exerted an effective pressure on a government which had found itself in an impossible situation. Elections were held on issues of economic prosperity and security. Under the apartheid system, however, the electorate could not have both.

Although the business community did achieve a measure of influence over Botha's reform agenda, this influence was limited by competing demands from the right. The recognition of black trade unions was made possible by the *de facto* acceptance of the system by the business community, before the government moved to make them legal. The business community was also instrumental in the repeal of the pass laws, by exerting pressure on the government and objecting to the costs of the system. By meeting representatives of the ANC the business community was also important in consolidating domestic opposition to apartheid, and demonstrating that a negotiated settlement could be possible.

The activity of the South African business community could have complemented Crocker's constructive engagement policy. Its focus was a negotiated solution to the apartheid problem. Unfortunately, Washington remained suspicious of the communist sympathies of the ANC, with whom South African business had chosen to negotiate. The overtures of the South African business community were in contrast to Crocker's own actions and they appeared to highlight the inflexibility of constructive engagement. Washington should have been putting its full support behind these actions, but rather it stuck to its entrenched approach of favouring other, moderate, groups. Washington's policy was beginning to look increasingly out of touch, both with the opposition groups inside South Africa, and the increased opposition to apartheid being voiced by the international community as a whole.

The International Community Opposes Apartheid

The changing international environment
Since the NP came to power in 1948, the international community had looked on with increasing concern as the unique system of codified racial segregation became more deeply entrenched – and increasingly out of step with changing international attitudes. As increasing numbers of African states gained their independence the agenda of the United Nations General Assembly shifted away from the great powers, which had primarily focused on the preservation of the status quo. As a result, the UN became more belligerent in its attitude towards South Africa. Washington found itself facing a dilemma, summarized in a 1949 CIA assessment of South Africa. This revolved around the relative merits of anti-communism and anti-racism. The CIA acknowledged the importance of South Africa's anti-Soviet stance, but also warned against the 'propaganda' liability of Washington's association with apartheid.[27] By 1963 the UN had imposed a voluntary arms ban on sales to South Africa

– this became mandatory in 1977. The US had also announced its own unilateral voluntary arms ban on 2 August 1963. Also in 1963, the newly independent African nations founded the Organization of African Unity (OAU). Its very first resolution addressed the situation in South Africa, and it subsequently passed many resolutions calling for member states to break off diplomatic relations and boycott all trade with South Africa and Portugal – then still a colonial power. When H. Kamuzu Banda of Malawi established diplomatic relations with South Africa on 10 December 1967 he was widely criticized at the OAU. Few members could afford to abide by the strict trade boycotts, however. South Africa was also targeted by the Organization of Petroleum Exporting Countries (OPEC) when it imposed an oil ban in 1977, although South Africa continued to receive supplies from Iran until the fall of the Shah in 1979. The changing international order was brought closer to home for Pretoria in 1974 after the Portuguese coup.

Not all the changes in the international environment were to Pretoria's detriment, however. The election of Margaret Thatcher in 1979 in the United Kingdom, followed by Reagan's 1980 electoral victory over Carter, demonstrated a shift to the right in two vital Western countries. The leaders of the old and the new worlds (Britain and the United States respectively) were now being led by governments who would clearly show more sympathy for Botha's staunch anti-communist stance, and would be more reluctant to damage either the economic interests of their own countries, or those of South Africa itself. This conservative perspective contrasted with the increasingly vocal demands of the newly independent Third World, and nowhere were these two opposing international trends more clearly illustrated than in the increasingly acrimonious debates within the United Nations.

The United Nations and South Africa

In the meetings of the General Assembly, the African states demanded that both South Africa and Portugal be expelled from the UN. By 1974 the calls in the General Assembly had become so vociferous that Pretoria decided to jump before she was pushed. South Africa retained her delegation to the UN, but did not take her seat (with the exception of the Namibia debates). Despite its high international profile, however, the UN had little real impact on the situation in South Africa. UN Security Council Resolution 569 (1985) was passed on 26 July in reaction to Pretoria's declaration of the State of Emergency. The resolution placed voluntary sanctions on South Africa, banning new investment and nuclear cooperation and preventing the sale of Krugerrands (the South African gold coins) outside South Africa. The resolution was passed over the abstentions of Britain and the United States. But this was as close to direct action as the UN came, restrained mainly by the overriding influence of the Security Council. France, Britain and the US vetoed any attempt by the General Assembly to impose mandatory economic sanctions on South Africa, much to the chagrin of the weaker Assembly members. The US even vetoed or abstained on measures expressing solidarity with the oppressed of South Africa, or proposing multilateral sports boycotts.[28] The United States also vetoed a UN Security Council Resolution calling for mandatory sanctions that were very similar to the sanctions already imposed on the US by Congress under the auspices of the CAAA. When questioned on this point Crocker stated 'We are not going to turn our foreign policy over to the United Nations Security Council.'[29]

This highlights an important issue with regard to the UN – the question of sovereignty. Many of the great powers were, by their very nature, supporters of the status quo and the principle of non-interference was held as sacred by the whole range of UN members. No country would welcome such interference into its own affairs. This partly explains why the larger powers in the UN, such as the United States, were quicker to criticize South Africa with regard to its dealings in Namibia, but were reluctant to criticize its internal policies. The principle of non-interference had long been South Africa's defence when criticized in the UN. The main debate between South Africa and its critics within the UN lay in two opposing views of the organization's original Charter. South Africa quoted paragraph 7 of Article 2 in its own defence, which states: 'Nothing contained in the present Charter shall authorize the UN to intervene in matters which are essentially within the domestic jurisdiction of any state.' Pretoria firmly believed that this ought to preclude UN criticism of their internal apartheid policies. Those opposed to South Africa said that the UN was within its jurisdiction when dealing with 'threats to peace' – and that was how apartheid could be viewed. Article 55 paragraph C also stated that governments should maintain 'Universal respect for, and observance of, human rights, fundamental freedoms for all without distinction as to race, sex, language or religion.'

South Africa remained unmoved by the criticisms of the UN, and with good reason. Not only did the principle of sovereignty reign supreme in international law, but Pretoria could also accuse its critics of gross hypocrisy – and with some justification. The human rights records of some of the states that were Pretoria's most vocal critics were themselves extremely poor. The fact was that, despite some psychological pressure being put on Pretoria, the UN achieved very little influence over South Africa's policies. Indeed, the 'harangues' of the UN were used as ammunition by the right wing in South Africa to bolster the will of the white community in its resistance against being dictated to by outside powers. Thus, South African obduracy was encouraged by public criticism from the international community.

It was just such an effect, Crocker maintained, that constructive engagement had been designed to avoid. It could be argued that this was a valid point at the start of Crocker's time in office. If public criticism was proving counter-productive, maybe private encouragement could work. However, as South Africa's intransigence continued throughout Reagan's first term, serious questions were raised about the efficacy of this new approach, both in Washington and in the wider international community.

The Commonwealth

Another international organization that attempted to influence events within South Africa was the Commonwealth. This organization was not held to ransom by superpower vetoes. Even though Thatcher was adamantly opposed to any joint mandatory measures against South Africa, the Commonwealth managed to establish an 'Eminent Persons Group' (EPG) of seven senior Commonwealth politicians, led by General Olusegun Obasanjo (former Head of the Nigerian Government) and Malcolm Fraser (former Prime Minister of Australia). They were joined by representatives from Tanzania, Barbados, Britain, Canada and India. During February and March 1986 the EPG undertook a trip to South Africa, meeting and entering into dialogue with a wide range of South Africans, both black and white. The group also had meetings with President Botha and Nelson Mandela. The proposal they made on 13 March 1986 called on the South African government to allow normal political activity. This should include the unbanning of the ANC and the PAC, the release of political prisoners including Mandela, freedom of assembly and speech, and the removal of the army from the townships. For his part, Mandela had agreed that in return the ANC would suspend violence and enter into negotiations with the government. Although Pretoria was known for its intransigence – and its objection to external interference – its reaction to this report still managed to shock much of the international community. On 19 May 1986, while the EPG was still in South Africa, South African forces launched cross-border attacks on Zimbabwe, Zambia and Botswana. The South African government claimed that they were targeting ANC bases, but such attacks at such a time – and against countries that were all members of the Commonwealth – sent an unmistakeable message to the EPG. South Africa was not interested in being dictated to by anyone. The EPG's mission was terminated abruptly. The final report of the EPG scathingly condemned the conditions in South Africa and called for swift action, including sanctions.[30] This damning report signalled the end of any productive dialogue with Pretoria. The Commonwealth's sanctions initiatives were successful in keeping apartheid on the international agenda, but its ability to achieve direct results had been hampered by Pretoria's obvious hostility. Washington's view was reflected in a confidential NSC memorandum dated 9 March 1987, which concluded that the situation at that time stood thus: 'further initiatives by the EPG are not likely to be fruitful. Since the group recommended sanctions, they are not likely to be welcomed back by the South African government ... the EPG is probably moribund.'[31]

The European Community

A further forum for debate was the European Community (EC), although here the debate was hamstrung by Thatcher's determined opposition to sanctions. Until the mid-1980s the EC's voluntary Code of Conduct for corporations with operations in South Africa (similar to the US's Sullivan Principles) was its only real contribution. The violent uprisings in South Africa during 1985 and 1986 caused a sea-change in international opinion. In July 1985 the EC issued a statement condemning South Africa and the EC governments temporarily withdrew their ambassadors. In September 1985 nuclear cooperation with, and oil exports to, South Africa were terminated, military attachés were withdrawn and sales of sensitive equipment to South Africa's army and police force were banned. Germany, Holland and France imposed their own bilateral investment restrictions, Ireland banned all agricultural imports and Denmark followed the example of other Scandinavian countries by imposing comprehensive sanctions. Britain continued to procrastinate and in June 1986 Thatcher sent the Foreign Secretary Geoffrey Howe on a mission to South Africa. Pretoria was irritated by yet another attempt by an outside power to threaten or prescribe to them. Mandela and Tambo refused to meet Howe, thereby demonstrating their frustration with Britain's approach towards South Africa. In sum, the visit achieved nothing. By October 1986, just as Congress was passing its own sanctions Bill, Britain had agreed to participate in EC sanctions. Krugerrands were banned, as were South Africa's steel and iron exports. New investment in South Africa was also banned, but Britain insisted that the ban remained voluntary. However, the EC sanctions, together with individual bilateral measures, ensured that international pressure on South Africa was publicly maintained.

Botha's reaction to international pressure

Despite Crocker's, Reagan's and Thatcher's insistence that sanctions were unhelpful and counter-productive, they did play a significant role in altering Pretoria's actions. Sanctions were vital in communicating international opinion on South Africa's apartheid policies. Botha's reform measures – although reflecting his own opinions – were also carefully constructed with the international audience in mind. However, as Schrire explained, apartheid to Botha meant the 'obsolete socio-economic policies of previous governments'.[32] When Botha said 'apartheid is dead', he did not actually mean the power structure of apartheid, but its outdated policies of privilege and prejudice. His reforms were sufficiently misinterpreted by Western heads of government to allow Botha to undertake an official tour of Western Europe beginning on 29 May 1984. Botha met the heads of government of Portugal, Switzerland, Britain, West Germany, Belgium, France, Austria and Italy. He also met the Pope at the Vatican. This was the first overseas mission by a South African head of state in 20 years.

Botha was not as impervious to international opinion as he led both the outside world and his domestic constituency to believe. In a secret memorandum, issued ahead of the Venice Economic Summit in 1987, Botha requested support from the summit participants, still trying to convince them of his plans for reform. He explained that the 1987 electoral victory gave him a mandate for his reforms, which would lift blacks through better housing, education and welfare. He even told the US government that: 'there will be an evolutionary program to bring blacks into the governmental process, *beginning* on an advisory status' [my emphasis].[33] This prevarication on Botha's part succeeded in veiling his ultimate aim regarding black political participation, although he was open to his own voters that he would never allow full black political participation. These overtures show that Botha did sometimes temper his language for his international audience. The fact was that he did need to retain a certain element of sensitivity to the views of the West, regardless of how vehemently he denied it at home. He fervently wanted to cultivate allies who would cooperate in containing Soviet power in Africa – something Botha viewed as a very real threat. He also 'sought to retain membership of the Western economic system, with its vital network of trade, technological transfers, and investment'.[34]

If this was the case, why then was Botha so vocal in publicly denouncing Western interference? Why, during the international criticism and threats of sanctions of the mid-1980s, did Botha defiantly declare that South Africa would not 'crawl before anyone' to avert sanctions and would 'go it alone'? The fact was that international threats had different effects on different South African constituencies. Threats of sanctions and disinvestment were received with alarm by the better-off and higher-class whites. They were successful business people, and were dependent on international trade and investment for their own prosperity – threats and actions by the international community had a very real impact upon them. Therefore, as we have seen above, they became significant actors in the campaign for reform. Lower-class, poorer whites, on the other hand, felt that they had less to lose from foreign embargoes than they would if these embargoes forced real reform of the apartheid system. These poorer whites felt the threats from below, not from above. Traditional apartheid practices of job reservation, with lower wages and worse conditions for black workers, were vital in maintaining the protected position of the lower-class whites above a huge pool of labour which would otherwise be in direct competition for their jobs, their higher wages and their (relative to blacks) privileged status. This constituency pressed the government even harder in a direction opposite to that urged by the affluent business community. They insisted that the government must not bow to outside pressure and this had a significant effect on Botha's agenda – in effect cancelling out much of the pressure from the international community. The more the international community demanded, the more indignant the right wing became.

Did foreign pressure – from the UN, the EC, the Commonwealth and individual governments – actually achieve any influence over Pretoria's policies? In some ways, the actions were entirely counterproductive. Partly in response to the threats to their oil supply, South Africa established the South African Oil and Gas Corporation (SASOL) in 1950. The increased threats in the mid-1970s simply encouraged it to increase greatly its own oil production. In 1968 South Africa also established its own arms manufacturer – Armscor – in response to the 1963 UN arms embargo. This company became so successful that, at the height of international pressure in the mid-1980s, South Africa had become a net arms exporter.

Yet international pressure did achieve some concrete results. Certain actions, such as the awarding of the Nobel Peace Prize to Bishop Desmond

Tutu on 16 October 1984, and the sight of diplomatic representatives of Western governments[35] attending the funeral of the black teacher Matthew Goniwe, murdered by the South African Police, did place great psychological pressure on the whites of South Africa. International pressure also achieved more tangible results. Just such publicity and pressure was instrumental in, for example, the moratorium on forced removals of blacks to 'homelands', which was declared by Pretoria in 1985. Virtually the entire international community refused to recognize the independent homelands. Without such recognition, this policy was rendered an embarrassing and expensive farce for Pretoria. Another concrete example of international pressure altering Pretoria's policies is that of the international sports boycott, which resulted in South Africa modifying the apartheid laws in their application to South African sports teams.

When eight aging black nationalist leaders – including Walter Sisulu – were unconditionally freed from prison on 15 October 1989, the UDF hailed the releases as a 'massive victory' for both the South African people and the international sanctions campaign.[36] Sanctions also had a profound impact on the confidence of the South African business community. But, despite the examples of success, it was the actions of international business that had a more direct effect. It was Chase Manhattan Bank's refusal to roll over South Africa's debt that sparked off the economic crisis that sent the rand into freefall, rather than international sanctions. As Crocker himself explained, 'the closing down of the capital markets bothered [South Africa] far more than the US threatening sanctions. We didn't cause the closing down of the markets ... but capital goes where there is confidence, and both were rapidly leaving South Africa.'[37]

The one remaining aspect of the international environment that had an impact on apartheid was something beyond the control of any individual government. The collapse of the Soviet Union and the subsequent end of the Cold War had a very real significance for the South African situation. The demise of the USSR meant that Afrikaners lost some of their fears and some of their excuses. As Crocker explained in *High Noon in Southern Africa*, Pretoria could no longer paint itself as the regional bulwark against communism. It is also important to remember that many Afrikaners harboured a very real fear of Soviet influence in the African continent. The removal of this fear enabled many to face up to the prospect of a negotiated settlement for South Africa. Crocker also highlighted the fact that without their superpower patron the ANC, too, had reason to push harder for a negotiated settlement – although this seems to overlook the fact that this had been the original stated aim of the ANC. Cohen also points out that the fear of the Western governments was also removed – making them more willing to understand the black point of view, rather than simply fearing black activists as agents of Moscow.

It seemed as though, by the mid-1980s, Crocker had taken his eye off the ball with regard to South Africa. His policy needed to be flexible to reflect the changing environment both within South Africa and among the international community. Unfortunately, the main alteration in Washington in response to these changing circumstances was to bolster the Public

Diplomacy Programme for constructive engagement within the US. The policy itself was not altered. Its main *implicit* aims with regard to South Africa – anti-communism and an acceptable *appearance* for the Washington–Pretoria relationship – became more obvious as the rest of the international community began to take concrete steps against apartheid. For Washington, the real significance of these international moves was the fact that they placed an unwelcome spotlight on just how little constructive engagement was doing in order to persuade Pretoria away from apartheid. Constructive engagement was shown to be an inflexible and self-motivated policy.

Notes

1   The Freedom Charter was declared at the Congress of the People in Kliptown on 26 June 1955. It was notable for its commitment to a non-racial South Africa, in contrast to the Pan-Africanist Congress's Africanist position. The full text of the Charter can be consulted at www.anc.org.za/ancdocs/history/charter.html

2   Meredith, Martin, *In the Name of Apartheid: South Africa in the Post War Period*, New York: Harper and Row, 1988, p. 193.

3   Riley, Eileen, *Major Political Events in South Africa 1948–1990*, Oxford and New York: Facts on File, 1991, p. 181.

4   As quoted in Barber, James and J. Barratt, *South Africa's Foreign Policy*, Cambridge: Cambridge University Press, 1990, p. 288.

5   As quoted in Meredith, *In the Name of Apartheid*, p. 177.

6   Baker, Pauline H., *The United States and South Africa: The Reagan Years. Update South Africa: Time Running Out*, Ford Foundation and Foreign Policy Association, 1989, p. 27.

7   Thompson, Alex, *Incomplete Engagement: United States Foreign Policy Towards the Republic of South Africa 1981–1988*, Aldershot and Brookfield: Avebury, 1996, p. 190.

8   Meredith, *In the Name of Apartheid*, 1988, p. 201.

9   Beinart, William, *Twentieth Century South Africa*, Oxford and New York: Oxford University Press, 1994, p. 242.

10 *The New York Guardian*, 3 October 1984.

11 Thompson, Leonard, *A History of South Africa*, New Haven and London: Yale University Press, 1990, p. 235.

12 Crocker, Chester, 'South Africa: Strategy for Change', *Foreign Affairs*, Vol. 59, No. 2 (Winter 1980–1), p. 343.

13 As quoted in Alex Thompson, *Incomplete Engagement*, p. 197.

14 Van Heerden, D., 'The New Nats', *Frontline*, March 1986, p. 36.

15 Worden, Nigel, *The Making of Modern South Africa: Conquest, Segregation and Apartheid*, Oxford and Cambridge, MA: Blackwell Publishers, 1994, p. 134.

16 Thompson, *Incomplete Engagement*, p. 251.

17 Kline, Benjamin, *Profit, Principle and Apartheid 1948–1994: The Conflict of Economic and Moral Issues in United States–South African Relations*, Studies in African Economic and Social Development, Volume 10, Lewiston, Queenstown and Lampeter: Edwin Mellen Press, 1997, p. 151.

18 Ohlson, Thomas and Stephen John Stedman with Robert Davies, *The New Is Not Yet Born: Conflict Resolution in Southern Africa*, Washington, DC: The Brookings Institution, 1994, p. 60.

19 Grundy, Kenneth W., *South Africa: Domestic Crisis and Global Challenge*, Boulder, San Francisco and Oxford: Westview Press, 1991, p. 70 and Riley, *Major Political Events in South Africa*, p. 168.

20 Crocker, Chester, *High Noon in Southern Africa: Making Peace in a Rough Neighborhood*,

New York and London: W. W. Norton and Company, 1992, p. 87.

21 Schrire, Robert, *Update South Africa: Time Running Out. Adapt or Die: The End of White Politics in South Africa*, London: Hurst & Co., 1991.

22 Ovenden, K. and T. Cole, *Apartheid and International Finance: A Program for Change*, Victoria: Penguin, 1989, p. 83.

23 Schrire, *Adapt or Die*, p. 83.

24 Crocker *High Noon in Southern Africa*, p. 308.

25 Meredith, *In the Name of Apartheid*, p. 185.

26 Personal interview with Herman Cohen, 22 June 2001, Washington, DC.

27 Schraeder, Peter J., *United States Foreign Policy Toward Africa: Incrementalism, Crisis and Change*, Cambridge: Cambridge University Press, 1994, p. 194.

28 See, for example, UN General Assembly Resolution 37/69/G (9 December 1982) regarding the issue of apartheid in sport (vetoed by Britain and the US); UN General Assembly Resolution 36/172 K (17 December 1981) expressing solidarity with the oppressed women and children of South Africa (Britain and US abstained); and UN General Assembly Resolution 39/2 (28 September 1984) rejecting South Africa's new constitution (Britain and US abstained).

29 ARC Identifier: 59926 *Current Situation in South Africa – Crocker 1987*. Creator: United States Information Agency (1982–) (Most Recent). Broadcast 27 February 1987. Item from Record Group 306: Records of the USIA 1900–1988. Video Recordings from the 'Worldnet Today' Program Series. NAIL Locator: 306-WNET-356 Motion Picture, Sound and Video Recordings LICON, National Archives at College Park, Maryland USA.

30 For full details see Commonwealth Group of Eminent Persons, *Mission to South Africa: The Commonwealth Report*, London and Harmondsworth: Penguin for the Commonwealth Secretariat, 1986 and Commonwealth Secretariat, *Racism in Southern Africa: The Commonwealth Stand*, London: The Commonwealth Secretariat, 1985.

31 Ronald Reagan Library, CA. White House Staff and Office Files: Cohen, Herman J., Files 1987–8. African Affairs Directorate, NSC. Boxes 91875 and 91876. Confidential Memorandum. From: Herman J. Cohen (NSC). To: Frank C. Carlucci. Subject: South Africa: Malcolm Fraser and Eminent Persons Group Request Appointment 9 March 1987. Declassified 1 June 1999.

32 Schrire, *Adapt or Die*, p. 118.

33 Ronald Reagan Library, CA. White House Staff and Office Files: Cohen, Herman J., Files 1987–8. African Affairs Directorate, NSC. Boxes 91875 and 91876. Secret Memorandum. From: Herman J. Cohen. To: Frank C. Carlucci. Subject: Letter from South African President Botha 26 May 1987. Declassified 1 June 1999.

34 Schrire, *Adapt or Die*, p. 22.

35 The officials represented the governments of France, Norway, Denmark, Canada, Australia and Sweden. For futher details see T. R. H. Davenport, *South Africa: A Modern History*, fourth edition, Basingstoke and London: Macmillan, 1991, p. 440.

36 Riley, *Major Political Events in South Africa*, p. 212.

37 Personal interview with Dr Chester Crocker 19 June 2001, Washington, DC.

6

Constructive Engagement inside
South Africa: Addressing Local Realities?

Constructive Engagement:
in the Interests of Pretoria?

Although constructive engagement was frequently criticized for presenting South Africa with too many concessions, the extent to which Pretoria actually benefited from this policy has never been clear. Constructive engagement did provide the South African government with material benefits from early in Reagan's first term. In 1981–2 'grey area' exports, including non-lethal military equipment, were resumed, together with military training and liaison. Increased consular interchange was also established. Although the US continued to criticize Pretoria openly for refusing to sign the Nuclear Non-Proliferation Treaty, the US continued in the role of Pretoria's most important foreign source of nuclear expertise. In September 1982 seven American companies were granted licences – worth $50 million in total – to service South Africa's Koeberg nuclear power plant.

From the beginning of the constructive engagement policy US trade and investment in South Africa increased, but the role of this increased trade was contested. Although many argued that foreign investment was vital for the welfare and advancement of South African blacks, opponents warned that this masked a lack of any real progress in achieving black political rights. This economic advancement could simply succeed in creating a black middle class which Pretoria could co-opt into supporting the apartheid system. As Greenberg explains: 'Constructive engagement under these circumstances may unwittingly facilitate the motives of the South African Government to create a privileged urban African stratum, economically and politically divorced from the majority of the African population.'[1]

As well as the tangible benefits of increased trade and technology transfer, constructive engagement also provided Pretoria with much-needed legitimacy on the world stage. The US supported South Africa by preventing or softening many UN resolutions which would have been disadvantageous to Pretoria. Peter Vale is damning in his account of the advantages this aspect of constructive engagement afforded Pretoria:

> Constructive engagement deliberately chose South Africa's government – and its supporting establishment – over the country's people. South Africa's rulers recognised this: they knew, too, that it provided them with much valued space

in an international community which was closing in on them.... They saw in [Crocker] a means to conduct their foreign policy in a higher league than they deserved.[2]

Commentators also criticized this diplomatic support for providing South Africa with an aura of respectability and a degree of tolerance, whilst it pursued its policy of destabilization of the Frontline States (FLS): Angola, Zimbabwe, Zambia, Mozambique, Botswana, Lesotho and Swaziland (see Chapter 9). Constructive engagement provided an umbrella under which South Africa could target the ANC points of operation in the FLS, eventually succeeding in forcing the organization out of the immediate neighbourhood, but at a great cost to the FLS themselves.[3]

An unsatisfactory feature of the benefits that constructive engagement was providing to South Africa was that they all appeared to be granted with no specific *quid pro quo*. South Africa was led to believe that, in the final analysis, the US under Reagan could be counted on for support. When Crocker was asked to identify just what he saw as America's 'coercive' power over South Africa – if there was any – he explained: 'Our coercive power was to remove legitimacy and to isolate them with our rhetoric, pointing out to them what we would see as acceptable.'[4] This seems a rather lean analysis from a man who took up his post strongly condemning the futile and counterproductive use of rhetoric during the Carter administration. It also demonstrates what Pretoria had already appeared to grasp – that there was no flip side to constructive engagement. A failure to respond to the increasing number of concessions being offered by Washington was not going to be met by any tangible negative alternative.

This survey of the benefits constructive engagement presented to Pretoria begs the question – how did South Africa respond to constructive engagement? Was it viewed in a positive light? Did Pretoria identify with constructive engagement as being in its own interests, and therefore worth cooperating with? The answer was, unfortunately, no. Botha made it clear to Crocker that he greatly resented the implication that South Africa had a price to pay for constructive engagement.[5] In an article in the South African publication *Optima* Gerrit Olivier – Chief Director of Communication and Planning in South Africa's Department of Foreign Affairs – explained the South African government's response to any external policy that attempted to influence South Africa's domestic concerns:

> Events of the last three years have demonstrated that foreign interference in South Africa's domestic affairs will be futile. In fact, such interference is counterproductive, demonstrated by the decline of foreign government influence on South African politics.'[6]

It would appear from this statement that Pretoria and Botha should have welcomed constructive engagement, but even this policy of concession and support went too far in its attempts to dictate to Pretoria. Indeed, any indication to fellow Afrikaners that policy could be affected in such a way would have reflected very badly on Botha in the eyes of his domestic audience. One example is the release of a group of black labour leaders from custody in South Africa at the end of 1984. Reagan publicly described the release as 'the result of three weeks of work.... I don't think we're being too bold in taking the credit.' Unfortunately, this *was* far too bold, according to Pretoria. Botha was incensed and subjected Crocker to a 'furious diatribe' on the 'counterproductivity of Mr Reagan's remarks' when they met in Cape Town in February 1985.[7] Crocker was in an impossible situation. His policy was based on maintaining a friendly and open dialogue with South Africa, but for it to be politically acceptable back home, tangible results were imperative to avoid accusations of appeasement. Botha's reaction demonstrates that these two things were simply not compatible. Crocker's political necessity was to demonstrate constructive engagement's ability to achieve influence over Pretoria's treatment of black South Africans. This, however, was at odds with Botha's political necessity of demonstrating the exact opposite to *his* domestic audience – that the South African government would not be dictated to by meddling external powers.

Curiously for a government that was so adamantly against foreign interference, South Africa was also very critical of the US and other foreign governments for not giving them sufficient credit for their reforms. As Olivier explained:

> South Africa is paying a high price for its exclusion from the mainstream of international trade, culture and diplomacy. There is no easy remedy and the whole problem is exacerbated by the inverse relationship between progressive change in South Africa and the international response to it.[8]

Although constructive engagement represented a decisive shift in US policy in Pretoria's favour – providing it with increased legitimacy and useful concessions over trade – the fact remained that Pretoria did not see in constructive engagement enough to benefit its own interests. South Africa was still indignantly holding on to the principle of sovereignty that it knew all other nations would cling to with just such tenacity if their own internal policies came under international scrutiny and condemnation. Pretoria was furious with what it saw as the inconsistent and hypocritical application of international law. Olivier continued: 'Of particular concern to South Africa in relations with the West is the cavalier fashion in which the rules and norms of conventional intercourse have been applied in some cases.'

It appears that South Africa had seriously overestimated what was on offer from constructive engagement. This was not helped by Crocker's early statements promising a new relationship. It seems remarkable that Pretoria did not expect to pay a price for constructive engagement but this belief became more understandable as concessions continued with no direct return. Botha had a deeper understanding of constructive engagement than Crocker might have liked – making it clear that he knew it was a policy based on America's own interests – and he was not about to compromise the interests of his own country just to make things easy for Crocker. The South African line was: 'The endeavour to regain international moral legitimacy, desirable as it may be, cannot be pursued at any price.'[9] It is true to say that constructive engagement did benefit

South Africa to an extent. Botha knew, however, that his interests as Prime Minster, and then President, rested on listening more carefully to his domestic constituency than to outside voices. It seems that, in both Pretoria and Washington, Crocker's initial assertion in 1981 that constructive engagement would 'underpromise and overdeliver' was turned on its head.

Constructive Engagement: in the Interests of the Black Opposition?

The ANC was widely recognized as the opposition group with the largest support base, but Crocker remained reluctant to engage with them, mistrusting their communist links. This decision proved an important stumbling block for the constructive engagement policy. The result was that the policy gained no support from the anti-apartheid movements in either South Africa or the United States. Crocker made it clear very early on that the strategy of constructive engagement would not sacrifice Pretoria's interests to the interests of black South Africa. Even before his appointment he had warned against: 'the twin dangers of abetting violence in the Republic and aligning ourselves with the cause of white rule'.[10] Such a statement had already succeeded in filling many blacks with dismay at this demonstration of his judgement that the black opposition to apartheid was on a par with the original oppression itself. In a situation where blacks were systematically robbed of the ability to speak out on the injustice they faced, this apparent refusal to recognize the seriousness of their plight caused great concern. Chabani Manganyi spoke for many in the black community when he explained that blacks 'interpreted the policy of constructive engagement as an act of choice – or moral choice.'[11] This refusal to address the interests of the oppressed population explicitly was seen as an unethical and immoral stance.

Such criticism had little impact on Crocker, who steadfastly continued to explain his support for gradual reform to the South Africans. His constructive engagement strategy was based on a firm belief in the efficacy of white-led change. He went as far as criticizing those who focused 'on the wrong issue: the ultimate goal, instead of the process of getting there'.[12] For South African blacks – unrepresented, dispossessed, banned or in detention – this comment represented a real lack of appreciation of the urgency of their cause. He also firmly refused to endorse the question of 'one man one vote' in a unitary South Africa. When pressed on this issue, he simply stated: 'We are determined *not* to answer that question … the question of what formula, what blueprint, is for South Africans themselves to negotiate.'[13] It was through statements such as these that Crocker spelt out constructive engagement's approach to the intractable apartheid issue – a message heard by blacks and whites alike, but with sharply differing responses.

Constructive engagement and Botha's reforms

Constructive engagement's encouraging attitude towards Pretoria continued throughout the 1980s, particularly in its response to P. W. Botha's reforms. Bearing in mind Schrire's distinction between reform of the politics of privilege and prejudice and reform of the politics of power, together with Botha's open admission that he would never allow blacks full power sharing, the attitude of the Reagan administration towards Botha's reforms exasperated many in the black community. The issue of the 1983 constitution caused particular grievance. In 'Strategy for Change', Crocker stated that piecemeal power-sharing steps deserved support if they were demonstrably agreed to by the participants in them. Yet, under constructive engagement, the new constitution was hailed as a step in the right direction, despite obvious black opposition. In a speech in San Francisco in June 1983, Under Secretary of State Lawrence Eagleburger applauded the fact that 'the South African government had taken the first step towards extending political rights beyond the white minority'.[14]

Reagan often exacerbated the situation with his ill-informed sentiments. During the mid-1980s crisis in South Africa, Reagan stated: 'In recent years, there's been a dramatic change. Black workers have been permitted to unionize.... The infamous pass laws have been ended.... Citizenship, wrongly stripped away, has been restored to nearly 6 million blacks....'[15] Reforms had indeed been undertaken, but as they went hand in hand with repression under the State of Emergency, and went no way towards addressing the question of black political rights, many in the black community saw Reagan's endorsement as particularly unhelpful. Even after it became clear that Botha's reforms had stalled and repression was now his main instrument, Crocker maintained: 'South Africa's government *is* a reformist government. We stand by that statement.'[16] Constructive engagement's prescription for the shift away from apartheid – gradual white-led change – had already indicated to blacks that the strategy had not been formulated with their immediate interests high on the agenda. This understanding was confirmed by the patent imbalance in Crocker's 'engagement'.

Washington engages the black opposition: 'all power to the moderates'

Although Crocker said he was attempting to help create conditions for a negotiated settlement, his own negotiations were largely confined to meeting representatives of the South African government. On the few occasions that Crocker did meet with black South Africans, the US concentrated on such black Africans as were sympathetic to American policy: 'The Africans telling them what they wanted to hear, like Buthelezi, got a big audience in the States.'[17] So how did Washington relate to the various black groups within South Africa? How true was constructive engagement to Crocker's initial statement that 'neither do we have the right to decide which black groups and leaders are "legitimate" representatives of the majority'?[18] Or, on the other hand, did Washington really only listen to the blacks who told them 'what they wanted to hear'?

Professor Lewis Gann (Senior Fellow of the Hoover Institute) championed the beliefs of the right wing in a testimony to Congress in March 1986 when he reiterated the importance of working through the whites in South Africa and *not* with the ANC 'which is totally unsympathetic toward the US and the system that the US represents'. Our slogan, Gann stated, should be 'all power to the moderates'.[19] With regard to other South African figures, Reagan had already met with both the Zulu Chief Gatsha Buthelezi and Desmond Tutu before the controversial Shultz/Tambo meeting in 1987. Indeed, the Reagan administration found in Buthelezi an articulate ally for some aspects of constructive engagement, particularly his opposition to sanctions. In a secret White House memorandum to the President, dated 4 February 1985, this usefulness was identified:

> Buthelezi's visit to the US comes as forces are gathering steam in Congress toward the passage of anti-South African legislation, including penalties and restrictions on US business dealings with South Africa. During his various meetings here ... he will be a forceful advocate opposing any punitive legislation.[20]

The Reagan administration did not attempt to conceal the fact that they were more attentive to certain moderate black groups – although these links never matched those established with the white government in Pretoria. At the same time, they were openly hostile to the ANC.

Relations with the ANC

From the very early stages of constructive engagement, Washington did not encourage any contact with the ANC. Indeed, when in late 1981 the ANC requested a meeting with the American Ambassador to the UN, Jeane Kirkpatrick, their letter was not even acknowledged.[21] This was in sharp contrast to the welcome afforded to the South African military officials whose visit of the same year – in March 1981 – had caused such controversy. Washington continued to support Pretoria in apparent reforms which were in direct opposition to the aims and interests of the ANC. The Nkomati Accord of 1984 between South Africa and Mozambique (a non-aggression pact under which Mozambique would refuse to allow the ANC to operate or have bases inside its borders – see Chapter 9) was hailed as a great success by Crocker. He presented it as the first tangible achievement of constructive engagement. The ANC, however, was bitter that Pretoria, with Western encouragement, had succeeded in forcing Mozambique to desert its cause.

The debate over relations with the ANC raged in Congress, where the right wing strongly supported Reagan's sentiments. Republican Congressman Jack Kemp wrote to the President directly, complaining of Shultz's planned meeting with Oliver Tambo of the ANC. The meeting, asserted Kemp, would send a message that 'the US has abandoned those who are working for peaceful and democratic change in South Africa. The Marxist ANC represents only a tiny minority of black South Africans.'[22]

Democrats on the Foreign Affairs Committee felt differently, however. Congressman Crockatt explained to a Congressional hearing in 1986 that the ANC had been founded in 1912 as a non-violent anti-apartheid organization. For almost fifty years its peaceful protests and boycotts had been met with mass arrests and detentions, repressive police action and oppressive laws to control dissent. After the protests over the Sharpeville shooting in 1960 in which 69 unarmed blacks had died, the government moved swiftly to ban both the ANC and the Pan-African Congress (PAC), and it was only then that the ANC turned to armed resistance. In a 1986 article even the 'New Nats' (as a liberal section of the NP *verligtes* were known) were said to understand – better than Washington – why the ANC could not now renounce violence:

> [The 'New Nats'] regard the government's insistence that the ANC should renounce violence before any talks can start as specious ... violence is the only picture card that the ANC still holds and if he is asked to abandon this, he is giving away his only basis for negotiation.[23]

Near the end of his time in office, Crocker wrote that it had long been obvious to observers that South Africa would not become free through revolutionary violence and actions aimed at physically destroying its economy and infrastructure. He went on to state that black leverage would principally develop through non-military means projected from black organizations created and based inside South Africa.[24] He appears to have discounted the fact that to call for disinvestment, or simply to profess 'unconstitutional opinions', was illegal in South Africa. Blacks were not in a position to plan strategies, or negotiating positions, let alone be admitted to the table. Yet he continued to insist: 'We believe that there are many openings, many opportunities in terms of the peaceful organization by black South Africans for acquiring a greater stake, acquiring a greater position and a better bargaining stance in the future.'[25] When asked directly how he thought blacks could have achieved this improved position, Crocker said they should have stopped working on the assumption of ending apartheid. They should first have been looking for a way into negotiations.

The fact remains that, despite the *raison d'être* of constructive engagement being presented as the promotion of negotiations in South Africa, this was not the policy's main priority. Professor Thomas Karis (Senior Research Fellow of the Ralph Bunche Institute, Graduate School of the City of New York) explained in his 1986 testimony to the House of Representatives that there was much wishful thinking about mobilizing a broad centre of black 'moderates' against 'extremists'. He went on to point out: 'In South African history and current circumstances, the political and economic program of the ANC is not "extreme". And there are no black leaders of credibility who can mobilize a substantial coalition that is anti-UDF, anti-COSATU and anti-ANC.' He also dismissed Washington's favourite, Chief Buthelezi, as 'a tragic figure who attracts from blacks more intense hostility than probably anyone else in South African politics'.[26]

Constructive engagement failed in its promise to promote negotiations by demonstrating to Pretoria that it would not have a price to pay for refusing to talk with the ANC. Indeed, not only did Washington itself avoid such communication, it even expressed outright hostility towards the organization. Also, although Nelson Mandela was widely acknowledged as the most popular black leader in South Africa, and therefore vital for credible negotiations, his release from detention was not officially demanded by the Reagan administration until 1985, for fear of upsetting Pretoria. Recently declassified documents emphasized the need to end the legitimization of 'terrorist, pro-Soviet groups', including the ANC, as one of the key goals for US policy in South Africa.[27] An article in the *New York Times* of 23 January 1986 also revealed that, under the Reagan administration, the CIA had supplied intelligence information on the ANC, and on Oliver Tambo's movements, to Pretoria throughout Reagan's presidency. In return, the South African government provided information on Soviet shipping movements in southern African waters and Cuban activities in Angola.[28]

In 1986, Washington began its first, tentative, official contacts with the ANC. On 30 July 1986 Paul Hare, the US Ambassador to Zambia, held talks with three senior ANC officials. This was followed by a meeting between Oliver Tambo and Chester Crocker in London in September 1986. The most high-profile – and controversial – meeting took place when US Secretary of State George Shultz met Tambo on 24 January 1987, in Washington, DC. The ANC was officially described by the State Department as having 'a legitimate voice' in South Africa. This represented a definite broadening of US policy, even though the talks themselves did not mask the very real reservations each had about the other. Shultz was open in his condemnation of the ANC's communist links and espousal of violence. In an address to the International Management and Development Institute in 1986, Shultz reiterated that the existence of such contacts did not signal American approbation of the ANC or the PAC. This was in reply to the vocal criticism from the right, who strongly objected to any dealings with the ANC.

Indeed, even after the Shultz/Tambo meeting, the US continued to pursue an anti-ANC policy. The Foreign Assistance Supplementary Appropriations Bill for fiscal year 1987 (passed on 11 July 1987) allowed for approximately $40 million for SADCC projects.[29] The bill stipulated, however, that assistance would not be granted to countries allowing terrorists to operate from their territory. This clearly was going to cause the ANC, still banned in South Africa, serious difficulty in obtaining external support. Even throughout the last few years of constructive engagement, Crocker did not demonstrate a full understanding of the no-win situation in which the ANC found itself. Professor Karis stated: 'It is important to emphasize that President Botha excludes from negotiations not only those who do not renounce violence, but also those who have "unconstitutional aims".'[30] Despite this, Crocker continued to insist: 'If the ANC is serious and wants negotiations and wants them now, it's going to have to face the issue of what choices *it's* prepared to make, what compromises *it's* prepared to make, just like the South African government has.' Shultz also stated: 'We do not ask that black South Africans temper their passion for change – we share it. We only ask that it be channelled into constructive strategies for reconciliation.'[31]

All of this begs the question: to what extent did constructive engagement address the interests and aspirations of the South African blacks – and what concrete actions did Washington take, under the auspices of this strategy, to help them? When Crocker was asked directly 'What did the US do to try to help the blacks enter into negotiations with the government?' he replied 'We refused to legitimate Pretoria's system. We declared it illegitimate ... this was a very powerful tool.'[32] This did not provide much practical help to South Africa's black community. When asked what *tangible* help Washington had provided, he pointed to the US aid programme as an example of just such assistance.

American aid to South African blacks

The US government undertook a number of entrepreneurial, educational and trade union 'empowerment' schemes in South Africa. At the beginning of 1984, the government established a scholarship fund of $10 million annually to enable black South Africans to gain a university education, together with a $2 million programme to help black high school graduates prepare for university entrance examinations. Another $1 million was channelled through the American Federation of Labor to train black trade union leaders in management skills.[33] Crocker also made much of the assistance provided by US companies that subscribed to the 'Sullivan Principles'. By 1985, these companies had provided over $80 million to be spent on community aid programmes.

Unfortunately, the fact remained that neither the Sullivan companies, nor the American government's aid programmes, addressed the fundamental concerns of the black community. Nor did the sums they were providing make any significant impact in the context of South Africa's $80 billion economy. The reality was that, by their very nature, these programmes could only ever touch a small proportion of South Africa's black community. They did nothing to assist the millions more, particularly those in the isolated homelands, who remained in poverty without a legitimate voice. It was not only the scale of these programmes that rendered them impotent in the face of apartheid, it was also the attitude and thinking behind their implementation. Crocker had made his views clear when he stated: 'Washington needs to stop thinking of African policy as a philanthropic venture and start defining *US interests* in the economic relationship with Africa.' He also criticized the growing focus of aid on 'basic needs', pointing out that this 'almost rules out using aid as a tool for the promotion of any US interest – either developmental or political'.[34]

This thinking was reflected in US aid to the black majority in South Africa. Although most observers accepted the fact that South Africa's black trade unions were at the forefront of black political awareness and representation, the US government carefully limited any aid to them, as they were perceived as not politically neutral enough. Many in the trade union movement were angered by the fact that Washington would provide no aid at all to the training initiatives they had developed under the auspices of their own unions. All funds had to be received through the African-American Labor Center (AALC) in Washington.

In a 1985 article, Stephen Weissman provides an example of how apartheid was affecting the daily lives of many blacks – and how little meaningful help they received from the constructive engagement strategy of the Reagan administration. In the summer of 1984 a group of American Congressmen visited South Africa for themselves and heard from community representatives how their historically black-owned settlement of Mgwali was to be eliminated. The South African government was going to relocate the residents to the barren 'homeland' of Ciskei. Despite repeated pleas from the Mgwali Residents Association, the US Embassy in South Africa would not provide any assistance to help towards their legal fees, not even from its 'Human Rights Fund'. This fund was specially designed to 'contribute $1.5 million in small grants to organizations in South Africa promoting human rights in the face of apartheid'. The Residents Association should therefore have been an eligible candidate. Neither did the embassy make any public statements on the issue. Washington did protest regarding the eradication of another 'black spot' – Magopa – but when the forced removals went ahead regardless, the Reagan administration's relations with Pretoria were unaffected.

Did constructive engagement address the interests of black South Africa?

The reality was that constructive engagement did not address the interests of South African blacks. Little meaningful communication was established, particularly with those groups, such as the UDF and the ANC, which were widely accepted as being the most representative voices of the black majority. Any attempts to criticize Pretoria or to extend economic aid were constantly tempered by constructive engagement's dictum that Washington should strive to maintain an open and friendly relationship with Pretoria. Blacks themselves were under little illusion as to what constructive engagement could mean for them. Their opinions on constructive engagement were damning. The outspoken recipient of the Nobel Peace Prize, Desmond Tutu, made no apologies for clearly stating his opinion of constructive engagement. In 1982, when asked for his opinion on how constructive engagement was developing, he stated: 'I frankly don't care ... I have written off the Americans as a government.' His reaction to Reagan's 22 July speech was also reported in the *Washington Times*: 'Your President is the pits as far as I am concerned ... the West, for my part, can go to hell.'[35] American commentators also remarked that: 'Reagan's coddling of South Africa had intensified the immiseration of black South Africa.'[36]

The situation was not helped by the fact that many of the overtures to Pretoria were made while restrictions on blacks were being tightened, particularly during the State of Emergency. The South African writer Jack Bloom also identified the fact that, for many black politicians, 'the realm of the symbolic is exceptionally important because of their very real powerlessness'.[37] Despite much caution in the signals sent to Pretoria, Washington did not take the same care over how constructive engagement was being presented to black South Africa. In Congressional testimony, Tutu testified that constructive engagement had worsened the situation under apartheid and he claimed that constructive engagement was saying that blacks were dispensable. In an article of April 1985, in the *New York Times*, the Reverend Beyers Naude – the Secretary General of the South African Council of Churches – warned that the US 'must recognize that its lack of meaningful support for the South African black community and its struggle for liberation has created feelings of deep anger and animosity ... toward Washington and its policy of "constructive engagement"'.[38] Weissman quotes a prominent UDF official as stating:

> We feel [the US is] going all out to prop up Prime Minister Botha ... and apartheid ... we're disappointed. You've given a morale booster to the government. The South African Broadcasting Corporation highlights constructive engagement as a definite change from the Carter Administration. Carter made no bones that South Africa has a racist government.[39]

After Senator Edward Kennedy's visit to South Africa, he testified in front of the Senate Committee on Foreign Relations that: 'It is no secret that the US is now despised by large numbers of blacks inside South Africa. As Winnie Mandela said to me during our visit, "Tell the people of the United States that constructive engagement is just another shoulder to the wheel of apartheid."'[40] Winnie Mandela put her words into action when she refused to accept US government help to rebuild her home, which had been petrol-bombed (although she did receive assistance from individual US senators). Her daughter said she would not accept help from the 'unprincipled' Mr. Reagan whose administration: 'has so insulted the black people with its so-called constructive engagement policy ... the American government must think that, like them, we have no values'.[41] Washington was further embarrassed when increasing numbers of moderate black South African leaders – and liberal whites – refused to attend diplomatic functions at the US Embassy in South Africa.

Although Crocker's failure to address the interests of the black majority in South Africa was obvious, it was not surprising. Despite the numerous rejections of the 'abhorrent' and 'repugnant' apartheid system that issued from the Reagan administration – and Crocker himself – constructive engagement was simply not designed with the interests of the black majority in mind. Indeed, the hostility which the Reagan administration held towards the Marxist-oriented ANC was such that any policy aimed at furthering the goals of this organization would have been viewed as hostile to American interests. Crocker's aim was to achieve a policy that contributed to the creation of a South African society that was not only amenable to US interests, but one that Washington could deal with without suffering political embarrassment. He was certainly not working to establish conditions in which a radical black Marxist government could take over a country with strategic mineral resources, geopolitical significance and a useful role in the international economic system. If he had indeed pursued constructive engagement *throughout* South Africa, he might have gained a better understanding of the aims and motives of the ANC, as did the South African businessmen who did speak with them at length. To say that constructive engagement failed to address the interests of black South Africans presupposes that this issue was a priority for Crocker in the first place. He did want to encourage a moderate black opposition, which Washington would have been happy to support at the negotiating table. He did not, however, seem to appreciate or acknowledge the realities on the ground for South African blacks – nor how a moderate opposition would have been viewed by its own black constituency in South Africa.

The fact was that, even after Congress imposed sanctions, the constructive engagement policy of the Reagan administration was still firmly rooted within the white South African government system, and still pinned its hopes on white-led evolutionary change. This outlook appeared to ignore the needs and the abilities of blacks, who were apparently expected to wait in the wings, making discreet gestures to demonstrate their willingness to negotiate – even from their position of subjugation. As Thompson points out, even if engagement with Pretoria can be: 'justified to a degree … there seems little grounds to justify the Reagan Administration's lack of contact with the black community'. Thompson concludes: 'Twenty-twenty hindsight is not required to see this failure to engage all South Africans as being the largest mistake the Reagan Administration made in its implementation of constructive engagement.'[42] This chapter agrees with this analysis, but sees this mistake as two-fold. Failure to connect with the black opposition was a major obstacle to assisting any apartheid settlement. Yet this failure to engage the black community also badly damaged Crocker's underlying aim of continuing a friendly and productive relationship with Pretoria 'without embarrassment' – in other words, without engendering criticism at home or abroad. The anti-apartheid movement in America would have more readily accepted continued engagement, if only Crocker had made some attempt to demonstrate that this policy could include, and engage with, black South Africa too.

Notes

1   Greenberg, Stanley B., 'Economic Growth and Political Change: The South African Case', *Journal of Modern African Studies*, Vol. 19, No. 4 (1981), p. 704.

2   Vale, Peter, 'Crocker's Choice: Constructive Engagement and South Africa's People' review article, *South African Journal of International Affairs*, Vol. 1, No. 1, 1993, p. 104.

3   See Windrich, Elaine, 'Review – Chester Crocker, *High Noon in Southern Africa: Making Peace in a Rough Neighborhood*', *Africa*, Vol. 65, No. 1, 1995, p. 135, and David E. Kyvig, (ed.), *Reagan and the World*, New York: Praeger, 1990, p. 124.

4   Personal interview with Dr Chester Crocker, 19 June 2001, Washington, DC.

5   *Ibid.*

6   Olivier, Gerrit, 'Recent Developments in South African Foreign Policy' *Optima*, Vol. 36, No. 4 (December 1988), p. 200.

7   *The Economist*, 'America and South Africa', 30 March 1985, p. 26.

8   Olivier, 'Recent Developments', p. 202.

9   *Ibid.*, p. 203.

10 Crocker, Chester, 'South Africa: Strategy for Change', *Foreign Affairs*, Vol. 59, No. 2 (Winter 1980–1), p. 325.

11 See N. Chabanyi Manganyi, 'The Washington–Pretoria Connection: Is There a Black Perspective?' in *The United States and South Africa: Continuity and Change*, Johannesburg: South African Institute of International Affairs, 1981.

12 Crocker, 'Strategy for Change', p. 327.

13 ARC Identifier: 59724 *US Policy in Southern Africa – Crocker, 1985*. Creator: United States Information Agency (1982–) (Most Recent). Broadcast 26 September 1985. Item from Record Group 306: Records of the USIA 1900–1988. Video Recordings from the 'Worldnet Today' Program Series. NAIL Locator: 306-WNET-152 Motion Picture, Sound and Video Recordings LICON, National Archives at College Park, Maryland USA.

14 As quoted in K. A. Oye, R. J. Lieber and D. Rothchild (eds), *Eagle Resurgent? The Reagan Era in American Foreign Policy*, Boston, Toronto: Little, Brown and Company, 1987, p. 246.

15 ARC Identifier: 54679 *President Reagan's South Africa Policy Speech, 22nd July 1986* Creator: United States Information Agency (1982-) (Most Recent). Item from Record Group 306: Records of the USIA 1900-1988. Series: Motion Picture Films 1944-1999. NAIL Locator: 306.9633 Motion Picture, Sound and Video Recordings LICON, National Archives at College Park, Maryland USA

16 ARC Identifier: 59724 *US Policy in Southern Africa – Crocker, 1985*.

17 Personal interview with Professor Donald Rothchild, Washington DC, 12 June 2001.

18 Crocker, 'Strategy for Change', p. 348.

19 *Developments in South Africa: United States Policy Responses* Hearing before the Subcommittee on Africa of the Committee on Foreign Affairs House of Representatives, 12 March 1986. See p. 36 and p. 44.

20 Ronald Reagan Library, CA. Executive Secretariat, NSC: Records Boxes 91340 and 91343. Secret Memorandum – From: Robert C. McFarlane. To: Ronald Reagan. Subject: Meeting with Chief Gatsha Buthelezi, 4 February 1985. Declassified 6 January 1999.

21 *Internal Political Situation in South Africa* Hearings before the Subcommittee on African Affairs of the Committee on Foreign Affairs House or Representatives, 1st Session, September 1983 – testimony of Frank Wisner, Deputy Assistant Secretary of State for African Affairs.

22 Ronald Reagan Library, CA. WHORM Subject Files: 'South Africa, US Policy Towards', File Number FG011 – 468690. Letter to President Reagan, 9 January 1987.

23 Van Heerden, D. 'The New Nats', *Frontline*, March 1986, p. 36.

24 Crocker, Chester, 'Southern Africa: Eight Years Later', *Foreign Affairs*, Vol. 68, No. 4 (1989), p. 149.

25 ARC Identifier: 59633 *Status of the Peace Process in Southern Africa – Crocker, 1984*. Creator: United States Information Agency (1982–) (Most Recent). Broadcast 16 May 1984. Item from Record Group 306: Records of the USIA 1900–1988. Video Recordings from the 'Worldnet Today' Program Series. NAIL Locator: 306-WNET-56 Motion Picture, Sound and Video Recordings LICON, National Archives at College Park, Maryland USA.

26 Testimony of Thomas Karis, City University of New York, *Developments in South Africa: United States Policy Responses* Hearing before the Subcommittee on Africa of the Committee on Foreign Affairs, House of Representatives, 12 March 1986, pp. 29–30.

27 Mokoena, Kenneth (ed.), *South Africa and the United States: The Declassified History*, A National Security Archive documents reader, New York: The New Press, 1993, p. 36.

28 *New York Times*, 23 January 1986.

29 SADCC – the Southern African Development Coordination Conference (now SADC –

the Southern African Development Community) was a grouping of 10 southern African states then attempting to strengthen regional stability, whilst exploring ways of reducing their dependence on South Africa.

30 *Developments in South Africa: United States Policy Responses* Hearing before the Sub-committee on Africa of the Committee on Foreign Affairs, House of Representatives, 99th Congress, Second Session, 12 March 1986, p. 33.

31 ARC Identifier: 54794, *Secretary Shultz's Speech on South Africa, 1987*. Creator: United States Information Agency (1982–) (Most Recent). Item from Record Group 306: Records of the USIA 1900–1988. Series: Motion Picture Films 1944-1999. NAIL Locator: 306.9758 Motion Picture, Sound and Video Recordings LICON, National Archives at College Park, Maryland USA.

32 Personal interview with Dr Chester Crocker, 19 June 2001, Washington, DC.

33 For further details of these programmes, see Holladay, J. Douglas, 'Using Our Leverage', *Africa Report* (March–April 1986), p. 32 and Crocker's statement to *United States Policy on South Africa* Hearing before the Subcommittee on African Affairs of the Committee on Foreign Relations, United States Senate, 98th Congress, Second Session, 26 September 1984, pp. 10–11.

34 As quoted in Rothchild and Ravenhill in *Eagle Resurgent?* p. 418.

35 *Washington Times*, 24 July 1986.

36 Kyvig, *Reagan and the World*, p. 128.

37 Bloom, Jack Brian, *Black South Africa and the Disinvestment Dilemma*, Johannesburg: Jonathan Ball Publishers, 1986, p. 231.

38 *New York Times*, 12 April 1985.

39 As quoted in Weissman, Stephen, 'Dateline South Africa: The Opposition Speaks', *Foreign Policy*, No. 58 (Spring 1985), pp. 162–3.

40 Testimony of Senator Kennedy, *United States Policy Toward South Africa* Hearings before the Committee on Foreign Relations, United States Senate, 24 April, 2 May and 22 May 1985, p. 11.

41 As quoted in Bloom, *Black South Africa and the Disinvestment Dilemma*, p. 235.

42 Thompson, Alex, *Incomplete Engagement: United States Foreign Policy Towards the Republic of South Africa 1981–1988*, Aldershot and Brookfield: Avebury, 1996, p. 162.

II
Linkage: South Africa, Angola & Namibia

7
Washington's Interests & Crocker's Linkage Strategy

The International Community & Linkage

In 1976 the United Nations Security Council passed a resolution (UNSCR 385) calling for the independence of Namibia and UN-supervised elections. In 1977 the Contact Group of Western Nations was established to investigate how this resolution could be implemented. The Contact Group consisted of five Western members then sitting on the UN Security Council – Britain, the United States, France, West Germany and Canada. This Group organized negotiations with South African and SWAPO representatives and by 1978 they had persuaded both opposing parties to agree to a final resolution on Namibian independence. The United Nations Security Council Resolution 435 (UNSCR 435) was adopted by the Security Council at its 2087th meeting on 29 September 1978. The Resolution established a timetable for the cessation of hostilities between South Africa and SWAPO and the gradual restriction to base of the opposing troops. It also detailed the role of the UN in assisting the transition to independence, which would be carried out under the auspices of the UN Transition Assistance Group (UNTAG), also established under UNSCR 435. The military element of this group would be deployed as the other troops began to withdraw.[1] Unfortunately the South Africans' distrust of the UN's impartiality meant that, although they had agreed in principle to the resolution, they could not be pinned down to act upon it. Pretoria was also very unhappy that the UN had declared SWAPO to be the 'sole authentic representative of the Namibian people'. Pretoria demanded that this recognition be withdrawn.

A conference was held from 7 to 14 January 1981 in Geneva to begin the pre-implementation negotiations on Namibian independence. Indications that the Reagan administration might take an ambivalent attitude towards UNSCR 435 were strengthened when the incoming administration declined to send an official observer to Geneva. The UN agreed to withdraw their official recognition of SWAPO as the 'sole authentic representative' in Namibia if South Africa would set a date for elections in Namibia. The South Africans said that this was premature and claimed that 'trust and confidence' between the parties had to be established before implementation of UNSCR 435 could begin. The talks collapsed without agreement on a date for a ceasefire or for implementation of the UN proposals. This was how Pretoria's relationship with the international community stood when the Reagan administration took office.

The Contact Group

Crocker met with the Contact Group in London on 22 and 23 April 1981. Their conclusions were outlined in the communiqué issued at the end of a meeting of the foreign ministers of the Contact Group held in Rome on 3 May. They confirmed that 'only a settlement under the aegis of the UN would be acceptable to the international community'.[2] They also reaffirmed their commitment to UNSCR 435. Crocker, on the other hand, had begun to raise the prospect of linking Namibian independence to the withdrawal of Cuban troops from Angola (see below). The major division between the US and the rest of the Contact Group was that the Contact Group regarded the linkage proposal with great suspicion and continued to insist upon the inviolability of UNSCR 435. In a memorandum to Crocker, Paul Hare, the director of the State Department's Southern African Affairs Office, pointed out that the Contact Group were:

> very leery of holding out the prospect to the SAG [South African government] that we are willing to change UNSCR 435. They feel that will induce South African creativity, in particular a reinforced SAG assault on UNTAG which they see as the guts of 435.[3]

The Contact Group was adamant that they would only agree to 'complement' UNSCR 435, rather than change it. On 26 October 1981 the Group presented a set of new proposals in the hope that they would break the impasse. The new proposals stipulated that the new Namibian constitution would have to be approved by a two-thirds majority in an assembly composed of representatives from all of Namibia's significant racial ethnic groups. The plan aimed to address South Africa's fears of SWAPO dominating any settlement. This initiative managed to get the stalled talks moving again. Due largely to a shared colonial history and cultural and historical links, the Europeans had a much better relationship with the Frontline States (FLS) than the Americans did. As Crocker explained: 'With the FLS, our allies could say things on our behalf we couldn't say ourselves. But it fell essentially to us Americans to bring South Africa along.'[4]

The Contact Group began its series of meetings with representatives of Angola, Botswana, Mozambique, Nigeria, Tanzania, Zambia, Zimbabwe and SWAPO at the United Nations headquarters in New York on 6 July 1982. With regard to furthering the American proposals, the activities of the Contact Group had mixed results, depending on the sympathies of the individual governments. As Shultz explained in a memorandum to Ronald Reagan: 'Our posture on the Cuban issue has been significantly strengthened by messages from our Contact Group partners (particularly the British, but excluding the French)....'[5] The differing views between the partners reflected to an extent their various interests in the region, which were largely economic. The motivation of South Africa's 'three most consistent' supporters in the West – the US, Britain and West Germany –

also had the largest economic stakes in both South Africa and Namibia. (Namibia's extractive economy had been developed by and for the benefit of foreign companies.)[6] Political ties also affected the perspectives of these countries. It was no coincidence that all three were under staunchly Conservative governments – Reagan, Thatcher and Kohl respectively. Even with these sympathetic governments as important members of the Contact Group, however, the Group as a whole remained very wary of Washington's intentions – and Washington could never persuade it to back the linkage strategy publicly, nor to move on the issue that any settlement must proceed under UN auspices. In public, the State Department characterized the relationship between Washington and the rest of the Contact Group as 'all rowing in the same direction'. A State Department press briefing claimed that, although Washington and the Contact Group may have had different public formulations, they still shared the same assessment of reality.

Behind the scenes, however, this division was proving very difficult, particularly in impairing America's attempt to cajole South Africa. In a direct message from Secretary Haig to Pik Botha, Haig stressed that the rest of the Contact Group did recognize the *de facto* relationship between Angola and Namibia. Haig had to admit, however, that Washington's allies would not consider Angola to be on the agenda of the Contact Group. Yet the linkage element remained vital to Washington. Haig went on to stress to Botha that 'it might be helpful if you did not raise [linkage] in your response or in other communications with the Contact Group'.[7] These confidential parallel discussions undermined the Group from the very beginning of the Reagan administration. While South Africa was apparently negotiating in good faith with the Contact Group members, it was secretly holding out for a result that both Washington and Pretoria were determined to achieve – the removal of the Cuban forces in Angola in return for Namibia's independence. The Contact Group, whilst resisting any formal linkage of the Namibian and Angolan issues, was in an impossible situation. They were caught between the need for US leadership and concern about the US approach. But Crocker also admitted that the reluctance of America's allies to acknowledge linkage publicly greatly complicated Washington's position.

The failure of the Contact Group
The collapse of the Contact Group initiative had begun, in effect, when South Africa walked out of the Geneva conference, hoping to bypass the 'Western Five' and obtain a better deal by working with the new Reagan administration directly. With the rest of the Contact Group refusing officially to endorse linkage, divisions began to grow. On 25 April 1983, the French Foreign Minister Claude Cheysson stated that it was 'not appropriate the Namibian people should serve as hostages'.[8] On 29 May 1983, in a meeting with Secretary Shultz, the British, French, West German and Canadian foreign ministers 'express[ed] their frustration over the slow pace of the Namibia effort and the need for new momentum, if the five [were] to stay together'.[9] They were sceptical about South Africa's

intentions. Shultz stated: 'I find all of this quite exasperating and was blunt with our allies in letting them know that if they have a better way to proceed, they are welcome to take over the effort.' As the linkage issue increasingly became recognized as the driving force in the negotiations, the role of the Contact Group began to diminish. The French initially suspended their membership of the Contact Group because of the disagreements over linkage. For his part, the UN Secretary-General Javier Pérez de Cuéllar 'vigorously refuted' the linkage correlation between Namibia and Angola, and on 28 October 1983 the UN Security Council adopted Resolution 539. This was a resolution condemning the linkage of Namibian independence to Cuban withdrawal from Angola. The resolution rejected:

> South Africa's insistence on linking the independence of Namibia to irrelevant and extraneous issues [and] declares that the independence of Namibia cannot be held hostage to the resolution of issues that are alien to Security Council Resolution 435 (1978).[10]

The resolution also reiterated that 435 was the only basis for peaceful settlement of the Namibian problems. The Resolution was passed 14–0, with the US abstaining, but after it was passed the Contact Group effectively ceased to function. In December 1983 the French formally withdrew, blaming the lack of progress in the negotiations. From this point on the failure of the Western Contact Group was acknowledged and negotiations continued under the auspices of Crocker's linkage strategy. The importance of the international community – and the UN in particular – receded into the background as Crocker and Pretoria took the reins.

The Explicit Aims of Crocker's Linkage Strategy

In one of the earliest articulations of his policy, Crocker identified a primary objective as the aim to promote peace and regional security in Africa; and to deny opportunities to all those who sought contrary objectives.[11] He included in his list of objectives a commitment to support proven friends and to support open market opportunities, access to key resources and expanding African and American economies. He summarized his aims before Congress thus: 'Our objectives are clear: to restore and advance US influence; to deny the Soviets a chance to extend and solidify their own; and, of course, to expand our cooperative relationships with African states.'[12]

Yet the way in which he presented his objectives changed over time, particularly in response to prevailing political pressures. He was later to place a good deal more emphasis (in words if not in action) on how his regional policy could aid an internal settlement in South Africa – in response to the increased public interest in this issue post-1985. The emphasis on this aspect of his policy was particularly apparent during the mid-1980s, at the height of public and Congressional anti-apartheid awareness and activity. In August 1985 Crocker again outlined the goals of his policy. This time he began by identifying South Africa as his first priority: 'We seek to hasten peaceful evolution in South Africa away from apartheid and to reduce the violence and instability that threaten lives and livelihoods throughout the region. The two goals are mutually dependent.'[13] In this way, he had moved away from his explicit recognition of 'US influence' and 'market opportunities' as the main objectives of his policy. These were emphasized less as the public focus shifted to helping the black majorities of South Africa and Namibia.

The right wing in Washington

The shift of emphasis in the public presentation of Crocker's policy, away from global and towards regional considerations, was due to real divisions within the Republican party regarding the Namibian and Angolan questions. Groups such as the Heritage Foundation and the Conservative Caucus[14] were vocal disciples of the Reagan Doctrine, and wanted the Soviet- and Cuban-backed Angolan government to be treated as a test case. Senator Jesse Helms strongly objected to constructive engagement in general, not because it would involve talking to the apartheid regime in Pretoria, but because its regional aspect would involve talking to the governments of Angola and Mozambique. Indeed, it was not just the extremists to whom the removal of the Cubans was more important than either Namibian independence or ending apartheid. Both Reagan and Crocker's (then) direct superior, Secretary of State Al Haig, shared these views. In fact, they found that talking to the Cubans was the hardest aspect of this policy for them to bear. The strength of these views put a good deal of pressure on Crocker. Ex-Secretary Moose described constructive engagement as being 'trapped between good sense and the right wing; it is talking tougher while trying to protect the promising diplomatic initiatives, which it has underway'.[15] Linkage was vital for Crocker in preserving the support of a majority of his own party, including the President, for his policies. He knew that without the incentive of Cuban troop withdrawal, he would have had great difficulty convincing either Reagan or Haig to put pressure on South Africa to leave Namibia. Linkage was a vital element in the policy debates in Washington.

American Interests in the Region

Although the way Crocker *presented* his aims might have altered over time – or with respect to the audience he was addressing – nevertheless, his policy remained firmly based on the set of American interests which had guided its formulation in the first place. In an early statement to Congress on 16 September 1981, he described southern Africa as a region of unquestioned importance to US and Western economic and strategic interests. Southern Africa was identified in the US as a potential regional locomotive for economic growth. In Washington's view, the increased political tension, unrest and cross-border violence also made it a potential target for Soviet adventurism. Safeguarding the region from Soviet influence and developing and opening its economies to the international markets were both seen as important American interests. Approximately 60 per cent of the total of US direct investment in sub-Saharan Africa was located in southern Africa. Washington was also very aware of the significance of southern Africa's mineral wealth. The main and guiding priority in the region, however, remained the containment of the perceived Soviet threat.

The Soviet threat

From the moment Angola gained its independence in 1974, the US was concerned about its instability and its potential susceptibility to Soviet influence. The timing of this independence was crucial because, only six years later, when Reagan was elected in 1980, memories of Vietnam were still very prominent in the American psyche. As the Reagan administration began to focus its attention on the Cubans in Angola, the American public and the Democrats in Congress were still experiencing the effects of the Vietnam Syndrome. They were extremely apprehensive about getting involved in another proxy Cold War battle in an obscure country far away from America's borders. Congressman Siljander, a member of the House of Representatives Committee on Foreign Affairs, exclaimed in a debate on intervention in Angola: 'Somehow every time we lift our head proudly in the support of others fighting for freedom the cries go out this is another Vietnam … what I call … creeping cowardice.'[16] Crocker himself accused previous administrations of allowing themselves to become distracted by Vietnam, saying that once the Soviets became aware of the extent of the US preoccupation with this issue, they realized they would get a 'free ride' into Angola. He identified in particular the Senate's decision on 19 December 1975 to deny any additional funding to Angola beyond the $32 million already committed – a figure which even then only represented between 15 and 20 per cent of Soviet levels of funding.

It was in response to these very fears that the Reagan Doctrine was established (see Chapter 1), and this approach guided much of the later American activity in Angola. The Reagan administration was convinced that the Soviet plan was to exploit the tension in the region. Secretary of State Shultz explained how Soviet aid to the region had been almost totally military in nature. He went on: 'Our adversaries have no constructive stake in the region, seeing rather in instability their best chance to expand their influence.'[17] Crocker stressed the importance of regaining the initiative. As early as 1978, he had warned against complacency in the region, identifying Russian and Cuban military activity as the single most destabilizing factor in an already fragile environment. The fact that apartheid and South Africa's intentional destabilization of the region, combined with chronic poverty there, opened the doors to Soviet influence, was never fully addressed by Crocker.

In a televised interview on 26 June 1985, Crocker was asked if the only reason the US was in the region was due to the presence of Soviet influence and Cuban troops. The interviewer pointed to the fact that the US had never been this involved in the region until Cold War questions were raised by Soviet activity there. Crocker disputed this by stating: 'It isn't the US that brought the Cold War into Africa.' However, he went on to point out that, 'like it or not', Africa is part of the world system and to ignore Soviet activity there would be 'to bury one's head in the sand'.[18] In *High Noon in Southern Africa* he explained that: 'To me, the West was on trial in southern Africa.'[19]

Crocker was often critical of Carter's reaction to Soviet influence in the area. He stated that some administration pronouncements under Carter seemed to imply that Moscow and Havana had a right to work actively against US and Western interests. In 1978 he asked what interest was served by encouraging the perception that only Soviet-Cuban sponsored adventures should succeed in Africa? It was in 'Strategy for Change', published two years later, just before Reagan's election victory, that he directly linked the resolution of the Namibian question with a reduction in the potential for Soviet interference in the region. Crocker saw the solution as increased stability of the region, and explained that conflicts in Namibia and Angola were very close to some resolution. This eventuality would further erode a Soviet position already weakened by Robert Mugabe's policy line in Zimbabwe. He also linked the resolution of this question directly to Western interests: 'There can be no presumed communist right to exploit and militarise tensions, particularly in this region where important Western economic, resource and strategic interests are exposed.'[20] But the fact remained that some of his most fundamental aims actually clashed. To reduce Soviet influence Crocker believed that he needed to reduce regional tensions, yet he never fully accepted the fact that South Africa was largely to blame for so much of this instability. Its apartheid policies, deliberate destabilization of the region, continued illegal occupation of Namibia, and frequent incursions into Angola could – and did – lead many Africans in the region to conclude that the US had chosen to confront the wrong enemy.

Economic benefits and relations with the region
Among other considerations that affected Crocker's planning, the strategic and resource benefits that the US gained from favourable relations with the white governments in the region also had to be taken into account. Many in the Reagan administration placed a good deal of emphasis on the importance of these interests, and made it clear that preserving this access must be a priority. Reagan himself described the strategic importance of southern Africa thus:

> Around the Cape of Good Hope passes the oil of the Persian Gulf, which is indispensable to the industrial economy of Western Europe. Southern Africa and South Africa are repositories of many of the vital minerals ... for which the West has no other *secure* source of supply. The Soviet Union is not unaware of the stakes.[21]

Crocker's regional policy therefore faced a dilemma. He needed to serve some American interests by placating South Africa. However, he also knew that US interests would be served by extending and improving relations with black Africa. Instead of seeing South Africa as the cause of many of the problems faced by the countries of the region, he chose instead to focus on the Soviet Union as the 'main destabilizing factor' in the region. Yet he still maintained that relations with the rest of black Africa would be an important part of his policy. In a statement to Congress on 17 June 1981, made very soon after his eventual confirmation in his new role as Assistant Secretary of State for African Affairs, he explained to the House: 'We are fully aware that the continuation of the conflict in Namibia complicates our relations with black Africa at a time when there appears to be more and more common ground between black Africa and the West.'[22] When interviewed for the US Information Agency on the impact he hoped his policy would have on the region, he explained: 'The policy is aimed at developing and improving the best possible relations with all the countries of the region who wish to have good relations with us.'[23] This had to be reconciled, however, with 'the inescapable fact that Pretoria holds the main key to a [regional] settlement and, therefore, must have a minimum of confidence in any settlement if it is to be implemented'.[24]

Crocker Addresses the Regional Situation & Chooses his Strategy

In order to reconcile these objectives and interests, Crocker concluded that he had three basic policy options. These he outlined in an interview with the author:

The US could soldier on with the UN Security Council Resolution 435, negotiated under Carter. Crocker explained that 'it hadn't worked for Carter, so we saw no reason why it would work for us'.[25] Also, he admitted that 'we didn't really *want* to pursue UNSCR 435 without linkage'. This first option was quickly dismissed. It did not provide the US with any Cold War leverage, nor did it address South Africa's security concerns – or America's interests in the region.

'We could just take a walk.' By this, Crocker meant that southern African diplomacy could be downgraded, and efforts to pursue US interests could be directed elsewhere. It was this issue that split the right wing of the Republican Party, because many Republicans favoured this option. Their opinion was 'You don't get any political gain from having a credible Africa policy.' Yet the geopolitical considerations would not go away, particularly in the climate created by Reagan's tough anti-communist rhetoric in his recent election campaign.

This left Crocker's chosen approach: linkage. This provided the US with the vital leverage it needed to get South Africa to move on the Namibian independence issue, whilst addressing Washington's own concerns over Cuban troops in Angola. He stressed the importance of linkage in gaining Pretoria's cooperation, but the truth was that linkage was just as important in gaining the cooperation of the rest of Washington, who would otherwise have been in no hurry to assist in the handover of Namibia from friendly South Africa's control to a potentially Marxist SWAPO government.

The regional situation had shifted since the 1974 Portuguese coup. A vacuum had been created by the departure of the Portuguese and, according to Crocker, the Russians wanted to fill it. He said that once the regional situation had changed in this way, 'we knew we had to keep the bad guys out'. He knew that linkage was the only option available to address the aim of getting the Cubans out of Angola – a goal that in fact had priority over all others in the region, including Namibian independence.

The Genesis of Linkage

Neither Washington nor Pretoria was in a hurry to lay claim to the linkage strategy as its own, while both espoused its benefits and its logic. It is generally accepted that the intrinsic logic of a link between Cuban withdrawal from Angola and Namibian independence had been recognized by previous administrations in Washington. What does cause some contention, however, is just how far the acceptance of this logic had gone. Barber states: '[Linkage] was an objective reality [that] had already been tacitly accepted by the Carterites. The new Administration's only departure was to formalize it and give it a name.'[26] Baker, however, indicates that the Carter administration had not gone as far down the road towards linkage as Barber suggests. She states that Carter's view was that once Namibia had been granted independence, 'Angola would no longer feel threatened' and could then 'fulfil its publicly stated promise to send the Cubans home'.[27] It seems that the difference in these views is exaggerated by Barber's statement that the Reagan administration's '*only* departure' [my emphasis] was to formalize linkage and give it a name. In fact, this understates what a significant step the movement towards explicit linkage was. Barber and Baker agree that Carter acknowledged the logic of linkage, but that he was not about to act upon it. The required combination of brave conviction and self-interested risk taking was left to Crocker to supply.

One of the first explicit discussions of the linkage formula occurred in June 1981. Crocker, Deputy Secretary of State William Clark and Assistant Secretary of State for Human Rights Elliott Abrams met a South African delegation including South African Foreign Minister Pik Botha in Cape Town. The details of this meeting were kept very quiet, particularly any indication of who had first raised the linkage issue. In previous discussions between Secretary of State Al Haig and Pik Botha during Pik's May 1981 visit to the US, Washington and Pretoria had reached 'a common understanding that the first requirement is to establish momentum on Namibia and to avoid explicit public linkage of the Angolan and Namibian situations'.[28] Crocker made the first public statement on linkage on 17 April 1981, telling government representatives in Angola that the

Namibian settlement was related to Cuban troop withdrawal, but the US remained very cautious about taking the credit for it. In reference material prepared by the Bureau of Public Affairs of the State Department, the State Department's public explanation was that: 'South Africa has made clear its readiness to proceed only in the context of a parallel commitment to resolve the longstanding problem of Cuban troop withdrawal from Angola.'[29]

Crocker explained the genesis of linkage as a logical progression. He said that the essential question was – if the regional security equation were to change, would it make a difference to South Africa? He believed that the answer would be yes, if the Cubans left Angola. This, then, was linkage. Crocker therefore argued that, in reality, linkage was not invented, but written into the history and geography of the region. In fact, Crocker would have preferred linkage never to have been made public. The linkage was useful in maintaining pressure on the various actors, but Crocker accused his colleagues of drifting towards the 'hard line' of 'explicit linkage'. This was not how he had planned to exercise his strategy. 'The subtlety and flexibility I considered essential were rapidly going out the window.'[30]

With regard to Washington's own input into the linkage formula, the administration was anxious to present itself, particularly in the early stages, as having no influence at all on the matter. Crocker pointed to the 'factual relationship' between the two elements of the linkage policy, but added: 'I would like to emphasize that we are not laying down precon-ditions to any party.'[31] When the spokesman for the State Department, John Hughes, was asked in a press briefing whether Washington had 'relaxed' its position on linkage, he said:

> the United States doesn't have a position, the United States has an observation. There are certain realities in play here … it's not really the United States who is saying you have a situation; you have a reality and somebody has to work at that.[32]

The reality was quite different. The United States *did* have a position, and linkage was an important part of it. The American Ambassador to the United Nations, Jeane Kirkpatrick, told ambassadors of the Frontline States that 'even if South Africa agrees to implement Resolution 435 on Namibia's independence, the US will raise objections because of the Cuban troops in Angola'.[33] Unfortunately for Crocker, his memorandum to Haig on 7 February 1981 was leaked to the *New York Times*. In it he had stated: 'African leaders would have no basis for resisting the Namibian–Angolan linkage once they are made to realize that they can only get a Namibian settlement through us.'[34]

Questioning Crocker's Explicit Aims

In public interviews and statements at the time, Crocker explained linkage in terms of its importance in gaining a settlement on Namibian independence. He concluded, in a statement to Congress in February 1983, that Namibia's independence could not be achieved in the absence of conditions giving all participants reasonable confidence that their security interests would be protected. He also pointed out, with reference to the UN Security Council Resolution 435, that having a resolution, a package and a plan, without having any political basis for implementing it, left the settlement as 'half a loaf'. There had to be something in the overall package for everyone. In his 1992 account of this time in office, Crocker is a little more candid regarding the order of his priorities. He explains that, on the first level, linkage 'was an exercise in American strategy',[35] hoping to advance American interests. He explains that, on the second level, it was an attempt to address the interests of all the parties involved.

It is evident that the settlement Washington had in mind was a very specific one, and not one that necessarily focused on Namibian independence. In a leaked 'memorandum of conversation' detailing a meeting between Crocker, Pik Botha and South African Defence Minister Magnus Malan in April 1981, Crocker states: 'We have said we believe SCR 435 is a basis for transition to independence for Namibia, but not for a full settlement.'[36] Indeed, Crocker openly admitted later that the Reagan administration 'viewed the merits of a Namibian settlement as utterly dependent on the context in which it occurred. Failure to achieve a settlement was not necessarily the worst possible outcome.'[37] In its determination to ensure a pliable and friendly regime in Namibia, the US did not accord a high priority to the interests of the Namibian people themselves.

Jeane Kirkpatrick made a statement before the United Nations Security Council denying that the US policy was driven by its own interests. When discussing the 'role and objectives of [the US] government' in the Namibian negotiations, she explained:

> I wish to stress above all that the United States neither desires nor seeks any special advantage or position for itself in these negotiations. It is not our intention, nor is it within our power, to impose our own views or wishes on those whose interests and aspirations are most directly involved.[38]

In fact, a secret cable from the Secretary of State to the US Embassy in Pretoria belied these public statements. It detailed the contents of a confidential letter from Secretary of State Haig that Crocker had personally delivered to Brand Fourie (South African Deputy Minister for Foreign Affairs) for Pik Botha on 13 January 1982. In it, the Secretary explained:

> The key motivation on our part has been our firm belief that in southern Africa, as in other important strategic regions of the world, we must seek to control and guide the course of events. For too long … the West has stood back and … allowed things to happen to us, which we should not have permitted. I have in mind in particular the unfortunate events in Angola in 1975–6.[39]

Here, the Secretary is referring to the cessation of US aid to Holden Roberto's FPLA and Savimbi's UNITA, which was partly responsible for allowing the Marxist-oriented MPLA regime to gain power in Angola in 1976.

The fact was that Crocker had proposed linkage because it served US goals and interests, but it also had the potential to create great hostility among liberals and, particularly, other black African states. This would have undermined a further aim of expanding positive relations in the region, which explains why he was reluctant – at the time – to make the linkage explicit. Another way in which Crocker protected himself and his policy was to obfuscate his reasons for pursuing the link itself. To a large extent it worked. Many observers at the time, and even now, still accept that:

> Crocker's primary goal ... was to reduce regional tensions so that Pretoria would feel more confident about accelerating domestic reform. Namibian independence, an important prize in itself, was a central part of that; so was the removal of foreign forces.[40]

He therefore succeeded in presenting his aims in reverse order of what he was actually hoping to achieve. He managed it so well that even informed commentators present his motivation in the way he had planned to present it, rather than in its reality. This book argues that this perception, however, was wrong. Crocker's *primary* goal was not to reduce tensions in order to accelerate domestic reform in South Africa. His primary goal was an implicit agenda which included economic as well as geopolitical considerations.

Crocker's Implicit Aims

Much of the difficulty faced by Crocker in the formulation and implementation of his southern African policy was caused by the fact that he was having to address the interests of so many constituencies at once. He never hid the fact that concern regarding the spread of Soviet influence was a guiding factor in his policy, but the public emphasis on the goal of Namibian independence was always stated as the top priority. To what extent was Cuban withdrawal a useful and mutually beneficial (for Washington and Pretoria) device to gain Namibian independence, and to what extent was it in fact the main objective of the Reagan administration, regardless of the outcome in Namibia? Did the cause of Namibian independence simply provide a moral justification for the United States to interfere in the region to pursue their own aims, or were American actions, at least in part, provoked by the plight of the Namibian people?

Many in American foreign policy circles – for example, National Security Adviser and White House Staff Member Robert McFarlane, Bill Casey in the CIA and Jesse Helms in Congress – found the Angolan regime abhorrent. Right-wing Republican members of Congress made statements in the House strongly condemning a regime that they believed was inimical to American interests, and they pointed out that the MPLA government of Angola did not try to disguise this fact. In May 1985 the State Department's annual report to Congress on voting practices in the UN showed that Angola had only a 4.9 per cent level of coincidence with

Washington's votes in the UN. Only Mozambique, Cuba, Swaziland, Algeria and the People's Democratic Republic of Yemen had a lower level of coincidence. Even the Soviet Union managed to coincide with American voting patterns more frequently, with a level of coincidence of 13.2 per cent. Those on the right in Republican circles brandished these statistics to demonstrate just how anti-American this Angolan regime was. They believed that the US, still reeling from Vietnam, had taken its eye off the ball and allowed the Soviet Union many opportunities to advance its influence. These advances needed to be halted and, where necessary, overturned. George Wright accused the Reagan administration of actually targeting Angola for destabilization, as part of a revived US Cold War-militarist project to roll back revolutionary regimes.[41] Wright stated that Reagan's globalist foreign policy makers were looking to 'avenge the US defeat' in the 1975–6 Angolan war. Indeed, this was how Republicans characterized the events in 1975–6, which saw the MPLA regime taking the reins of government in Luanda. In fact, Crocker explains that at the time of the 1974 Portuguese coup and the scramble for Angola, the United States *was* still totally preoccupied with events in South East Asia: 'If we hadn't been, we wouldn't have tolerated what happened in Angola.'[42] The Reagan administration and the Republican Party welcomed the Reagan Doctrine as an opportunity to reverse the losses that had been countenanced in the wake of Vietnam. Angola was seen as a good example of a loss that could, and should, have been averted.

Despite continued public assurances that America's main aim in the region was to facilitate Namibian independence, the fact remained that Crocker's priority, together with the rest of the Reagan administration, was to get the Cubans out of Angola. A secret memorandum from Secretary of State Haig to the President in May 1981 reports just these sentiments being discussed during Pik Botha's visit to Washington in May 1981.

> [The South Africans] know that we are determined to *roll back Soviet influence* throughout the world and in their region. They understand our determination to *get the Cubans out of Angola* and that we will *not allow UNITA to be sacrificed*.[43] [original emphasis]

Crocker's successor, Herman Cohen (a career diplomatist who was Senior Director for Africa on the NSC staff at the time), explained that Washington's main objective was to get the Cubans out of Africa, and that, second, they wanted to see Namibian independence. In fact, Crocker's aims in the region did not stop at getting the Cubans out of Angola, or gaining Namibian independence. Just as in South Africa, he also wanted to ensure that the final internal settlement in each of these countries could be sanctioned by Washington. Crocker believed very strongly that change in southern Africa must be controlled. In a secret letter to Pik Botha from Secretary Haig, dated 13 January 1982, Haig explained some of the reasoning behind American involvement in the region:

> the Namibia negotiation ... is playing a key role in our effort to take control of events in the region. It provides the West with essential leverage to improve our

relative strategic position in the region and to establish a track record of success.[44]

This demonstrates the side of the negotiations which Crocker hoped would remain outside the public realm. Entering into negotiations on Namibia with a hidden agenda would not further his aim of improving relations with all the states in the region. However, a cable from Haig to Pik Botha in January 1981 had already stated that the new administration would not be 'steamrollered on Namibia'[45] by the international community. At the time this communication, and the aims it represented, was kept secret. It would not look good to be colluding with the very government who was illegally occupying Namibia, regarding negotiations on Namibian independence which the US was itself planning to mediate. The cable went on to state: 'It is in our interests that the solution we find should not put into jeopardy the interests of those who share our values – above all, our interests in a broad strategic sense.'

This was the message Pretoria was receiving from an administration it firmly believed would take a far more understanding view of its position. Little wonder that Pretoria now felt able to proceed with its internal arrangements in Namibia regardless of international and UN calls to the contrary – and particularly as the US held the purse strings at the UN. Indeed, both Crocker and Haig were open, at least to the South Africans, in their intention to control the internal Namibian settlement. Washington and Pretoria agreed that US policy in the region must proceed by first accepting the premise that Soviet domination was the danger. Crocker went on to assure Botha that: 'The ideas the US has in mind don't include Soviets in Windhoek.'[46] Haig reported to the President that in his meeting with Pik Botha in May 1981, the South Africans: 'want firm assurances that the agreement [in Namibia] will not simply lead to a "one-man, one-vote, one-time" outcome. We agree.' Haig also went on to confirm: 'While neither the South Africans nor ourselves want a SWAPO victory, both sides recognize SWAPO must be included in the settlement if it is to be internationally acceptable.' The communication also explained that keeping the Soviets out of Windhoek 'will require a provision for Namibian non-alignment (no foreign bases or troops) as part of the settlement package'.[47] Clearly, this was another aim which remained implicit. The idea of binding a legitimately elected government after it had been liberated from illegal occupation – particularly binding it to agreements decided between the US and Namibia's former occupiers – would be a breach of sovereignty, and would certainly cast doubt on America's role as a fair (albeit admittedly partisan) mediator. Crocker took a huge risk by linking Cuban withdrawal to Namibian independence. Washington thereby effectively presented South Africa with an open invitation to control the pace and direction of the Namibian independence process. Yet, in reality, the risk was not being faced by Washington, but by the Namibian people. From Washington's perspective, the public goal of Namibian independence was worth risking for the real aim of Cuban withdrawal and reduced communist influence in the region.

Notes

1 For the full text of UNSCR 435 (1978) see Crocker, Chester, *High Noon in Southern Africa: Making Peace in a Rough Neighborhood*, New York and London: W. W. Norton and Company, 1992, Appendix 1, p. 495.

2 Quoted in State Department Summary, Subject: Overview of US Policy Toward Southern Africa 31 May 1981. Reproduced in Baker, Pauline H., *The United States and South Africa: The Reagan Years. Update South Africa: Time Running Out*, Ford Foundation and Foreign Policy Association, 1989, Appendix A.

3 Memorandum from Paul Hare, Director of State Department's Southern African Affairs Office, to Crocker on Contact Group Meeting of 13 May 1981. Reproduced in Baker, *The United States and South Africa*, Appendix A.

4 Crocker, *High Noon in Southern Africa*, p. 125.

5 Ronald Reagan Library, CA. White House Staff and Office Files: Cohen, Herman J., Files 1987–8. African Affairs Directorate, NSC. Boxes 91875 and 91876. Secret Memorandum. To: Ronald Reagan. From: George Shultz. Subject: South Africa: Progress in the Angolan and Namibian negotiations, 26 August 1982

6 Hackland, B., A. Murray-Hudson and B. Wood, 'Behind the Diplomacy: Namibia 1983–5', *Third World Quarterly*, Vol. 8, No. 1 (January 1986), pp. 52–3.

7 Ronald Reagan Library, CA. White House Staff and Office Files: Cohen, Herman J., Files 1987–8. African Affairs Directorate, NSC. Boxes 91875 and 91876. Cable. From: Secretary of State Washington, DC. To: American Consulate Cape Town. Subject: Message from the Secretary for Pik Botha 30 September 1981.

8 Mokoena, Kenneth (ed.), *South Africa and the United States: The Declassified History*, a National Security Archive documents reader, New York: The New Press, 1993, p. 32.

9 Ronald Reagan Library, CA. White House Staff and Office Files: Cohen, Herman J., Files 1987–8. African Affairs Directorate, NSC. Boxes 91875 and 91876. Memorandum. To: Ronald Reagan. From: Secretary of State George Shultz. Subject: 'South Africa: Status of our Negotiation Effort', 6 June 1983.

10 United Nations Security Council Resolution (UNSCR) 539 (1983), enacted 28 October 1983.

11 *US Policy Toward Southern Africa: Focus on Namibia, Angola and South Africa* Hearing and Mark Up before the Subcommittee on Africa of the Committee on Foreign Affairs, House of Representatives, on House Resolution 214; Congress Resolution 183, 16 September 1981, p. 57.

12 *Angola: Options for American Foreign Policy* Hearings before the Committee on Foreign Relations, US Senate, 18 February 1986, p. 3.

13 *America*, Vol. 153, No. 3 (3–10 August 1985), published by the Jesuits of the United States and Canada, New York: America Press, p. 49.

14 The Heritage Foundation is a conservative think tank that publishes research on domestic, economic, foreign and defence policy. The Conservative Caucus is an ultra-conservative grassroots lobbying group, established in 1974 by Senator Jesse Helms (Republican, North Carolina) and his staff member Howard Phillips.

15 Testimony of Richard Moose in *Angola: Options for American Foreign Policy* Congressional Hearings, 18 February 1986, p. 30.

16 *Angola: Intervention or Negotiation* Hearings before the Subcommittee on Africa of the Committee on Foreign Affairs, House of Representatives, 31 October and 12 November 1985, p. 69.

17 'Southern Africa: Toward an American Consensus', address by Hon. George P. Shultz, Secretary of State, before the National Press Club, Washington, DC, 16 April 1985.

18 WNET 128 ARC Identifier: 59701, *Role of the US in Southern Africa – Crocker, 1985*. Creator: United States Information Agency (1982–) (Most Recent). Broadcast 26 June 1985. Item from Record Group 306: Records of the USIA 1900–1988. Video Recordings from the 'Worldnet Today' Program Series. NAIL Locator: 306-WNET-128

Motion Picture, Sound and Video Recordings LICON, National Archives at College Park, Maryland USA.

19 Crocker, *High Noon in Southern Africa*, p. 27.

20 Crocker, Chester, 'South Africa: Strategy for Change', *Foreign Affairs*, Vol. 59, No. 2 (Winter 1980–1), p. 346.

21 ARC Identifier: 54679, *President Reagan's South Africa Policy Speech, 22 July 1986*. Creator: United States Information Agency (1982–) (Most Recent). Item from Record Group 306: Records of the USIA 1900–1988. Series: Motion Picture Films 1944–1999. NAIL Locator: 306.9633 Motion Picture, Sound and Video Recordings LICON, National Archives at College Park, Maryland USA.

22 *US Policy Toward Namibia* Hearing before the Subcommittee on Africa of the Committee on Foreign Affairs House of Representatives, 17 June 1981, p. 3.

23 ARC Identifier: 54305 *Challenges to United States Foreign Policy: Chester Crocker Responds, 1983* Creator: United States Information Agency (1982-) (Most Recent). Item from Record Group 306: Records of the USIA 1900-1988. Series: Motion Picture Films 1944-1999. NAIL Locator: 306.9172 Motion Picture, Sound and Video Recordings LICON, National Archives at College Park, Maryland USA

24 *US Policy Toward Namibia* Congressional Hearing, 17 June 1981, p. 4.

25 Personal interview with Dr Chester Crocker, 19 June 2001, Washington, DC.

26 Barber, Simon 'Shadows on the Wall', *Optima*, Vol. 35, No. 2 (June 1987), p. 70.

27 Baker, Pauline H., *The United States and South Africa: The Reagan Years Update. South Africa: Time Running Out*, Ford Foundation and Foreign Policy Association, 1989, pp.15–16.

28 Ronald Reagan Library, CA. White House Staff and Office Files: Cohen, Herman J., Files 1987–8. African Affairs Directorate, NSC. Boxes 91875 and 91876. Secret Memorandum – From: Secretary of State Alexander Haig. To: The President, 20 May 1981. Subject: Summing up of Pik Botha Visit. Declassified 21 January 1999.

29 Culley, Harriet (ed.), 'Gist Southern Africa: Constructive Engagement', Bureau of Public Affairs, Department of State, February 1985.

30 Crocker, *High Noon in Southern Africa*, p. 65.

31 *US Policy Toward Southern Africa* Congressional Hearing and Markup, 16 September 1981, p. 61.

32 'Secretary Shultz's Meetings with African Foreign Ministers', transcript of a Department of State Press Briefing, New York, 26 May 1983, in *American Foreign Policy: Current Documents Annual*, 1983, Washington, DC, GPO (1981–), Document number 547.

33 As quoted in Novicki, Margaret 'Southern Africa: Behind the Scenes at the UN', *Africa Report*, Vol. 32, No. 3 (1987), p. 7.

34 *New York Times*, 1 June 1981, p. A1, as cited in Alex Thompson, *Incomplete Engagement: United States Foreign Policy Towards the Republic of South Africa 1981–1988*, Aldershot and Brookfield: Avebury, 1996, p. 171.

35 Crocker, *High Noon in Southern Africa*, p. 72.

36 'Memorandum of Conversation – Participants: SA Foreign Minister Pik Botha, SA Defence Minister Magnus Malan, US Assistant Secretary – Designate Chester Crocker, Alan Keyes. Subject: Discussion with SAG in Pretoria. Date: 15–16 April 1981'. Reproduced in Baker, *The United States and South Africa*, Appendix A.

37 Crocker, *High Noon in Southern Africa*, p. 69.

38 Statement by the Representative at the United Nations (Kirkpatrick) Before the UN Security Council, 25 May 1983, *American Foreign Policy: Current Documents Annual*, 1983, Washington, DC, GPO (1981–), Document number 546.

39 Ronald Reagan Library, CA. WHORM Subject Files: 'South Africa, US Policy Towards', File Numbers FG001–FG013; PR003-PR007-02. Secret Cable. From: Secretary of State Haig. To: US Embassy Pretoria and American Consulate Cape Town. Subject: Message From the Secretary to Pik Botha, 29 January 1982.

40 Barber, 'Shadows on the Wall', p. 70–1.

41 Wright, George, *The Destruction of a Nation: US Policy toward Angola Since 1945*, London and Chicago: Pluto Press, 1997, p. 99.

42 Personal interview with Dr Chester Crocker, 19 June 2001, Washington, DC.

43 Ronald Reagan Library, CA. White House Staff and Office Files: Cohen, Herman J., Files 1987–8. African Affairs Directorate, NSC. Boxes 91875 and 91876. Secret Memorandum – From: Secretary of State Alexander Haig. To: The President, 20 May 1981. Subject: Summing up of Pik Botha Visit. Declassified 21 January 1999.

44 Ronald Reagan Library, CA. White House Staff and Office Files: Cohen, Herman J., Files 1987–8. African Affairs Directorate, NSC. Boxes 91875 and 91876. Cable. From: Secretary of State Haig. To: US Embassy in Pretoria and American Consulate Cape Town. Subject: Containing text of Letter from Haig to Botha, 29 January 1982.

45 See Alex Thompson, *Incomplete Engagement*, p. 138.

46 'Memorandum of Conversation – Participants: SA Foreign Minister Pik Botha, SA Defence Minister Magnus Malan, US Assistant Secretary – Designate Chester Crocker, Alan Keyes. Subject: Discussion with SAG in Pretoria. Date: 15–16 April 1981'. Reproduced in Baker, *The United States and South Africa*, Appendix A.

47 Ronald Reagan Library, CA. White House Staff and Office Files: Cohen, Herman J., Files 1987–8. African Affairs Directorate, NSC. Boxes 91875 and 91876. Secret Memorandum – From: Secretary of State Alexander Haig. To: The President, 20 May 1981. Subject: Summing up of Pik Botha Visit. Declassified 21 January 1999.

8
Pretoria & UNITA:
The Beneficiaries of Linkage?

Pretoria's Perspective: Obstacles to Resolution

Crocker was adamant in his belief that the international community did not possess enough influence to force Pretoria to change its tactics – in the region just as much as with regard to its internal situation. What was needed, in the regional context as in the domestic one, was an approach which would address Pretoria's interests and its regional security concerns. He argued that South Africa was under no military pressure to leave Namibia. The only way they could be persuaded to go would be if their concerns and interests were addressed.

The Geneva conference held in January 1981 to find a way to implement the United Nations plan for Namibian independence had reached a total impasse just days before the Reagan administration came to power. It appeared that Pretoria wanted to delay agreeing to a settlement, believing that it could get a better arrangement under Reagan. His statements during his election campaign on the threat of the spread of communism had already convinced Pretoria that he would be a far more sympathetic interlocutor than the outgoing Carter administration. Crocker denied this inference, calling it 'illusory' and stating that the negotiations had reached an impasse over 'unresolved issues'. So what were the obstacles in the way of South Africa agreeing to a settlement, and what were their policy goals in the region?

Anti-communism/anti-SWAPO

It has been argued above that the government of South Africa had a very real fear of the spread of communism in its region, and that this fear formed the basis of much of Pretoria's regional policy. The South Africans saw the influence of Moscow in many of the liberation movements on their borders (and within their borders, in the case of the ANC and the PAC). This fear was particularly strong when it came to the possibility of a SWAPO victory in Namibia. In a meeting with the Republican senator Nancy Kassebaum, Pik Botha described the Namibian situation as a very serious, almost critical problem for Pretoria. In the early stages of Pretoria's negotiations with the Reagan administration, the fear of a SWAPO victory in Namibia was seen as an even more immediate threat than the presence of the Cubans in Angola (reversing the priorities as they were held in Washington). In their discussions with Washington, South African officials stressed the military threat of SWAPO and their very real fear of SWAPO winning any UN-supervised elections in Namibia. In contrast, the issue of Cubans in Angola was barely mentioned in discussions regarding Pretoria's security agenda.[1] During Pik Botha and Magnus Malan's meeting with Crocker in April 1981, the South Africans pointed out that SWAPO's representatives were indoctrinated in Marxism every day. The bottom line of the South African government was 'no Moscow flag in Windhoek'. The South Africans said they thought that the United States wanted to stop Soviet gains, but they didn't think the US believed Pretoria's view of SWAPO. They accused Washington of being 'soft' on SWAPO. Botha explained that developed moderate blacks were not communists – and whites could see them as allies. 'But if we all come under Moscow's domination, that's the end.'[2]

Mistrust of the United Nations

The next obstacle to a settlement was Pretoria's profound distrust of the United Nations. The UN, and the General Assembly in particular, had not hidden its disgust when reacting to South Africa's apartheid regime. It was equally outspoken when it came to denouncing South Africa's illegal occupation of Namibia. Pretoria had been incensed when the UN had declared SWAPO 'the sole authentic representative of the people of Namibia' in UNSCR 435 (1978). UNSCR 435 had also established the UN Transition Assistance Group (UNTAG) to assist in the implementation of the UNSCR 435 plan for the decolonization of Namibia. The South Africans dismissed UNTAG as 'a stalking horse for SWAPO'[3] and said that 'the UN's blue helmets were SWAPO helmets'.[4] This was despite the fact, as Faundez points out, that UNTAG was established by the Security Council, on which South Africa had many powerful friends. UNSCR 435, however, had been negotiated during the Carter administration. The most powerful of South Africa's 'powerful friends' was now under a new administration, one that shared Pretoria's misgivings. Both Washington and Pretoria wanted South Africa to maintain a military and political presence in Namibia until the settlement was completed, implying that they would prefer South Africa to oversee the independence process rather than the UN. The UN's sympathy for SWAPO did not bode well from the standpoints of the US and South Africa, neither of whom wished to see this potentially Marxist organization governing Namibia.

Concerns regarding Namibia's internal settlement

Pretoria placed great emphasis on retaining control of events within Namibia, particularly the way in which it would be governed. Namibia was seen by Pretoria as a vital security buffer zone against hostile black states in the region. This view was strengthened after the 1974 Portuguese coup, which resulted in the sympathetic white states of Angola and Mozambique falling into the hands of radical left-wing black governments. Just before Reagan came to power, Zimbabwe, the final remaining white state in the region (bar South Africa itself and the occupied Namibia) gained independence in 1980 under the black government of Robert

Mugabe. Pretoria could not envisage an independent Namibia which would not follow Zimbabwe's path, thereby seriously damaging South Africa's own security interests.

At the same time as they were grappling with this problem, however, the South African policy makers realized that their long-held objective of incorporating Namibia into South Africa was no longer tenable. The only way Pretoria could guard against the communist 'total onslaught' on their borders would be to install a client regime in Namibia. Pretoria put a good deal of effort into building up a credible opposition – and the result was the Democratic Turnhalle Alliance (DTA). In the South African-sponsored (whites only) 1978 election in Namibia, the DTA won 82 per cent of the vote, confirming it as South Africa's choice as SWAPO's opponent in Namibia. Unfortunately for Pretoria, the international community did not look with favour on their orchestrated 'internal settlement' for Namibia. In statements and publications even Washington made it clear that it would not endorse South Africa's internal settlement. Crocker stated: 'The internal government institutions South Africa has created are null and void and we do not recognize them.'[5]

Economic interests

Pretoria had another reason behind wanting to maintain control of events within Namibia. The South African government was very concerned that an undertaking should be sought in talks with the Namibian parties to honour the loan agreements and financial commitments that Namibia incurred before independence. In other words, those incurred by Pretoria itself while it had governed Namibia, as well as by private South African companies and individuals. In a cable to the Secretary of State, the American Consulate in Cape Town explained: 'South Africa does not want in Namibia their situation in Zimbabwe where their financial exposure is sizeable, vulnerable and politically embarrassing at home.'[6] In a communication to Crocker, the Chargé d'Affaires said that the South African government had prepared a list of South African investments, loans and credits in Namibia for the Western Contact Group. Pretoria wanted to discuss with the Contact Group 'ways of assuring the SAG [South African Government] about that financial exposure'. Yet it was not just the prospect of a SWAPO victory that prompted these fears. Another cable in October 1981 mentioned that 'Pik told me that the DTA, too, had made eyebrow-raising noises about how it might not fully meet Namibia's financial obligations to Pretoria, or, at least, not in the way that South Africa would want'.[7]

There was a further dimension to South Africa's concerns regarding the future running of the Namibian economy. As well as being concerned about the security of its own loans and investments, Pretoria was also concerned on behalf of the white Namibians. This worry was prompted by its own domestic interests. A telegram from the US Embassy in Pretoria to Crocker described how South African officials had made it clear to the US representatives that politically P. W. Botha would not be able to accept the flight to South Africa of large numbers of Namibian whites. Whites would leave, according to South African officials, only if there was a threat to their economic interests; the exodus would not be prompted merely by fear of a black government – 'even a SWAPO one'.[8] Botha was very concerned about accusations from the right wing that he was abandoning the whites, and any exodus would serve to confirm this accusation. As the cable explained, however, while one of Botha's main fears in the region was communism, the real threat to many of the ordinary white South Africans and Namibians was to their own pockets. The majority would remain under a SWAPO government if their financial freedom and security, and the health of the economy, could be guaranteed.

Botha's domestic battle

Unfortunately for the people of Namibia and Angola, economic guarantees were not the only issue to be taken into consideration in the region. A serious political split in the South African cabinet meant that the negotiations on Namibian independence were badly compromised. P. W. Botha constantly had to tread the line between the moderates and right wing of his party. At the time of the Geneva conference on Namibian independence, Botha was facing his first national election as the leader of the National Party. A 'sell out' on Namibia would have been seized on by his right-wing opponents as excellent political capital. This was undoubtedly one of the reasons behind the conference's collapse.

In the South African cabinet itself, the moderate wing was largely represented by Pik Botha and the Foreign Ministry. Although, like the rest of South Africa, they were anxious regarding communist encroachment in their region, these moderates took a balanced view of events both in Namibia and Angola. The Foreign Ministry wanted to recognize whoever came into power in Angola, even if it was the MPLA. In Pik Botha's meeting with Nancy Kassebaum in January 1983, he pointed out that, six months before, he would not have predicted that he would have been meeting with Angolan (and Mozambican) ministers. Botha explained that this had indicated to him how practical problems could override ideological hostility.

This view, however, was certainly not shared by South Africa's military. A cable to the Secretary of State from Ambassador Nickel stated: '[P. W.] Botha's ruminations on Soviet intentions seem to reflect a genuine split of opinions within the SAG, with the military most sceptical of [Mozambican President] Machel's and Dos Santos's motives and freedom of maneuver.'[9] The military, therefore, was adamantly opposed to recognition of any regime in Angola that they believed to be unfriendly or under communist influence. Certainly, they did not believe that the MPLA could be weaned away from Soviet influence. The military's view was that South Africa must go on the attack and bully its neighbours into showing South Africa more respect. They should: 'press on to victory, not make deals with Marxists to suit "Pik Botha's cocktail party friends"'.[10]

The fact was that the military believed South Africa could win the destabilization war in the region, and that their favoured party in Angola – UNITA – could win the civil war there. These aims went directly against much of Crocker's policy in the region. They also contradicted his view of the situation. He believed that the military route was not a realistic option, and that UNITA could not win an outright military victory in Angola. His aim was to assist UNITA in order to provide it with a strong position at the negotiating table, not with an outright military victory. As Shultz explained in a letter to Reagan: 'It is essential that our views get directly to Savimbi, and not through the filter of the South African military which is taking the line with him and others that a military solution in Angola is possible.'[11] Indeed, although the State Department worked hard to restrain the influence of the South African military, this effort was compromised by the splits in Botha's cabinet, and the fact that the competing parties were constantly undermining each other in their discussions with the US. A good example was the launch of Operation Protea, a large-scale South African invasion of Angola, in August 1981 (see Chapter 9) just as Crocker's diplomacy in the region had begun.

With regard to P. W. Botha, *The Economist* stated that, although he tended to the hawkish view, he preferred to mediate rather than lead. In fact, it seems that Botha's preference went further than this. An unnamed source from the South African government was asked by the US Embassy in Pretoria to evaluate the relative influence of the diplomatic and military camps in the South African government:

> XXXX [still classified] said the military definitely had the upper hand. P. W. Botha et al. regarded them highly because they were concerned with the bigger picture in the region. Diplomacy tended to break down the issues and solve each part independently which could lead to an overall result not in SAG's favour.[12]

This section has discussed the problems that Pretoria was facing with regard to the situation in Namibia and Angola. A number of complex interests were present, and these were exacerbated by the splits within the South African cabinet. This chapter now turns to an evaluation of just how successful Crocker's policy was in addressing these competing interests in Pretoria, and what impact they, in turn, had on his linkage strategy.

Linkage Addresses Pretoria's Concerns

Crocker himself describes linkage as both a pressure and a gift. He saw it as a 'face saver' for the South Africans. Within Botha's cabinet, the right wing gave linkage a cautious welcome, although the moderates were far more enthusiastic. At a meeting in Geneva, Pik Botha told Crocker that he saw great diplomatic and public relations value in the concept. 'It's too good to be true.'[13] Although many in Botha's cabinet remained genuinely fearful of SWAPO's communist leanings, they were also aware of the reality of their situation, and that maintaining the occupation was becoming increasingly difficult due to international pressure and the costs – human and financial. A secret CIA report of August 1982 stated: 'Pretoria recognizes that the political strength of the South West Africa People's

Organization (SWAPO) has not been diminished by South Africa's military operations during the past year....'[14] The report continued: 'The Botha government probably believes that it needs the political ammunition of a Cuban withdrawal to defuse a domestic right wing reaction to a probable SWAPO victory in Namibia.'

But it was not just the effects in Namibia that interested Pretoria. The effects of a Cuban withdrawal in Angola were also significant. Cuban withdrawal would vastly improve the security situation for UNITA – the South African-funded resistance movement in Angola. The CIA report explained that South Africa viewed UNITA as a valuable source of leverage that cost very little. South Africa had long been funding UNITA against the MPLA, and was determined to ensure Jonas Savimbi a good settlement deal in Angola – preferably at the expense of the MLPA. Crocker also maintained that Botha's strong pro-Savimbi stance was calculated to win over conservatives in America, Britain and Portugal. The conservatives in these Western countries had long viewed Savimbi as 'their man' in Angola – a practical man who would be sympathetic to Western security and economic interests in the region. Crocker states that South Africa's reasoning was that 'Angola was perhaps the best place to force the feckless Western powers to choose between South Africa and the more militant black African states.'[15]

As well as the potential benefits that linkage offered South Africa, its timing was also important. Although South Africa was benefiting from exploiting Namibia's economic and mineral reserves, many saw the war in Namibia as an economic drain. The American Department of State concluded that Namibia was not a profitable exercise for the South Africans. Rather, it was a drain in economic and military terms. The press also began to comment that South Africa appeared weary of a war it was not losing but apparently could not end.[16] A settlement in Namibia also had the potential of improving relations with the other countries of the region. South Africa was keen to gain maximum trade benefits with its neighbours. As a Director at South Africa's Department of Foreign Affairs explained, Pretoria 'strives for national security, economic cooperation and good neighbourliness in the region'.[17] He went on to point out: 'In spite of the official OAU trade boycott against South Africa, the country's total exports to African states amount to R4 billion a year.'

As well as the trade benefits of improved relations with the regional governments, South Africa craved political acceptability, both on the continent and abroad. In 1979, Botha announced his intention to establish a 'Constellation of States' known as CONSTAS. This would be an association of South Africa, its 'independent homelands' and the sovereign black states of the region. Regional ties and trading links would be established, together with a series of mutual security pacts. South Africa saw this as a good way to ensure its influence over the region, but all of South Africa's neighbours rejected the plan outright, adding insult to injury in 1980 by forming their own regional association – the Southern African Development Coordination Conference (SADCC), later to become the Southern African Development Community (SADC).

Pretoria Remains Cautious

Despite the obvious benefits that linkage provided, much of Botha's cabinet remained cautious of Washington's motives. Pretoria had witnessed the election of the new Reagan administration with optimism, and its rejection of the compromises on the table in Geneva in 1981 reflected a belief that the incoming administration would offer a better deal. Nevertheless, history had made the South Africans sceptical. In 1975 Kissinger had indicated to P. W. Botha – then the South African Defence Minister – that a South African invasion to install UNITA in Angola would be actively assisted by the US. Commentators remarked that 'the failure to deliver on that promise is deeply etched on Mr Botha, and conditions his attitude to every American initiative'.[18] In a meeting with US Embassy official Howard K. Walker, Pik Botha said that, as South Africa's Ambassador to Washington during the 1975–6 period, he had advised Prime Minister Vorster not to rely on President Ford and Secretary Kissinger. Walker reported that 'Pik said that he is giving similar advice today.'[19] Pik also reported to the US Embassy that great difficulty had been caused by the publishing of an interview given by US Secretary of State Al Haig. As the South Africans understood it, Haig had said that Washington was keeping a low profile on South Africa in order to achieve a Namibian settlement. This was interpreted in South African circles as: 'as soon as Namibia is out of the way, you will get down to seriously giving us hell'.[20] Reports such as these merely exacerbated the reservations harboured by all the South African policy makers, particularly since 1975. Olivier (Chief Director of Communications and Planning in South Africa's Department of Foreign Affairs) explained that South Africa knew linkage was not a 'benevolent, altruistic policy' but one based on American interests in a region where Washington would like to broaden its influence. 'In short, this is a policy prescribed by American interests; should these interests change, the policy will change as well.'[21] Olivier concluded with this assessment of the South African perspective: 'South Africa regards her policy towards the United States as unaltered, i.e. acknowledgement by American leadership and the pursuance of friendly, normal interstate relations, and not expecting too much.'

UNITA

When assessing South Africa's policies towards Angola and Namibia, it is vital to take into account the role played by UNITA. Depictions of this group have ranged from freedom fighters and champions of liberal democracy to South African proxy agents of destabilization in Angola. But what was the reality – and what function did UNITA perform in Crocker's linkage strategy? By the time of Reagan's inauguration in January 1981, Jonas Savimbi's UNITA was the main opposition in Angola. Savimbi was a resourceful opponent, and attempted to turn events, allies and beliefs to his advantage to such an extent that it is often difficult to identify just what his aims were. Savimbi's own statements painted him as a model African nationalist – fighting for nothing more than freedom from colonialism. Savimbi described his own position thus:

> The political program of UNITA is simple and clear. We fight for an independent Angola, free of all foreign troops. We believe that peasants, not the state, should own farm land. We favour democratic elections, freedom of religion and respect for tribal customs and languages.[22]

Savimbi was also careful to paint himself as a good anti-communist, continuing: 'The goals of UNITA are clear and open ... we will drive the Cubans and Soviets and Eastern-bloc personnel from Angola.... We reject foreign ideologies that presuppose masses of industrial workers and men without souls.' UNITA's strategy was to raise the costs of the foreign occupation of Angola until the Cubans and the Soviets would simply have to withdraw. This strategy had a devastating effect on Angola as a whole. Damaging Angola and damaging the MPLA came to be indistinguishably interrelated. Infrastructure and agriculture were destroyed. This, combined with further sabotage of industry, went a long way to fulfilling Savimbi's professed aim of destroying the Angolan economy – large parts of which were being used to fund the presence of Savimbi's enemies – the Cubans. Savimbi stressed the fact that the MPLA government was paying Havana $1,000 per month for each Cuban soldier in Angola. Attacking diamond and mineral mines and petroleum instalments, explained Savimbi, did not harm his Angolan brothers as they did not see this wealth anyway. 'It is taken by the Cubans and Soviets to pay for their repression here and to finance Cuban expeditions in other nations.'

Savimbi's elusive ideology
Although Savimbi believed he had laid out his aims and his strategy clearly, his politics and ideology were far less clear. Even Gerald Bender states: 'In spite of twenty years of reading statements by and about Mr Savimbi, I have not always been able to point with confidence to what his position is or would be on a variety of issues.'[23] In correspondence from UNITA to the Chairman of the House Foreign Affairs Subcommittee on African Affairs, the organization itself said that its 'guiding philosophy ... espouses individual freedom, free enterprise, human liberties and respect for cultural national identity'.[24] With regard to the charges of former Marxist sympathies – mainly arising from Savimbi's training in and funding from communist China and his early statements, UNITA stated: 'Dr [sic] Savimbi has never accepted the principles of Marxism. UNITA's political and economic system is clearly of a Western style and orientation.'[25] Yet observers remarked on Savimbi's 'relatively short political history marked by what might appear to be a remarkable agility in switching allegiances, but is in fact a consistent allegiance to his personal

ambition to rule Angola'.[26] If this was the case, and his loyalties were so easily swayed, it seems surprising that Savimbi and UNITA could command such a range of external support – and be depended upon by South Africa and the United States.

UNITA's external support

Possibly the most controversial of Savimbi's alliances, even more so than his accord with South Africa, was an earlier understanding with Angola's old colonial masters – the Portuguese. After the Portuguese coup of 25 April 1974, Portuguese officers gained access to the files of the PIDE (the Portuguese colonial police force). In these files they found correspondence between Savimbi and General Luz Cunha, Commander-in-Chief of the colonial army in Angola. In this correspondence both parties referred to the MPLA as 'the enemy'. In one letter dated 29 September 1972, Savimbi wrote to Cunha of the need for 'the weakening of the MPLA forces in Angola, leading to their liquidation. This task can be accomplished through the combined efforts of the [Portuguese] military forces and UNITA's forces.'[27] As well as collaboration with Portugal, and receiving aid and training from China, UNITA also received external support from the Middle East, Morocco, Zaïre and multinational companies interested in Angola's mineral wealth.

Yet Pretoria was without doubt UNITA's most important ally. After the MPLA had declared an independent Angola under its government in 1975, Pretoria's immediate response was to launch an (abortive) invasion to install UNITA as the new government. In 1978 South Africa made an official request to the UN Secretary-General that UNITA should be included in the talks on Namibian independence – a request that was denied. Pretoria was determined to assist UNITA into power – a situation which would have helped to address South Africa's regional security questions. Even if UNITA could only gain control of the Namibian border area, this would greatly facilitate South Africa's role in the region, as it would ease SWAPO pressure inside Namibia. Indeed, as well as arms, Pretoria supplied UNITA with food to distribute in this region to win the hearts and minds of the people. As one observer commented: 'For a low cost (continued supplies to UNITA) South Africa could realize the benefit (continued disruption of SWAPO) of a stalemate on the independence of Namibia.'[28]

Although UNITA was to become almost entirely dependent upon South Africa, this aid was a mixed blessing. The fact that the black liberation movement UNITA would accept aid from the apartheid regime in South Africa was very damaging for the rest of UNITA's external relations. Even the left wing in Washington, arguing against the resumption of funding to UNITA, utilized the argument that to do so would be to place the US on the side of Pretoria too publicly. In Savimbi's first visit to the United States – as a guest of the New York-based Freedom House in 1979 – he denied receiving South African support. He simply admitted that some of the arms bought with stolen diamonds happened to come from South Africa and that UNITA traded with South Africa. In the

Winter 1986 edition of *Policy Review*, however, Savimbi admitted to receiving aid from South Africa, but stated that that did not mean he condoned apartheid, calling it a 'dead ideology'. He also pointed out that: 'Stalin's acceptance of war material from America and Britain during World War Two did not constitute an endorsement of liberal democracy on Stalin's part'.[29] The fact was, Savimbi explained, that his organization's ties with South Africa were those of necessity. In testimony on 13 March 1986 to the House Permanent Select Committee on Intelligence, Professor Rotberg stated that UNITA was an important instrument of South Africa's regional policy. Rotberg went further, dismissing the organization thus: 'UNITA is a proxy for South Africa just as the National Resistance Movement is a proxy in Mozambique for South Africa.'[30] The result was that South African assistance to UNITA was a double-edged sword. The organization became so dependent on South African assistance as to be unable to survive as a credible military force without it. However, it was this very support that most damaged UNITA's credibility and precluded further support from many black African nations and many in the international community.

In the United States, however, a powerful lobby group was forming, calling for a resumption of American support for UNITA. On 14–15 March 1981 Senior Deputy Assistant Secretary of State for African Affairs Lannon Walker met privately with Savimbi in Morocco. Savimbi's first official visit to Washington came in December 1981, during which he outlined his platform: all foreign troops out of Angola; national elections to be held; and free elections in Namibia. Savimbi was certainly adept at playing the statesman, and impressed his audiences with both his oratorical skills and his willingness to negotiate. Savimbi was also extremely skilful in adapting his message to his audience, ensuring that he told them what they wanted to hear. In American journals Savimbi wrote articles explaining how his war was a war against Soviet colonialism and communism, and referred to the common enemy of Soviet imperialism. He continued: 'Our struggle in Angola ... is the battle for the West and its values.'[31] Savimbi had also managed to judge the post-Vietnam Syndrome mood, and appealed to the very fundamentals upon which the Reagan Doctrine was based. Savimbi described Angola as the 'Munich of Africa', stating:

> Hesitation, the refusal to aid UNITA in its fight against the Cubans and the Soviets, will be taken as a signal by all the countries in the region that the United States has abandoned them to the Soviets as the West abandoned Czechoslovakia and Eastern Europe to Hitler in 1938.[32]

Yet, back in 1970, the UNITA organization held a very different view. UNITA spoke of its admiration for the Vietnamese people 'in fighting dauntlessly American imperialism and their lackeys'.[33] Savimbi, when outlining his reasons for leaving the then US-funded FNLA, stated at the time: 'No progressive action is possible with men who serve American interests ... the notorious agents of imperialism.'[34] Indeed, when talking to a Third World organization in 1970, the UNITA Secretary for External

Affairs identified the organization's challenge thus: 'UNITA is aware that the struggle against US-led imperialism in Angola is a vital key to the heart of the entire Southern African problem.'[35]

It is a testament to Savimbi's skill that such a dramatic *volte-face* could have been accepted in the West – largely thanks to Savimbi's remarkable ability to match his message to his audience. Indeed, many in Washington were keen to point to Savimbi as a great and brave man, fighting for the same principles that America held dear – anti-communism, freedom and democracy. It was clear in Washington circles that an end to the civil war in Angola would only be acceptable if the needs of their client group were met. In heavy fighting near Luanda in November 1982, reports were heard in Washington that government troops were defecting to UNITA. In a meeting between Assistant Secretary Abrams and Pik Botha, Washington and Pretoria saw the chance of victory for their proxy in the region. A report of the meeting explained: 'it was not impossible that Savimbi might end up on top. If that happened SAG and the US should immediately call for elections in both Angola and Namibia.'[36] This demonstrated that South Africa would have been able to call for Namibian elections as early as 1982 – and Washington knew it, and colluded with Pretoria in avoiding them. Yet the opportunity was missed because South Africa and Washington had their own goals in the region, and this was reflected in UNITA's relationship with them both. As Peter Vale concluded:

> men like Savimbi were – to self-styled realists like Chet Crocker – mere instruments in the regional ambitions of the US. Launched without clear political goals, they were compliant partners and were used constantly to block the goals of Africa's liberation.[37]

Notes

1   Baker, Pauline H., *The United States and South Africa: The Reagan Years. Update South Africa: Time Running Out*, Ford Foundation and Foreign Policy Association, 1989, p. 14.

2   'Memorandum of Conversation – Participants: SA Foreign Minister Pik Botha, SA Defence Minister Magnus Malan, US Assistant Secretary – Designate Chester Crocker, Alan Keyes. Subject: Discussion with SAG in Pretoria. Date: 15–16 April 1981'. Reproduced in Baker, *The United States and South Africa*, Appendix A.

3   Faundez, Julio, 'Namibia: the Relevance of International Law', *Third World Quarterly*, Vol. 8, No. 2 (April 1986), p. 552.

4   'America and South Africa', *The Economist*, 30 March 1985, p. 19.

5   National Archives MD. ARC Identifier: 59701, *Role of the US in Southern Africa – Crocker, 1985*.

6   Ronald Reagan Library, CA. White House Staff and Office Files: Cohen, Herman J., Files 1987–8. African Affairs Directorate, NSC. Boxes 91875 and 91876. Secret Cable. To: Secretary of State Washington, DC. From: American Consulate Cape Town. Subject: 'Pik/Chargé Conversations', 10 November 1981.

7   Ronald Reagan Library, CA. White House Staff and Office Files: Cohen, Herman J., Files 1987–8. African Affairs Directorate, NSC. Boxes 91875 and 91876. Secret Cable. To: Secretary of State, Washington. From: American Consulate Cape Town. Subject: 'Pik and the Prospects of a SWAPO Victory', 23 October 1981.

8   *Ibid.*

9 Ronald Reagan Library, CA. Executive Secretariat, NSC: Records Boxes 91340 and 91343. Cable – From: Herman Nickel US Ambassador to SA. To: Secretary of State. Subject: SAG View of Soviet Influence, 4 February 1983.

10 *The Economist*, 30 March 1985, p. 20.

11 Ronald Reagan Library, CA. White House Staff and Office Files: Cohen, Herman J., Files 1987–8. African Affairs Directorate, NSC. Boxes 91875 and 91876. Memorandum. To: Ronald Reagan. From: Secretary of State George Shultz. Subject: 'South Africa: Status of our Negotiation Effort', 6 June 1983.

12 Ronald Reagan Library, CA. White House Staff and Office Files: Cohen, Herman J., Files 1987–8. African Affairs Directorate, NSC. Boxes 91875 and 91876. Cable. To: Secretary of State, Washington. From: US Embassy Pretoria, 17 November 1982.

13 Ronald Reagan Library, CA. White House Staff and Office Files: Cohen, Herman J., Files 1987–8. African Affairs Directorate, NSC. Boxes 91875 and 91876. Secret Cable. From: Crocker. To: Poindexter (The White House). Subject: Geneva Meeting with Pik Botha, February 1986. Declassified 26 May 1999.

14 Ronald Reagan Library, CA. White House Staff and Office Files: Cohen, Herman J., Files 1987–8. African Affairs Directorate, NSC. Boxes 91875 and 91876. Secret CIA Memorandum. To: William P. Clark Asst. to the President for National Security Affairs. From: John N. McMahan Acting Director of Central Intelligence. Subject: The Namibia Settlement Process: Obstacles and Regional Implications, 20 August 1982.

15 Crocker, Chester, *High Noon in Southern Africa: Making Peace in a Rough Neighborhood*, New York and London: W. W. Norton and Company, 1992, p. 56.

16 *Economist*, 30 March 1985, p. 19.

17 Olivier, Gerrit 'Recent Developments in South African Foreign Policy', *Optima*, Vol. 36, No. 4 (December 1988), p. 201.

18 *Economist*, 30 March 1985, p. 19.

19 Ronald Reagan Library, CA. Secret Cable. To: Secretary of State, Washington. From: American Consulate Cape Town. Subject: 'Pik and the Prospects of a SWAPO Victory', 23 October 1981.

20 Ronald Reagan Library, CA. Secret Cable. To: Secretary of State, Washington. From: American Consulate Cape Town. Subject: 'Pik/Chargé Conversations', 10 November 1981.

21 Olivier in Kapp, P. H. and G. C. Oliver, *United States–South African Relations: Past, Present and Future*, Human Sciences Research Council Publication Series, No. 87, Cape Town: Tafelberg Publishers, 1987, p. 156.

22 Savimbi, Jonas, 'The War Against Soviet Colonialism: The Strategy and Tactics of Anti-Communist Resistance', *Policy Review*, No. 35 (Winter 1986), p. 77.

23 *Angola: Intervention or Negotiation* Hearings before the Subcommittee on Africa of the Committee on Foreign Affairs, House of Representatives, 99th Congress, First Session, 31 October and 12 November 1985, p. 161.

24 Ronald Reagan Library, CA. White House Staff and Office Files: Cohen, Herman J., Files 1987–8. African Affairs Directorate, NSC. Boxes 91875 and 91876. Letter. From: Jeremiah Chitunda Secretary of Foreign Affairs, UNITA. To: Congressman Howard Wolpe, Chairman, Subcommittee on African Affairs, 11 November 1985.

25 *Ibid.*

26 Stockwell, John, 'The Angolans' Perennial Loser Without A Cause', *New York Times*, 22 November 1979.

27 'Memorandum of Conversation' between Assistant Secretary of State Chester Crocker and South African Foreign Minister Pik Botha and Defence Minister Magnus Malan, Pretoria 15–16 April 1981. Photocopy of document sent to the author by the Namibian Embassy in London.

28 James III, W. Martin, *A Political History of the Civil War in Angola 1974–1990*, New Brunswick, NJ and London: Transaction Publishers, 1992, p. 152.

29 Savimbi, Jonas 'The War Against Soviet Colonialism The Strategy and Tactics of Anti-Communist Resistance' in *Policy Review*, No. 35 Winter 1986 p.82. When pressed about his relationship with the apartheid state, Savimbi stated: 'Of course, a black man like me will not say that apartheid is a good thing. How are we going to get rid of the mistreatment of blacks in South Africa? I don't know because I'm busy with my own

problems.' Quoted from 'UNITA Leader Lives with his Men' Jack Foise, *Los Angeles Times* 4 June 1980.

30 *Angola: Should the United States Support Unita?* Hearing before the Permanent Select Committee on Intelligence, House of Representatives, 99th Congress, Second Session, 13 March 1986, p. 15.

31 Savimbi, Jonas, 'The War Against Soviet Colonialism', p. 82.

32 *Ibid.* p. 82.

33 Puna, Miguel, Secretary-General UNITA, in *Kwacha-Angola* (Official UNITA Organ), 19 August 1970, p. 7.

34 As quoted in Gerald Bender, 'The Quintessential Savimbi', June 1984, Appendix to *Angola: Intervention or Negotiation* Congressional Hearings, 31 October and 12 November 1985, p. 171.

35 *Ibid.*, p. 171.

36 Ronald Reagan Library, CA. WHORM Subject Files: 'South Africa, US Policy Towards' File Numbers FG001–FG013; PR003-PR007-02. Secret Cable – From: Pretoria US Embassy. To: White House Situation Room and Secretary of State, 22 November 1982. Subject: Meeting with Pik Botha, 18 November 1982. Declassified 19 January 1999.

37 Vale, Peter, 'Crocker's Choice: Constructive Engagement and South Africa's People', review article, *South African Journal of International Affairs*, Vol. 1, No. 1 (1995), p. 105.

9
Linkage Policy Undermined: Destabilization & the Funding of UNITA

Crocker had had to overcome many obstacles when he first proposed a formal link between Namibian independence and the removal of Cuban troops from Angola. He faced vocal opposition from both African states and America's Western allies in the international community. Apart from South Africa's endorsement, no other country wished to be publicly linked to such a policy. However, Crocker persevered and linkage soon became the only viable policy option in the region – only with linkage in place would America lend its credibility to the goal of achieving Namibian independence. Unfortunately, the implementation of the linkage strategy was to prove at least as problematic as its conception. Although general opposition had complicated Crocker's pursuit of linkage, it was the actions of the two governments who had most supported linkage that eventually succeeded in inflicting serious damage on the policy.

South Africa's Destabilization of the Region

After the Portuguese coup of April 1974, the leverage and advantages South Africa had obtained in the region through 'guile, diplomacy and economic leverage'[1] now had to be imposed forcibly on the new and hostile governments in the region. The significance and impact of Pretoria's destabilization tactics throughout the region cannot be under-estimated. They had a profound effect on both the governments and the people of the Frontline States (FLS). They also caused severe damage to constructive engagement, undermining a policy that was aimed at helping South Africa regain international legitimacy.

Representatives of the South African government stated that even when the region changed – and in a way which was largely understood to be detrimental to the Republic's own security interests – the South African government 'adhered to its policy of peaceful coexistence and economic cooperation'.[2] Pretoria claimed that it hoped interstate relations could be based on mutual interest and non-interference in the domestic affairs of other states. It pointed to the fact that certain states in the region adopted an unfriendly stance towards South Africa by making their territories available to the ANC for bases from which to launch terrorist attacks on South Africa. It was these decisions that compelled the government to defend the country's territorial integrity. Pretoria was left with no choice. As Pik Botha warned: 'Terrorism … has a boomerang effect – it hits back at those who allow it.'[3] The fear of terrorism was indeed one of South Africa's primary motives for the repeated military raids that the South African Defence Force (SADF) perpetrated against countries throughout the region. Pretoria viewed this as an effective way of crippling both the ANC and SWAPO's ability to mount cross-border operations in Namibia or South Africa. SADF's full-scale invasion of Angola was an extreme form of this anti-terrorist destabilization. Damage to the MPLA government would jeopardize SWAPO's freedom to use Angola as a base for its missions into Namibia itself.

However, although the South African government portrayed destabilization as a form of self-defence against those neighbours who were supporting terrorism, destabilization was not simply a *reactive* strategy. South Africa had its own goals in the region that it actively pursued, in part, through the destabilization of its neighbours. In Angola, for example, elements within South Africa – the military in particular – wanted to bring down the MPLA government in the hope that it would then be replaced by South Africa's own client group, UNITA. Another objective behind Pretoria's actions in Angola was to prevent, or at least delay, the UN independence settlement for Namibia as laid down in UN Security Council Resolution 435 (1978). Botha had made it clear 'that South Africa would never allow the Territory [Namibia] to be "handed to SWAPO on a plate"'.[4] Once the implementation of this resolution was tied to the withdrawal of Cuban troops from Angola, Pretoria could delay any progress by making it impossible for the MPLA to dispense with the services of the Cuban troops without facing almost certain defeat at the hands of the SADF and UNITA. Botha was determined to build up a credible opposition to SWAPO in Namibia and, as Gerald Bender explains, 'Pretoria needed to buy time, and linkage provided the perfect vehicle'.[5]

As well as wishing to punish neighbours that cooperated with the terrorist organizations of the ANC and SWAPO, Pretoria was also determined to create a neighbourhood of pliant states, with governments who could be persuaded or coerced into following policies which were consistent with Pretoria's interests. The shield of instability created by the destabilization tactics not only helped to deter the incursion of ANC and SWAPO guerrillas, but also rendered the governments of the region more unstable and therefore more vulnerable to Pretoria's influence.

The tactics and operations of destabilization – Pretoria in Angola
Pretoria utilized a number of strategies and tools in its destabilization of the southern African region. Lesotho, Angola and Mozambique were all subject to military raids. Economic pressure and proxy wars were also significant tools in South Africa's armoury. In Angola, South Africa began supporting UNITA and the FNLA before the Portuguese left. Crocker stated that the presence of South African troops on Angolan soil began in July 1975 when they moved a short way across the Angolan/Namibian border into Angola to protect the Calueque dam. This was a South

Table 9.1 Major South African Military Operations inside Angola (after Angolan Independence)

Operation	Date	Dead (d) Captured (c)	Comments
Reindeer	May 1978	SWAPO 1,000 (d) SWAPO 200 (c) RSA 6 (d)	Raid on Kassinga
Safron	March 1979	Unknown	Raid on SWAPO near Zambian border
Crossbar	March 1979	Unknown	Raid on SWAPO base in SE Angola
Smokeshell	June 1980	SWAPO 380 (d/c) RSA 17 (d)	Raid lasted 3 weeks
Klipklop	July 1980	Unknown	Angolan town of Chitado destroyed as a base for SWAPO
Protea	August 1981	SWAPO 1000 (d/c) RSA 10 (d)	Defensive radar systems eliminated
Carnation	August 1981	SWAPO 225 (d)	Offshoot of Protea
Daisy	Oct./Nov. 1981	Unknown	RSA's deepest penetration since 1975, first air clashes between RSA/PRA
Super	March 1982	SWAPO 200 (d) RSA 3 (d)	Quick sweep against Cambeno in SW Angola
Meebos	July/Aug. 1982	SWAPO 345 (d) RSA 29 (d)	PLAN Eastern Front HQ raided
Phoenix	April 1983	SWAPO 309 (d) RSA 27 (d)	Raid on SWAPO near Namibia border
Askari	Dec. 1983	FAPLA 324 (d) RSA 21 (d)	Cubans directly in fighting for first time, SAM sites destroyed
Bush Willow	June 1985	SWAPO 27 (d)	25-mile sweep against SWAPO
Modular	Dec. 1987	FAPLA 382 (d) RSA 6 (d)	Military incursion to assist UNITA
Hooper	Dec. 1987	FAPLA 525 (d) RSA 16 (d)	To inflict maximum casualties on retreating Cuban/FAPLA forces
Packer	June 1988	Unknown	To force Cuban/FAPLA to retreat west of Cuito River

PRA = People's Republic of Angola; PLAN = People's Liberation Army of Namibia (SWAPO); FAPLA = Popular Armed Forces for the Liberation of Angola.
Source: James III, W. Martin, *A Political History of the Civil War in Angola 1974–1990*, New Brunswick, NJ and London: Transaction Publishers, 1992.

African-run hydroelectric and water supply project which was important to Namibia's economy. Pretoria's tactics did not remain defensive for long, however. In October 1975 the SADF launched 'Operation Savannah' in which 2,500–3,000 troops – mainly 'under FNLA and UNITA banners' invaded Angola to fight against the MPLA.[6]

The number of SADF soldiers along the 'Operational Area' (the Namibia/Angola border) increased from 15,000 in 1974 to 45,000 in 1976. By 1977 the frequency of South African incursions into Angola had increased. By 1981 the incursions included air strikes and ground forces up to 200 miles inside Angola's territory. South Africa claimed that these attacks were aimed at SWAPO, but it appeared that they had been coordinated with UNITA. This suspicion was heightened by the fact that towns taken by South African forces were given to UNITA to administer.[7] During the late 1970s and the 1980s the South Africans undertook regular military operations within Angola (see Table 9.1).

Although South Africa characterized the raids as straightforward military operations against the SWAPO terrorists, some of the invasions clearly had alternative motivations. Operation Protea, for example, was a huge operation launched in August 1981, just before a UN General Assembly session on Namibia, and when the Contact Group was coordinating its approach to new negotiations. Some in the West saw this as a deliberate action to demonstrate that Pretoria would not be dictated to by external powers. Pretoria's invasions continued deep into Angolan territory. On 17 March 1981 the South African Air Force (SAAF) attacked a SWAPO base 200 kilometres north of the Namibian–Angolan border. On 24 August 1981 Angola claimed that 45,000 South African troops were involved in attacks 130 km into Angolan territory. The South Africans called the figures 'totally laughable'.[8] However, the 1985 Report by the Commonwealth Secretariat described South Africa as 'occupying the southern third of the country'.[9] As the military campaign continued, moreover, South African confidence was badly shaken. There was an outcry in South Africa when the major December 1983 operation, Askari, met with far heavier resistance than anticipated. Although dwarfed by the number of Angolan casualties – 324 dead – the loss of 21 South African soldiers began a call from many white liberals to stop the fighting in Angola. Unfortunately for the region, the perceived security concerns outweighed these calls in the minds of the South African government.

With these destabilization tactics, Pretoria could gain maximum influence with minimum cost. They found this particularly through their use of 'proxy' organizations. Achieving outright military victory was not necessary. The dislocation caused by the resulting civil wars would force governments to divert scarce resources into fighting off the military threat. In South Africa's view, this had the virtue of causing dissatisfaction with the government and therefore rendered these governments far more vulnerable – either to being deposed or to South African influence. The costs of this destabilization to the target countries were huge. Eileen Riley described Botswana's Finance Minister as 'summing up the mood' when he commented in January 1983: 'It's not much use to develop ports and pipelines, roads and railways, and then watch in silence as they are blown up.'[10]

The FLS were frustrated at their own impotence in the face of South Africa's onslaught. They were also disappointed by the reluctance of the international community to act. Western governments, the US and Britain in particular, strongly resisted sanctions against Pretoria. They pointed to the fact that neighbouring countries would suffer just as much as South Africa from sanctions, because their economies were so closely linked. However, replying to this argument at the UN, the FLS said that they were currently suffering *more* at the hands of Pretoria – and that the current situation was more expensive for them because of the costs of South Africa's destabilization policy towards them. The Executive Secretary of the Southern African Development Coordination Conference (SADCC) estimated the costs of South African destabilization to his organization's nine member states at $2 billion annually, 'more than the total official development assistance all nine countries received from outside the region in the same period'.[11] He concluded that, for the countries of the region, sanctions were a sacrifice worth making.

Non-aggression pacts – the fruits of destabilization
The most tangible results from South Africa's destabilization policy were the non-aggression security pacts that it signed with the FLS. One by one, South Africa's neighbours were forced to sign a security pact with Pretoria. The first such pact was made in secret with the government of Swaziland in February 1982. The threat of incursions was coupled with financial inducements in order to extract a promise from the Swazi government that it would expel ANC activists from its territory.

The agreements reached with Luanda and Maputo were more public and high-profile in nature. This was largely due to the fact that Washington – and Crocker in particular – played a major role in bringing them about. On 16 February 1984 South Africa and Angola signed an agreement in Lusaka, Zambia. The South Africans had just undergone the sobering experience of Operation Askari (see above) and were temporarily of a mind to sign the deal with the Angolans. The South Africans promised a staged withdrawal from southern Angola while the Angolans pledged an end to cross-border incursions from Angola by SWAPO. An Angolan/South African Joint Monitoring Commission (JMC) was also established to detect or investigate any alleged violation by either party. The signing of the Nkomati Accord between South Africa and Mozambique on 16 March 1984 was even more dramatic. In a highly publicised ceremony on the banks of the Nkomati River, at the South African-Mozambique border, the governments promised to 'respect each other's sovereignty and independence, and … to refrain from interfering in the internal affairs of the other'.[12] Each government also agreed to prevent terrorists using its territory as a base for actions against the other.

These security pacts brought a range of benefits to Pretoria. The pacts were largely successful in driving the ANC out of South Africa's immediate neighbourhood, which was a severe blow to the organization.

The public agreements between South Africa and the FLS helped to overcome Pretoria's regional and international isolation, with Botha taking on the role of regional peacemaker. The white electorate was delighted with the agreements, and believed that their pariah status was coming to an end. The accords had great propaganda value and by June 1984 P. W. Botha was invited on an eight-nation tour of Europe, where he was received by – among others – Thatcher, Kohl and Pope John Paul II. The tour was a great coup for Botha – the first official tour of Europe by a South African head of state since the 1950s.

Washington's Reaction – the Impact of Destabilization on Constructive Engagement

Washington's reaction to South African destabilization was one of the most striking and controversial elements of Crocker's early constructive engagement policy. Crocker stressed that his policy was regional in scope, and was an attempt to engage all the countries of the region who were keen to enter into a constructive relationship with the US. The early actions of the US government, however, filled the FLS with alarm. After South Africa's 'Operation Protea' invasion of Angola in August 1981, both London and Bonn summoned their South African ambassadors to register a protest against the South African action. Washington did not follow suit. Instead, on 31 August 1981, the US vetoed a UN Security Council Resolution condemning South Africa for 'an unprovoked and persistent armed invasion' of Angola. The US representative said Washington was voting against the resolution because it 'placed all the blame on South Africa for the escalation of violence'.[13] Washington abstained on further Security Council resolutions condemning South African military actions in Angola in 1983 and 1984. The US also refused to single out South Africa for condemnation when the South African Air Force (SAAF) launched air strikes against Maputo in 1983.

In his May 1981 memorandum to Haig, Crocker had stated that Washington 'couldn't afford to give [South Africa] a blank check regionally'. Nevertheless, in Crocker's own account, he asserted that: 'We did not intend that pro-Western states like South Africa would be written off as fair game for Moscow, Havana, Luanda and their SWAPO guerrilla allies.'[14] This view did not take into account the legitimate security concerns of Angola, nor the legal arguments behind SWAPO's aims. Instead, he argued that it was important for Luanda, SWAPO and their Soviet and Cuban backers to know that it was a new situation after 1981: 'South African power was one of the anvils of our diplomacy.'[15] With comments such as these, it is hard to understand how Crocker hoped to avoid the perception that Washington was 'riding on a South African tank to the negotiating table'.

Unfortunately for Washington, protecting its anti-communist allies was no excuse in the eyes of the FLS for its failure to condemn South African destabilization. These states watched in horror as the Reagan administration continued to relax export restrictions against South Africa (three times in less than a year between February 1982 and January 1983) during a period of intense military destabilization by the SADF against its neighbours. In Congress, too, the attitude of the Reagan administration was strongly criticized. In a debate on Namibia before the House sub-committee on African Affairs, Chairman Howard Wolpe took issue with Crocker's insistence on condemning 'cross-border violence' by all parties. When Wolpe objected to the use of this term, asking 'Is there any point at which Angola has invaded South Africa?', Crocker stated that 'the issue is more complex than that', pointing to SWAPO raids into Namibia and ANC raids launched from Angola.[16] For the FLS, looking for support against repeated South African incursions into their territories, Crocker had a warning. It was, he stated, important for Angola, SWAPO and their Soviet and Cuban backers to know that 'If they obstructed our settlement terms, the price and the pain would grow.'[17]

A SADCC statement, issued on 13 July 1983, expressed the desperation felt by the governments of the FLS: 'South Africa can invade and occupy sovereign states, blow up vital installations, and massacre populations at no apparent cost to its relations with its main allies.'[18] In one meeting in September 1982, between P. W. Botha and CIA director William Casey, it was reported in the press that Casey had agreed with Botha that South African incursions against the FLS need cease only when the ANC had been eliminated from the region.[19] These actions, and US abstentions and vetoes against UN Security Council resolutions critical of South Africa's actions, led Chief Jonathan of Lesotho to state that US constructive engagement was exacerbating the situation.

Unfortunately for Crocker, South African actions were making it increasingly difficult for him to stick to the spirit of constructive engagement, which had indicated that a friendly and open relationship with South Africa would reap far more rewards than a relationship based on public criticism. The more aggressive Pretoria became in the region, the harder it was for Crocker to turn a blind eye to its actions. In an early and embarrassing episode, the SADF launched a raid into Angola in June 1982 at the same time as Reagan's roving Ambassador, General Vernon Walters, was in Luanda to discuss the US linkage initiative. The situation worsened when Pretoria launched Operation Askari in December 1983 (see Table 9.1) into Angola. Crocker was furious at the way Pretoria was openly undermining his diplomatic track, and allowing the military track to become an end in itself. He stated that he would not allow his diplomacy to be stalled while South Africa stoked regional wars. Thus he found it difficult to maintain a constructive dialogue when South Africa was becoming an increasingly embarrassing political ally, under fire for its actions in the region as well as its domestic policies.

One element of South Africa's behaviour caused particular difficulties for Crocker and his constructive engagement strategy. The conclusion of the Lusaka Accord between South Africa and Angola and the Nkomati

Accord between South Africa and Mozambique were seen as a major step forward in the region – and a triumph for constructive engagement. An April 1984 cable from Shultz to diplomatic posts in southern Africa described the Nkomati accord thus: 'In a nutshell, we are witnessing a potential watershed in southern Africa's evolution.'[20] A background briefing prepared for Robert McFarlane (Reagan's National Security Adviser) for Congressional Hearings on southern Africa on 21 and 23 May 1985 pointed to the Nkomati Accord of 16 March 1984 as 'tangible evidence of the increased willingness' of the parties of the region to solve their differences through negotiation.[21] The document asserted that: 'Constructive Engagement has brought about a lessening of major regional tensions in southern Africa.' The optimism created by these accords was, however, an illusion. The South Africans halted their withdrawal from Angola, a withdrawal which had been a stipulation of the Lusaka Accord, in May 1985, whilst still 40 kilometres inside Angolan territory. They stated that Angola was incapable of preventing SWAPO incursions into Namibia, so they remained on Angolan territory. Pretoria also soon resumed its support for RENAMO in Mozambique, contrary to the provisions of the Nkomati Accord. The Accord collapsed in the wake of these revelations.

The collapse of the Lusaka and Nkomati bridgeheads was a great embarrassment for Washington, and Crocker in particular. He had been very instrumental in achieving the US-brokered treaties, persuading each of the parties to talk to the other. The accords had been hailed as the one tangible success in the region for constructive engagement and had been viewed as a victory for his diplomatic approach. But, rather than the parties having been successfully persuaded to compromise, Pretoria had successfully forced Angola, Mozambique and Swaziland into submitting to an agreement to refuse assistance to the ANC. The alternative was to fall victim to Pretoria's destabilization. South Africa achieved the promises it wanted. It was destabilization, rather than US diplomacy, that could claim the accords as a victory. The failure of the accords was thus a major blow for constructive engagement. Crocker described how his painstakingly negotiated non-aggression pacts in Angola and Mozambique were deliberately violated and stated that: 'Pretoria seemed for a time determined to scuttle the embryonic regional framework that offered its only real prospect of obtaining an end to Soviet-Cuban military presence and cross-border guerrilla violence.'[22] There was a feeling that Washington had lost any influence over South Africa's actions. Christopher Coker described the situation thus: 'South Africa like Israel seemed to be a client state that had long escaped the control of its patron.'[23] A secret memorandum from Phillip Ringdahl to Robert C. McFarlane in July 1985 discussed 'the impasse in the Namibian Peace process (State prefers to call it "stepping back")' and commented on Crocker's fear that the White House was starting to distance itself from the constructive engagement policy.[24]

Yet more serious damage to constructive engagement through South African actions came in 1985, and was caused by two separate incidents occurring in quick succession. On 22 May 1985, a three-man South

African commando team was ambushed in the Angolan oil enclave of Cabinda by Angolan government forces. Two were killed and one was wounded. The South African government was forced to admit that its troops were on 'intelligence-gathering missions' against SWAPO. Pretoria denied the Angolan government's accusation that they were planning to attack the American-owned Gulf Oil installation in Cabinda. The incident embarrassed Pretoria, who had announced on 17 April 1985 that they had withdrawn their troops from Angola in order to concentrate on negotiating the removal of Cuban troops with the Angolan government. The Angolan government called off the negotiations in the light of the Cabinda revelations. The incident came at a difficult time for Crocker, as the American anti-apartheid movement was then gathering pace – and was calling into question the efficacy of his constructive engagement approach. He had to admit that the South African raid clearly was aimed at a Gulf Oil installation and declared that Washington was 'deeply troubled' by the raid. A secret memorandum from Shultz to US diplomatic missions throughout southern Africa stated that: 'The Cabinda raid was a definite setback to our negotiating efforts.'[25] Although the Reagan administration was clearly embarrassed by the incident, the South African government offered no apology, saying that it had warned Angola about a build-up of ANC rebels in its territory.

In fact, the very next month – on 14 June 1985 – a SADF unit carried out another raid, this time in the Botswanan capital of Gaborone. The South African government said that Botswana had been warned that it must expel ANC terrorists. Sixteen people were killed in the raid, including women and one child. Washington had been vocal in its condemnation of cross-border violence and its insistence on respect for national sovereignty. As Shultz pointed out: 'Coming on the heels of those statements, the Gaborone raid only added to our displeasure with the SAG [South African government] and called even more into question its intentions.'[26] In a move that clearly went against the spirit of constructive engagement, US Ambassador to South Africa Herman Nickel was recalled to Washington on 15 June 1985 in response to South African actions. Shultz described the recall as a signal of Washington's intense displeasure. In an NSC memorandum dated 3 July 1985, Phillip Ringdahl commented on the fact that there had been much debate in the State Department since Nickel's recall 'regarding suggested policy changes in the light of recent developments'. However, he went on to say that Crocker 'has not accepted any suggestions – at least not yet'.[27] Crocker maintained that Nickel had been recalled to review the situation, not the policy.

Unfortunately for Crocker, things were to get even worse the following year. In October 1985 the Commonwealth Eminent Persons Group (EPG) had launched its own diplomatic initiative to encourage talks between the South African government and black opposition groups. In April and May 1986, while the EPG initiative was still under way, Pretoria launched a series of strikes in Zambia, Zimbabwe and Botswana against ANC targets. Crocker said it seemed almost as though South Africa wanted to scuttle the EPG exercise. His policy was now facing a new onslaught as suddenly the Hill and the media were 'in uproar'. The policy of quiet diplomacy was showing signs of irreversible damage, particularly when Crocker himself was forced to join the chorus of public criticism of Pretoria's actions.

From 1985 onwards, Crocker's regional policy was forced to mirror the changes taking place in his policy towards South Africa itself. On both fronts condemnation of Pretoria's actions was stepped up and important symbolic moves took place which showed the extent to which the US–South African relationship had degenerated. In the light of the May 1986 cross-border raids, and less than a year after the three-month recall of Ambassador Nickel, Washington chose to withdraw permanently its military attaché from Pretoria. On 20 May 1986, Brigadier Alexander Potgieter, the South African military attaché to Washington, was expelled. Only a handful of countries had maintained their military attaché link with South Africa and this link had served as a symbol of Washington's constructive relationship with Pretoria. These actions were, therefore, of a particular symbolic significance regarding the fate of the constructive engagement policy.

It was through South African actions that Crocker's regional policy was discredited. South Africa had made it very clear that it would not be reciprocating his overtures. Crocker's image had been badly damaged when the Nkomati and Luanda accords – which he had presented as key achievements in his regional constructive engagement policy – collapsed in the face of continued South African aggression. During President Carter's administration, South Africa had made one incursion into Angola, but during Reagan's time in office there were many (see Table 9.1). An alarmed Howard Wolpe, Chairman of the House Subcommittee on African Affairs, called the Committee's attention to South Africa's increased regional violence through direct and covert action in Angola, Mozambique, Zimbabwe and Lesotho in Hearings on Namibia held on 21 February 1985. He stated that the actions were 'particularly worrisome, because these developments have occurred against the backdrop of the American government's policy of "constructive engagement"'.[28] Critics asserted that the South African government's actions in Namibia – and throughout the region – demonstrated to the US that constructive engagement had no teeth. Indeed, in the report on constructive engagement by the Secretary of State's Advisory Committee on South Africa the Committee explained how, under constructive engagement, the South African government had hardened its bargaining position. Mokoena remarked on how 'Pretoria exploited the optimistic new Administration's easing of pressure to turn the apparent rapprochement to its own advantage.'[29]

In the region, just as in the domestic setting, South Africa strongly resisted making any concessions in return for the Reagan administration's continued policy of constructive engagement. In fact, constructive engagement had been undermined to such an extent – in part due to South Africa's continued destabilization tactics – that not only had Washington come to accept that it had little influence over South Africa, but even the friendly relationship was in jeopardy. Baker quotes the pro-government

South African newspaper *The Citizen*, at the end of 1987, asserting: 'Looking back over the past year, it is clear that the United States has become South Africa's enemy number one (leaving aside Russia and the Communist Bloc countries...)'.[30] Despite all the signals that constructive engagement could not achieve its regional goals, the Reagan administration decided to pursue the policy further. Shultz stated, in a secret cable of June 1985, that Washington's interests were still best served in a continuing relationship with Pretoria. 'We fully intend to remain "constructively engaged" throughout southern Africa as the best means of keeping the US a relevant player.'[31] Shultz also pointed out that Washington would make it clear to Pretoria that continued cooperation could only be viable if Pretoria ceased its destabilizing activities. However, this comment did not appear to influence US actions. The Executive in Washington continued to support South Africa against the threat of sanctions, and the administration and the Republicans on Capitol Hill remained more suspicious of the Marxist regional governments than of Pretoria.

Destabilization proved to be extremely damaging, not just to Washington's constructive engagement but also to Washington's other main aim in the region – getting the Cubans out of Angola. On 4 February 1981 the Cubans and the Angolans had signed an accord which stated that: 'The withdrawal of Cuban forces stationed in Angola will be carried out once every eventuality of acts of aggression or armed invasion ceases to occur.'[32] In 1985, the UN Secretary-General was in Cuba discussing, among other issues, potential Cuban withdrawal from Angola. It so happened that the South African raids on Cabinda and Gaborone during May and June 1985 occurred at just this time. Instead of hearing plans for the withdrawal, the Secretary-General instead heard that Castro would reinforce his 25,000 troops if necessary to protect Angola. Indeed, South African attacks – which increased under Reagan's administration – achieved the very result that Pretoria's Republican supporters in the administration and on the Hill feared most. When Reagan was elected, there were 15,000 Cuban troops in Angola. By the end of 1988 there were 50,000.[33]

UNITA & the Funding Debate

The effects of destabilization on constructive engagement – and on Cuban troop withdrawal – led to another important decision in the region which was also to have a huge impact on the fortunes of Crocker's southern African policy. Washington had maintained an interest in the civil war in Angola since the Portuguese coup of 1974. The US had begun an attempt to determine the outcome as early as 1975, in order to ensure that the FNLA and UNITA would not lose out to the Marxist MPLA. In the wake of Vietnam, the attempt had soon been abandoned, however, much to the chagrin of America's right wing. The more conservative Republicans had been waiting for ten years to avenge the defeat of UNITA at the hands of the Soviet-backed MPLA. Yet again, circumstances beyond Crocker's control were about to deal a huge blow to his constructive engagement policy. This time, however, the circumstances were brought about by his colleagues in Washington.

Reagan's interest in Africa was limited to the role it would play in the Cold War, and this was reflected in his attitudes towards the Angolan parties. With Savimbi successfully presenting UNITA as anti-communist freedom fighters battling against a Soviet-imposed Marxist MPLA government, Reagan had no difficulty deciding whom America should support. In 1980, even before his appointment to the Presidency, Reagan stated: 'I don't see anything wrong with someone who wants to free themselves from the rule of an outside power which is Cubans and East Germans. I don't see why we shouldn't provide them with the weapons to do it.'[34] This comment sent an early signal of hope to Savimbi and heralded a major and divisive debate among American politicians regarding the funding of UNITA. Early actions confirmed the Reagan administration's positive stance. On 14–15 March 1981 Deputy Assistant Secretary for African Affairs Lannon Walker met privately with Savimbi in Morocco. This was followed in November 1981 by Savimbi visiting the US. As Chapter 8 demonstrated, Savimbi's anti-communist rhetoric was very effective in garnering support from conservative Republicans, both in the administration and on the Hill.

At the height of the debate on whether to resume funding to UNITA, Savimbi's carefully orchestrated 10-day visit to Washington – including a meeting with President Reagan at the White House on 30 January 1986 – was an important step. Savimbi took no chances. In a deal signed in the summer of 1985, he hired a well-connected lobbying firm – Black, Manafort, Stone and Kelly – under a $600,000-a-year public relations contract. For Savimbi it seems that the money was well spent. A *Washington Post* article commented on the way in which: 'He was meticulously coached on everything from how to answer his critics to how to complement his patrons.'[35] The article also commented on the fact that Savimbi received as much press and television exposure as a US Presidential candidate. Savimbi said the right things to gain US support, and in Washington he found a willing audience.

The Clark Amendment and the history of external funding
The history of the funding of the Angolan parties is a complex one. For the first nine months of 1975, after the Portuguese had withdrawn, the three Angolan political movements – the MPLA, the FNLA and UNITA – fought to gain overall control of Angola. Each group was receiving support from a variety of foreign donors in what Howard Wolpe described as a 'rapidly escalating' cycle. China, Zaïre and the US funded the FNLA and UNITA. South Africa armed and funded UNITA and actually invaded southern Angola. The Soviet Union armed the MPLA and Cuba dispatched 300 advisers and then 700 troops. During October and early November 1975, the MPLA was under threat from a South African invasion from the south and an FPLA/Zaïrian thrust from the north. The Cuban troops responded by sending in thousands of troops, which tipped

the balance in the MPLA's favour.

The timing for the US was critical. Although Holden Roberto's FNLA had had links with the CIA since 1962 (see Introduction), and received several hundred thousand dollars in support in January 1975, it was only after months of delay that this aid was extended to UNITA. In what Republicans condemned as a 'knee-jerk reaction to the withdrawal from Vietnam'[36] Congress adopted the Clark amendment – a ban on military aid to any Angolan party. When the amendment was passed in December 1975, it was originally adopted for one year. Fears that the US could find itself drawn into another costly and obscure venture meant that the ban was extended in 1976. Reagan's early comments regarding UNITA made it clear that he was not happy with this situation – and that the funding of UNITA would be just the sort of action prescribed by his 'Reagan Doctrine'. In the election year of 1980, questioned by the *Wall Street Journal* on aid to the Angolan rebels, Reagan stated flatly: 'Well, frankly, I would provide them with weapons.'[37]

The issue eventually came to a head during Reagan's campaigning for a second Presidential term in office in 1984. By the beginning of 1985 there were heated debates in Congress on the issue. A member of the House Subcommittee on African Affairs, the Republican Mark Siljander, asserted that the failure of Congress to repeal the Clark amendment 'forbids us to perform our responsibility ... of assisting democratic movements in the Third World'.[38] Secretary of State George Shultz went even further in a May 1985 Senate Hearing, stating that with the Clark amendment 'the Brezhnev Doctrine – which declares that Communist revolutions are irreversible – was, in effect, enacted into American law'.[39] Although Shultz disagreed with the restriction on executive power, an influential Conservative lobby was growing which wanted to take things further. Groups such as the Heritage Foundation and the Conservative Caucus were calling, not just for the repeal of the Clark amendment, but also for the resumption of funding to UNITA. The right-wing *Washington Times* endorsed this view in the media, and Reagan himself had made it clear that he would support such an approach. In the House, Siljander voiced the right wing's dissatisfaction with the direction southern African policy was taking. He complained that opponents of aid to UNITA argued against funding because UNITA was supported by an apartheid government, but they called for support to the ANC in spite of its strong communist links overseas.

For the Republicans, to whom communist sympathies were the litmus test of international actors, this approach simply did not make sense. The right wing was still hoping to overturn the defeat in Angola that had been so carelessly accepted during the US withdrawal of aid in 1975–6. Crocker described how funding UNITA had become a call for revenge and 'an article of Conservative faith'. One of the most ardent advocates of assisting UNITA was CIA Director William J. Casey. He was a vocal supporter of Savimbi, and visited him at his headquarters in Jamba, Angola in 1985. Crocker accused Casey of wanting to be Reagan's Secretary of State, commenting: 'If the political leadership tolerates it, the director of the CIA can try to be a rival foreign minister.' He was clearly furious at the way Casey attempted to undermine his policy in the region, and accused him of persuading Savimbi to stick to a hardline position just before Crocker presented his basis for negotiation in March 1985. The pro-funding lobby was given a boost when, in September 1985, Angolan forces expelled UNITA forces from Cazombo in the Moxico province of Angola. This spectre of a total UNITA defeat strengthened the pro-funding voices in the more conservative agencies – the Pentagon, the CIA and the NSC. Influential voices argued forcefully that the US could not allow UNITA to be decisively weakened. On 11 June 1985 the Senate voted 63 to 34 to repeal the Clark amendment. The surprise came when the House of Representatives followed suit, voting to overturn the amendment by 236 votes to 185 on 10 July 1985. The debate had always been a close-run thing, but with the Reagan Doctrine guiding policy towards Nicaragua, Afghanistan and Angola, and memories of Vietnam fading, the anomaly of the Clark amendment restricting Presidential action had been on borrowed time since the Senate had voted to repeal it in 1981. On 9 August 1985 President Reagan signed the Foreign Aid Authorization Bill, thereby repealing the 1976 Clark amendment.

The Resumption of Funding

Once the amendment was repealed, the debate over the resumption of funding began in earnest. In Congress, the right wing talked of '10 years of United States ambivalence toward the Cuban occupation of Angola'[40] and voiced fears of Cuban-Soviet expansion in the region. Opponents argued that aid to UNITA would ally the US too closely with the apartheid regime in South Africa and insisted that increased US intervention would result in increased Soviet and Cuban involvement. Opponents also questioned the perception of UNITA as a staunchly pro-US democratic organization.[41] The State Department had been openly supportive of the campaign to repeal the Clark amendment, agreeing that it placed an unusual and unwarranted restriction on the President's executive authority. This support did not extend to welcoming a resumption of funding to UNITA, however, and the department now found itself facing a battle to maintain control of its diplomacy-led policy in southern Africa.

When Representatives Pepper and Kemp sponsored a proposal for $27 million in non-lethal aid for UNITA, Shultz felt that the control of the State Department policy was being usurped by Congress. On 12 October 1985 he wrote a confidential letter to House Republican Minority Leader, Robert H. Michel (Republican, Illinois), asking him to oppose the legislation. Unfortunately for Shultz, Michel chose to reprint the letter and circulated it at the House of Representatives, along with a 'scathing denunciation of State Department policy toward UNITA'.[42] The main problem was that, for the State Department, any assistance would have been particularly ill-timed, as negotiations were at a delicate stage and Angola had recently been more open in discussing the possibility of a Cuban withdrawal. The Reagan administration agreed to postpone covert assistance as a sign of 'good faith' towards the State Department's US–Angolan negotiations which recommenced on 27 November 1985.

Nevertheless, on 1 October 1985 Congress introduced the Bill authorizing $27 million in humanitarian aid for UNITA, and, just after Savimbi's successful visit to Washington in January 1986, the White House announced that UNITA would receive $15 million of US military assistance during 1986. Crocker accused the Angolans of bringing it upon themselves by refusing to be more flexible in the negotiations. He was also irritated that Reagan had allowed the debate to degenerate into an inter-agency skirmish. The traditionally conservative agencies – the Department of Defense, the CIA and the NSC – had been allowed to override the State Department in what should have been an area of policy under State's control. Crocker was furious and blamed Reagan's lack of leadership for the result.

The diplomatic track of Crocker's policy was not the only target for the right-wing lobby groups. They were furious that American oil companies, Chevron in particular, were instrumental in propping up the Angolan government. They were the leading force in Angolan oil production (Chevron alone had $600 million in Angolan assets) and this in turn was responsible for the majority of the MPLA government's access to foreign exchange. The major conservative lobby groups launched a campaign to force Chevron to abandon its oil operations in Angola. Chevron claimed that the results of the campaign had been negligible and argued that it took no political position in Angola. Its operations were purely commercial. However, right-wing pressure did gain a victory when, in November 1986, Congress cancelled an agreement which had permitted companies operating in Angola to deduct taxes paid to Angola from their US taxes.

On 18 February 1986 the Reagan administration informed Congress that it had decided to provide UNITA with military aid and by June of that year the promised $15 million in military aid had been issued, including Stinger anti-aircraft missiles. By June 1987 UNITA had received a second grant of $15 million in covert military aid, which included more Stingers and TOW anti-tank missiles. Herman Cohen said that, from this point, US assistance to UNITA averaged about $25 million per year, although George Wright contends that the increase in aid was steeper – from $15 million in 1987 to $30 million in 1988 and $50 million in 1989.[43] Crocker points out that, in fact, these amounts of aid were tiny in comparison with the $1 billion of Soviet aid that was being channelled into Angola in the form of arms deliveries and in-country technical assistance. This then begs the question – what was the thinking behind providing aid if it was too small an amount to effect any significant change in outcome?

One of the major problems behind the aid allocation was this confusion regarding Washington's objectives in the region. There appeared to be no clarity of purpose behind the decision and much of the debate over funding involved a debate over just *what* Washington's objectives in the region were – and what they *should* be. Congressmen wanted to know if the aim was an eventual overthrow of the Angolan government, and if so, 'Will $27 million or $200 million or $20 billion be sufficient? How many people will be killed?... What will be the fruits of victory if victory is achieved?'[44] Crocker explained that the aid was more symbolic in reality.

Washington wanted to demonstrate that it was not prepared simply to abandon the region to Cuba and its allies. He also asserted that the aid was a coercive measure – a way to bring the Angolan government to the negotiating table. Cohen also explained the objectives of the aid in these terms. He stated that the Reagan administration never had the intention that Savimbi should defeat the government and take power. The aim was to create a hurting stalemate that would force all parties to the negotiating table.

Aid to UNITA – the Impact on Crocker's Policy

Crocker made it clear that he was sympathetic to UNITA. In Congress, he praised its long and brave fight against the Soviet and Cuban adventurism in Angola. He also stated: 'We intend to be supportive of UNITA ... as the President said in his State of the Union Message, we want to support all those who are fighting for freedom.'[45] The repeal of the Clark amendment was useful in sending a signal to Moscow, Havana and Luanda that Washington had options and the aid was useful as a signal of support and a morale booster for UNITA. In fact, however, when one assesses the impact this decision had on his own policy, it becomes apparent that this description of the aid as a useful symbol was not so much a statement of his beliefs, but rather putting a brave face on a decision that seriously undermined both Crocker himself and his constructive engagement policy in the region. The funding decision came at just the wrong time for Crocker. The Angolan government was beginning to demonstrate a level of flexibility, as seen in their Lusaka agreement the year before. It was also clear that the amount of aid given was not going to enable UNITA to win the war in Angola. As Barber pointed out, constructive engagement was supposed to reduce foreign intervention in the region rather than encourage more. In an especially damning assessment of the situation, Barber concluded: 'Steamrollered, Crocker would lamely explain (and tragically perhaps even come to believe) that the idea was to try and push Luanda back on to the "negotiating track".'[46]

Was this really a fair assessment of just how far US policy had strayed from Crocker's objectives? A policy of quiet diplomacy was certainly undermined by the decision to provide military aid to one of the parties. Earlier comments by Crocker himself appear to confirm that such funding did not fit into his constructive engagement strategy. When asked in an earlier interview (on 26 June 1985) about possible US aid or intervention in Angola, Crocker clearly stated: 'We are not playing a role, unlike some other parties I could think of who are intervening there, and we don't intend to.'[47] Crocker had also commented, in regard to South Africa's internal situation: 'We don't recognize movements and political parties ... we recognize governments.... It's not our business from 8,000 miles away to endorse ... one party out of many parties.'[48] This demonstrates how the decision to fund UNITA made it very difficult for him to maintain consistency in his policy towards South Africa's internal situation and his policy throughout the region.

The immediate result for Crocker of the decision to begin funding UNITA was that the Angolan government broke off talks in February 1986. They were not to recommence until more than a year later – on 7 April 1987. Another problem was that aid to UNITA painted Washington as an ally of Pretoria – a charge consistently levelled at constructive engagement and one that Crocker was always at pains to refute. Washington's relationships with the FLS were also damaged by the decision. The Organization of African Unity sent an *aide memoire* to the UN on 4 November 1985, noting with deep concern the action taken by the United States Congress in abrogating the Clark amendment. In the document, Rameschand Seereekissoon (Chairman of the African Group at the UN) drew the UN's attention to a declaration published by the Heads of State and Government of the OAU meeting in Addis Ababa in July 1985 which read: 'Any American covert or overt involvement in the internal affairs of the People's Republic of Angola, directly or through third parties, will be considered a hostile act against the Organization of African Unity.'[49]

Crocker was left in an impossible situation. In Congress he attempted to defend his policy, taking the opportunity to 'categorically state here that the basis and goals of our policy remain unchanged'. It is difficult, however, to see how a policy based on negotiation could remain unchanged in the light of the fact that one of the parties had broken off talks in direct response to another branch of Washington's policy. His difficulties in Congress continued, as he found himself defending a policy he had not directed. In March 1986, for example, when Crocker asserted: 'We do not associate ourselves in any way with those using violent means', Chairman Wolpe was quick to respond: 'Only in Angola.'[50]

Notes

1   Grundy, Kenneth W., *South Africa: Domestic Crisis and Global Challenge*, Boulder, San Francisco and Oxford: Westview Press, 1991, p. 118.
2   Olivier, Gerrit, 'Recent Developments in South African Foreign Policy', *Optima*, Vol. 36, No. 4 (December 1988), pp. 201–2.
3   'Pretoria's Bloody Friday', *South African Digest*, 27 May 1983, p. 3.
4   Jaster, Robert S., *South Africa in Namibia: The Botha Strategy*, Lanham, New York and London: University Press of America and Center for International Affairs, Harvard University, 1985, p. 44. The quotation from Botha is taken from *P. W. Botha: A Political Backgrounder*, London: South African Embassy, 1978.
5   Bender, Gerald J. 'Peacemaking in Southern Africa: the Luanda–Pretoria Tug-of-War', *Third World Quarterly*, Vol. 11, No. 1 (January 1989), p. 16.
6   Dale, Richard, 'Melding War and Politics in Namibia: South Africa's Counterinsurgency Campaign, 1966–1989', *Armed Forces and Society*, Vol. 20, No. 1 (Fall 1993), p. 11.
7   See Barber, James and J. Barratt, *South Africa's Foreign Policy*, Cambridge: Cambridge University Press, 1990, p. 153.
8   Riley, Eileen, *Major Political Events in South Africa 1948–1990*, Oxford and New York: Facts on File 1991, p. 175.

9   Commonwealth Secretariat, *Racism in Southern Africa: The Commonwealth Stand*, London: The Commonwealth Secretariat, 1985, p. 16.

10 As quoted in Riley, *Major Political Events*, p. 182. As stated at a SADC conference in Lesotho held on 27 January 1983.

11 Makoni, Simba, 'SADCC's New Strategy', *Africa Report*, May–June 1987, p. 32.

12 Barber and Barratt, *South Africa's Foreign Policy*, p. 294.

13 See Mokoena, Kenneth (ed.), *South Africa and the United States: The Declassified History*, a National Security Archive documents reader, New York: The New Press, 1993, p. 29: 'Department of State Bulletin, Security Council Meeting on Angola, 5 September 1981, p. 18.

14 Crocker, Chester, *High Noon in Southern Africa: Making Peace in a Rough Neighborhood*, New York and London: W. W. Norton and Company, 1992, p. 105.

15 *Ibid.*, p. 170.

16 *Namibia: Internal Repression and US Diplomacy* Hearing before the Subcommittee on Africa of the Committee on Foreign Affairs, House of Representatives, 99th Congress, First Session, 21 February 1985, Washington: US Government Printing Office, 1985, p. 30.

17 Crocker, *High Noon in Southern Africa*, p. 170.

18 Thompson, Alex, *Incomplete Engagement: United States Foreign Policy towards the Republic of South Africa 1981–1988*, Aldershot and Brookfield: Avebury, 1996, p. 172.

19 Marsden, E., 'US Plans "Cordon"', *Sunday Times*, 10 October 1982, p. 22.

20 Mokoena, *South Africa and the United States*, p. 184.

21 Ronald Reagan Library, CA. White House Staff and Office Files: Cohen, Herman J., Files 1987–8. African Affairs Directorate, NSC. Box No. 92241. Background Report – For: Robert McFarlane. Subject: Congressional Briefings arranged for 21 May 1985 and 23 May 1985.

22 Crocker, Chester 'Southern Africa: Eight Years Later', *Foreign Affairs*, Vol. 68, No. 4 (1989), p. 150.

23 Coker, Christopher, *The United States and South Africa 1968–1985: Constructive Engagement and its Critics*, Durham, NC: Duke University Press, 1986. See especially pp. 228–30.

24 Ronald Reagan Library, CA. Executive Secretariat, NSC: Records Boxes 91340 and 91343. Secret Memorandum – From: Phillip Ringdahl. To: Robert McFarlane. Subject: South Africa – Your Meeting with Crocker and Nickel, 3 July 1985. Declassified 7 June 1999.

25 Ronald Reagan Library, CA. White House Staff and Office Files: Cohen, Herman J., Files 1987–8. African Affairs Directorate, NSC. Boxes 91875 and 91876. Cable. From: Secretary of State. To: American Embassies Southern Africa. Subject: Southern Africa Update, June 1985.

26 *Ibid.* The cable continued that Washington was particularly displeased because 'the Botswana government had indicated its willingness to be cooperative in resolving those complaints'.

27 Ronald Reagan Library, CA. Memorandum – From: Phillip Ringdahl. To: Robert McFarlane. Subject: South Africa – Your Meeting with Crocker and Nickel 3 July 1985.

28 *Namibia: Internal Repression and US Diplomacy* Congressional Hearing, 21 February 1985, p. 2.

29 Mokoena, *South Africa and the United States*, p. 182.

30 As quoted in Baker, Pauline H., *The United States and South Africa: The Reagan Years. Update South Africa: Time Running Out*, Ford Foundation and Foreign Policy Association, 1989, p. 52.

31 Ronald Reagan Library, CA. Cable from Secretary of State. Subject: Southern Africa Update, June 1985.

32 Riley, *Major Political Events*, p. 175.

33 Bender, 'Peacemaking in Southern Africa', p. 16.

34 As quoted in Wright, George, *The Destruction of a Nation: US Policy Toward Angola since 1945*, London and Chicago: Pluto Press, 1997, p. 103.

35 Tyler, P. E., 'The Selling of Jonas Savimbi: Success and a $600,000 Tab', *Washington Post*, 9 February 1986.

36 Statement by Stratton in *Angola: Intervention or Negotiation* Hearings before the Sub-committee on Africa of the Committee on Foreign Affairs, House of Representatives, 99th Congress, First Session, 31 October and 12 November 1985, p. 78.

37 Hunt, A. R. and Bray, T., 'An Interview with Ronald Reagan', *Wall Street Journal*, 6 May 1980, p. 26. Reagan later described UNITA as 'a black liberation movement which seeks for Angolans the same right to be represented in their government that black South Africans seek for themselves'. 'Ending Apartheid in South Africa', address by President Ronald Reagan, 22 July 1986. US Department of State, Bureau of Public Affairs. Reproduced in Baker, *The United States and South Africa*, Appendix C, p. 128. Reagan did not, however, address the logical question that this comment seemed to raise – if that was the case, why not fund the ANC too?

38 *Namibia: Internal Repression and US Diplomacy* Congressional Hearing 21 February 1985, p. 3.

39 *United States Policy Toward South Africa* Hearings before the Committee on Foreign Relations, United States Senate, 24 April, 2 May and 22 May 1985, p. 60.

40 See Siljander testimony in *Angola: Intervention or Negotiation* Congressional Hearings, 31 October and 12 November, p. 7.

41 See, for example, Bender, *Angola: Intervention or Negotiation* Congressional Hearings, 31 October and 12 November, p. 40: 'No American citizen or property has been touched by the [Angolan] government. Any destruction of American property or murder of American citizens in Angola has been carried out by South Africa and by UNITA.' See also Baker, *The United States and South Africa*, p. 54 for a discussion of the views held in Congress.

42 James III, W. Martin, *A Political History of the Civil War in Angola 1974–1990*, New Brunswick, NJ and London: Transaction Publishers, 1992, p. 167. In the letter, Shultz had asserted that 'there are better ways to help'. Crocker says that this was code for covert action, but the truth was that his diplomatic track would have been badly damaged if any hint of assistance had been leaked.

43 Wright, G., *Destruction of a Nation*, p. 127.

44 Testimony of Ted Weiss, Representative from the State of New York, *Angola: Intervention or Negotiation* Congressional Hearings, 31 October 1985, p.115. For a further discussion of the funding of UNITA see particularly the testimony of Randall Robinson of TransAfrica in *ibid.*, pp. 31–2. See also the testimony of Representative Stephen Solarz in *ibid.*, pp. 73–5, which raises the point that aid to UNITA was more likely to increase the number of Cuban troops in Angola.

45 *Angola: Options for American Foreign Policy* Hearing Before the Committee on Foreign Relations, US Senate, 99th Congress, Second Session, 18 February 1986, p. 5.

46 Barber, Simon, 'Shadows on the Wall', *Optima*, Vol. 35, No. 2 (June 1987), p. 74.

47 ARC Identifier: 59701, *Role of the US in Southern Africa – Crocker, 1985*. Creator: United States Information Agency (1982–) (Most Recent). Broadcast 26 June 1985. Item from Record Group 306: Records of the USIA 1900–1988. Video Recordings from the 'Worldnet Today' Program Series. NAIL Locator: 306-WNET-128 Motion Picture, Sound and Video Recordings LICON, National Archives at College Park, Maryland USA.

48 ARC Identifier: 59926, *Current Situation in South Africa – Crocker 1987*. Creator: United States Information Agency (1982–) (Most Recent). Broadcast 27 February 1987. Item from Record Group 306: Records of the USIA 1900–1988. Video Recordings from the 'Worldnet Today' Program Series. NAIL Locator: 306-WNET-356 Motion Picture, Sound and Video Recordings LICON, National Archives at College Park, Maryland USA.

49 *Aide memoire* from OAU to UN, 4 November 1985, as reprinted in *Angola: Intervention or Negotiation* Congressional Hearings, 31 October 1985, p. 82.

50 *Developments in South Africa: United States Policy Responses* Hearing before the Sub-committee on Africa of the Committee on Foreign Affairs, House of Representatives, 12 March 1986, p. 113.

10
Factors Behind
the Angolan/Namibian Settlement

The Final Settlement

By the middle of 1986 Crocker's diplomacy was seriously undermined, and temporarily derailed, by circumstances beyond his control. These circumstances, however, were not the product of decisions made by foreign governments or the United Nations, or even by the business community. The hiatus in his constructive engagement was caused by decisions made in Washington itself. Chapter 2 discussed how the Congressional victory in passing the Comprehensive Anti-Apartheid Act in 1986 caused a deep divide in the Washington–Pretoria relationship. The decision to resume funding UNITA in January 1986 after the repeal of the Clark amendment equally drove a rift between Washington and the MPLA government in Angola. Under these circumstances, the talks on the regional settlement were suspended, as none of the parties involved trusted Washington as a mediator. In fact it was external circumstances that once again combined with Crocker's own diplomatic skill and determination to reverse this situation. The Reagan–Gorbachev Summits of 1987 and 1988 signified a gradual thawing of US–USSR relations and, sensing the opportunity, Crocker returned to Angola on 14 July 1987 in the hope of rescuing the linkage negotiations. The Angolan government responded positively by issuing a new set of proposals on 4 August 1987. The new moves, combined with increased international pressure on South Africa to withdraw its forces from Angola, resulted in a South African announcement on 5 December 1987 of its intention to withdraw its troops. The fighting continued, however, both in Angola's civil war and with South Africa's attacks on SWAPO from southern Angola.

Meanwhile, Crocker's re-started diplomacy was beginning to progress. On 28 January 1988 a series of talks began in Lusaka and, for the first time, senior Cuban officials were also present. The talks resulted in a significant achievement when Angola and Cuba agreed in principle, for the first time, to the eventual total withdrawal of the approximately 40,000 Cuban troops from Angolan soil. For the next six months the military and diplomatic tracks proceeded in tandem.[1] On 1 June 1988 Crocker visited the Deputy Soviet Foreign Minister Anatoly Adamishin in Moscow. They declared a deadline of 29 September 1988 for achieving an international accord on a southern African peace settlement.

While the civil war in Angola continued, the negotiations progressed.

Crocker and Adamishin met again in Geneva on 31 July and 1 August 1988 to prepare for the next round of negotiations scheduled to commence the following day. Adamishin commented that he believed there was a positive momentum forming in the search for a settlement. Adamishin's optimism was well-founded. In a press conference at the end of the year, Crocker described the understandings achieved at Geneva as playing: '… a major role in bringing about a de-escalation of military tensions along the Angola–Namibia border and in southern Angola'.[2] It was the South Africans who had seized the initiative in Geneva that August. They came to the talks armed with their 'comprehensive review' of the situation and proposed 1 November 1988 as 'D-Day' – the start of the implementation of UNSCR 435. The UN plan stipulated that Namibian elections would be held seven months later. All SADF units would have had to leave Namibia by this point, and the South Africans proposed a parallel Cuban withdrawal from Angola. The other significant element of the South Africans' proposals was a *de facto* ceasefire – to commence on 10 August 1988. The Angolans and Cubans did not table their proposal for the Cuban withdrawal timetable (which had merely been a reduction from 48 to 42 months) and the Cuban withdrawal issue was set aside until the next round of negotiations. The ceasefire proposal, however, had a more immediate effect. Crocker described the breakthrough thus: 'These military steps unlocked the way to broader progress … we had effectively ended the war ….'[3] The Angolan, Cuban and South African governments announced the ceasefire on 8 August 1988, although the main deficiency of the ceasefire was the fact that neither SWAPO nor UNITA had been involved in the decision. During the same announcement, the target date of 1 November 1988 was established for the implementation of UNSCR 435 – although it was later renegotiated to 1 April 1989.

The Joint Monitoring Commission (JMC) was established to oversee the implementation of any agreement. The JMC would consist of members from South Africa, Angola and Cuba – with the US and the USSR as observers. The JMC was officially formed on 15 August 1988 when the officials met at Raucana on the Angola–Namibia border. It was not long before the agreements, to be overseen by the JMC, took on a more definite form. On 13 December 1988 the South African, Cuban and Angolan governments signed the Brazzaville Protocol, in the Congolese capital. The agreement was of great significance, establishing 1 April 1989 as the beginning of Namibia's transition to independence. The phased withdrawal of Cuban troops was to start at this time, and be completed by July 1991. The Namibian election was scheduled for 1 November 1989, and would proceed under UN supervision. By this point, half of the Cuban troops should have departed, and the remainder would be confined to north of the 13th parallel. The South Africans were to remove almost all of their 60,000 strong force within a week of the elections – with only 1,500 to remain at that stage.

The final treaty signings took place on 22 December 1988, and were based on the agreements known as the New York Principles – these were the commitments to implement UNSCR 435 and the Cuban withdrawal timetable agreed at a meeting between the parties in New York in July 1988. There were two signings reflecting the agreements reached in the New York Principles. The trilateral agreement between South Africa, Cuba and Angola committed the parties, through a binding treaty, to the undertakings that had been agreed in New York: the implementation of UNSCR 435 and the commitment to Cuban troop withdrawal. The second treaty was a bilateral treaty between Angola and Cuba, which formalized the timetables and details of the Cuban troop withdrawal.

On 10 January 1989 the Cubans began their withdrawal from Angola, while Namibia was preparing for its transitional phase to commence on 1 April. Unfortunately, the commencement of the transition phase resulted in some of the bloodiest fighting of Namibia's struggle for independence. South Africa detected up to 1,200 SWAPO fighters infiltrating Namibia from Angola – in clear violation of the ceasefire agreement. South Africa hunted down the guerrillas and killed more than 250 of them, injuring hundreds more.[4] Nevertheless, by November, as planned, Namibia's first non-racial elections took place to elect a 72-seat assembly to draft Namibia's new constitution. Although SWAPO was victorious (with 57.3 per cent of the vote and 41 seats) it did not obtain the two-thirds majority needed to draft the constitution alone. Sam Nujoma made it clear, however, that he was happy to cooperate with his political rivals – the largest of which was the Pretoria-backed Democratic Turnhalle Alliance, with 28.5 per cent of the vote and 21 seats.

In fact the discussions did proceed cordially, and on 20 December 1989 the final document was agreed in principle. Namibia would be a multi-party democracy with an executive President, a Bill of Rights and an independent judiciary. The bicameral Parliament was to be elected by proportional representation. Nujoma made a significant gesture by offering positions in his Cabinet to members of Namibia's six other political parties. On 31 January 1990 the assembly announced that the day of Namibian independence would be 21 March 1990. In Angola the last of the Cuban troops departed on 24 May 1991. Exactly a week later the MPLA government and UNITA signed a peace agreement ending the 16-year civil war and preparing Angola for democracy.

Almost 10 years after Crocker first outlined his 'linkage' strategy in the context of his constructive engagement policy, the Cubans were out of Angola and Namibia had achieved its independence. The signing of the peace accords on 22 December 1988 has been called Crocker's 'finest hour'.[5] The settlement had been reached and it reflected his linkage strategy: the Cubans had withdrawn from Angola and, in return, the South Africans had withdrawn from Namibia, granting its independence at last. When assessing the settlement, however, it is important to determine the extent to which this linkage approach had actually helped to achieve it. Much praise had been afforded to Crocker for achieving both Namibian independence and Cuban withdrawal. To understand the significance of his role, however, one must first ask: what were the other factors that played a role in the settlement – and how important was their role? The following section begins by looking at the impact of the linkage strategy and its effect on the final negotiations. It will then address the key question of what other factors, if any, contributed to achieving the final settlement.

The Impact of the Linkage Strategy

One of the most contentious aspects of linkage is whether it hastened or delayed the settlement of the Namibian independence issue. Critics of linkage complain that South Africa could have been persuaded or cajoled into accepting the UNSCR 435 settlement by 1981, if the Reagan administration had not made it clear that by procrastinating, Pretoria would obtain a far more beneficial settlement under the new administration in Washington.[6] Crocker, on the other hand, explained that linkage was a vital approach in that it addressed the needs of *all* the parties involved – only by achieving this could Washington begin to mediate a settlement that no-one would want to wreck. Crocker's deputy, Charles Freeman, outlined the way in which such a settlement could successfully address the objectives of each party. He explained that the MPLA would gain a security buffer once the South Africans were out of Namibia; South Africans would achieve their objective of getting the Cubans out of Angola, as would UNITA; Cuba would receive credit for securing Namibian independence; and the Soviets would improve relations with the West and would be saved from the expense of financing the war. Indeed, this final consideration of expenses was of vital importance to all the groups involved.

Critics of the linkage approach denounced its unethical stance, complaining that handing South Africa a further delaying tactic would only result in more suffering for the Namibian people. Lawyers pointed out that the approach was illegal under international law. South Africa was already obliged to fulfil the provisions of UNSCR 435, without sovereign governments such as Angola and Cuba being forced to make further concessions. Observers stated that it was likely to be unworkable due to Cuban and South African intransigence – and FLS opposition. Yet, despite the criticisms, the negotiations held under the auspices of the linkage approach made good headway. The *quid pro quo* of Cuban withdrawal was successful in persuading South Africa to enter into the negotiations in a more positive frame of mind. During 1981 and 1982, talks between Pretoria and Washington succeeded in resolving many of the outstanding issues in UNSCR 435 to which South Africa had previously objected. The election formula, the monitoring of the settlement and the composition of the international peacekeeping forces had all been resolved by July 1982.

The feared South African intransigence began to surface, however, and Angola frustrated Crocker by refusing to present an acceptable timetable for Cuban withdrawal, even after they had accepted the notion of linking the withdrawal of Cuban forces to Namibian independence. Unhappily for Crocker, the unravelling of his diplomacy coincided with, and was caused by, events beyond his control. While the left wing undermined his dialogue with South Africa by the passing of the Comprehensive Anti-

Apartheid Act in 1986, the same year saw the right wing's victory over the liberals in the administration, including the State Department, on the issue of funding UNITA. It was not until late 1987 that Crocker managed to regain his hold on policy and re-start the negotiations. It was at this point that the efficacy of the linkage approach was demonstrated. In January 1988 the Cubans joined the negotiations and accepted the principle of total Cuban withdrawal from Angola. The fact that the South Africans, Cubans and Angolans all had items on the agenda to their benefit was vital in re-starting the stalled negotiations.

After the final settlement was signed on 22 December 1988, Charles Freeman described the way in which the negotiators: 'raised their glasses to the historic achievements of an American mediation effort that they had spent nearly a decade denigrating and obstructing'.[7] Crocker, in his work on the US role in African peacemaking, said of the Angola/Namibia settlement that linkage 'was the specific key to success in this instance'.[8] The eventual resolution and signing of the Angola/Namibia accords was a dramatic and significant achievement. But what role was played by Crocker's linkage strategy in the negotiation process, and what contribution was made by the other parties interested in achieving a settlement?

The Negotiating Process

One of the major stumbling blocks during the course of the negotiations – particularly in the initial stages – was the deep mistrust between East and West. The Reagan administration was hoping to thwart the expansionist ambitions of the Soviet Union: Washington saw Cuba as an enemy on its doorstep, and the MPLA was viewed with deep suspicion by the American government. Although there was much constructive dialogue between American businessmen and diplomats and the Angolan government during the 1980s, the US government remained ideologically opposed and hostile towards it. Indeed, with hindsight Crocker himself admits that 'a cool analysis of the situation in 1981 might suggest we should have talked to Moscow (or Cuba)'.[9] However, it was not just the Americans who were hostile to the inclusion of the Soviet or Cuban parties to the negotiations. The South Africans were intensely suspicious of both governments, and viewed the Cuban presence in Angola as part of the perceived Communist total onslaught, threatening South Africa and its Western interests. By 1988 the Cubans and the Soviets were being invited to participate in the negotiations, but even at this late stage, President Botha was still defiant. In an interview with the *Washington Times* on 14 March 1988 he stated that South Africa would remain in Angola until the Cubans left.

Splits in the South African camp hindered progress further. The civilian and military staff argued bitterly over the direction Pretoria's southern Africa policy should take, with some in the security forces deeply opposed to sitting down and talking with the Cubans or the Soviets. Soon, however, events overtook the negotiations. The winds of change were about to alter the equation dramatically: in a year when Botha had been insisting adamantly that South Africa would not cease its incursions into Angola, the peace accords were finally signed.

The Soviet contribution

When evaluating the importance of the contribution of each actor in the negotiations, probably the most significant factor of all was the radical change in Soviet foreign policy thinking. Gorbachev came to power determined to address the question of Soviet priorities. He had been horrified to discover just how much Moscow had been spending on its overseas adventures and military commitments in the Third World. He wanted to use these same resources to address the domestic problems in the USSR – particularly the faltering economy. Gorbachev heralded a seismic change in Moscow's approach: instead of looking either to gain influence in regional disputes or, at least, to reduce American influence – Moscow now wanted to cooperate with the US in order to solve these disputes. The Soviet Deputy Foreign Minister Anatoly Adamishin explained to Crocker in a meeting on 21 March 1988 that Moscow was keen to help the progress of the negotiations – and would not seek 'ideological purity'.[10] Cohen stated that the Soviets even made it clear to Washington that the costs of funding the war were no longer in line with Soviet policy, and that they were ready to work for a settlement. When the formal negotiations between Angola, Cuba and South Africa began in London in May 1988, the Soviet Union was invited as an observer.

Crocker's evaluation of the Soviet contribution is somewhat mixed. When asked directly if the Soviets helped to achieve a settlement, Crocker replied: 'No, not really.' He stated that the Russians just 'made sure to get on the train as it was leaving the station'.[11] In *High Noon in Southern Africa* he says that it was difficult to pinpoint the Soviet contribution. In one sense, they were 'hitching a ride' on American diplomacy, but he does concede that Soviet involvement strengthened Washington's hand with each of the parties. However, he still qualifies any credit that the Soviets are given. Of the praise given at the time, Crocker says: 'We gave them credit to keep them sweet.' He explained that credit, even unwarranted, is worth it if you want to keep someone involved in your diplomacy. Herman Cohen, present with Crocker at the linkage negotiations, has a more positive view of the Soviet contribution. He states that they were helpful and very important in achieving a settlement: 'Crocker was turning to them constantly: "Go see the Angolans and talk some sense into them". And sometimes the Cubans were stubborn: "Go see the Cubans and explain that what Crocker is proposing is sensible".'[12]

Overall, it appears that the Russians did provide significant assistance in achieving the settlement. Although there is some measure of contention regarding the role played by the Soviets in the actual discussions, one factor must not be overlooked. The regional situation in Angola and Namibia was a surrogate war with the Soviets and Cubans on one side, pitted against the Americans and South Africans on the other. It is for this reason that the advent of Gorbachev's 'new thinking' was so vital.

Once the major partner of the Eastern coalition in the war decided to find an honourable exit from its regional entanglements, both super-powers decided to channel their energies into a settlement – and they had the power to achieve it. The regional players may have fought on (as happened in Angola), but the withdrawal of their patrons meant that the international significance of their struggle was greatly reduced, and the attention of the international community was soon directed else-where. General observers assumed that the worst of the southern African region's problems were now over, thanks to the Angola/Namibia settlement.

The Cubans join the talks

The other major factor in the course of the negotiations came when the Cubans were allowed to join. During the first half of 1987, the Cubans had little control over the direction of the stalled negotiations, or the struggling military campaign. However, Crocker describes the second half of 1987 as the Cubans' magic moment. As the Cubans had not been directly involved in the negotiations, they were free to take over the leader-ship of the communist allies – without being tainted by failed stratagems. Castro was also undertaking to tip the military balance by sending another 15,000 Cuban troops to Angola (see below). The Cubans were in a better position when, on 28 January 1988, they joined the negotiations in Lusaka for the first time.

The Cubans were unusual in that theirs was probably the only delega-tion at the table not struggling with factions and infighting back home. As Crocker pointed out: 'Castro had the clearest strategy of any of the parties.' The Cuban delegation was also helped by the fact that the head of their negotiating team, Carlos Aldana Escalante, made a very good impression – he was an excellent negotiator and won the confidence and respect of the other parties. He gave an important speech stressing the 'sovereign nature' of each country's contribution, and recognized the importance of each delegation's domestic audience. The Americans and South Africans were impressed and the South Africans openly saluted his contribution. Like the Soviets, the Cubans proved to be of vital impor-tance during the negotiations. Crocker praised their contribution, saying that Castro's clear strategy pulled Angola along in its wake. The South Africans had no such clarity, and 'might still be at the table today if it wasn't for the Cuban factor'.[13]

The Angolan delegation was suspicious of the negotiation process – and particularly of the US role as mediator. On 18 March 1986 President dos Santos had written to the UN Secretary-General Javier Pérez de Cuéllar to request that the UN take over the coordination of the Namibian negotia-tions. Dos Santos stated that Washington's open support of South Africa and funding of UNITA 'jeopardized its credibility as a mediator'.[14] Nevertheless, after meetings with Secretary of State Shultz in Washington, the Angolan delegation announced on 22 June 1988 that Angola was willing to negotiate the issue of Cuban troop withdrawal from its territory without first getting assurances that the US would cease its assistance to

UNITA. This was a vital step in the progress of the negotiations. This Angolan flexibility was essential in the face of American intransigence regarding the funding of UNITA.

Although the contributions of all parties were vital to a successful outcome, one must not overlook the tireless effort of Crocker himself in bringing the negotiations about. Berridge singles out the third round of talks at Cairo, on 24–25 June 1988, as being where 'the importance of Crocker's mediation was perhaps seen most vividly'.[15] There were reports of a build-up of Cuban troops at the Namibian border, and there was a rise in military tension in southern Angola. Berridge asserted: 'Had it not been for the presence of Crocker, it seems highly likely that the negotiations would have foundered in Cairo.' His ceaseless efforts to bring the parties together and to guard against a breakdown of talks were essential. At a conference held in July 1992 to evaluate the Namibian peace process, the Head of the Soviet delegation, Adamishin, stated: 'Victory has many pretenders, defeat only one. Had the Namibia operation ended in failure, only Chester Crocker would have been here. But the winners are many, so let us not divide the victory.'[16]

The Military Campaigns

The importance of the military dimension alters depending on who is doing the analysis. At some points, Crocker recognizes its significance. He says that the early stages of his negotiations were affected by the military situation. By mid-1983 the MPLA were under immense pressure in the civil war, and Crocker characterized this changing military balance as distracting dos Santos, and as damaging the MPLA's ability to pursue Washington's diplomatic strategy. Yet the real impact of military achievements came during the endgame – from mid-1987 to mid-1988.

The beginning of the end came in late summer of 1987. The Soviet Union instigated a major MPLA offensive against UNITA, attempting to capture the town of Mavinga near the Lomba River. The size of the attack was unprecedented, and it was backed by huge amounts of Soviet military hardware. There was virtually no Cuban input for this attack. The result was a fiasco for the Angolan government and their Soviet backers. The South Africans did not stand by and allow UNITA to be beaten. Not only did Pretoria move to help UNITA achieve a decisive defeat of the government forces, but the South African government was also 'tempted to go for a knock-out blow against the MPLA at Cuito Cuanavale'.[17] UNITA and the South Africans continued their offensive against the retreating Angolans, inflicting serious losses. UNITA claimed that the Angolans had lost 2,032 troops, 156 armoured vehicles and 26 combat aircraft.

The combined UNITA and South African forces drove the government troops back to Cuito Cuanavale, the MPLA's southernmost fortified air-base. Thus began a protracted siege, with the South African government and UNITA hoping to defeat the government troops and force a surrender at Cuito. Castro, however, had other ideas. He had not agreed with the initial Soviet offensive in the late summer of 1987, and had not therefore suffered Angolan criticism or loss of confidence with the defeat. He took the opportunity to reverse the losses the Angolan government had suffered. In a dramatic move, Cuba sent a further 15,000 troops to assist the approximately 10,000 Angolan troops under siege at Cuito. Rather than another contingent of young and inexperienced soldiers, Castro – for the first time – committed experienced frontline troops. This move tipped the balance, but it was a gamble, as Castro was not in a position to maintain such levels of support indefinitely. However, Castro was hoping that his decision not to allow an Angolan government defeat would force South Africa to reassess its options in Angola. Cuban planning proved successful in this stand-off, because the plan to alleviate the situation at Cuito Cuanavale involved sending a large proportion of the 15,000 well-equipped Cubans deep into south-west Angola near the Namibian border. Until this point, this area had been 'SADF's unimpeded hunting ground against SWAPO'.[18] The Cuban move created the threat that SADF forces could be cut off inside Angola by the Cuban forces stationed on the Namibian border.

Another decisive blow to Pretoria came with the realization that South Africa had lost air superiority over the Cuban and MPLA forces. During the fighting at Cuito the Cubans and Angolans, equipped with radar, shot down two out of South Africa's twelve operational fighter aircraft. Baker describes South Africa's loss of air superiority as the most significant result of the clashes. International embargoes meant that lost aircraft were very difficult to replace. It was over the skies of Angola that South Africa fully realized that apartheid had a real cost – they were falling behind technologically.

Pretoria also faced a vital domestic battle – opposition to the war in Angola was mounting among the white electorate. Angola was extremely hostile terrain for the combat forces and the inadequate infrastructure rendered the logistics of troop support very difficult. Although South African casualties were small compared to the losses suffered by the rest of the warring parties (31 soldiers from July 1987 to the end of 1988), this relatively small number was still politically unacceptable to Botha's domestic constituency, which was beginning to wonder *why* the war was being fought.

As the siege of Cuito Cuanavale settled into a costly stalemate, the parties began to question the value of their positions. Once the Cubans had joined the frontline battle in earnest, the war had the potential to escalate, but the troops remained balanced. This would simply result in an expensive extension of the war, to no-one's definitive advantage. Pretoria had demonstrated that it would not abandon UNITA, but it was facing an uncomfortable choice of either defeat or stalemate at Cuito. The problem facing each party now was how to make an honourable exit. The Cubans, from their position of relative strength (Angola was financing their troops and their territory was not under threat) joined Angola in talks with the US in January 1988. For the first time, they were prepared to discuss total

Cuban withdrawal in return for Namibian independence under UNSCR 435. In the summer of 1988 Pretoria made a crucial decision – they would withdraw from Angola and concentrate on the negotiations. The New York Principles, negotiated during July 1988, set down the goals of territorial integrity and non-interference in internal affairs. This laid the groundwork for the ceasefire agreed in Geneva in August 1988. By the end of August, the siege of Cuito Cuanavale was over and South African units had pulled back across the Namibian border.

Crocker was reluctant to identify the importance of the military campaigns in achieving a final settlement. When questioned on the significance of the Cuban intervention in Cuito Cuanavale, he explained that when the Cubans played their cards in 1987, it was Castro's recognition that Angola was a quagmire. Christopher Pycroft described how Crocker characterized the Cuito standoff as a 'legend' created by Fidel Castro and 'sold to the gullible liberal press'.[19] Crocker does not allow that Cuito Cuanavale held a strategic importance for either UNITA or SADF. The legend, he maintains, only went uncontested by Washington at the time as it provided the Cubans with an escape route in the form of an honourable exit.

Although one must heed Brian Wood's warning against a belief in monocausality in the settlement negotiations, particularly when assessing the significance of Cuito Cuanavale, it can certainly be argued that the military stand-off was one of the most significant factors behind the final settlement. The prospect of an indefinite, unwinnable war was politically and economically unacceptable, and the realization of this fact was what finally drove the parties to the negotiating table. A Defense Intelligence Agency report stated that it was the Cuban build-up of forces that had: 'provided new impetus to peace negotiations and resulted in the December 1988 accords among South Africa, Angola and Cuba'.[20] Peter Vale goes further when he questions the notion of linkage, and asserts: 'it seems precisely the opposite of Cuban withdrawal which brought about Namibia's independence. Had Castro not bolstered his troops in Angola … would the South Africans have agreed to withdraw?'[21]

The Role of Internal Pressure

The strategy of linkage itself, the role of the parties in the negotiations and the military campaigns were all instrumental in affecting the eventual Angola/Namibia peace accords. However, the 'most forgotten determinants' of the 1988 peace accords were 'the actions of the Namibian people'.[22] Wood identifies the two largest-ever worker stayaways in South Africa (6–8 June 1988) and Namibia (20–21 June 1988) and the campaigns of civil disobedience as being very effective in forcing concessions from P. W. Botha and making him re-evaluate South Africa's presence in Namibia. He accuses the censored media of underestimating SWAPO/PLAN's successes against the SADF. Afrikaner businessmen were also impressed by SWAPO's overtures to business leaders from 1986 onwards. From mid-1988, SWAPO made public statements allaying fears about nationalization of Namibia's companies after independence. Wright also pointed out that the internal opposition to apartheid within South Africa – and the domestic crisis it caused – also forced South Africa to reassess its regional policies in the light of how far it could stretch its security apparatus in the suppressing of internal discontent.

Charles Freeman, however, does not recognize the veracity of Wood's complaint that the actions of the Namibian people were overlooked. On the contrary, he categorically denies that internal opposition *had* been a significant factor. When SWAPO decided to cross the Angola/Namibia border the very day after the Geneva ceasefire accords of August 1988, Freeman argues, the attack could have been undertaken in order to lay a basis for the myth 'that armed struggle inside Namibia had made a decisive contribution to independence, when it had not'.[23]

The Impact of Economic Factors

The impact of cost and economics affected all the parties. In South Africa in particular, the economy was facing obstacles at every turn. With South Africa's reserve bank warning that Pretoria would have difficulty in meeting its foreign debt payments, Botha announced that South Africa faced a $4 billion loss of capital over the next five years. Sanctions were also taking their toll, as has been seen in the question of South African military technology and air power in Angola. The war in Angola and the occupation of Namibia were expensive undertakings – and Pretoria was fast running out of foreign exchange.

The problem of financing the war itself was not restricted to South Africa alone. In 1986, just as Luanda was embracing the military route in earnest, a dramatic fall in the price of oil made things very difficult for the government. Oil accounted for 80 per cent of the government's foreign exchange, and Luanda was forced to adopt stringent austerity measures, just as it most needed the support of the people. This dramatic loss of foreign exchange also severely hampered its ability to meet the cost of the Soviet arms deliveries. As the debt to Moscow rose, the burden of this debt was shouldered by the Soviets too. It was mainly the huge cost ($1 billion in Angola) of the involvement that made Gorbachev reassess the Soviet role there. The only party in a potentially stronger position was Havana, as it had been receiving up to $1,000 per month from the MPLA government for each soldier it sent to Angola. However, as the Angolan economy continued to falter, and Luanda ran out of foreign exchange, the financial costs of involvement were set to rise dramatically for Cuba.

The fact was that a timely combination of factors was altering the perceptions and priorities of all the parties. One of the most fundamental changes, and the most significant of all in this instance, was the thawing of Soviet–US relations and the imminent collapse of the Soviet Union. The international aspect of the war in Angola and the battle for Namibian independence had all been linked, in part, to the Cold War and fears of the spread of communism in the region – fears held by Pretoria and Washington alike. The military stalemate created largely by Castro's decision to increase his troop deployment in Angola provided the catalyst that finally drove all the parties to the table. As the escalating costs of the war threatened to spiral indefinitely, the balance of power between the combatants meant that no decisive result could be achieved. Thus, the economic considerations drove home to each party that the hurting stalemate had reached such a point that no benefit could be gained by continuing in such a manner.

Notes

1   A detailed picture will not be presented here as very detailed accounts are available elsewhere, most notably by Crocker himself in *High Noon in Southern Africa: Making Peace in a Rough Neighborhood*, New York and London: W. W. Norton and Company, 1992 See also Mokoena, Kenneth (ed.), *South Africa and the United States: The Declassified History*, a National Security Archive documents reader, New York: The New Press, 1993, p. 41.

2   'Significance of the Angola/Namibia Agreements', press conference by Chester Crocker, USUN Mission HQ, New York, 21 December 1988, in *American Foreign Policy: Current Documents Annual*, 1988, Washington, DC, GPO (1981–), Document No. 395.

3   Crocker, *High Noon in Southern Africa*, p. 433.

4   Riley, Eileen, *Major Political Events in South Africa 1948–1990*, Oxford and New York: Facts on File, 1991, p. 210.

5   Thompson, Alex, 'Incomplete Engagement: Reagan's South Africa Policy Revisited', *Journal of Modern African Studies*, Vol. 33, No. 1 (March 1995), p. 85.

6   See for example Ben T. Gurirab in Arnold Bergstraesser Institute, 'The Namibian Peace Process: Implications and Lessons for the Future', *Review of International Conference at the Arnold Bergstraesser Institute and International Peace Academy Freiburg, Germany 1–4 July 1992*, Freiburg: Arnold Bergstraesser Institute, 1994.

7   Freeman, Charles, 'The Angola/Namibia Accords', *Foreign Affairs*, Vol. 68, No. 3 (1989), p. 126.

8   Crocker, Chester and William H. Lewis, 'Missing Opportunities in Africa', *Foreign Policy*, No. 35 (Summer 1979), p. 65.

9   Crocker, *High Noon in Southern Africa*, p. 135.

10   *Ibid.*, p. 386.

11   Personal interview with Dr Chester Crocker, 19 June 2001, Washington, DC.

12   Personal interview with Herman Cohen, 22 June 2001, Washington, DC.

13   Crocker, *High Noon in Southern Africa*, p. 408.

14   Mokoena, *South Africa and the United States*, p. 36.

15   Berridge, Geoff, 'Diplomacy and the Angola/Namibia Accords', *International Affairs*, Vol. 65, No. 3 (Summer 1989), p. 463.

16   Arnold Bergstraesser Institute, *The Namibian Peace Process*, p. 37.

17   Freeman, 'The Angola/Namibia Accords', p. 134.

18   *Ibid.*, p. 134.

19   Pycroft, C., 'Review – *High Noon in Southern Africa: Making Peace in a Rough Neighborhood*, Chester Crocker', *Journal of Modern African Studies*, Vol. 32, No. 1 (1994), p. 171.

20   Defense Intelligence Agency briefing text, 'The 1987–88 Combat in Southern Angola:

Lessons Learned', as quoted in Mokoena, *South Africa and the United States*, p. 185.

21 Vale, Peter, 'Crocker's Choice: Constructive Engagement and South Africa's People', review article, *South African Journal of International Affairs*, Vol. 1, No. 1 (1995), p. 103.

22 Wood, Brian, 'Preventing the Vacuum: Determinants of the Namibia Settlement', *Journal of Southern African Studies*, Vol. 17, No. 4 (December 1991), p. 753.

23 Freeman, 'The Angola/Namibia Accords', p. 139.

11
Effects of the Settlement on Less Powerful Actors

SWAPO

Most assessments of Washington's linkage strategy evaluate its results according to a Western perspective, concentrating on its results for America or Pretoria. A comprehensive evaluation needs to take into account the policy's impact on all relevant parties – and how the goals of these parties, in turn, had an impact on the development of the linkage strategy. One cannot ignore the fact that SWAPO stood to gain most of all from a settlement. The truth remained that one of the two main aims of the linkage policy was the realization of Namibia's independence – something SWAPO had been fighting for since 1966. The debate regarding what benefits linkage provided for SWAPO rests on the question of whether South Africa would have settled in 1981, implementing UNSCR 435 as the international community insisted it should. Did linkage provide the only mechanism to force Pretoria to follow this path, or did it distract South Africa from its intention by offering a package that cost the people of Namibia dearly? The Namibian independence to which Crocker referred was of a particular kind. Washington was not about to campaign to install a Marxist government in a country that had some strategic value, both politically and in its possession of important minerals. Washington's foremost ally in the region – South Africa – was even more adamantly against the prospect of a SWAPO victory in Namibia than was Washington. In Crocker's meeting with Pik Botha and Magnus Malan on 15 and 16 April 1981, Malan flatly declared that Pretoria could not accept a SWAPO victory in Namibia. Although Crocker pointed to the fact that neither Pretoria nor Washington could have veto power, Malan repeated Pretoria's initial line: 'SAG's [South African Government's] bottom line is no Moscow flag in Windhoek.'[1]

Although some elements in Washington had a more nuanced view of SWAPO, the administration was still optimistic that a settlement could be reached that would avoid overall SWAPO power in Windhoek. Indeed, Crocker was criticized by other countries – and by many in Congress – for conducting negotiations on Namibian independence as though only SWAPO and the Frontline States were supposed to make concessions – rather than South Africa. His response was to state that:

> In South Africa they are being asked ... for the big concession [granting Namibian independence], so it is in that understanding and spirit that we

approach this problem ... there is not going to be a Namibian settlement until such time as South Africa agrees to it.[2]

In reality, the bottom line in Washington was that 'in the Reagan Administration there was a total rejection of SWAPO as anathema'.[3] When the role of SWAPO was debated in a Congressional Hearing held on 22 May 1985, Crocker made it very clear that the Reagan administration would not be following the UN's example of extending any special recognition to SWAPO, stating that Washington did not accord any special status to SWAPO and would strongly resist any effort to do so. He later explained that he also hoped the Cuban withdrawal from Angola would leave SWAPO so weakened that they would be forced into a deal with South Africa, thus ensuring that SWAPO would not gain full control over Namibia.[4] SWAPO itself was under no illusions with regard to Crocker's views, which he made perfectly clear at the outset. In April 1981, before he was confirmed in his post, he went on a two-week trip to Africa, visiting twelve countries including South Africa 'with the express purpose of reviewing the negotiations for Namibia's independence ... he refused to meet SWAPO anywhere on his trip'.[5]

Linkage clearly had been developed, not simply with a neglect of SWAPO's interests, but based on a reasoning that was *purposely* detrimental to a party that neither Washington nor Pretoria wanted to see in power. Any opportunity of delaying a settlement in Namibia gave Pretoria much needed time to build their internal opposition to SWAPO in Namibia. Linkage also provided Pretoria with legitimacy – instead of being blamed for the delay, South Africa could simply point to the Cuban presence in Angola as the major stumbling block for a settlement. SWAPO itself had immediately and roundly condemned the linkage strategy. It was simply not right that Namibian independence – which South Africa was obliged to grant by international law – could be held hostage to extraneous matters in this way. SWAPO maintained that the provisions laid down in UNSCR 435 in September 1978 had been agreed to by all the relevant parties – including SWAPO and South Africa. This was the plan that ought to be pursued under the auspices of the UN. At the Geneva conference on 14 January 1981, when South Africa refused to set a date for elections in Namibia, SWAPO's reaction was to condemn the South Africans for their 'manifest intransigence and prevarications' and to demand that the UN set up sanctions against them. SWAPO was exasperated at the way the agreed resolution could so easily be ignored by South Africa. Crocker, however, remained unconcerned by SWAPO's views. When discussing the fact that SWAPO wanted to put all the issues of independence under the control of the UN, he stated: 'This would have killed off the negotiations – Moscow's real aim. We ignored the suggestion.'[6] He cannot have been insensible to SWAPO's position, and to dismiss it as some communist plot compromised his image as a diplomat who was skilled at balancing globalist and regionalist demands in the difficult arena of Reagan's Washington.

Just as serious in the eyes of SWAPO and their supporters was the fact that Crocker's proposed linkage was actually illegal under international law. Cuban presence in Angola was legal, while South Africa's presence in

Namibia was not. American legal scholars condemned the trade-off as violating the right of the Namibian people to national self-determination by imposing conditions totally extraneous under law to the realization of that right. Attempts to influence the *internal* settlement were also 'void under international law. Negotiations are only to secure the transfer of power to the people of Namibia, not to determine how they exercise their sovereignty when they are a sovereign state.'[7] One fact that was often dismissed in the linkage discussions within the Reagan administration was the way in which the costs of these 'politics of postponement' were being paid by the thousands of innocent Namibians. While machinations continued to ensure that a Namibian government amenable to the regional interests of Pretoria and Washington could be achieved, thousands of Namibians – some SWAPO members or sympathizers, some with little knowledge or understanding of the political process – were detained and tortured in Namibia. Many of these were the victims of South Africa's notorious special police counter-insurgency unit Koevoet ('Crowbar'). Reading the evidence of the treatment of many Namibians – whose own opportunity to legally challenge the occupation of their country was undermined by the reticence of the international community, and then held hostage to the regional interests of Pretoria and Washington – reveals a clear testament to how little the goals and aspirations of the Namibian people were taken into account under the linkage strategy. In a conference held in 1992 to discuss the implications of the Namibian settlement, Theo-Ben Gurirab (of SWAPO) concluded that: 'Linkage kept Namibia's independence hostage for almost seven years',[8] although it is not possible to say with certainty what could have been achieved in the absence of the linkage strategy.

The MPLA

The Portuguese coup of 25 April 1974 and the subsequent news of forthcoming independence eventually led to the three warring nationalist movements in Angola – the MPLA, the FNLA and UNITA – agreeing to a ceasefire. At a conference in Kenya in January 1975 they signed the 'Alvor Agreement'. This allowed for a transitional government to be inaugurated on 31 January 1975, to govern until November, when independence would finally be realized. Unfortunately, as Henderson points out, without a genuine consensus on the agreed rules or an authoritative body to enforce them, the exercise was destined to fail – yet neither of these requirements existed. The nationalist movements, who from their inception had been illegal guerrilla groups, were not accustomed to abiding by legal provisions or agreed rules. The skeleton police force left by the Portuguese was too weak to maintain order. Within days of the inauguration of the transitional government, the scramble for Angola had resumed.[9] Although the legitimacy of the MPLA government in Luanda was contentious, even American politicians accept that external interference began when South Africa sent several thousand troops into Angola in the autumn of 1975. As Congressman William Gray, member of the House Foreign Affairs Committee, explained: 'In an attempt to stave off this massive onslaught Angola made an international appeal for assistance, resulting in a bilateral agreement with the Cubans.'[10] The MPLA was still in a very precarious position at the time of Reagan's election and Washington was well aware of this. A secret memorandum to the White House from the CIA in August 1982 stated: 'We believe that Luanda could not afford to lose more than 5,000 to 7,500 members of the total Cuban military force without suffering appreciable territorial losses to UNITA.'[11]

When Crocker met the Angolan Foreign Minister Paulo Jorge in Paris in January 1982, Jorge pointed to Article 51 of the UN Charter – regarding the right of states to self-defence. He said that this was what the MPLA was trying to achieve, with the assistance of the Cubans. Jorge also flatly rejected linkage, explaining that they had consistently supported the plan for a settlement in Namibia, but to agree to linkage would be to equate the aggressor – South Africa – with the victim – Angola. Crocker dismissed Jorge's argument thus: 'True, but this conflict wasn't going to be solved by legal argument.'[12] He also described the MPLA as a 'weak and fragmented regime'. Indeed, the former President Neto had died in 1979 and dos Santos was still consolidating his role. However, there is contention over how broad the MPLA's support was throughout the country. As *mestiços*, the MPLA formed an intellectual elite, many of whom had Portuguese names and did not speak African languages. However, testimony from the former Secretary of State for African Affairs Richard Moose describes how Moose flew to Angola himself in August 1975 and met Savimbi. He reported that: 'The MPLA at the time of independence was the most broadly based of all the parties.'[13] Although this support may have been limited, there was no other broad-based Angolan party. By this stage, UNITA formed the main opposition, and it relied heavily on the Ovimbundu people for its support.

The MPLA was not in overall control, however, and there was a need to achieve some form of settlement in Angola. The pressure on the MPLA was both military and economic. The Soviet Union was notoriously reluctant to provide the economic aid that the MPLA needed, and the MPLA was therefore very keen to secure both aid and recognition from the US. In early 1982 the MPLA initiated tentative contacts with UNITA. A memorandum to Reagan in 1982 also stated that, by August 1982, the MPLA had:

> for the first time moved away from the February 4, 1982 joint Angolan-Cuban communiqué which has been the basis of their position to date. They have dropped their demand that Cuban troop withdrawal cannot be considered until Namibia is fully independent.[14]

In fact, Luanda also made a serious effort to improve relations with the US. Randall Robinson of TransAfrica noted how Luanda had offered a phased withdrawal of Cuban troops and had, in September 1985, reopened negotiations on the Namibian question. He also pointed to a meeting between President dos Santos and Crocker in New York in October 1985, where dos Santos had offered to improve ties with the United States.[15] By the time of Reagan's election, the United States and South Africa were the only two governments who refused to recognize the legitimacy of the Angolan government. Crocker explained that this stance represented the US's 'principled rejection' of the MPLA victory and the manner in which it took place. He continued to maintain that Angola did not have a properly elected government. The country had been in the middle of a civil war 'which the Cubans and their patrons had decided to cut off in the middle. It was like a game of musical chairs and when the music stopped, the MPLA were the ones in the chair.'[16] He did not acknowledge the significance of the many other external forces, especially South Africa and Zaïre, who were equally to blame for attempting to determine the result of the war. Although Crocker maintained that for diplomacy to succeed, the security concerns of all parties ought to be taken into account, his focus on South Africa's legitimate security interests overrode concerns about the security situation facing the MPLA.

The costs of the civil war to the government of Angola were high, and were hugely increased by the fact that Angola had become the venue for a proxy struggle between the two superpowers. The government had to bear the costs of the physical and economic dislocation of the country, and these costs were increased because American and South African aid to UNITA – and incursions by South Africa itself – meant that UNITA's potential to wreak havoc within Angola was greatly enhanced. In addition, the MPLA was having to pay Havana up to $1,000 per soldier per month for helping to defend its position of power. In a speech in August 1987, Angolan President dos Santos estimated that the war had resulted in $12 billion worth of damage to the country and that, between 1975 and 1987, the war had cost over sixty thousand Angolan lives.[17]

One element of Crocker's linkage package was very attractive to the Angolan government. They wanted South Africa out of Namibia. The destabilization on the Angolan/Namibian border was costing them dearly. South African incursions into Angola – ostensibly to root out SWAPO, but in reality also to aid UNITA in undermining the MPLA government – were one of Angola's most pressing problems. Indeed, on this score Washington was prepared to help, and one of the aims of the State Department was to obtain a South African commitment to non-aggression against Angola, in order to facilitate Cuban withdrawal. Unfortunately, this aim was undermined by Washington's eventual decision to fund UNITA.

By 1988 the MPLA had suffered some of its worst military losses since the beginning of the war and was on the defensive, economically and militarily.[18] It looked as though linkage could provide them with a much-needed get-out clause. And yet, the MPLA government regarded this strategy with both intense distrust and dissatisfaction. Dos Santos was under no illusions that Washington's strategy was an attempt to further its own interests. The resumption of funding to UNITA made it clear what result Washington intended to bring about. The Angolan government complained bitterly that, while the Reagan administration had done everything to address South Africa's security concerns, Angola's legitimate fears had been ignored – and this was while South Africa's territory remained secure from Angolan government forces, while Angola was subject to attacks from internal parties and outside forces.

The secret 'National Security Decision Directives' (NSDD) which guided US policy demonstrate that the MPLA were right to be suspicious of Washington's intentions. NSDD 212, dated 10 February 1986 and entitled 'United States' Policy Toward Angola', and the follow-up NSDD 274, under the same title and dated 7 May 1987, gave a clear delineation of American policy towards the Angolan government. NSDD 274 ordered a review of support to UNITA to ensure that it was 'effective in raising the cost incurred by the MPLA regime and its Soviet and Cuban backers'. The Department of State was to convene an interagency review to 'consider feasible and effective means of increasing economic pressures on the MPLA regime'. The Department of State was also instructed to work on 'more effective information programs' to increase UNITA's stature both within Angola and in the wider international community. Economic pressures had already been put in place by NSDD 212 a year previously, where the EXIM bank was instructed to 'neither seek nor accept any new business in Angola which would, broadly construed, enhance the ability of the MPLA to wage war or acquire the military or economic resources necessary to sustain its war effort'.[19]

Luanda's aims had never included the intention of alienating Washington. In fact, the trading relationship between the two was of vital importance to Angola. By the middle of 1985 Angola was the fourth-largest US trading partner in sub-Saharan Africa, despite its lack of diplomatic relations, with trade between the two countries totalling over $1 billion per annum. The MPLA's communist leanings apparently did not affect America's interest it its commercial viability, nor did it prevent Angola's willingness to enter into such agreements with the US. As one Congressman asked:

> The government of Angola, with all the charges of Marxism, having its prime commitment and involvement in trade partnership with the West and especially with the United States, how do we characterize that as being some assignation that is in the thralls of the communist Soviet Union?[20]

Crocker's fixation on who was Washington's 'enemy' and who was a 'friend' meant that he appeared to overlook Luanda's willingness to enter into negotiations on a settlement and, by ignoring those overtures, he could have missed an important opportunity to bring about a settlement sooner.

Another aspect of American policy also cost the MPLA very dearly. Washington had consciously avoided addressing the internal situation in Angola during the linkage negotiations. To have attempted to address this issue could have derailed the whole process. Crocker's critics in Washington called his diplomacy 'a sham. Unless you get national reconciliation in Angola it's a sellout.'[21] He responded: 'This will come once the Cubans have left – you've got to get the foreigners out of the kitchen before the cooks can cook.' However, while mediating the linkage negotiations,

Washington continued to fund UNITA. The Angolan government was furious at this, telling Washington that the only reason Angola did not have peace was because the US continued to assist Savimbi.

Although the Angolan government benefited from linkage because the South Africans were removed from Namibia, the benefits were decidedly mixed. On the whole, the Angolan government suffered under Crocker's linkage policy. The Cuban withdrawal left the MPLA facing a determined UNITA which was still receiving American funds. Although Crocker claimed that an internal settlement in Angola would be the logical result of the Namibia/Angola accords, the civil war continued, with no apparent end in sight. In fact, the next stage of Angola's history was even more violent than before.[22]

UNITA

Unfortunately for Savimbi, Washington's favoured party in Angola fared little better under the linkage agreements. Crocker insisted in a press conference held in New York on 21 December 1988 (the day before the signing of the peace accords) that US funding to UNITA was 'non-negotiable'.[23] The fact remained, however, that this issue had placed him in a very awkward situation. Pressure from the right wing meant that he was forced to defend a policy which he knew had greatly complicated his own strategy in the region. When the regional ceasefire was arranged in Geneva in August 1988, UNITA declared that it would not observe it. South Africa soon after announced a halt to its support of UNITA. Washington, however, proceeded to commit $50 million worth of aid to UNITA, despite its rejection of the ceasefire proposals. Grundy describes Washington's decision as thereby undermining the ceasefire Crocker had worked hard to achieve.[24]

Despite continued funding from the US, Savimbi reacted angrily to the settlement. UNITA had not been included in any of the negotiations – as Angola's civil war had not been an issue under discussion. UNITA had lost South African funding, and the independence of Namibia meant that it had lost one of its best supply routes: 'In his only public statement about the tripartite agreement, Savimbi expressed bitterness that Secretary Crocker had been either unable or unwilling to include an internal settle-ment in the package.'[25] Washington was not ready to abandon UNITA, however. The incoming Bush administration had decided to retain support for UNITA as a matter of policy. On 6 January 1989 Bush's first foreign policy commitment was to send a letter to Savimbi promising to 'continue all appropriate and effective assistance to UNITA'.[26] The letter also pointed out that, although the US had mediated the tripartite accords, Washington was not bound by their provisions. The new Deputy Assistant Secretary of State for African Affairs, Clark, made clear in a statement to Congress in September 1989 that 'the United States will continue appro-priate and effective assistance to UNITA until national reconciliation is achieved'.[27] As Cohen explained, Washington's main objective in Angola, after Cuban troop withdrawal, was 'ending the war with justice for Savimbi – he'd been our guy, and he'd been working for us in the Cold War'.[28] Yet the American goal was a dangerous one. Their assistance to UNITA was not designed to help UNITA win the war, but to prevent the MPLA from winning. The aim was to force the MPLA to the negotiating table, where they would have to listen to UNITA's demands. Creating this hurting stalemate, however, would involve the continuation of the bitter and brutal civil war in Angola. In fact, even when the Angolan Peace Accords were finally signed in May 1991, Savimbi did not accept the outcome of the elections for which he had been fighting.

The Organization of African Unity & the Frontline States

As well as the dissatisfaction among SWAPO, the MPLA and UNITA regarding the outcomes of Washington's linkage, another group of regional actors was unhappy with the way in which this policy had been conducted. Crocker's policies in southern Africa were designed to further American interests, and this included improved relations with the black African states. NSDD 212 stated that the US should 'work actively with our allies, the Frontline States, and other parties' to press the MPLA for a peaceful settlement.[29] However, this set of actors was frustrated by the turn of events under Crocker and was opposed to the threat to sovereignty that his linkage formula implied. Washington's early invitation to Pik Botha was condemned in the United Nations by the African Group Chairman Ambassador Rupia of Tanzania as showing 'the utmost contempt' for international opinion. He stated that African nations considered it an unfriendly act. The continued links drew more criticism from the African nations, with the OAU openly condemning the 'emerging unholy alliance between Pretoria and Washington'.

Any inclination Crocker might have had to balance his deepening ties with South Africa with a more meaningful dialogue with the Frontline States was obstructed by the right wing in Washington. They were suspicious of the FLS's support of the ANC and the governments which were either openly Marxist or sympathetic to that approach, particularly Jose Eduardo dos Santos in Angola, Machel and later Chissano in Mozambique, and Mugabe in Zimbabwe. Indeed, Congress went as far as forbidding aid to Mozambique and Angola and made $40 million of US economic aid to southern Africa conditional on governments denouncing any group that condoned the brutal practice of 'necklacing'. These provisions were enacted in an amendment introduced to the supplementary appropriations Bill by Senator Larry Pressler (Republican – South Dakota) in July 1987. The Pressler amendment was very controversial, with Mugabe pointing out that no government of the region had ever condoned necklacing, and that the amendment was merely an attempt to punish any support for the ANC.[30]

Meanwhile, the FLS had their own solution to the Namibian question, which they spelt out to Crocker on his tour of twelve African nations from 6 to 23 April 1981. They insisted that the only acceptable solution would be the immediate implementation of an unchanged UNSCR 435, which should be brought about by Western pressure on South Africa. Some of the FLS leaders had already started to call for sanctions. Crocker insisted that Washington would not be imposing blueprints or timetables, and that the US had neither 'the leverage or a mandate' for such a role. Rather, he maintained, Washington should work to foster 'a regional climate conducive to compromise and accommodation' in both southern and South Africa.[31] The African states did call on the UN to propose resolutions which would have resulted in sanctions if South Africa did not implement UNSCR 435 unconditionally. Their moves were blocked, however, by Security Council vetoes from the United States, Britain and France. The African states continued in their opposition, attempting to utilize the various channels open to them. At the Commonwealth conference in India in November 1983, 15 African heads of state and government leaders asked Thatcher to attempt to persuade Reagan to drop the linkage demand – but to no avail.

For his part, Crocker stressed that the African states saw the logic in his methods. He pointed to President Kaunda of Zambia and President Nyerere of Tanzania as agreeing with his proposed sequence, in which the problem of Namibia should be tackled before the question of apartheid within South Africa. He also pointed to the strong relationship that Zaïre and Zambia had with UNITA. However, this did not represent the majority view, as confirmed by a confidential CIA report which stated that 'the Frontline States for the most part support Angola's view that Savimbi is a "traitor" and a South African "puppet"'.[32] The fact was that the Africans were being pushed hard by Washington to accept the linkage strategy – with Washington making it clear that there were no alternative solutions. Shultz outlined his position in a secret memorandum to the President:

> The Africans now appear grudgingly to understand our position that further progress will depend on a credible commitment to ... Cuban troop withdrawal. Your 13 August letters to the [FLS] leaders put them firmly on notice that we will not agree to take the Namibia package to the Security Council until we have that commitment.[33]

The FLS had put their faith in the UN and the UNSCR 435. They publicly and adamantly opposed the linkage formula, but by late 1983 the linkage formula was no longer under debate. As the FLS had rejected this approach, Crocker explained, 'this was to be the last time they would play a substantive role in the negotiations'.[34] The FLS governments resented the fact that, once again, superpower interests had been imposed and had guided developments in their region. It was clear that Washington was not to be influenced by the views or interests of the African nations. Rather, the African nations, like the Contact Group, knew that if they wanted the leadership only Washington could provide, they would have to accept Washington's solutions.

Dissatisfaction with Washington's role was widespread among the regional actors, but the fact was that their interests had remained subordinate to America's wider globalist goals. The regional actors were always going to remain subject to the pressures of the Cold War. But this begs the question – how successful was Washington in achieving these goals? What was the policy's impact on the Soviets and Cubans?

The Soviet Union

Just before his appointment to the post of Assistant Secretary, Crocker had warned that the Soviet Union was motivated by a range of interests in the southern African region. He explained that the Soviets were keen to reduce Western and Chinese influence in the region; that they aimed to acquire naval and military facilities there; and that they wanted to demonstrate to the African nations that the Soviet Union was a more reliable and powerful security partner than the West. He also explained that their financing of guerrilla groups benefited their fundamental aim of undermining Western interests. The disruption of transport lines and mineral production would deter investment and damage the international economy. The fact that Angola was the second largest oil producer in sub-Saharan Africa (behind Nigeria) and that Namibia had rich reserves of uranium, as well as diamonds, meant that disrupting the region and therefore the West's access to it was seen as an important incentive for Soviet action in the region. While this might have been the case regarding the ANC actions in South Africa, it is impossible to see how Crocker could have maintained this argument in the Angolan case. The MPLA government, supported by Moscow, was reliant upon its own oil and mineral exports – for which America was its biggest customer. It was UNITA, funded by the US ally South Africa, and later by the US itself, which perpetrated acts of sabotage to undermine and destabilize the Soviet-backed MPLA government – and the Angolan economy.

South Africa maintained that it was a victim of a Soviet-sponsored 'total onslaught' – the Soviet Union had the region in its sights and was determined, through pacts with Marxist governments and the funding of Marxist guerrillas, to undermine legitimate governments and subjugate the region to communist influence. Pretoria pointed to Soviet 'treaties of friendship and cooperation' with the Angolan and Mozambican governments and its funding of the ANC and SWAPO, as proof of these fears. Crocker argued that the Soviet Union had purposely installed the MPLA regime in Angola, describing the assertion that the Cubans were in Angola to protect the government from South African incursions and South African-funded rebels as a 'myth'.[35] He stated that the Soviet Union relied on the MPLA to 'parrot the Soviet line' and to 'legitimize [Soviet] support for the "liberation struggle" in Namibia and South Africa'. He also pointed to the financial incentives the Soviets had for remaining involved in the region, and highlighted the fact that, of the $4.5 billion that Angola spent on arms in its first ten years of independence, 90 per cent went to the Soviet Union. This 'wasn't a charitable relationship on Moscow's part'. Grundy also points to the Soviet Union's increased profile in the region, which contributed significantly to its effort to be recognized as a global power on a par with the US.[36]

The fact was, however, that the Soviet Union was reluctant to get involved deeply in the region, or to put itself to great expense in order to achieve influence there. It sold arms to regimes it endorsed, but was far more reluctant when it came to providing economic aid. As *The Economist* explained: 'Eastern aid to the region was primarily military. Russia did not see why its valuable foreign exchange should end, like much economic aid to southern Africa, in a Johannesburg bank.'[37] Evidence does not point to a grand strategy or master plan for a total onslaught. Russian intervention in the region appears to have been largely opportunistic. Soviet policy in the region was largely low-risk and low-cost. Indeed, it seems that much of the Soviet benefit was gained by the actions of Washington allying itself to unpopular groups or regimes – to Pretoria in particular. Simply by opposing Western actions and interests, the Soviets could gain great credibility as the anti-colonial superpower in the region.

The secrecy surrounding the Kremlin did make it difficult to understand Moscow's true aims in the region, but Vale says observers ignored this fact. Instead, he asserts, 'a political megaphone called the 'Total Onslaught' passed for analysis'.[38] Pretoria's insistence on the reality of the total onslaught played into the Soviet Union's hands and gave it undeserved credit for much of the opposition to apartheid. The truth was that limited Russian activity in the region garnered very few benefits of real significance to Moscow. At the time observers remarked that: 'After two decades of trying, the Soviets have acquired neither one true African satellite or even constant friend.'[39] Although anti-colonialism meant that many African countries still harboured resentment against the West, this did not make them automatic allies of the East. National self-interest was the top priority of all governments (although self-aggrandizement and financial gain was the first aim of many of the dictators) regardless of where the money came from. Angola and Mozambique strove to protect their non-aligned status in deference to their vital trade links with the West. Although the Soviet Union was granted use of an airfield in Angola (to monitor long-range shipping in the South Atlantic), requests for further military facilities in southern Africa were publicly refused.

Moscow's intentions in the region were limited and opportunistic, but instead of capitalizing on this, Crocker's policy was counterproductive. He painted the Soviet Union as far more determined and involved in the region than it actually was. By allying with Pretoria and the ex-colonial powers, while stressing opposition to Moscow, the US did far more than Moscow itself to paint the Soviet Union as being on the side of the black African states. In Moscow, on the other hand, the government was becoming far more pragmatic, rather than simply ideological, in its calculations. Anatoly Adamishin, Vice-Minister of Foreign Affairs for Africa, later explained to Herman Cohen that when Gorbachev came to power, he was 'horrified' at the $1 billion a year that the Soviet Union was spending in both Angola and Ethiopia on arms deliveries and in-country military technical assistance. Adamishin admitted that Moscow did not believe either conflict could be solved and 'wanted to bow out' – but in a way which would not humiliate its clients. In Angola in particular, the plummeting oil price had hit hard. Angola stopped paying for arms, and Bender estimates the Angolan debt to the USSR as between $2.5 and $3 billion by early 1988.[40]

This opportunity was wasted by Washington and Pretoria's myopic fixation on the threat of the total onslaught. A cable to the Secretary of State from Howard Walker at the US Embassy in Cape Town referred to Soviet proposals for a settlement in Angola as early as 1981. Although the details of the Soviet settlement plan remain classified, reports of a conversation between Pik Botha and the US Chargé d'Affaires in South Africa show that Pretoria was willing to discuss this potential plan:

> Pik does not agree with Ambassador Sole that the Soviet approach should not be taken seriously ... his own view is that the Soviet Ambassador in Salisbury [Harare] would not have mentioned such a possible initiative without instructions.[41]

The conclusion to this episode was that Washington was able to convince Pretoria, against Pik Botha's better judgement, to ignore early Soviet initiatives to achieve a settlement. The report stated: 'Foreign Minister Botha still thinks there is something in the Soviet Ambassador's approach for USG [United States Government]/SAG/USSR talks on Angola, but he accepts our decision not to pursue it at this time.'[42] Soviet intentions in the region appear far more flexible than Washington gave them credit for – and this proof of Soviet overtures shows that an early opportunity for agreeing a settlement might have been missed by the Reagan administration's refusal to meet this flexibility with a modicum of its own.

When evaluating the benefits that the Soviet Union obtained through linkage, one must be aware of just how completely Soviet goals changed during this period. At the beginning of the 1980s, linkage was seen as a way of heading off the determination of the USSR to extend its sphere of influence in southern Africa – and to simultaneously increase American influence there. By the end of the decade the *glasnost* era meant that linkage was now well suited to a very different set of Soviet priorities –how to withdraw with honour from expensive African entanglements. Crocker's linkage strategy, with its globalist underpinnings (inadvertently) provided Moscow with just such a solution. It is fair to characterize this result as inadvertent, as neither Washington nor Moscow could have foreseen the changing objectives of the Soviet Union when this strategy was first launched in 1981.

The Cubans

The role and intentions of the Cubans in the region remains a contentious issue. Gerald Bender maintains that the Cuban presence in post-colonial Angola was both welcome and valuable. The departing Portuguese left an

Angolan population that had a 90 per cent illiteracy rate. The Portuguese also stripped Angola of its resources and failed to establish a functioning civil society before they left. Bender stresses the fact that the Angolan population was in dire need of the 900 Cuban doctors and nurses who arrived to sustain Angola's health services. The Cubans were also 'extremely helpful' in the area of civil construction.[43]

After only a month in office, President Carter had received signals from Angola and Cuba that Cuban troop reduction from Angola was imminent. This reduction did take place, and was verified by US officials, until May 1977. The South African-sponsored attempts to destabilize the MPLA regime meant that the Cuban troop withdrawal was halted. On 19 March 1984, the governments in Luanda and Havana issued a joint statement detailing the four conditions necessary for Cuban troop withdrawal from Angola:

1 'unilateral withdrawal' of South African troops from Angola;
2 'scrupulous implementation' of UNSCR 435 and the withdrawal of South African troops from Namibia;
3 'cessation of all types of direct aggression' against Angola by 'South Africa, the United States and its allies';
4 a withdrawal of support for 'UNITA and any other puppet group' by South Africa, the United States and its allies.[44]

These, therefore, were Cuba's aims as stated by Havana. Crocker, however, made it clear that he believed Havana's own political considerations were the driving force behind Castro's actions. He pointed to Castro's ideological focus as being even sharper in Angola than Moscow's. In a report on a 1987 meeting in Luanda with the Cubans and Angolans, Crocker told Shultz that he believed the Cubans 'were holding a fairly tight leash on the Angolans'[45] and that Cuban political considerations were preventing Angolan agreement in the negotiation process. Critics of Cuba also cited the considerable financial benefits Havana received through its assistance to the MPLA. In a Congressional debate reports were used to demonstrate the extent of these financial rewards: 'The BBC and Reuters have also cited intelligence reports which variously estimate that the Angolan government pays between $500 and $800 million a year to Cuba for the use of Cuban troops.'[46] Crocker does, however, point to the fact that by mid-1987 the Cubans definitely wanted out of Angola – and that Castro wanted to be seen as a partner of the US. The Angolan entanglement was complicating improved links with the West. Despite the financial payments and political benefits, the Cubans were forced to remain in Angola longer than suited their own interests in order to support the MPLA while it faced attacks from South Africa and UNITA. To do otherwise would have risked the loss of credibility among Cuban allies and throughout the Third World.

Cuba – the accidental victor?

Cuba was not one of the parties Crocker intended to help through his linkage proposals. During this period of resurgence of anti-communist sentiment under the Reagan Doctrine, Cuba was a sworn enemy, particularly among the Republicans in Washington. Crocker had devised linkage in order to reduce Cuban influence by getting them out of southern Africa, and Washington had strongly resisted including the Cubans in the negotiation process. It was the MPLA government's decision whether or not the Cubans should be afforded a place at the negotiating table. The Cubans wanted the prestige that would result from involvement in the settlement process and were keen to join. Crocker admitted to stretching the truth in order to avoid this outcome: 'We exaggerated to the MPLA Castro's implication that Cuban involvement would make a major difference. Dos Santos was indeed upset when he learnt of Castro's signal to Washington.'[47] However, dos Santos's visit to Havana on 30 July 1987 successfully healed the breach.

Crocker himself admits that including the Cubans in the negotiations earlier could have been beneficial[48] – but as he viewed them as the enemy, and as such a move would be politically unacceptable in the domestic arena, the option was closed to him until late in the negotiations. When discussing the linkage settlement, the American team all pointed out that the Cubans wanted to leave. Crocker, his deputy Charles Freeman and his successor Herman Cohen all highlighted the fact that the Cubans were finding that lives lost in Angola were creating pressure to get out; that soldiers were returning to Cuba bringing AIDS; and that the influx of battle-hardened troops was creating a threat to Castro's regime.[49] But the Cubans were not as desperate to withdraw as these assertions would indicate. They had wanted to ensure a clear victory before their withdrawal. By January 1988 they had joined the negotiations and when a final settlement was reached, they found that the linkage formula had served their interests well. Overall, Cuba had incurred negligible costs from supporting Luanda. South African incursions and support of UNITA meant that there was little African support for UNITA, and therefore little African opposition to the role played by Cuba in Angola.

The Cubans were also successful at the negotiating table. Crocker explained that they wanted to leave Angola by mid-1987. By the end of 1988 the agreement was signed. Cuba secured great credibility in the Third World, and had gained in prestige by helping the superpowers negotiate an end to the Namibian conflict. The Cuban withdrawal commenced on 10 January 1989, with all 50,000 Cuban troops scheduled to depart by July 1991. In the farewell ceremony President José Eduardo dos Santos thanked the Cubans, saying: 'You have fulfilled your mission with honour and glory, and your contribution to our country is unforgettable and indestructible.'[50] Crocker had achieved his aim of getting the Cubans out of Angola, but was not wholly successful in reducing Cuban influence in this sphere. The Cubans gained more friends and respect by their actions in the region than Washington did through its close association with South Africa and UNITA.

Notes

1   'Memorandum of Conversation', Participants: SA Foreign Minister Pik Botha, SA Defence Minister Magnus Malan, US Assistant Secretary-Designate Chester Crocker, Alan Keyes. Subject: Discussion with SAG Pretoria 15–16 April 1981. Photocopy of document sent to the author by the Namibian Embassy in London.

2   See *US Policy Toward Namibia* Hearing Before the Subcommittee on Africa of the Committee on Foreign Affairs, House of Representatives, 97th Congress, First Session, 17 June 1981, pp. 7–8 for a discussion of this point between the Chairman Wolpe and Crocker.

3   Personal interview with Herman J. Cohen, Washington, DC, 22 June 2001.

4   Crocker, Chester and David A. Smock (eds), *African Conflict Resolution: The US Role in Peacemaking*, Washington, DC: US Institute of Peace Press, 1995, p. 62.

5   'Memorandum of Conversation', 1981.

6   Crocker, Chester, *High Noon in Southern Africa: Making Peace in a Rough Neighborhood*, New York and London: W. W. Norton and Company, 1992, p. 124.

7   Faundez, Julio, 'Namibia: the Relevance of International Law', *Third World Quarterly*, Vol. 8, No. 2 (April 1986), p. 555.

8   Arnold Bergstraesser Institute, 'The Namibian Peace Process: Implications and Lessons for the Future', *Review of International Conference at the Arnold Bergstraesser Institute and International Peace Academy Freiburg, Germany, 1–4 July 1992*, Freiburg: Arnold Bergstraesser Institute, 1994, p. 47.

9   Henderson, Lawrence W., *Angola: Five Centuries of Conflict*, Ithaca and London: Cornell University Press, 1979, pp. 207–8 and 246–9.

10 *Angola: Intervention or Negotiation* Hearings before the Subcommittee on Africa of the Committee on Foreign Affairs, House of Representatives, 31 October and 12 November 1985, p. 137.

11 Ronald Reagan Library, CA. Secret CIA Memorandum. To: William P. Clark Assistant to the President for National Security Affairs. From: John N. McMahan Acting Director of Central Intelligence. Subject: The Namibia Settlement Process: Obstacles and Regional Implications, 20 August 1982.

12 Crocker, *High Noon in Southern Africa*, p. 141.

13 *Angola: Should the United States Support UNITA?* Hearing before the Permanent Select Committee on Intelligence, House of Representatives, 99th Congress, Second Session, 13 March 1986, p. 55.

14 Ronald Reagan Library, CA. White House Staff and Office Files: Cohen, Herman J., Files 1987–8. African Affairs Directorate, NSC. Boxes 91875 and 91876. Secret Memorandum. To: Ronald Reagan. From: George Shultz. Subject: South Africa: Progress in the Angolan and Namibian negotiations, 26 August 1982.

15 Testimony of Randall Robinson in *Angola: Intervention or Negotiation* Congressional Hearings, 31 October and 12 November 1985, p. 32.

16 Personal interview with Chester Crocker, 19 June 2001, Washington, DC.

17 Bender, Gerald J., 'Peacemaking in Southern Africa: the Luanda–Pretoria Tug-of-War', *Third World Quarterly*, Vol. 11, No. 1 (January 1989), p. 24.

18 *Ibid.*, p. 26.

19 Ronald Reagan Library, CA. National Security Decision Directive 212, 10 February 1986.

20 *Angola: Intervention or Negotiation* Congressional Hearings, 31 October and 12 November 1985, p. 115.

21 Arnold Bergstraesser Institute, *The Namibian Peace Process*, p. 44.

22 Wright, George, *The Destruction of a Nation: US Policy Toward Angola Since 1945*, London and Chicago: Pluto Press, 1997, p. 141.

23 'Significance of the Angola/Namibia Agreements', press conference by Chester Crocker, USUN Mission HQ, New York, 21 December 1988, in *American Foreign Policy: Current Documents Annual*, 1988, Washington, DC, GPO (1981–), Document No. 395.

24 Grundy, Kenneth W., *South Africa: Domestic Crisis and Global Challenge*, Boulder, San Francisco and Oxford: Westview Press, 1991, p. 115.

25 Cohen, Herman J., *Intervening in Africa: Superpower Peacemaking in a Troubled Continent*, Basingstoke and London: Macmillan, 2000 and New York: St Martin's Press, 2000, p. 88.

26 *Ibid.*, p. 88 and personal interview with Herman Cohen, 22 June 2001, Washington, DC.

27 'Review of US Policy Toward Angola', statement by Deputy Assistant Secretary of State for African Affairs Clark, 27 September 1989, in *American Foreign Policy: Current Documents Annual*, 1989, Washington, DC, GPO (1981–), Document No. 395.

28 Personal interview with Herman Cohen, 22 June 2001, Washington, DC.

29 Ronald Reagan Library, CA. National Security Decision Directive 212, 10 February 1986.

30 Baker, Pauline H., *The United States and South Africa: The Reagan Years. Update South Africa: Time Running Out*, Ford Foundation and Foreign Policy Association, 1989, p. 56.

31 Crocker, *High Noon in Southern Africa*, p. 75.

32 Ronald Reagan Library, CA. Secret CIA Memorandum. To: William P. Clark Assistant to the President for National Security Affairs. From: John N. McMahan Acting Director of Central Intelligence. Subject: The Namibia Settlement Process: Obstacles and Regional Implications, 20 August 1982.

33 Ronald Reagan Library, CA. Secret Memorandum. To: Ronald Reagan. From: George Shultz. Subject: South Africa: Progress in the Angolan and Namibian negotiations, 26 August 1982.

34 Crocker, *High Noon in Southern Africa*, p. 133.

35 *Ibid.*, p. 47.

36 Grundy, *South Africa: Domestic Crisis and Global Challenge*, p. 47.

37 *The Economist*, 16 July 1983, p. 27.

38 Vale, Peter, 'Crocker's Choice: Constructive Engagement and South Africa's People', review article, *South African Journal of International Affairs*, Vol. 1, No. 1 (1995), p. 101.

39 Weissman, Stephen, 'Dateline South Africa: The Opposition Speaks', *Foreign Policy*, No. 58 (Spring 1985), p. 168.

40 Bender, 'Peacemaking in Southern Africa', p. 27.

41 Ronald Reagan Library, CA. White House Staff and Office Files: Cohen, Herman J., Files 1987–8. African Affairs Directorate, NSC. Boxes 91875 and 91876. Secret Cable. To: Secretary of State, Washington, DC. From: American Consulate Cape Town. Subject: 'Pik/Chargé Conversations', 10 November 1981.

42 *Ibid.*

43 Bender, Gerald J. 'Angola, the Cubans and American Anxieties', *Foreign Policy*, No. 31 (Summer 1978), pp. 8–10.

44 Mokoena, Kenneth (ed.) *South Africa and the United States: The Declassified History*, a National Security Archive documents reader, New York: The New Press, 1993, p. 33.

45 Ronald Reagan Library, CA. WHORM Subject Files: 'South Africa, US Policy Towards', File Numbers FG001–FG013; PR003-PR007-02, Confidential Report for Secretary Shultz, 'Crocker's Meeting in Luanda' undated.

46 Testimony of Mr Sorzano, President of the Cuban American National Foundation, in *Angola: Intervention or Negotiation* Hearings before the Subcommittee on Africa of the Committee on Foreign Affairs, House of Representatives, 31 October and 12 November 1985, p. 35.

47 Crocker, *High Noon in Southern Africa*, p. 357.

48 *Ibid.*, p. 223.

49 Personal interview with Dr Chester Crocker, 19 June 2001, Washington, DC and personal interview with Herman Cohen, 22 June 2001, Washington, DC. See also Freeman, Charles, 'The Angola/Namibia Accords', *Foreign Affairs*, Vol. 68, No. 3, p. 133 and Chester Crocker, *High Noon in Southern Africa*, p. 356. It was estimated that over 2,000 Cuban soldiers died in Angola. See Riley, Eileen, *Major Political Events in South Africa 1948–1990*, Oxford and New York: Facts on File, 1991, p. 209.

50 Riley, *Major Political Events in South Africa*, p. 209.

III
Conclusions

12
Successes & Failures
of Constructive Engagement

The Impact of Concepts, Aims & Implementation

The first question posed by this book identified the conceptual basis of Crocker's policy. Constructive engagement was an attempt to reconcile two agendas that were at the forefront of American foreign policy. The US historically believed it had an important 'mission' to fulfil – to lead the free world and spread values of liberty and democracy throughout its sphere of influence. The realization of this mission was affected, however, by another agenda which outweighed all others in the foreign policy of the Reagan administration – the shift back to the policy of containment. This was in contrast to the reluctance to get involved in world affairs due to the Vietnam Syndrome and President Carter's emphasis on human rights, which had characterized the foreign policy of the mid- to late 1970s. The Reagan Doctrine was presented as a method of achieving both of these agendas – leading the free world and maintaining a vigilant containment policy. This work has examined the extent to which Crocker's constructive engagement followed the dictates of the Reagan Doctrine. The basic assumptions of this Doctrine stated that Africa was only important in an East–West context, and that regional problems were caused not so much by local factors as by an all-enveloping Soviet threat. Human rights were also moved down the agenda, in favour of the support of proven friends, regardless of their human rights records.

Crocker's policy, at least in its public aspect, was an attempt to reconcile both regional and global concerns. The conceptual basis of his policy recognized four important factors: that American interests were paramount; that a synthesis could be created to address these regional and global concerns together; that his policy must be understood as a regional policy; and that there was a real possibility of gradual, white-led change within South Africa. What this book has argued, however, is that the re-ignited Cold War zeal of the Reagan administration overshadowed each one of these issues. David Newsom, an earlier Assistant Secretary of State for African Affairs, warned in Congress in 1983 against the difficulty of attempting to reconcile working with Pretoria and maintaining credibility with the black African states – both of these factors were in the American interest, yet they conflicted. In the end, South Africa's importance to the US in the struggle against communism meant that American credibility among black African states was badly damaged. With regard to creating a

Conclusions

globalist/regionalist balance, Crocker maintained that, in his relationship with Pretoria, he could avoid the 'clandestine embrace' of the Nixon administration and the 'polecat treatment' of Carter.[1] In the event, he failed. Again, Washington ended up in this 'clandestine embrace' in pursuit of global calculations. Crocker failed to connect with the black opposition in South Africa because its Africanist, and potentially Marxist, views were perceived as a threat to Washington's globalist agenda.

Although Crocker was adamant that constructive engagement could only be understood as a 'regional policy', the fact remains that his initial description of the policy was in an article entitled 'South Africa: Strategy for Change' (my emphasis). He was later to claim that his regional policy would help to end apartheid in South Africa by reducing South Africa's external security worries. He only emphasized this aspect of his regional policy, however, after the black uprisings of the mid-1980s, which had elevated apartheid on the American political agenda. The fact was that his regional policy was more important to Washington's containment strategy – particularly in its efforts to remove the Cubans from the region – than was his policy against apartheid. These regional aims, far more in line with Washington's globalist considerations, ended up obscuring the parallel aim of dealing with apartheid in South Africa.

Finally, Crocker used the emphasis on white-led change within South Africa as a justification for building a stronger and closer relationship with Pretoria. Unfortunately for Crocker, this policy was a miscalculation. Pretoria simply refused to listen to his overtures about reform, and proved far more intransigent than he had ever envisaged. The black opposition, too, surprised him. He had underestimated their ability, not to overturn apartheid, but to reduce South Africa to a state of ungovernability and to achieve a stalemate with the government. Again, the overriding globalist calculations came into play. Washington did not simply want a move away from apartheid. It wanted a change to a society that would maintain an anti-communist, pro-capitalist perspective. The white government in Pretoria was vital in this calculation, which meant that, even when it became apparent that it was not interested in fundamental political reform inside South Africa, the Executive's hands were tied with regard to increasing the pressure for change. Pretoria was too important in the struggle against communism to risk alienating on the basis of its domestic policies. This increase in pressure was eventually forced upon the Executive by Congress in 1986.

The conceptual basis of Crocker's policy strongly influenced his aims in the region – particularly his implicit agendas. The second question called for an analysis of his aims, both within South Africa and towards the Angola/Namibia situation. Trying to identify these aims requires a distinction to be drawn between the 'explicit' and 'implicit' goals behind Crocker's South and southern African policies. His early explanations of his constructive engagement policy clearly couched it in terms of a method of persuading Pretoria away from apartheid. He also explained his policy in terms of US interests, explaining that it would enable Washington to preserve its beneficial relationship with Pretoria without public or political embarrassment. What Crocker did not admit until after his time in office, however, was that the survival of apartheid was not necessarily the worst outcome for his policy. Relations between the Reagan administration and the potentially Marxist ANC were extremely poor. Subsequent actions – as we have seen throughout this book – demonstrated that Crocker's anti-communist agenda in South Africa, together with his emphasis on a positive appearance for US policy, outweighed his explicit aim of persuading Pretoria away from apartheid.

In evaluating Crocker's linkage policy, this work has examined the dichotomy between those aims that were publicly stated and those that remained implicit. A confusing element of the intentions behind his linkage strategy was the way he presented his main objectives in the region. He began by painting linkage as a strategy designed to achieve Namibian independence but, particularly after the shift in public and political opinion during the uprisings of the mid-1980s in South Africa, and the passing of the CAAA in 1986, he presented the main aim behind linkage as a strategy designed to help the domestic situation within South Africa (see Chapter 8). This alteration can be explained by the fact that, although these were both desirable aims, neither had formed the main reasoning behind Crocker's linkage strategy. The roots of the policy lay in the 1976 US withdrawal from Angola – seen as a Cold War 'defeat' in the eyes of the right wing in Washington, and one that they were determined to avenge. The main aim remained constant throughout – to achieve a total withdrawal of Cuban troops from the region and therefore to reduce communist influence in this sphere. With regard to Namibia's independence, Crocker admitted that achieving a settlement in Namibia was not his first priority. Washington was determined to maintain influence over the final settlements in the region, and was very wary of an outright SWAPO victory. These aims are explored further when this chapter turns to an analysis of the results of Crocker's policies.

Firstly, however, it is important to note here how one of the themes of this book became apparent in the analysis of Crocker's goals. This is the question of whether constructive engagement went beyond an exercise in *realpolitik*. Crocker claims that it did, because his goal to persuade Pretoria away from apartheid demonstrated the fact that his policy was an attempt to address ethical as well as *realpolitik* considerations.[2] He stated that American involvement in South Africa should be pursued for 'reasons both ideological and humanitarian, both strategic and moral, in helping to bring about change in South Africa'. His failure to influence the apartheid issue in South Africa reflected his failure to address this moral dimension of foreign policy, and therefore his failure to take constructive engagement beyond the dictates of *realpolitik*.

The third question posed by this study was to identify the impact of implementation on the results of Crocker's policy. This book emphasizes the significance of policy implementation. It also addresses the idea that a policy such as constructive engagement, so dependent upon sending a clear message to both South Africa and critics at home about what it was trying to achieve, was simply impossible to implement successfully when it involved an issue (apartheid) that so split the Republican Party, the Reagan administration, Congress and even public opinion. Any attempt to exercise real influence over Pretoria was thwarted by the menu of policy choices presented to the South African government by the competing voices emanating from Washington. The linkage strategy was also seriously undermined and almost derailed by the actions of two parties whose interests it had most at heart. As was argued in Chapter 9, Washington almost ruined the negotiations by its insistence on the resumption of funding to UNITA, as did Pretoria, through its continued destabilization of the region.

It was in addressing this question of implementation that the two further themes of this study were developed. The extent to which bureaucratic infighting and political opposition can undermine a particular foreign policy is clearly shown throughout this work. Crocker's own account of his time in office makes no bones about the difficulties he had with rival government departments and agencies (in particular Central Intelligence Agency director Bill Casey). Chapters 2 and 9, in particular, confirm the belief that a fragmented bureaucracy altered the results of his policy. This situation was made far worse for Crocker by Reagan's 'hands off' approach to the presidency and the resulting lack of leadership within the administration.

The final theme was that of the impact of commercial decisions taken by business, independent of government strategy. Indeed, business activity within South Africa and Angola, as well as withdrawal from South Africa, remained decisions that were taken independently by private companies, regardless of whether they reinforced or undermined Crocker's own approach. The concrete achievement of constructive engagement most often pointed to was that of the Sullivan Code, which had not been a government initiative and, although encouraged by the government, was not made mandatory by it. The difficulty became apparent when, after claiming credit for the success of the Sullivan Code, the American government could do nothing when it began to collapse in the face of an absence of any real political change within South Africa. The company signatories began to withdraw from South Africa entirely, and even the founder, Reverend Leo Sullivan of General Motors, disowned the Code in the face of continued political oppression inside South Africa. Continued disinvestment from South Africa undermined constructive engagement's goal of continuing a normal, open relationship with South Africa – but there was nothing Crocker could do to force these companies to remain.

Evaluating the Results: South Africa

The first three questions have dealt with the conceptual basis of Crocker's policy, the aims behind it, and the obstacles and impact of the implementation process. This chapter now turns to the fourth, and most important, question – regarding the results of his policy. The first task is to evaluate the results of this policy as compared with his explicit aims in South Africa. Crocker stated that his aim was to convince Pretoria to move towards a gradual, white-led reform of the political system, leading to the eventual dismantling of the apartheid system. In order to evaluate the success of this declared aim, this analysis begins by looking at the way in which the constructive engagement policy was perceived in South Africa – by the government in Pretoria and by the black opposition.

With regard to Pretoria, constructive engagement was not a success. Pretoria was not as immune to international opinion as it wished both its domestic and its international audience to believe. It saw itself as part of the Western system – a liberal, capitalist, anti-communist ally that provided a stability in the southern African region which was important to Western interests, both economic and strategic. As this view was shared by Crocker and Reagan, it seems difficult to understand why constructive engagement should have gone so badly wrong. The fact was that constructive engagement was about American, not South African interests – and Pretoria was well aware of this. What Pretoria should have realized, however, was that many of its interests (continued investments, anti-communism and concern that changes in South Africa should be gradual and white-led) were in line with Washington's aims. If Pretoria had been less intransigent and isolationist, it could have gained more from constructive engagement, rather than squandering the benefits that this strategy could have brought. What Pretoria did realize was that it could not and would not undertake the level of reform required to make constructive engagement acceptable to the American public. Pretoria made this clear to Crocker when Pik Botha privately explained to him, in February 1986 that 'we simply cannot meet your price'.[3] The fact that Crocker did not revise his approach in the light of these revelations was one of constructive engagement's primary stumbling blocks. Neither Washington nor Pretoria could afford to ignore their electorates, and these two electorates were pulling in opposite directions. The American public became increasingly vocal in their denunciation of apartheid – and their government's links with that regime. However, South Africa's electorate – the Afrikaners in particular – were demanding that their government should stand firm and resist the pressures of external influence.

With regard to black South Africa's opinion towards constructive engagement, reaction was mixed. Washington assiduously courted some of the black moderates, most notably the Zulu leader Chief Buthelezi. Washington would have been well pleased with a government of whites and black moderates, working together in pursuit of regional stability, rejecting communism and participating fully in the international capitalist economy. From the moderate black leaders, therefore, Crocker and his constructive engagement strategy received a cautious welcome. Yet, as was demonstrated in Chapter 5, no unified black support could be given without the engagement of the United Democratic Front (UDF) and the African National Congress (ANC). Far from taking the interests of the ANC into account, Washington was openly hostile to the organization, wary of its communist links and critical of its 'armed struggle' tactics. The

Conclusions

ANC was equally hostile towards Washington, viewing it as in league with Pretoria. Washington's attitude towards the UDF umbrella organization, however, was particularly disappointing to black South Africa. This body represented the mainstream of black opinion and did not espouse violence. Crocker's patent reluctance to engage either with the ANC or the UDF led many blacks to question his commitment to their cause – the ending of apartheid.

Unfortunately for Crocker, he did not seem to appreciate the extent of desperation and anger in the black community. His insistence on gradual, white-led change infuriated the black population. He criticized the black opposition for focusing on the wrong issue: the ultimate goal, instead of the process of getting there. He also stated that black South Africans had 'many openings, many opportunities' to acquire a better bargaining position.[4] This seemed to ignore the fact that simply to profess 'unconstitutional opinions' or to call for disinvestment was illegal in South Africa. Instead, Crocker suggested, blacks could improve their negotiating position if they would just stop working on the assumption of ending apartheid. To blacks, to whom ending apartheid was the crucial issue, and whose every route to the negotiating table, save total capitulation, was proscribed by the South African government, this attitude caused genuine anger.

A lack of concrete results did not help to improve the negative view of constructive engagement held by most black South Africans. Blacks were dismayed by the fact that additional concessions were being offered to Pretoria without being linked to any specific concrete actions of reform on the part of the South African government. The black opposition made it clear that they believed America to be no ally in the fight against apartheid, and were furious with Crocker's insistence on promoting gradual, white-led change. They saw this approach as completely ignoring the urgency of their situation.

The policy of engagement actually resulted in very little tangible influence over Pretoria's behaviour. This study shows that the reforms implemented were entirely at Botha's own pace – addressing only the areas of privilege and prejudice that he saw it expedient to reform. None of Washington's overtures were met with any tangible reforms. When establishing constructive engagement's success in influencing Pretoria's behaviour, one must also take into account the other possible influences and causes that came into play. Genuine influence over Pretoria's actions was usually exerted a lot closer to home. Chapter 5 evaluated the three main sources of influence over Pretoria's policies that came from domestic sources – the black opposition, the right-wing opposition and the South African business community. Chapter 5 also looked at alternative sources of potential influence from elsewhere in the international community.

The black opposition did prove to be effective in influencing Pretoria's behaviour to a certain extent. Intimidation and determined opposition succeeded in dismantling the Black Local Authority System that had been imposed by the 1983 constitution in lieu of more meaningful black political representation. Strikes and demonstrations were also instrumental in achieving some measure of reform, particularly regarding trade union rights and the abolition of pass laws and forced removals. The nightly scenes of violence that were witnessed by the international media were also important in galvanizing world opinion against apartheid – one of the most significant manifestations of this was the passing of the Comprehensive Anti Apartheid Act (CAAA) by the US Congress in 1986. Finally, the sustained black opposition also proved its vital importance by demonstrating, once the uprisings of the mid-1980s had subsided, that the government now faced a stalemate. Black opposition forced Pretoria to look for a way out of the impasse that apartheid had created.

The next internal source of influence was the fear of a right-wing backlash against reforms – a fear that became a reality. For most of Botha's time in office, the National Party (NP) did not look as though it could actually lose power. However, the growth of right-wing electoral support – and the partial shift of Afrikaner allegiance from the NP to Treurnicht's new Conservative Party, forced Botha to tread very carefully when attempting to implement reform. Botha's agenda was significantly affected when, in the 1987 election, the CP replaced the *verligte* Progressive Federal Party (PFP) as the new opposition. By the 1989 election, the NP had gained less than 50 per cent of the vote. These conspicuous trends all served to slow Botha's reform programme.

Together with the black opposition, the business community provided a source of influence that was pulling in the opposite direction from the right-wing critics. Chapter 2 discussed the way in which economic growth and apartheid were eventually accepted by the business community, both in South Africa and abroad, to be incompatible. Although through his actions Botha seemed more concerned by the threat from the right, he did appease the business community to an extent with his reforms on trade union rights and, particularly, the abolition of job reservation legislation in 1983 and the scrapping of the pass laws in 1986. Although these reforms were on Botha's agenda, it is likely that business influence was important in hastening them. The combined pressure from the South African Federated Chamber of Industries and the Associated Chamber of Commerce in particular led to the eventual abolition in 1983 of the restrictive job reservation laws.

The international community made little progress towards the elimination of apartheid through the 1980s. The United Nations and the Commonwealth were strongly criticized by Pretoria for misunderstanding South Africa's plight, and the sanctions threat was openly dismissed by Botha. Yet certain pressures did have dividends. Examples of this include the sports boycotts, which forced apartheid rules to be relaxed in the selection of sports teams. Of even greater significance was the continued international non-recognition of the 'independent homelands', which helped to derail Pretoria's 'grand apartheid' strategy. The international community did keep South Africa on the international agenda, and did exert psychological pressure on many white South Africans, but the only

Conclusions

real action it threatened was limited sanctions. This threat was itself largely negated as Pretoria knew that loss of business confidence and capital market disinvestment were far more serious economic threats than limited, voluntary economic sanctions.

This analysis argues that Botha faced many competing pressures while implementing apartheid and pursuing his reform agenda. The fact remained, however, that Pretoria was simply not ready to undertake a fundamental reform of apartheid. The system was being put under increasing pressure by the influences discussed above, but Crocker's policy of constructive engagement exerted little pressure or influence on Pretoria with regard to the dismantling of apartheid. The fact was that constructive engagement failed in South Africa. It failed to address the interests of Pretoria – and to anticipate just how uncompromising Pretoria would be. When this attitude became apparent, the policy itself was not reviewed, even though, by its own admission, it needed Pretoria's cooperation to succeed. It failed to demonstrate any sincere concern for black interests – and then failed to anticipate how successful the black opposition could be. Although unable to overthrow the government, black opposition did make it impossible to govern South Africa in a normal manner. There is no convincing evidence to show that constructive engagement was instrumental in hastening the demise of apartheid, and there were no signals from Pretoria that they had any intention of dismantling it. This was despite the fact that Crocker had initially presented his policy as a useful contribution towards achieving these aims. In a Congressional hearing in 1989 Senator Cranston outlined the human rights abuses that were still in place in South Africa at the end of Crocker's constructive engagement strategy:

> Many are still the victims of arbitrary arrest and imprisonment. Church and labor groups remain banned. Housing remains segregated and unequal. The homelands policy, which compels blacks to live in the least desirable areas, remains intact. The black majority still has no vote and no representation.[5]

Indeed, Crocker himself, when he left office, envisioned apartheid continuing for many years to come. The situation he had left gave no indication of a government ready to negotiate. As his successor, Herman Cohen, explains: 'In fact, I think that, until the time he left office, Crocker didn't see any change coming in apartheid. And we saw dispatches from the US embassy in Pretoria saying the same thing – apartheid will be here for twenty years.'[6]

The failure to influence South Africa to change the apartheid system is seen by many as the reason *why* constructive engagement can be considered a failure in South Africa. But this is only part of the reason. Chester Crocker's strategy of constructive engagement was designed as a way of enabling Washington to continue its developing relationship with South Africa, while attempting to deflect the controversy that would be created by critics of Pretoria's apartheid regime. Crocker *presented* constructive engagement as a way of addressing the issues raised by the anti-apartheid lobby in the context of an open relationship with Pretoria.

He pointed to the fact that Carter's more aggressive approach towards Pretoria had achieved little with regard to furthering black rights in South Africa. Constructive engagement would mean an end to hostile rhetoric towards Pretoria, and the beginning of an open dialogue in order to increase US influence in persuading Pretoria to engage in a gradual, white-led change away from apartheid.

Although this is the way in which Crocker presented constructive engagement's general approach, the realities behind this policy proved more complex. This study has explored the difference between his implicit and explicit aims, and has attempted to untangle the real motivation behind his actions, as opposed to the occasionally misleading reasoning Crocker himself has presented. Without an understanding of all of his goals, a comprehensive analysis of the success of his policy is impossible. Certainly, Crocker did not deny that his guiding aim was to address US interests in the southern African region, but some of these interests would have proved controversial if addressed in the public arena. In both the questions regarding Namibian independence, and the discussions over apartheid itself, the fact remained that a failure of the Namibian settlement, or a failure to address the question of full political rights for South African blacks, was never the worst possible scenario for Crocker's policy. Nor, accordingly, were these aims given priority in guiding his policy. In both cases, his first priority was to ensure a gradual, non-radical change to a government – whether black or white – that was non-Marxist, sympathetic to American interests, and easily assimilated into the global capitalist economy, whereby America could then benefit from the presence of a political and strategic ally and a further opening of markets without having to face criticism from the international community or the American public.

In fact, constructive engagement failed to achieve Crocker's foremost goal. Constructive engagement failed to successfully address *America's* interests in South Africa. He stated that his main aim was a South Africa 'with which the United States can pursue its varied interests in a full and friendly relationship, without constraint, embarrassment or political damage'.[7] His fundamental goal was to devise a policy in which pursuing American interests in South Africa would not be dogged by controversy or criticism. This book discusses the way in which the Reagan administration focused, in vain, on the American public's perception of the policy, rather than the policy itself. Unfortunately for Crocker, Pretoria's leaders made it very clear that they understood the reasoning behind this policy – in other words, that it was guided by US interests – and that America's public opinion would demand greater reform than Pretoria was prepared to concede. Although they sacrificed potential benefits by not cooperating with this policy, to Pretoria any additional reform was a far higher sacrifice. In the end, Pretoria did not need to make the choice between the benefits of constructive engagement and internal reform, because, until Congress imposed sanctions, the strategy of constructive engagement meant that benefits and allowances kept being issued to South Africa regardless of their actions.

Conclusions

This book also asks if Crocker was able to maintain the credibility of his policy in the United States. The answer appears to be no. Once Congress had passed the CAAA in October 1986, constructive engagement was effectively dead. Crocker tried valiantly to explain how a significant sanctions package did not undermine his policy of open dialogue and friendly persuasion. Chapter 3 discusses the 'Working Group on South and Southern Africa', established to oversee the Public Diplomacy Program on South Africa. The reasoning behind this was to 'sell' constructive engagement to the American public. This Working Group employed more staff than the State Department's southern Africa desk. Despite these efforts, however, it is noticeable that after the CAAA was passed, 'constructive engagement' dropped out of common parlance in Washington circles. Crocker was asked if he thought constructive engagement had survived the CAAA, and whether or not 'constructive engagement' was still the administration's policy. He stated: 'There are those who have wilfully misconstrued what constructive engagement was and is in order to try to discredit it. So we just don't use the word any more because all it does is to sow confusion. The basic approach remains the same.'[8] In fact, the policy was already being referred to by some in the State Department as 'the policy that dare not speak its name'.

Ironically, the CAAA actually spared the constructive engagement policy the additional bad publicity it would otherwise have received when the Secretary of State's Advisory Committee on South Africa published its report entitled *A US Policy Toward South Africa*.[9] After the CAAA the debate over US policy was put on the back burner and attention was focused on potential changes in Eastern Europe. Congress felt as though it had achieved something with the CAAA and the acrimonious debates were put on hold while the results of this new approach were awaited. Also, Pretoria's crackdown on media coverage within South Africa was extremely successful in removing images of violence from American television screens and newspapers – forcing the South Africa issue still further down the political agenda. However, for those still following the developments in US policy towards South Africa, the Advisory Committee's report came as a damaging blow to constructive engagement. The report stated that constructive engagement had 'failed to achieve its objectives'. Crocker was told that his approach must distance itself from the South Africa's white-led reforms and internationalize existing sanctions. Among all the varying recommendations, these two were the most damaging to the strategy of constructive engagement. They flatly contradicted two of its most fundamental aspects – support for white-led evolutionary change and resistance to further sanctions.[10] It is for these reasons that Crocker's constructive engagement failed in both its explicit and implicit aims within South Africa. No concrete proof could be offered to demonstrate that constructive engagement had contributed to the dismantling of apartheid, nor had the policy been accepted by the public as a genuine attempt to address and combat the problem of apartheid in South Africa.

Evaluating the Results: Angola & Namibia

The next task was to explore the results of Crocker's linkage policy towards the regional issues of Namibia and Angola. Linkage itself was bitterly resented by SWAPO, the Angolan government and the African states. The United Nations and the Western Contact Group both refused to endorse the approach, and were thereby sidelined from the settlement negotiations. This book has assessed whether the eventual granting of Namibian independence proved the critics wrong – and whether linkage did eventually succeed where previous administrations and policies had failed.

On the whole, the general evaluation of the results of Crocker's linkage policy in the available literature is a very positive one. Linkage has been termed 'constructive engagement's finest hour'.[11] Thompson states that it was in the Angola/Namibia accords that constructive engagement 'bore some fruit'.[12] Robert Rotberg asserted that: 'Only in the southern African corner of Namibia and Angola could the Americans claim to have helped improve the lot of Africans.'[13] Cohen described the settlement as being 'the most important diplomatic settlement we've had in Africa since 1960 – a magnificent achievement'.[14] Because of the linkage settlement, he explained, 'Our prestige in Africa has never been higher.'[15] Crocker himself said the settlement could not have been better: 'This was the deal that would end Africa's Thirty Years War ... and validate a concept that had been the object of abuse and ridicule.'[16] As Crocker claimed in 1989, after the settlement had been agreed 'the American flag flies high in Africa'.[17]

Indeed, there is certainly no denying the fact that Crocker deserved praise for his extremely effective diplomatic and negotiation skills. Berridge draws attention to the 'length, complexity and bitterness' of the Namibia/Angola accords, and the 'profound mistrust' on both sides. He explains that real diplomatic skill was needed to overcome these obstacles. The Soviet negotiator Adamishin praised Crocker's 'brilliant role'. Even one of Crocker's severest critics, TransAfrica's Randall Robinson, termed the settlement 'a significant achievement' and accepted that Crocker deserved 'kudos for a major effort'.[18] This book by no means dismisses the important role linkage played in getting the parties to the table, nor the considerable diplomatic skill of Crocker in keeping them there. With regard to achieving the final settlement, however, its conclusions are more circumspect.

Although Crocker was successful in bringing the parties to the table for the Angola/Namibia accords, it is important to question the extent to which those accords reflected and achieved the original goals he had set out in the region. In his press conference in New York – held on the eve of the signing of the accords – Crocker outlined his three aims: Namibian independence; the withdrawal of all foreign forces from Angola and Namibia – 'specifically' the Cuban forces in Angola; and to bring about an environment conducive to peace and reconciliation inside Angola.[19] The

Conclusions

confidential NSDD 212 of 10 February 1986 also listed improved relations between South Africa and its neighbours and a minimizing of violence and terrorism by any party.

The first of these objectives, the realization of Namibian independence, was achieved. There is, however, a contentious aspect to this part of the settlement. It is possible to argue that Crocker's constructive engagement approach to Pretoria actually delayed this settlement. It is impossible to say for certain how close the Carter administration had come to bringing about this result. Nevertheless, even Crocker appeared confident, when he took up his post in 1981, that an agreement could be reached by 1982. A State Department memorandum to Richard Allen (White House Staff Member) at the White House, dated 24 September 1981, described the way in which Crocker's positive meeting with Pik Botha's deputy Brand Fourie in Zurich on 21 September had:

> permitted the announcement of the adoption of a common objective of beginning implementation of a Namibian independence agreement during 1982. The very positive South African response is a clear, direct result of our new relationship of constructive engagement with South Africa.[20]

This aspect does not negate Crocker's achievement regarding Namibian independence, but it does qualify it.

The next objective of Crocker's policy was to achieve a total withdrawal of Cuban troops from Angola. Again, his linkage formula was directly instrumental in achieving this aim. Yet questions remain regarding what could have been achieved in the absence of this policy. The Angolans and the Cubans had already agreed to their own withdrawal schedule independently – a schedule only torn up in response to repeated South African incursions into Angolan territory. It is also important to note that Crocker wanted the Cubans out of Angola in order to reduce their influence in the region. The fact was that Cuban influence in the region was never very great – particularly as Cuba, unlike the West, was not in a position to provide the level of economic assistance the countries of the region so badly wanted. However, the signing of the accords did not succeed in diminishing Cuban influence still further. Rather, the Cubans had gained an important role on the international stage, and had been seen by other governments in Africa as defending a sovereign African government from the incursions of Pretoria. The Cubans also proved themselves successful in the military arena.

The third goal was to achieve a significant move towards peace and reconciliation in Angola. In 1989 Crocker stated that a move towards peace between the MPLA and UNITA was 'the logical and inexorable fruit of the December 1988 regional settlement in south western Africa'.[21] His optimism was sadly misplaced. Critics said that Washington's policy of aiding UNITA and refusal to recognize the MPLA government in Luanda: 'encouraged Jonas Savimbi to disregard the outcome of the September 1992 election and plunge Angola back into its devastating civil war'.[22] Far from aiding reconciliation, it can be argued that American policy was responsible for prolonging this bloody and brutal war. The aims of reduced violence and improved relations between South Africa and the FLS were not addressed by Crocker's policy. This is demonstrated by the fact that South African destabilization of the region actually increased during Crocker's tenure.

Indeed, certain factors that contributed to the settlement appeared to be in direct contradiction to Crocker's own prescription for achieving a settlement. A major factor was the thawing of American–Soviet relations. The changing attitude of the Soviets meant that including them in the negotiations proved very valuable. The role of the Soviets – and the Cubans – in the negotiations is often overlooked in the main body of the literature, yet in interviews with Crocker and Herman Cohen it appears that the Soviets were indeed valuable partners in the negotiating process. The strength of the Cuban military presence was also an important factor in forcing South Africa to accept that they could no longer maintain the *status quo* without a considerable – and increasing – cost. This contrasted directly with Crocker's insistence on securing Cuban troop withdrawal in order to achieve a settlement. Also, despite his adamant rejection of sanctions, the South Africans became genuinely concerned when export restrictions meant that they began to fall behind technologically and militarily, as was demonstrated to them in the fight against the Cubans in Angola.

Final Conclusions

This work therefore presents a critical evaluation of Crocker's policies – both within South Africa and with regard to the Angolan/Namibian settlement. It demonstrates the way in which the *public presentation* of his aims in the region and statements about what he hoped to achieve – through his policies of constructive engagement in South Africa and his linkage strategy in the regional settlement – were in need of further investigation in order to obtain a comprehensive understanding of his actions. This is because evaluations of his role in the Western literature have tended to concentrate on judging his achievements in the context of his publicly stated aims – the gradual dismantling of apartheid in South Africa and the twin goals of Namibian independence and Cuban troop withdrawal in the region. What these analyses tend to overlook, however, is the overriding goal which Crocker himself identified in his first public articulation of his constructive engagement policy in his 'Strategy for Change'. He stated then that he wanted to formulate a policy which would result in the US being able to pursue a relationship with South Africa 'without constraint, embarrassment or political damage'.[23] Once he was appointed to office, this goal became part of his *implicit* agenda in southern Africa. The aim was to achieve an acceptable public face for this policy of continued engagement with the apartheid regime in South Africa. This book argues that the substance of these explicit aims was lower on his list of priorities than this emphasis on appearance.

The conclusion in the current literature is that Crocker failed in South

Conclusions

Africa and succeeded in the regional settlement. As Baker states: 'In the

Africa and succeeded in the regional settlement. As Baker states: 'In the final analysis, constructive engagement ... will be associated with a major success in its regional diplomacy and a major failure in its South African strategy.'[24] Thompson also argued that although in the Angola/Namibia negotiations, constructive engagement 'bore some fruit' and was constructive engagement's 'finest hour ... [t]he fact remains that the Reagan administration operated an anti-apartheid strategy for eight years without any real positive results'.[25]

In South Africa it was clear that Crocker's constructive engagement had done nothing to hasten the end of apartheid – and little to address the interests of South Africa's black majority. Crocker failed, too, in his implicit agenda to achieve a publicly acceptable face for this policy. Within South Africa itself, Pretoria remained steadfastly suspicious of Washington's motives, whereas relations between the United States and South Africa's main black opposition groups verged on the openly hostile. Even the American public rejected the policy of constructive engagement, particularly after the South African uprisings in the mid-1980s, despite the fact that public acceptance of America's relationship with Pretoria was the driving force behind Crocker's constructive engagement policy.

Crocker failed in his goal to *present* his South Africa policy as a genuine attempt to redress the injustices of apartheid and he failed in his attempt to boost American credibility in the region at the expense of the Soviet Union and the Cubans. He had planned to support change in South Africa only to the extent that it would result in a pro-West, anti-communist society with an open economy. Ironically, it was this open, capitalist economy that finally rejected apartheid. De Klerk came to accept that modern, capitalist growth could not be reconciled with the anachronistic system of apartheid.[26] Also, Gorbachev's radical new thinking, a precursor to the collapse of the Soviet Union, meant that white South Africa could no longer hold on to its fear of the 'total onslaught' from the communist presence in the region. It also meant that the Soviet Union was rethinking its own exposure in the southern African region.

Far less universally accepted in the current literature is the idea that Crocker could be described as having, in part, 'failed' in the Angola/Namibia accords. This study, while focused on the conclusions reached in Western literature, also takes into account the perspectives of the other parties involved. Rather than furthering US credibility among the states of southern Africa, many of the Frontline States were vocal opponents of the linkage approach – as was the Organization of African Unity (OAU) as a whole. Even the SWAPO government of Namibia, elected after the independence achieved through the linkage settlement, resented the role played by Washington in the accords, seeing it as 'a policy of destructive engagement'.[27] While the hostility between the MPLA government in Angola and Washington was always open, even America's client group UNITA was furious with the final results of the settlement, believing itself to have been abandoned by the US and refusing to accept the eventual election results in Angola.

The real measure of failure – in Crocker's terms – is that American final analysis, constructive engagement ... will be associated with a major success in its regional diplomacy and a major failure in its South African strategy.'[24] Thompson also argued that although in the Angola/Namibia negotiations, constructive engagement 'bore some fruit' and was constructive engagement's 'finest hour ... [t]he fact remains that the Reagan administration operated an anti-apartheid strategy for eight years without any real positive results'.[25]

In South Africa it was clear that Crocker's constructive engagement had done nothing to hasten the end of apartheid – and little to address the interests of South Africa's black majority. Crocker failed, too, in his implicit agenda to achieve a publicly acceptable face for this policy. Within South Africa itself, Pretoria remained steadfastly suspicious of Washington's motives, whereas relations between the United States and South Africa's main black opposition groups verged on the openly hostile. Even the American public rejected the policy of constructive engagement, particularly after the South African uprisings in the mid-1980s, despite the fact that public acceptance of America's relationship with Pretoria was the driving force behind Crocker's constructive engagement policy.

Crocker failed in his goal to *present* his South Africa policy as a genuine attempt to redress the injustices of apartheid and he failed in his attempt to boost American credibility in the region at the expense of the Soviet Union and the Cubans. He had planned to support change in South Africa only to the extent that it would result in a pro-West, anti-communist society with an open economy. Ironically, it was this open, capitalist economy that finally rejected apartheid. De Klerk came to accept that modern, capitalist growth could not be reconciled with the anachronistic system of apartheid.[26] Also, Gorbachev's radical new thinking, a precursor to the collapse of the Soviet Union, meant that white South Africa could no longer hold on to its fear of the 'total onslaught' from the communist presence in the region. It also meant that the Soviet Union was rethinking its own exposure in the southern African region.

Far less universally accepted in the current literature is the idea that Crocker could be described as having, in part, 'failed' in the Angola/Namibia accords. This study, while focused on the conclusions reached in Western literature, also takes into account the perspectives of the other parties involved. Rather than furthering US credibility among the states of southern Africa, many of the Frontline States were vocal opponents of the linkage approach – as was the Organization of African Unity (OAU) as a whole. Even the SWAPO government of Namibia, elected after the independence achieved through the linkage settlement, resented the role played by Washington in the accords, seeing it as 'a policy of destructive engagement'.[27] While the hostility between the MPLA government in Angola and Washington was always open, even America's client group UNITA was furious with the final results of the settlement, believing itself to have been abandoned by the US and refusing to accept the eventual election results in Angola.

The real measure of failure – in Crocker's terms – is that American credibility, influence and prestige in South and southern Africa was not increased by his policies, and this is why this book is justified in stating that he failed to achieve his implicit aims in the region. In fact it was Cuba in particular that gained credibility and prestige, not only in the eyes of the states of southern Africa, but even on the international stage. The Marxist MPLA government remained in power in Angola, and the Marxist-oriented SWAPO was elected as the new democratic government of an independent Namibia – something neither Washington nor Pretoria wanted to see. In the final analysis, Crocker failed in his two most important goals: to conduct a policy with South Africa by which 'the United States [could] pursue its varied interests in a full and friendly relationship, without constraint, embarrassment or political damage'[28] and to 'win the Cold War in the Third World'.[29]

Notes

1 Crocker, Chester, 'South Africa: Strategy for Change', *Foreign Affairs*, Vol. 59, No. 2 (Winter 1980–1), p. 346.
2 Personal interview with Dr Chester Crocker, Washington, DC, 19 June 2001.
3 Ronald Reagan Library, CA. White House Staff and Office Files: Cohen, Herman J., Files 1987–8. African Affairs Directorate, NSC. Boxes 91875 and 91876. Secret Cable. From: Crocker. To: Poindexter (The White House). Subject: Geneva Meeting with Pik Botha, February 1986. Declassified 26 May 1999.
4 ARC Identifier: 59633, *Status of the Peace Process in Southern Africa – Crocker, 1984*. Creator: United States Information Agency (1982–) (Most Recent). Broadcast 16 May 1984. Item from Record Group 306: Records of the USIA 1900–1988. Video Recordings from the 'Worldnet Today' Program Series. NAIL Locator: 306-WNET-56 Motion Picture, Sound and Video Recordings LICON, National Archives at College Park, Maryland USA.
5 Testimony of Senator Cranston, *US Policy Toward South Africa* Hearings before the Committee on Foreign Relations, United States Senate, 101st Congress, First Session, 3 October 1989, p. 2.
6 Personal interview with Herman Cohen, 22 June 2001, Washington, DC.
7 Crocker, 'Strategy for Change', p. 324.
8 ARC Identifier: 60164, *United States – African Relations – Crocker, 1987*. Creator: United States Information Agency (1982–) (Most Recent). Broadcast 16 December 1987. Item from Record Group 306: Records of the USIA 1900–1988. Video Recordings from the 'Worldnet Today' Program Series. NAIL Locator: 306-WNET-597 Motion Picture, Sound and Video Recordings LICON, National Archives at College Park, Maryland USA.
9 Department of State Publication No. 9537, *A US Policy toward South Africa: The Report of the Secretary of State's Advisory Committee on South Africa*. Released to the Public 21 April 1987.
10 Other recommendations included more aid to South African blacks, improved communication and links with a range of black leaders, and a clearer statement of opposition to apartheid. All of these recommendations reflect the serious miscalculation Crocker made in not engaging with South Africa's black opposition.
11 Thompson, Alex, 'Incomplete Engagement: Reagan's South Africa Policy Revisited', *Journal of Modern African Studies*, Vol. 33, No. 1 (March 1995), p. 85.
12 *Ibid.*, p. 85.
13 Rotberg, Robert I. 'The Reagan Era in Africa', in David E. Kyvig (ed.), *Reagan and the World*, New York: Praeger Publisher, 1990, p. 120.
14 Personal interview with Herman Cohen, 22 June 2001, Washington, DC.
15 Cohen, Herman J., *Intervening in Africa: Superpower Peacemaking in a Troubled Continent*,

Basingstoke and London: Macmillan, 2000 and New York: St Martin's Press, 2000, p. 87.

16 Crocker, Chester, *High Noon in Southern Africa: Making Peace in a Rough Neighborhood*, New York and London: W. W. Norton and Company, 1992, p. 441.

17 Although, during a conference held at Chatham House in London on 25 April 1989, Chester Crocker related that, at a meeting he had held with Fidel Castro in late March 1989, he had heard Castro describe the December Accords as 'his [Castro's] settlement'. Cuba's flag was flying, too! See Geoff Berridge, 'Diplomacy and the Angola/Namibia Accords', *International Affairs*, Vol. 65, No. 3 (Summer 1989), p. 465.

18 Baker, Pauline H., *The United States and South Africa: The Reagan Years. Update South Africa: Time Running Out*, Ford Foundation and Foreign Policy Association, 1989, p. 70.

19 'Significance of the Angola/Namibia Agreements', press conference by Chester Crocker, USUN Mission HQ, New York, 21 December 1988, in *American Foreign Policy: Current Documents Annual*, 1988, Washington, DC, GPO (1981–), Document No. 395.

20 Ronald Reagan Library, CA. White House Staff and Office Files: Walker, Lannon. Secret Memorandum – From: L. Paul Bremer III Executive Secretary Department of State. To: Richard V. Allen, The White House. Subject: Namibia Contact Group Ministerial Meeting, 24 September 1981.

21 Crocker, Chester, 'Southern Africa: Eight Years Later', *Foreign Affairs*, Vol. 68, No. 4 (1989), p. 148.

22 Pycroft, C. 'Review – *High Noon in Southern Africa: Making Peace in a Rough Neighborhood*, Chester Crocker', *Journal of Modern African Studies*, Vol. 32, No. 1 (1994), p. 169.

23 Crocker, 'Strategy for Change', p. 324.

24 Baker, *The United States and South Africa*, p. 71.

25 Thompson, 'Incomplete Engagement', p. 85.

26 Herman Cohen, Crocker's successor, was one of the first American officials to meet de Klerk after he announced his intention to stand for the position of President of South Africa. In a private meeting in August 1989, when Botha had announced his retirement and de Klerk was on the campaign trail – already having taken over leadership of the NP – de Klerk outlined to Cohen his views on apartheid. He explained: 'I was born under apartheid and grew up under apartheid. I believed in it and I thought it was the best way for South Africa. But now, when my first grandchild has just been born, I know it won't work. I never believed it was immoral, but I know it won't work because we're trying to become a modern economy and you can't have a modern economy when 80 per cent of the population is not producing anything and is not consuming anything. My generation will be OK, but my grandchild's generation will have nothing – they won't be able to live here. We don't want to see the whites leaving and this is why we must dismantle apartheid.' As recounted by Herman Cohen. Personal Interview with Ambassador Herman J. Cohen (Retired), Cohen & Woods, Washington, DC, 22 June 2001.

27 Personal correspondence between the author and Jeroboam Shaanika of the Namibian High Commission in London, 26 January 1999.

28 Crocker, 'Strategy for Change', p. 324.

29 Crocker, *High Noon in Southern Africa*, p. 17.

13
Implications for
Today's Policy Makers

The analysis of Crocker's policy in southern Africa has an important relevance to the foreign policy dilemmas of today. The post 9/11 world in which we live has created a climate of fear. The need for a world view which balances both regional and global considerations is more pressing than ever, but the current context has made achieving this ever less likely. The events of 9/11 and the subsequent recognition of the global nature of the terrorist threat have not been the only change in context since Crocker was in office. The collapse of the Soviet Union has resulted in a shift from a bipolar to a unipolar world, with the United States now the world's only superpower. In this role, the US has been tempted to follow a foreign policy based on the calculations of a global war on terror. The understandable emphasis on national security has meant that, once again, some regional realities elsewhere in the world are being neglected in Washington. Meanwhile, the failure of sanctions and the war in Iraq, followed by the current chaos there, the regrouping of the Taliban on the borders of Afghanistan and the threat of terrorist attacks across the globe all point to the need for a balanced approach towards the pursuit of foreign policy goals. At the same time, it is feared that the widespread abuse of human rights, systematic in some parts of the world, could result in serious instability – producing, in turn, disenfranchised and disillusioned groups vulnerable to terrorist recruitment. Thus the need to ensure national security, whilst at the same time combating the abuse of human rights, is a matter of urgency. Throughout this book, the tension between the pursuit of national interest and concern for human rights has been obvious and this tension exists just as surely for policy makers throughout the West today.

Can a strategy of constructive engagement enable these governments to use their influence to address the moral and ethical concerns of human rights, without having to compromise security or sacrifice strategic and economic links with the country in question? This is how constructive engagement has been presented to the public by successive Western governments, in much the same way that it was used to explain the Reagan administration's dealings with South Africa.

The term 'constructive engagement' has once again found favour in the West. The UK's Foreign and Commonwealth Office (FCO), for example, has explicitly described its relations with a wide range of countries in terms of constructive engagement, including Iran, Uzbekistan, China and even such pariahs as Libya and North Korea. As the FCO explains: 'The aim is to encourage improved standards though dialogue, guidance and support as part of a constructive bilateral relationship.'[1] It is interesting to note the divergence between Western governments over engagement with certain 'rogue states', most notably Iran and Libya. Despite the Republican championing of engagement with Pretoria during apartheid, Washington has been more reluctant than Britain and its EU partners concerning engagement with some of today's hostile governments. Yet for both America and the EU constructive engagement with pariah states remains a vital diplomatic tool.

Constructive engagement, this book has argued, did not succeed in South Africa. Can it succeed today? The Cold War was instrumental in affording major strategic significance to certain states, including those guilty of abusing the human rights of their own citizens. The necessity of maintaining ties and influence meant that human rights abuses were sometimes overlooked or, as in South Africa, weighed in the balance with strategic interests. The fear remains that Bush's 'for us or against us' approach to the War on Terror could result in the same myopia in American foreign policy that was apparent during the Cold War. Although Washington has a menu of policy choices at its disposal,[2] constructive engagement could be used, in part, to disguise a 'business as usual' approach towards a rogue state, particularly in the face of domestic criticism, and the analysis of Washington's engagement with Pretoria has demonstrated the risks of this approach. Yet the fact remains that the most obvious alternative to engagement would be to simply leave misgoverned countries in isolation. It is true that refusing to have anything to do with such countries 'might provide us with clean hands, but ... is unlikely to provide their people with better rights'.[3] So the strategy of constructive engagement remains a vital policy alternative. This analysis of Crocker's experience demonstrates, however, certain lessons that can – and should – be learnt. This final chapter will identify the main problems revealed by Washington's engagement with Pretoria – in the hope that such stumbling blocks can be avoided today.

The Carrot & the Stick

The first lesson to be learnt is that for constructive engagement to be credible, it must utilize both the 'carrot' and the 'stick'. The problem with engagement is that it is often employed when a country's interests are at stake, whether these interests be economic, strategic or political. If this interest is apparent, a rogue state is well aware of the costs of disengagement to the other actors. It will therefore feel little inclination to alter its behaviour in order to maintain such engagement, knowing that continued engagement is in the interests of both parties. This is partly what happened during Washington's engagement with Pretoria. The over-arching concern of the Cold War, together with the strategic issues of the

Conclusions

Cape route, and access to minerals and trade, made any withdrawal from South Africa just as costly to the perceived interests of the US as it was to Pretoria. In these circumstances, Washington's hands were tied when faced with Pretoria's intransigence over the apartheid issue. It is just such a situation that appears to validate the accusation that engagement is merely a diplomatic fig leaf – an attempt to conduct 'business as usual' with a rogue state without attracting criticism from a domestic or international audience.

Such accusations are levelled at Western governments today. One example is the West's relationship with Beijing. On 3 and 4 June 1989, Beijing ordered the Chinese army to open fire on the large crowd of protesters who had gathered in Tiananmen Square to protest at the lack of democracy in China. There were no official estimates of the number of people killed, but the US State Department estimated that the casualties numbered in the hundreds at least. In response to this incident, Chinese relations with the West cooled considerably. The US suspended high-level official exchanges, weapons exports were put on hold and a number of limited economic sanctions were imposed. Despite the fact that grave human rights abuses continue in China, relations with the West have steadily improved – and this fact has greatly benefited the Chinese economy. Relations with China are often described in terms of 'constructive engagement' or 'critical dialogue' with the West, and it is argued that continued engagement not only promotes economic or strategic interests but also helps to improve human rights within that country. The experience of the British–Chinese relationship is a good example of this argument.

Under the auspices of the constructive engagement approach, the British government established a formal 'UK–China dialogue' in 1997. Twice a year, representatives of the two governments meet to discuss the human rights situation inside China. The meetings alternate between London and Beijing, and the UK government holds a debriefing session with NGOs after the talks. The British government maintains that the constructive engagement approach towards China has resulted in many benefits in the field of human rights. During the period of dialogue, China has acceded to the International Covenant on Economic, Social and Cultural rights and had dialogue with the UN High Commissioner for Human Rights. Communication with the British government has resulted in practical help, such as providing China with technical expertise in order to make the legal changes necessary to accede to the International Covenant on Civil and Political Rights. Constructive engagement is seen as a good way of reconciling the UK's 'broad objectives':

- To encourage China's closer integration into the international system (including economic, financial and trade structures) and to encourage a constructive approach towards international security issues;
- To promote positive change in human rights, with a particular emphasis on the rule of law;
- To advance British commercial interests.[4]

Certainly, attempts to integrate China into the world economy and to advance British commercial interests appear to be working well. China has now overtaken Italy as the sixth largest economy in the world. In 2002, with Foreign Direct Investment (FDI) reaching $52 billion, China overtook the US as the largest recipient of FDI in the world, and on 11 December 2001 China became a member of the World Trade Organization (WTO). Britain is the sixth largest foreign investor in China, and the leading EU investor there. The DTI states that China is a priority market for UK trade and investment and that British trade with China grew exponentially in the 1990s. Yet this growth in trade and investment occurred directly after the massacre in Tiananmen Square in 1989.

In an article condemning Europe's laissez-faire attitude towards human rights in China, *The Economist* stated: 'The lure of trade long ago detached human rights from matters economic.'[5] The British government points to the UK–China dialogue as the forum for encouraging change in this area. This dialogue is a good example of constructive engagement in action but dialogue can never be an end in itself. It must lead to practical change on the ground. Unfortunately, the British government's appraisal of the results of this dialogue admits that, with regard to its human rights agenda at least, many of its own objectives have resulted in disappointment: there has been no reduction in the use of the death penalty; no steps have been taken to reduce the use of 're-education through labour' (RTL) – a method of punishment to which the British government has particularly objected; pressure to reform the treatment of prisoners has not been heeded; and persecution of religious minorities persists. Indeed, the lack of progress made through this dialogue is perhaps unsurprising when the Chinese government itself has stated, at the UN Commission on Human Rights in April 2003, that international concern regarding human rights in China was 'unimportant, meaningless and irrelevant'.[6] Despite these disappointments, the West continues to engage constructively with China.

In the meantime, of course, the non-confrontational attitude allows trade to flourish. The trouble with this approach is that it does not seem to be working. Most independent observers, and the US Department of State, say that in recent years the Chinese government's treatment of its people has been getting worse.[7]

Even advocates of constructive engagement recognize this fact. In a speech on human rights and their priority in British foreign policy, former British foreign secretary and vocal campaigner for the role of ethics in foreign policy Robin Cook acknowledged that there was a paradox: 'while China has engaged more fully rights at an international level ... in the domestic arena the record on human rights is grave and even more dissidents are being arrested.'[8] With little apparent sanction applied, apart from 'meaningless and irrelevant' criticism, it appears that constructive engagement, once again, has failed in its attempt to reconcile the pursuit of economic interests with the ability to influence a move towards genuine change in the field of human rights. No Western government appears to have the will to provide any necessary 'stick' to counterbalance the carrot of improved relations. It is apparent that the important economic benefits of dealing with this huge and rapidly growing economy make it harder for any specific country to put access to such benefits at risk. The massive growth in the Chinese economy has been hard for governments to resist and constructive engagement continues to dominate the Western approach towards Beijing.

Such unity is not to be found in the West's approach towards all states, however, and a comparison of American and European approaches to certain rogue states illustrates some important points about using both a carrot and stick in engagement. Until recently, there was a marked contrast between American and European approaches towards Libya. The accession of General Quaddaffi to the office of President and his openly hostile attitude towards the West, and America in particular, led to a rapid worsening of Libya's relations with the West. On 29 December 1979 the US government declared Libya a 'state sponsor of terrorism' and in March 1982 Washington prohibited imports of Libyan crude oil into the US. By January 1986 a total ban on all direct import and export trade was in place, sanctions which were codified in the form of the Iran Libya Sanctions Act (ILSA). In Britain, diplomatic relations with Libya were broken off in 1984, in response to the shooting of WPC Yvonne Fletcher during the siege of the Libyan embassy in London. On 21 December 1988 an American passenger jet, Flight Pan Am 103, was brought down by an onboard bomb over Lockerbie in Scotland. Tripoli was suspected of complicity in the plot and its initial refusal to cooperate with the international community in bringing the Libyan suspects to justice resulted in UN sanctions being imposed in March 1992 (UNSCR 731 and UNSCR 748). Further obstruction by Libya meant that the sanctions were strengthened in November 1993 (UNSCR 883). Libya remained in political and economic isolation from the West for most of the 1990s.

Since this time, however, Tripoli has shown a definite wish to restore ties with Europe. In July 1999 the Libyan government accepted 'general responsibility' for the shooting of WPC Fletcher and apologized. Diplomatic relations with the UK were resumed, with the first British Ambassador for 15 years arriving in Libya in December 1999. Eventual cooperation regarding the Lockerbie bombing suspects meant that talks began on 13 February 2001 to determine how Libya could meet the rest of the requirements of the UN Security Council. On 15 August 2003 Britain tabled a resolution recommending that UN sanctions be lifted. It was passed on 13 September 2003, with abstentions from the US and France. Libya now has strong and growing trade links with the EU, and is an important British market. In 2002 the value of British exports stood at £215.7 million, while imports – almost all petroleum products – were valued at £167 million.

On 19 December 2003, Libya announced its intention to rid itself of weapons of mass destruction (WMD) and MTCR-class missile programmes, and has since cooperated with the international community in fulfilling this promise. The US responded by terminating the applicability of the ILSA, a five-year extension of which was approved by Congress in July 2001. On 28 April 2004 the US Office of Foreign Assets

Control issued a general licence, effectively opening Libya to US investment by making it permissible to engage in financial and commercial transactions with Libya. The ban on Libyan petroleum imports was also lifted. By July 2004 diplomatic presence had also been re-established, via a US Liaison Office in Tripoli and a Libyan Interest Section in Washington, DC. The US had been far more circumspect than Britain about lifting sanctions, maintaining economic and diplomatic penalties when the British government had already embarked on a policy of constructive engagement with Tripoli. Indeed, Washington believes that its resistance to any earlier lifting of sanctions brought about the pressure that was necessary to force Quaddaffi to cooperate with the West. The State Department explained:

> The US maintained its trade and travel embargoes and brought diplomatic and economic pressure to bear against Libya. This pressure helped to bring about the Lockerbie settlement and Libya's renunciation of WMD and MTCR-class missiles.[9]

This is an interesting claim, particularly as the British government prefers to see Libya's rehabilitation as an example of successful constructive engagement in action. Indeed, commentators speak of the way in which British constructive engagement has brought Libya 'back into the diplomatic fold' and they contrast the policy 'favourably with Washington's resolution of awkward international issues'.[10] Quaddaffi has been explicit in his intention to improve relations with the West and both constructive engagement and a determination to escape the damage being done by economic and diplomatic sanctions could have encouraged this reasonableness on his part. The likelihood appears to be a combination of both (although caution must be exercised when attempting to extrapolate lessons from Quaddaffi's notoriously erratic behaviour). Constructive engagement opened the channels of communication that were necessary for Quaddaffi to make his intentions known. The 'stick' of the damaging economic and diplomatic sanctions meant that engagement and the prospect of a thawing of relations had real value. On the other hand, the ability to remain, to an extent, open-minded about the intentions of this pariah state meant that such overtures could be encouraged.

Unfortunately, another recent example of constructive engagement in action is that of the relationship between Europe and Canada and the Sudan. The Sudan People's Liberation Army (SPLA) in the Christian South had been at war with the Islamic government in Khartoum since 1983. Although the 2003 peace talks between Khartoum and the SPLA in Kenya have established a ceasefire, the conflict in the Darfur region of western Sudan continues. This more recent conflict is caused by two main factors. The first was an uprising by two military resistance groups known as the Sudanese Liberation Movement/Army (SLM/A) and the Justice and Equality Movement (JEM). These groups resented the inferior treatment of the ethnic black Africans of the region at the hands of the Arab government in Khartoum. The second issue is that many of the African villages were situated either on potential oil fields ripe for exploration, or on the planned route of a pipeline intended to transport oil. The uprising was met by a government response of crushing brutality, carried out largely by the government-backed Arab militias known as the Janjaweed with the support of government air power. The Janjaweed have been responsible for widespread human rights violations against the civilian population in Darfur. This black African (although largely Muslim) population has been subject to a sustained campaign of murder, rape and abductions. The situation has been described by the UN Commissioner for Human Rights, Bertrand Ramcharan as a 'scorched earth policy' in the execution of which 'repeated crimes against humanity [are] happening before our very eyes'.[11] A report by the New York-based Human Rights Watch accused the Sudanese government of ethnic cleansing. The brutality is such that, in August 2004, the US Secretary of State Colin Powell categorized it in a speech to the United Nations as 'genocide'. The EU has shied away from going as far as this, which reflects its historically more cautious approach towards the Sudan. In 1993 the US designated the Sudan a 'state sponsor of terrorism' and in October 1997 Washington imposed comprehensive sanctions. In August 1998, in response to the bombings of US embassies in East Africa, the US launched retaliatory air strikes against Khartoum. The US Ambassador was withdrawn, and since that time the US embassy has been headed by a chargé d'affaires.

This approach contrasts with that of, for example, the British and Canadian governments, who chose to engage with the Sudanese government. Since 1999, oil has been the major source of revenue and economic growth for Sudan and the UK remains one of its major trading partners. Government policies have enabled British and Canadian firms to lead the way in exploiting Sudan's oil reserves – until, that is, public pressure held sway (see below). The actions and policies of the British government have left it exposed to charges of putting corporate profits before human rights. The response of the British government has been to explain that 'the UK is fully engaged. We have lobbied at the highest levels in Khartoum on this matter.'[12] London's approach has been strongly criticized. Peter Verney, author of *Oil and Conflict in Sudan*, pointed out: 'The British government has called on Premier Oil to pull out of Burma, saying "constructive engagement" doesn't work. Yet in Sudan we are still plugging away at constructive engagement, getting by with warm words of concern about the turmoil in the South.'[13] Almost a year later, the approach of the British government was still facing the same criticism: 'The British government's policy of constructive engagement has done nothing to dissuade Khartoum's bombing.'[14] Again it was the US, rather than Britain or the rest of Europe, who appeared determined to pressure Khartoum to stop the killing. In 2003 peace talks were held between the largely Christian South and the Islamic North, and the government of Sudan began talking seriously to the SPLA for the first time in May 2003. It was accepted that US pressure had been instrumental in bringing about this turn of events. *The Economist* stated that 'foreign pressure had been crucial', explaining that, if Khartoum refused to negotiate in good faith, the US 'threatened to choke it with economic sanctions and bankroll the SPLA'.[15] This forced

President Omar Bashir to make enough concessions to show good faith – at least on paper. It had been agreed in October 2002 that the continued normalization of EU–Sudanese relations would be tied to progress in the peace process. Once again, however, there has been nothing to demonstrate that a continued policy of engagement alone could or would produce such results.

The fact that the UN has been unwilling or unable to act in this case is also a depressingly familiar theme. The UN was rendered impotent when dealing with apartheid in South Africa, and was particularly undermined by the American 'linkage' efforts in the southern African region. Such limitations remain today. What the above discussion of constructive engagement has illustrated is that the international community needs to work together – both in its engagement with a pariah regime, and in its determination to impose some form of sanction should engagement fail. It has also demonstrated the necessity of using some form of pressure to bring about change. Such efforts should be coordinated by a powerful international body, but the UN in its current form is incapable of such a task. Since the time of Crocker's policy, the need for fundamental reform of the UN has become ever more pressing. It was designed to deal with wars between states, but now its principles of sovereignty and non-interference in internal affairs risk rendering it obsolete in the new climate of civil war and terrorism. When even clear-cut cases such as the abuses in the Sudan, for example, cannot be agreed upon in the Security Council, and successive General Assembly criticisms are ignored by the Sudanese government, the need for reform becomes still more obvious.

A final example of engagement with Iran again illustrates contrasting American/European approaches. The British government explains that its policy of constructive engagement with Iran does not imply satisfaction with Iran's human rights record. Rather, its 'policy of critical engagement enables it to put forward its views and concerns regularly and at all levels'. The government also denies that the issue of trade with Iran affects its judgement on human rights. It has stated that negotiations on the EU/Iran Trade Agreement are dependent on progress in the area of political reform. It also utilizes the argument, put forward by Crocker with regard to dealings with South Africa, that engagement with the rest of the world, an improved economy and improved living standards are much more likely to result in reform in Iran than isolation. Some commentators applaud this European view, and criticize America's heavy-handed response towards rogue states (for example, its characterization of Iraq, Iran and North Korea as an 'axis of evil'): 'The policies of the United States towards Iran contrast strongly with the policies of "constructive engagement" pursued by the EU and Britain which have re-established diplomatic relations with Iran and encouraged democratization.'[16]

Despite this assessment, however, the Iranian elections held in February 2004 indicated widespread intervention by the ruling Guardian Council, including the disqualification of over 3,000 candidates (including eighty members of the current parliament). Many foreign governments expressed grave doubts regarding the elections. Concern also remains regarding human rights within Iran, particularly the treatment of women and religious minorities. The British government states that such persecution is 'totally unacceptable'. However, there appears to be no sanction to balance the UK's engagement with Iran on this matter. With regard to the abuses of human rights, London only explains: 'Whilst such persecution persists we shall continue to raise these issues.' The conclusions of the US Department of State illustrate that Washington does not view this approach as sufficient:

> Relations with Western European nations have been uneven, with growing commercial ties largely having failed to deliver dividends on key European political concerns such as human rights, and WMD acquisition efforts. The IAEA [International Atomic Energy Agency] remains strongly critical of Iran.[17]

The situation has deteriorated further owing to Iran's insistence that it will continue its efforts to acquire nuclear technology, together with its recent threats to withdraw from the IAEA. Indeed, the nuclear situation is also forcing a re-think of policy in the EU. The EU–Iran Trade Agreement negotiations were suspended in July 2005 over Iran's resumption of uranium conversion in breach of its international agreements. The EU has also supported a critical UN resolution brought by Canada on 21 November 2005. Yet, despite these developments, the EU maintains that engagement must continue in order to reintegrate Iran into the international community. To this end it argues that a resumption of formal dialogue is essential. It would seem that neither engagement nor threats can alter a government's course when such vital interests are at stake. The recent news that Iranian President Ahmedinejad has written to President Bush suggesting 'new solutions for getting out of international problems and the current fragile situation of the world'[18] has come as a surprise. This letter represents the first official contact Iran has had with the United States since the US broke off all diplomatic contact in 1980. The US remains hostile, however, and continues to press for further UN sanctions against Tehran, stating its position thus:

> Now the world faces a test. If diplomacy is to work, Iran must see it will pay a price for defiance. The test is beginning now in the work that has begun at the United Nations.[19]

The lack of a 'stick' to counterbalance the 'carrot' of engagement has proved problematic, not only in Crocker's dealings with South Africa, but in many examples since. For Crocker, however, the global context of the Cold War severely limited his actions towards those countries that were recognized as important allies in the fight against the spread of communism. Unfortunately, the conduct of America's 'War on Terror' is exerting similar pressures today, badly skewing foreign policy calculations and obscuring the *longer-term* interests of the West. It is this fact that leads to the identification of the most important lesson that foreign policy makers of today must take from Crocker's experience – the imperative need to balance both globalist and regionalist considerations in the development of foreign policy.

The Global/Regional Balance

One of the most damaging aspects of the Reagan administration's approach to foreign policy was its calculation of each decision almost exclusively in globalist terms. Even local disputes were viewed in terms of their impact on the East/West balance. With the end of the Cold War, 'the extent to which the lens of anti-Sovietism distorted the United States' formulation of its post war foreign policy'[20] has become increasingly apparent. Such an approach can become self-defeating, and this is what happened in southern Africa. The polarized perspective of the US diverted the attention of local leaders away from state-building priorities, and towards 'externally determined ideological battles of little relevance to [their] immediate needs'. The lack of mutually beneficial outcomes meant that such governments came to resent the role played by the US. The real danger in this approach is the tendency to simplify the idea of 'friends' and 'enemies'.[21] In America's dealings in South Africa, and elsewhere, this simplification resulted in its being too soft on friends and too hard on enemies. Its leniency towards perceived allies in Pretoria lost it much credibility in the region, particularly when this leniency went unreciprocated by reform in South Africa. Even worse, the perception of the ANC as communist enemies meant that approaches made by its more pragmatic leaders went unheeded in Washington.

This same East/West dichotomy prevented the early overtures of both the Cubans and the Soviets from being reciprocated by Washington – overtures, Crocker comments, that with hindsight would have been useful to explore, but which the political reality of Washington at that time made it impossible to pursue. The overarching nature of the Cold War and its resultant 'containment' policy genuinely was damaging to the long-term interests of the United States. This was demonstrated not only in the ill-conceived Vietnam War, but also in the resentment caused by the many newly independent countries co-opted by either East or West as pawns in a global zero-sum game. The over-reliance on the categorization of states as 'friends' or 'enemies' damaged Washington's ability to determine policy based on rational calculation. The focus on states' roles in a global context overshadowed the importance of understanding *regional* concerns. This proved to be a great handicap in America's foreign relations. A good example was Washington's misconception of the African nationalism of newly independent states as being the same as Soviet bloc communism, rather than an expression of the rejection of *any* external interference as a threat to their newly won freedom.

Today, the parallels are clear in Bush's 'for us or against us' approach to the War on Terror, and in British foreign policy too. A good example is British and American relations with Uzbekistan – a 'key ally' of the coalition despite its own internal repression, 'disappearances' and the use of torture (which the UN Special Rapporteur for Torture has described as

Conclusions

'systematic'). It is possible to identify a parallel between some of the actions of the Uzbek government and the way in which Savimbi used the appeal of his (newfound) anti-communism to gain support in the United States. Much of the torture and disappearances in Uzbekistan have been against alleged Islamic extremists, although the truth of all of the allegations is difficult to determine in the culture of censorship and show trials. Recent events, however, have meant that relations between Uzbekistan and the West are now uncertain. In May 2005 mass protests were held against the jailing of large numbers of men on charges of 'Islamic extremism'. The Uzbek troops opened fire, killing hundreds of protesters. Uzbekistan's apparent reorientation towards Russia and regression towards authoritarian practices have damaged its relations with the West. Although President Karimov insists such repression is targeted on the threat of Islamic extremism, opponents argue that the conflict has been 'a product of the President's ongoing policy to suppress all forms of dissent in Uzbekistan'.[22] Washington and its allies in the War on Terror must remain vigilant against the fact that rogue states will be happy to use the threat of Islamic terrorism as a red herring in certain cases of political suppression.

These same calculations must also be apparent in the West's relations with, for example, China and Libya. Despite recurrent concerns over China's record on human rights, the fact that China has offered strong public support in the War on Terror has been one of the guiding interests of Washington's China policy. The State Department describes China as an important partner in US counterterrorism and welcomes both its support for the coalition campaign in Afghanistan and China's $150 million in bilateral assistance to that country following the fall of the Taliban. Libya was certainly aware of the way the wind was blowing. In its attempts at reconciliation with the West, Quaddaffi publicly renounced terrorism in a letter to the UN Security Council in August 2003. The US State Department says that Libya's record of support for terrorism remains under review, but the fact that most of Washington's sanctions were lifted the following April was welcomed in Tripoli.

That there must be some international reaction to the terrorist atrocities is inevitable, and that it be as unified as possible is certainly preferable. What this book argues, however, is that individual regional realities must also be taken into account. The American experience in South Africa demonstrated the importance of engaging with as many groups and representatives as possible. In fact, Washington's experience also demonstrated the difficulties caused by failing to acknowledge that constructive engagement should encompass both government and opposition – both 'friend' and 'enemy'. The risk of being too soft on friends and too hard on enemies is usually a result of not comprehending or acknowledging the *regional* dimension – not taking into account the specific interplay of domestic and international interests in the country in question. As a regionalist himself, Crocker did attempt to encompass the South African situation in its own context – as well as in terms of its significance in the Cold War. That this regional aspect did not play its full role in his policy can largely be blamed on the role of Reagan as President. Reagan's lack of leadership allowed Crocker's regional sensitivities to be overshadowed by the globalist world vision of the competing departments. And herein lies an important lesson for today. By the very nature of government, specific regional specialists will be in a minority. But the significance of their understanding is such that government leadership is vital if this knowledge is to play a proper part in policy calculation. Only a strong leadership can ensure that a proper regionalist/globalist balance is achieved, and that the knowledge of the specialist is not buried under the more widely understood – and more easily simplified – goals of the global context.

The National Interest:
Short-Term Versus Long-Term Calculations

A further lesson is that a failure to balance regional and global considerations when formulating policy can be detrimental to long-term interests. Many examples of constructive engagement, both during Reagan's administration and today, were formulated as a way of combining pressure (or, at least, the *appearance* of applying pressure) for change in a country where human rights were being abused, with a policy that preserved and protected interests in that country. It is apparent that the economic benefits of continued trade, or the strategic benefits of maintaining allies in the War on Terror, have been important factors in the decision to engage with, for example, China, the Sudan or Uzbekistan. But it is important to maintain a longer-term perspective of these 'interests', some of which appear to be based mainly on short-term goals. When the former British Foreign Secretary Robin Cook initially outlined his new 'ethical' approach to foreign policy in 1997, he condemned the fact that he had been criticized for 'sacrificing national interest for principle'. He went on to explain that national interest was 'promoted, not hindered, by a commitment to human rights [because] there is no such thing any more as a quarrel in a faraway country which is indifferent to our interests'.[23] States where rights are violated following a breakdown of the rule of law, or the repression and violence necessary to sustain the ruling group in power, are 'the main source of risk to our and our allies' security'.

The protection of human rights can often appear to be contrary to short-term strategic or commercial interests. But the growth of inter-dependent issues, the world economy and the ever-present yet nebulous threat of terrorism have all combined to increase the importance of international cooperation. Despite these changes, policy makers have not yet fully altered their perceptions of national interest to follow suit. What may superficially appear as expedient *realpolitik* at the time can, in fact, be damaging to those same interests in the long term. Could the failure today to apply pressure on the government of Uzbekistan to respect the rights of its people turn it into another breeding ground for terrorists tomorrow?

Conclusions

On the other hand, could isolation or condemnation of Iran preclude the possibility of constructive dialogue in the future? If the potential value of the constructive engagement approach is to be realized, governments should learn that, not only must one engage with one's enemies, but one must also have some form of sanction when engaging with friends – or those seen as strategically important.

Crocker – to an extent – was correct to dismiss an insistence on consistency as the 'hobgoblin of small minds'. One policy does not suit all, particularly when different governments can react in very different ways to the promise of engagement. But it is important to understand the *grounds upon which* this inconsistency is based. The problem with Washington's engagement under Reagan was that an appreciation of the differences – of interests, security fears, even cultures – of individual countries did not play a significant enough part in the decision to engage. Again, an overriding concern with the calculations of the Cold War formed the basis for these judgements, and this provided insufficient grounds upon which to form policies in the long-term interests of the US. Washington's continued engagement with Pretoria earned the hostility of both the South African black majority and the neighbouring governments of the region. With regard to Pretoria itself, it learnt to treat Washington's threats with contempt, until the Executive's constructive engagement was overruled by Congress and punitive sanctions were applied.

The Impact of Commerce

The comparison of Crocker's dilemmas with those of foreign policy practitioners today cannot be complete without the acknowledgement of one final problem that was to prove extremely damaging to the implementation of Crocker's policy. This is the fact that one can neither underestimate nor fully control the impact that independent commercial decisions can have on policy goals. If a government engages with pariah regimes, it could find the reins of foreign policy being taken from its hands by campaigners who oppose such engagement. The independence of market decisions, and the growth of communications resulting in more organized and better publicized lobby groups, can pose a real threat to government control of policy – just as experienced by Washington in October 1986. To Crocker's frustration, the exodus of corporations and investment from South Africa was significant in undermining Washington's constructive engagement with South Africa. These pressure groups and disinvestment campaigners influenced disinvestment from South Africa through their boycott campaigns years before Congress imposed sanctions. Indeed, this public pressure can and has forced Western companies to cease controversial operations today. Oil companies in Sudan are criticized as they can 'operate only with the approval of a government that is ruthlessly clearing local people out of the oil areas and using its oil revenue to finance the war'.[24] The vociferous campaign against Canada's

Talisman Energy in Sudan was eventually successful in achieving its goal – forcing Talisman to pull out of Sudan. This reflects the events in South Africa during the 1980s, when a sustained public campaign managed to influence the investment decisions of many major companies, regardless of their own government's policy. Indeed, it is through their power over big business in the role of investors and consumers that campaigners can often have the most direct effect on government policy.

As Crocker's experience showed, governments can attempt to maintain contacts via continued trade and investment (as in South Africa), or they can attempt to employ some form of sanction on the behaviour of a rogue state by limiting this activity (as in Angola). The difficulty arises when commercial decisions are incompatible with government policy. It then becomes apparent just how little influence a government has on the decisions of big business. The British government maintains that Premier Oil and British American Tobacco (BAT), the two largest remaining British investors in Burma, are withdrawing this investment 'in response to requests made by the British government'.[25] But it is Burma's own dire economic mismanagement that has led to a massive withdrawal of foreign investment, just as a lack of business confidence had caused the majority of US firms to withdraw from South Africa even before the 1986 Sanctions Act was passed. A government can promise constructive engagement to a rogue state, but the fact remains that continued investment relies on the economic conditions within a state. An example of a government's resources is demonstrated by the limited measures of control that the UK government has at its disposal regarding British companies operating in Burma:

> The UK discourages trade, investment or tourism with Burma. We do not offer any commercial services for companies wanting to do business with Burma, nor do we give financial support for trade promotion activities or organize trade missions.[26]

The US had gone further in its Iran and Libya Sanctions Act (ILSA), first enacted in 1996 and extended for a further five years in August 2001 (although this was suspended with regard to Libya in 2004 – see above). This not only banned American companies from operating in either Libya or Iran, but also allowed, through secondary sanctions, for the punishment of any *foreign* business that invested over $20 million per annum in the Libyan energy industry. However, when this Act forced Conoco to pull out of Libya, it was quickly replaced by a French-led consortium. Washington did not impose these secondary sanctions, for fear of starting a trade war. Libya remained a major oil producer despite the previous US sanctions, largely due to the presence of European energy companies there.

In reality, a government has a limited store of influence over the decisions of big business. Watertight sanctions are difficult to impose. On the other hand, companies cannot be co-opted into continuing trade or investment simply because a government wishes to pursue a programme of engagement – particularly if, as is often the case, political instability and/or

Conclusions

economic mismanagement in the rogue state have damaged business confidence in the economic climate there. Corporate decisions are based on commercial, not political, considerations. So what can governments do? A Christian Aid report recommends that an international monitoring body should be established to oversee the implementation of strengthened international guidelines on corporate responsibility. Christian Aid also calls for this body to have the power *in extremis* to impose sanctions on individual companies. The organization also calls on the British government to 'encourage the EU and other parties to support the development of an international agreement on competition'.[27] Possibly as a response to such calls from NGOs, governments, shareholders and consumers alike, big business has undergone a series of changes to demonstrate that their operations are 'socially responsible'. The Socially Responsible Investment (SRI) Movement is rather like the economic equivalent of political engagement. Rather than avoiding investment in pariah or rogue states, SRI activists use 'constructive engagement to improve corporate behaviour'.[28] In what appears to be a far-sighted move, the British government was the first to appoint a Minister for Corporate Social Responsibility (CSR) in March 2000. But John Jackson, of the UK-based Burma Campaign, rejects the notion of CSR. He believes 'there is no such thing as good practice if you are working [in Burma]'.[29] He advocates a total withdrawal of all companies.

The coercive options of sanctions or even war are not always feasible – and the instruments that they provide are too blunt to ensure that those suffering abuses of human rights will not simply suffer more. On the other hand, isolation of rogue states may provide us with 'clean hands', but will often do little to ameliorate the desperate situations in which so many citizens of the globe still live. What this exploration of Crocker's policy has shown is that governments should be honest in their reasoning when pursuing engagement with a rogue state: honest with themselves, with the international community and with their own domestic constituency. They should resist the simplified conclusions that come from viewing the world as a dichotomy between subjective definitions of good and evil – with states characterized as 'friends' or 'enemies'. The overarching nature of the Cold War damaged Washington's ability to do this – and to maintain a balance between the necessities of a global foreign policy and the regional realities and cultural sensitivities of the countries with which they were attempting to engage.

In the final analysis, states must understand that constructive engagement is too important a diplomatic tool to use simply as a diplomatic fig leaf. It is not, or should not be, an exercise in public relations strategy while governments engage in 'business as usual' relationships with rogue states. Only in this way can engagement be properly understood, and backed up with some form of sanction if necessary. Yet the final lesson must be not to allow the parallel, overarching nature of a 'for us or against us' War on Terror to curtail and skew foreign policy in this century as the Cold War did during the last.

Notes

1 www.fco.gov.uk June 2004.
2 See Oye, K., D. Rothchild and R. J. Lieber (eds), *Eagle Entangled: US Foreign Policy in a Complex World*, Boston and Toronto: Little, Brown, and Co., 1979, pp. 181–4, for a discussion of these various alternatives with specific examples.
3 Cook, Robin, 'Human Rights into a New Century', speech made at the Locarno Suite, FCO, London, 17 July 1997.
4 Adapted from FCO Country Profile at www.fco.gov.uk, May 2004.
5 'Who Will Condemn China?', *Economist*, 24 March 2001, p. 23.
6 Foreign and Commonwealth Office, *Human Rights Annual Report 2003*, Norwich: The Stationery Office 2003.
7 'Who Will Condemn China?', *Economist*, p. 23.
8 Cook, Robin, 'Human Rights – A Priority of Britain's Foreign Policy', speech made at the FCO, London, 28 March 2001.
9 Country Profiles, www.state.gov, August 2004.
10 MacAskill, Ewen, 'Analysis: Tough Love in Tripoli', *Guardian*, 11 February 2004.
11 'Big Powers Wary Over Sudan Crisis', BBC News, UK edition, 8 May 2004, at www.bbc.co.uk.
12 FCO Country Profiles www.fco.gov.uk, May 2004.
13 As quoted in Flint, Julie, 'Britain Backs Ugly War for Oil', *Observer*, 16 April 2000.
14 Flint, Julie, 'British Firms Fan Flames of War', *Observer*, 11 March 2001.
15 'Peace, the Unimaginable', *Economist*, 17 May 2003, pp. 62–3.
16 Bromley, Mark, 'Washington's Nuclear Bunker Busters', *Observer*, 28 July 2002.
17 Department of State Country Profiles www.state.gov, August 2004.
18 Fickling, David, 'Iran Breaks silence with US to offer nuclear "solutions"', *Guardian Unlimited* at www.guardian.co.uk/international/story/0,,1770118,00.html
19 US State Department Country Briefing, www.state.gov/p/nea/ci/c2404.htm
20 Donald Rothchild in Kenneth Mokoena (ed.), *South Africa and the United States: The Declassified History*, a National Security Archive documents reader, New York: The New Press, 1993, p. xi.
21 *Ibid.*, p. xi.
22 As quoted in State Department Background Note at www.state.gov/r/pa/ei/bgn/2924.htm#relations
23 Cook, 'Human Rights – A Priority of Britain's Foreign Policy'..
24 'War, Famine and Oil in Sudan', *Economist*, 14 April 2004, p. 61.
25 FCO Country Profiles: Burma www.fco.gov.uk, June 2004.
26 FCO Country Profiles: Burma www.fco.gov.uk, May 2004.
27 Green, Duncan and Claire Melamed, 'A Human Development Approach to Globalization', Christian Aid and CAFOD at www.christianaid.org.uk/indepth, June 2004.
28 Slavin, Terry, 'New Rules of Engagement', *Observer*, 1 September 2002.
29 *Ibid.*

Bibliography

Primary Sources

Interviews

Personal Interview with Chester Crocker, Georgetown University, Washington, DC, 19 June 2001.

Personal Interview with Professor Donald Rothchild, University of California, Davis – Washington Office, Washington, DC, 12 June 2001.

Personal Interview with Ambassador Herman J. Cohen (Retired), Cohen & Woods, Washington, DC, 22 June 2001.

Personal Correspondence

Letters from Jeroboam Shaanika, Counsellor, High Commission for the Republic of Namibia, London to the author (Joanne Davies), 26 January and 17 March 1999.

Official Letters, Cables & Memoranda

Ronald Reagan Library, CA. White House Staff and Office Files: Cohen, Herman J., Files 1987–8. African Affairs Directorate, NSC. Boxes 91875 and 91876. Secret Memorandum – From: Secretary of State Alexander Haig. To: The President 20 May 1981. Subject: Summing up of Pik Botha Visit. Declassified 21 January 1999.

Ronald Reagan Library, CA. White House Staff and Office Files: Walker, Lannon. Secret Memorandum – From: L. Paul Bremer III, Executive Secretary Department of State. To: Richard V. Allen, The White House. Subject: Namibia Contact Group Ministerial Meeting 24 September 1981.

Ronald Reagan Library, CA. White House Staff and Office Files: Cohen, Herman J., Files 1987–8. African Affairs Directorate, NSC. Boxes 91875 and 91876. Cable. From: Secretary of State Washington, DC. To: American Consulate Cape Town. Subject: Message from the Secretary for Pik Botha, 30 September 1981.

Ronald Reagan Library, CA. White House Staff and Office Files: Cohen, Herman J., Files 1987–8. African Affairs Directorate, NSC. Boxes 91875 and 91876. Cable. From: American Consulate Cape Town. To: Secretary of State Haig. Subject: Situation Listing, 10 November 1981.

Ronald Reagan Library, CA. White House Staff and Office Files: Cohen, Herman J., Files 1987–8. African Affairs Directorate, NSC. Boxes 91875 and 91876. Cable. From: Secretary of State Haig. To: US Embassy in Pretoria and American Consulate Cape Town. Subject: Containing text of Letter from Haig to Botha, 29 January 1982.

Ronald Reagan Library, CA. White House Staff and Office Files: Cohen, Herman J., Files 1987–8. African Affairs Directorate, NSC. Boxes 91875 and 91876. Secret CIA Memorandum. To: William P. Clark, Assistant to the President for National Security Affairs. From: John N. McMahan, Acting Director of Central Intelligence. Subject: The Namibia Settlement Process: Obstacles and Regional Implications, 20 August 1982.

Ronald Reagan Library, CA. White House Staff and Office Files: Cohen, Herman J., Files 1987–8. African Affairs Directorate, NSC. Boxes 91875 and 91876. Secret Memorandum. To: Ronald Reagan. From: George Shultz. Subject: South Africa: Progress in the Angolan and Namibian negotiations, 26 August 1982.

Ronald Reagan Library, CA. WHORM Subject Files: 'South Africa, US Policy Towards'. File Numbers FG001–FG013; PR003–PR007-02. Secret Cable – From: Pretoria US Embassy. To: White House Situation Room and Secretary of State, 22 November 1982. Subject: Meeting with Pik Botha 18 November 1982. Declassified 19 January 1999.

Ronald Reagan Library, CA. White House Staff and Office Files: Cohen, Herman J., Files 1987–8. African Affairs Directorate, NSC. Boxes 91875 and 91876. Cable. To: Secretary of State, Washington. From: US Embassy Pretoria. Subject [Still Classified] Discusses Regional Situation, 17 November 1982.

Ronald Reagan Library, CA. White House Staff and Office Files: Cohen, Herman J., Files 1987–8. African Affairs Directorate, NSC. Boxes 91875 and 91876 Secret Telegram. From: Secretary of State. To: American Embassy Pretoria. Subject: Message for Pik from Undersecretary Eagleburger, 20 February 1983.

Ronald Reagan Library, CA. WHORM Subject Files: 'South Africa, US Policy Towards'. File Numbers FG001–FG013; PR003–PR007-02 Confidential Cable – From: Nickel, American Consulate Johannesburg. To: White House Situation Room and Secretary of State, 1 October 1983. Subject: Senator Kassebaum's Meeting with Pik Botha. Declassified 22 January 1999.

Ronald Reagan Library, CA. Executive Secretariat, NSC: Records Boxes 91340 and 91343. Cable – From: Herman Nickel, US Ambassador to SA. To: Secretary of State. Subject: SAG View of Soviet Influence, 4 February 1983.

Ronald Reagan Library, CA. White House Staff and Office Files: Cohen, Herman J., Files 1987–8. African Affairs Directorate, NSC. Boxes 91875 and 91876. Secret CIA Memorandum. To: William P. Clark,

Assistant to the President for National Security Affairs. From: L. P. Bremer, III, Executive Secretary Department of State. Subject: Update on the Southern African Negotiations, 24 March 1983.

Ronald Reagan Library, CA. Executive Secretariat, NSC: Records Boxes 91340 and 91343. Secret Memorandum – From: Robert C. McFarlane. To: Ronald Reagan. Subject: Meeting with Chief Gatsha Buthelezi, 4 February 1985. Declassified 6 January 1999.

Ronald Reagan Library, CA. White House Staff and Office Files: African Affairs Directorate, NSC: Records Boxes 91026 and 91028. Secret Memorandum – From: Phillip Ringdahl (NSC). To: Robert McFarlane. Subject: South Africa: Botha's Letter to the President, 2 August 1985. Declassified 26 May 1999.

Ronald Reagan Library, CA. White House Staff and Office Files: African Affairs Directorate, NSC: Records Boxes 91026 and 91028. Confidential Memorandum – From: Phillip Ringdahl (NSC). To: Robert McFarlane. Subject: South Africa – Meeting with Ambassador Nickel, 19 June 1985. Declassified 7 June 1999.

Ronald Reagan Library, CA. Executive Secretariat, NSC: Records Boxes 91340 and 91343. Secret Memorandum – From: Phillip Ringdahl. To: Robert McFarlane. Subject: South Africa – Your Meeting with Crocker and Nickel, 7 March 1985. Declassified 6 July 1999.

Ronald Reagan Library, CA. White House Staff and Office Files: Cohen, Herman J., Files 1987–8. African Affairs Directorate, NSC. Boxes 91875 and 91876. Cable. From: Secretary of State. To: American Embassies Southern Africa. Subject: Southern Africa Update, June 1985.

Ronald Reagan Library, CA. WHORM Subject Files: Veto and Override of HR 4868. File number CO141– 437840. Memorandum – From: Mona Charen (White House). To: Patrick Buchanan (White House), 29 July 1985. Subject: Framing the Argument on S. Africa.

Ronald Reagan Library, CA. WHORM Subject Files: 'South Africa, US Policy Towards'. File Numbers FG001–FG013; PR003–PR007-02. Confidential Report – Bureau of Intelligence and Research – Analysis – South Africa: Economic Vulnerability, 31 July 1985.

Ronald Reagan Library, CA. White House Staff and Office Files: Cohen, Herman J., Files 1987–8. African Affairs Directorate, NSC. Boxes 91875 and 91876. Secret Cable. From: Crocker. To: Poindexter (The White House). Subject: Geneva Meeting with Pik Botha, February 1986. Declassified 26 May 1999.

Ronald Reagan Library, CA. Executive Secretariat, NSC: Records Boxes 91340 and 91343. 'Super Sensitive' (8624301). Memorandum. From: Nicholas Platt, Executive Secretary, US Department of State. To: John M. Poindexter, The White House. Subject: Letter from South African State President P. W. Botha to President Reagan, 8 May 1986. Declassified 5 September 2000.

Ronald Reagan Library, CA. White House Staff and Office Files: Dewhirst, Mary, File Number OA 17788. Memorandum - From: Office of Management and Budget. To: The President – Subject: Discussion/Background Paper on South Africa, 25 September 1986.

Ronald Reagan Library, CA. White House Staff and Office Files: Chumachenko, Katherine: File Number OA 19268. Report – 'South African Federated Chamber of Industries – Business Charter of Social, Economic and Political Rights' (Report of Workshops held during September and October 1986), 12 August 1986.

Ronald Reagan Library, CA. White House Staff and Office Files: Chumachenko, Katherine: File Number OA 19268. George Shultz, 15 February 1984, in US Department of State Bureau of Public Affairs: Public Information Series – April 1985.

Ronald Reagan Library, CA. WHORM Subject Files: Veto and Override of HR 4868. File No. TA 001. Press Briefing – From: Office of the Press Secretary, The White House, 9 September 1985. Subject: Executive Order – Prohibiting Trade and Certain Other Transactions Involving South Africa.

Ronald Reagan Library, CA. WHORM Subject Files: Veto and Override of HR 4868. File No. TA 001. Press Briefing – From: Office of the Press Secretary, The White House 9 September 1985. Subject: Press Briefing by Secretary of State Shultz on Executive Order Regarding South Africa.

Ronald Reagan Library, CA. White House Staff and Office Files: African Affairs Directorate, NSC: Records Boxes 91026 and 91028. Memorandum – From: Phillip Ringdahl (NSC). To: John M. Poindexter (White House), 26 March 1986. Subject: South Africa – Activities of US Corporate Council.

Ronald Reagan Library, CA. WHORM Subject Files: Veto and Override of HR 4868. File number CO141 – 437008. Memorandum – From: Phil Nicolaides (White House). To: P. Buchanan (White House), 25 August 1986. Subject: Congressional Suggestions Re: SA Policy.

Ronald Reagan Library, CA. WHORM Subject Files: Veto and Override of HR 4868. File No. TA 001. Memorandum – From: Executive Office of the President, Office of Management and Budget. To: The President, 25 August 1986. Subject: Discussion of HR4868 Veto.

Ronald Reagan Library, CA. WHORM Subject Files: 'South Africa, US Policy Towards'. File Numbers FG001–FG013; PR003–PR007-02. Letter – From: House of Representatives. To: Bernardus G. Fourie, South African Ambassador to the United States. Subject: SA View of Constructive Engagement, 12 April 1984.

Ronald Reagan Library, CA. White House Staff and Office Files: Cohen, Herman J., Files 1987–8. African Affairs Directorate, NSC. Boxes 91875 and 91876. Confidential Report 'South Africa: Impediments to Growth', Intelligence Research Report No. 77, 26 March 1987, US Department of State Bureau of Intelligence and Research.

Ronald Reagan Library, CA. White House Staff and Office Files: Cohen, Herman J., Files 1987–8. African Affairs Directorate, NSC. Boxes 91875 and 91876. Secret Memorandum. From: Herman J. Cohen. To: Frank C. Carlucci. Subject: Letter from South African President Botha, 26 May 1987. Declassified 6 January 1999.

Ronald Reagan Library, CA. White House Staff and Office Files: Cohen, Herman J., Files 1987–8. African

Bibliography

Affairs Directorate, NSC. Boxes 91875 and 91876. Secret Memorandum. From: Herman J. Cohen. To: Frank C. Carlucci. Subject: Canadian Prime Minister's Letter on the South African Question at Venice, 6 February 1987. Declassified 6 July 1999.

Ronald Reagan Library, CA. White House Staff and Office Files: Cohen, Herman J., Files 1987–8. African Affairs Directorate, NSC. Boxes 91875 and 91876. Confidential Memorandum. From: Herman J. Cohen (NSC). To: Frank C. Carlucci. Subject: South Africa: Malcolm Fraser and Eminent Persons Group Request Appointment, 3 September 1987. Declassified 6 January 1999.

Ronald Reagan Library, CA. WHORM Subject Files: 'South Africa, US Policy Towards', File Numbers FG001–FG013; PR003–PR007-02. Letter – To: Edwin Meese III, Attorney General. From: George P. Shultz, Secretary of State, 8 April 1987. Subject: State and Local Disinvestment Measures.

Ronald Reagan Library, CA. White House Staff and Office Files: Cohen, Herman J., Files 1987–8. African Affairs Directorate, NSC. Boxes 91875 and 91876. Secret Memorandum – From: Herman J. Cohen (NSC). To: Frank C. Carlucci (National Security Adviser), 1 June 1987. Subject: Meeting with Ambassador Edward Perkins, 2 June 1987. Declassified 7 June 1999.

Ronald Reagan Library, CA. WHORM Subject Files: 'South Africa, US Policy Towards'. File FG 011 – 533184. Letter – From: House Of Representatives Committee on Foreign Affairs. To: The President, 30 September 1987.

Ronald Reagan Library, CA. WHORM Subject Files: 'South Africa, US Policy Towards'. File Numbers FG001–FG013; PR003–PR007-02. Letter – From: J. Edward Fox (Assistant Secretary Legislative and Intergovernmental Affairs). To: Howard Wolpe (Chairman of House Foreign Affairs Committee), October 1987.

Ronald Reagan Library, CA. WHORM Subject Files: 'South Africa, US Policy Towards'. File Numbers FG001–FG013; PR003–PR007-02 Letter – From: J. Edward Fox (Assistant Secretary Legislative and Intergovernmental Affairs). To: Richard J. Lugar (Chairman of Senate Foreign Affairs Committee), February 1987.

Ronald Reagan Library, CA. White House Staff and Office Files: Cohen, Herman J., Files 1987–8. African Affairs Directorate, NSC. Boxes 91875 and 91876. Secret Memorandum. From: Larry Napper, US Department of State. To: Chester Crocker. Subject: Thoughts on the Next Round with the MPLA. Undated.

Ronald Reagan Library, CA. White House Staff and Office Files: Cohen, Herman J., Files 1987–8. African Affairs Directorate, NSC. Boxes 91875 and 91876. Department of State Confidential Briefing Paper. Subject: Meeting with South African Chief Gatsha Buthelezi. Undated.

Ronald Reagan Library, CA. WHORM Subject Files: 'South Africa, US Policy Towards'. File Numbers FG001–FG013; PR003–PR007-02. Report – By: Interagency Team, Departments of Commerce and Defence. Subject: South Africa: Source of Strategic Minerals, May 1985.

Ronald Reagan Library, CA. White House Staff and Office Files: Cohen, Herman J., Files 1987–8. African Affairs Directorate, NSC. Box No. 92295. Secret Report – By: The White House. Subject: Background for National Security Study Decision Directive Number 273. Undated.

Ronald Reagan Library, CA. White House Staff and Office Files: Cohen, Herman J., Files 1987–8. African Affairs Directorate, NSC. Box No. 92295. National Security Study Decision Directive Background 'United States Objectives in Southern Africa', April/May 1987.

Ronald Reagan Library, CA. White House Staff and Office Files: Cohen, Herman J., Files 1987–8. African Affairs Directorate, NSC. Box No. 92295. Secret Report – By: The White House. Subject: National Security Study Decision Directive Number 187, 7 September 1985. Declassified 16 March 1998.

Ronald Reagan Library, CA. White House Staff and Office Files: Cohen, Herman J., Files 1987–8. African Affairs Directorate, NSC. Box No. 92295. Secret Report – By: The White House. Subject: National Security Study Decision Directive Number 212, 'United States Policy Toward Angola', 10 February 1986. Declassified 17 May 1991.

Ronald Reagan Library, CA. White House Staff and Office Files: Cohen, Herman J., Files 1987–8. African Affairs Directorate, NSC. Box No. 92295. Secret Report – By: The White House. Subject: National Security Study Decision Directive Number 273, 7 May 1987. Declassified 17 May 1991.

Ronald Reagan Library, CA. White House Staff and Office Files: Cohen, Herman J., Files 1987–8. African Affairs Directorate, NSC. Box No. 92295. Secret Report – By: The White House. Subject: National Security Study Decision Directive Number 274, 'United States Policy Toward Angola', 7 May 1987. Declassified 20 December 1991.

Ronald Reagan Library, CA. Executive Secretariat, NSC: Records Boxes 91340 and 91343. Memorandum – From: Phil Nicolaides. To: Patrick Buchanan, 27 June 1986. 'Re: Lugar-Crocker Sanctions Bill Parley'.

Ronald Reagan Library, CA. Executive Secretariat, NSC: Records Boxes 91340 and 91343. Memorandum – From: Phil Nicolaides to Pat Buchanan [No Subject], 18 August 1986.

Ronald Reagan Library, CA. WHORM Subject Files: 'South Africa, US Policy Towards'. File FG 011 – 390429. Memorandum – By: The White House. Subject: The Reagan Doctrine, 10 April 1986.

Ronald Reagan Library, CA. WHORM Subject Files: Veto and Override of HR 4868. File number CO141 – 437995. Memorandum – From: Maseru, Ambassador to Lesotho. Subject: The View From the State Department, 30 July 1986.

Ronald Reagan Library, CA. White House Staff and Office Files: Cohen, Herman J., Files 1987–8. African Affairs Directorate, NSC. Box No. 91876. Report – By: NSC. To: Congress, 1 October 1987. Subject: Executive Summary Pursuant to Section 501 of CAAA of 1986.

Ronald Reagan Library, CA. White House Staff and Office Files: Cohen, Herman J., Files 1987–8. African Affairs Directorate, NSC. Box No. 92241. Secret Memorandum – From: NSC. To: Departments of State and Defense, US Information Agency and Agency for International Development, 26 September

1985. Subject: SPG Meeting – Public Diplomacy. Declassified 5 April 1995.

Ronald Reagan Library, CA. White House Staff and Office Files: Cohen, Herman J., Files 1987–8. African Affairs Directorate, NSC. Box No. 92241. Secret Memorandum – From: Nicholas Platt, Executive Secretary Department of State. To: Robert McFarlane (White House), 1 October 1985. Subject: Sustaining a Public Diplomacy Program on South Africa. Declassified 5 April 1995.

Ronald Reagan Library, CA. White House Staff and Office Files: Cohen, Herman J., Files 1987–8. African Affairs Directorate, NSC. Boxes 91875 and 91876. Letter From: Jeremiah Chitunda, Secretary of Foreign Affairs, UNITA. To Congressman Howard Wolpe, Chairman, Subcommittee on African Affairs, 11 November 1985.

Ronald Reagan Library, CA. White House Staff and Office Files: Cohen, Herman J., Files 1987–8. African Affairs Directorate NSC. Box No. 92241 Background Report – For: Robert McFarlane. Subject: Congressional Briefings arranged for 21 May 1985 and 23 May 1985..

Ronald Reagan Library, CA. WHORM Subject Files: 'South Africa, US Policy Towards'. File Numbers FG001–FG013; PR003–PR007-02. Letter – From: Jack Kemp (Congress). To: The President. Subject: Shultz/Tambo Meeting, 9 January 1987.

Ronald Reagan Library, CA. Executive Secretariat, NSC: Records Boxes 91340 and 91343. Memorandum – From: Fred Wettering (NSC). To: Bill Clark (NSC). Subject: Transfer of Commerce Positions, 7 April 1983.

Ronald Reagan Library, CA. Executive Secretariat, NSC: Records Boxes 91340 and 91343. Confidential Memorandum – From: Pat Buchanan. To: Donald Regan and John Poindexter (White House). Subject: Possible Botha/Reagan Meeting, 22 August 1986.

Ronald Reagan Library, CA. WHORM Subject Files: 'South Africa, US Policy Towards'. File Numbers FG001–FG013; PR003–PR007-02. Letter – From: President Ronald Reagan. To: State President Botha, 22 August 1988.

Ronald Reagan Library, CA. White House Staff and Office Files: Cohen, Herman J., Files 1987–8. African Affairs Directorate, NSC. Boxes 91875 and 91876. Report – South Africa: The Sanctions Mission. By: Dr James Mutambirwa. Report of the Eminent Church Persons Group World Council of Churches, 1989.

'Memorandum of Conversation', Participants: SA Foreign Minister Pik Botha, SA Defence Minister Magnus Malan, US Assistant Secretary – Designate Chester Crocker, Alan Keyes. Subject: Discussion with SAG Pretoria, 15–16 April 1981. Photocopy of document sent to the author by the Namibian Embassy in London.

Ronald Reagan Library, CA. WHORM Subject Files: 'South Africa, US Policy Towards'. File Numbers FG001–FG013; PR003–PR007-02. Department of State Publication No. 9537, 'A US Policy Toward South Africa: The Report of the Secretary of State's Advisory Committee on South Africa'. Released to the Public 21 April 1987.

Ronald Reagan Library, CA. WHORM Subject Files: 'South Africa, US Policy Towards'. File Numbers FG001–FG013; PR003–PR007-02. Cable. From: Ambassador Herman Nickel. To: Secretary of State, 4 February 1983.

Ronald Reagan Library, CA. White House Staff and Office Files: Cohen, Herman J., Files 1987–8. African Affairs Directorate, NSC. Boxes 91875 and 91876. Cable. From: US Embassy Pretoria. To: Chester Crocker, 23 November 1981.

Ronald Reagan Library, CA. White House Staff and Office Files: Cohen, Herman J., Files 1987–8. African Affairs Directorate, NSC. Boxes 91875 and 91876. Memorandum. To: Ronald Reagan. From: Secretary of State George Shultz. Subject: 'South Africa: Status of our Negotiation Effort', 6 June 1983.

Ronald Reagan Library, CA. White House Staff and Office Files: Cohen, Herman J., Files 1987–8. African Affairs Directorate, NSC. Boxes 91875 and 91876. Transcript of Department of State Press Briefing, 26 November 1982, Washington, DC: Office of Press Relations, Department of State.

Ronald Reagan Library, CA. White House Staff and Office Files: Cohen, Herman J., Files 1987–8. African Affairs Directorate, NSC. Boxes 91875 and 91876. Secret Cable. To: Secretary of State, Washington. From: American Consulate Cape Town. Subject: 'Pik and the Prospects of a SWAPO Victory', 23 October 1981.

Ronald Reagan Library, CA. White House Staff and Office Files: Cohen, Herman J., Files 1987–8. African Affairs Directorate, NSC. Boxes 91875 and 91876. Sullivan, Leon 'Give the Sullivan Principles Two More Years', 1985.

Ronald Reagan Library, CA. White House Staff and Office Files: Cohen, Herman J., Files 1987–8. African Affairs Directorate, NSC. Boxes 91875 and 91876. Secret Cable. To: Secretary of State, Washington, DC. From: American Consulate Cape Town. Subject: 'Pik/Chargé Conversations', 10 November 1981.

Statement by the Representative at the United Nations (Kirkpatrick) Before the UN Security Council, 25 May 1983. American Foreign Policy (1983). *American Foreign Policy: Current Documents Annual*, Washington, DC: GPO (1981–)

Ronald Reagan Library, CA. WHORM Subject Files: 'South Africa, US Policy Towards'. File Numbers FG001–FG013; PR003–PR007-02. Secret Cable. From: Secretary of State Haig. To: US Embassy Pretoria and American Consulate Cape Town. Subject: Message from the Secretary to Pik, 29 January 1982.

US Aid to South Africa. The Special Working Group on South and Southern Africa (SAWG), Department of State, Washington, DC, January 1987.

Culley, Harriet (ed.), *Gist Southern Africa: Constructive Engagement*, Bureau of Public Affairs, Department of State, Februrary 1985.

Bibliography

Statements & Congressional Hearings

US Policy Toward Namibia Hearing before the Subcommittee on Africa of the Committee on Foreign Affairs, House of Representatives, 97th Congress, First Session, 17 June 1981.

US Policy Toward Southern Africa: Focus on Namibia, Angola and South Africa Hearing and Markup before the Subcommittee on Africa of the Committee on Foreign Affairs, House of Representatives, 97th Congress First Session on House Resolution 214; Con. Resolution 183, 16 September 1981.

The Role of the Soviet Union, Cuba and East Germany in Fomenting Terrorism in Southern Africa Hearings before the Subcommittee on Security and Terrorism of the Committee on the Judiciary, United States Senate, 22 March 1982.

Controls on Exports to South Africa Hearings before the Subcommittees on International Economic Policy and Trade, and on Africa, of the Committee of Foreign Affairs, House of Representatives, 97th Congress, Second Session, 2 December 1982 and 9 February 1983.

Internal Political Situation in South Africa Hearings before the Subcommittee on African Affairs of the Committee on Foreign Affairs, House of Representatives, First Session, September 1983.

Foreign Assistance and Related Programs Appropriations for 1985 Hearings before a Subcommittee of the Committee on Appropriations, House of Representatives, 14 March 1984.

United States Policy on South Africa Hearing before the Subcommittee on African Affairs of the Committee on Foreign Relations, United States Senate, 98th Congress, Second Session, 26 September 1984.

The Current Crisis in South Africa Hearing before the Subcommittee on Africa of the Committee on Foreign Affairs, House of Representatives, 4 December 1984.

Namibia: Internal Repression and US Diplomacy Hearing Before the Subcommittee on Africa of the Committee on Foreign Affairs, House of Representatives, 99th Congress, First Session, 21 February 1985, Washington: US Government Printing Office, 1985.

'Statement of James B. Kelly – Department of Commerce' before the Subcommittee on Africa of the Committee on Foreign Affairs, House of Representatives, 17 April 1985.

United States Policy Toward South Africa Hearings before the Committee on Foreign Relations, United States Senate, 99th Congress, First Session, 24 April, 2 May, and 22 May 1985.

Angola: Intervention or Negotiation? Hearings before the Subcommittee on Africa of the Committee on Foreign Affairs, House of Representatives, 99th Congress, First Session, 31 October and 12 November 1985.

The Economics Division of the Congressional Research Service, *Review of Events Concerning Angolan Economic and Petroleum Developments as a Background to more Recent Articles and Clippings dealing with US Commercial Relations with Angola and Angola's Commercial Relations with Other Countries,* Report requested by Hon. Ted Weiss, 8 November 1985, in *Angola: Intervention or Negotiation?* Hearings before the Subcommittee on Africa of the Committee on Foreign Affairs, House of Representatives, 99th Congress, First Session, 31 October and 12 November 1985, pp. 124–36.

Angola: Options for American Foreign Policy Hearing before the Committee on Foreign Relations, US Senate, 99th Congress, Second Session, 18 February 1986.

Developments in South Africa: United States Policy Responses Hearing before the Subcommittee on Africa of the Committee on Foreign Affairs, House of Representatives, 99th Congress, Second Session, 12 March 1986.

Angola: Should the United States Support Unita? Hearing before the Permanent Select Committee on Intelligence, House of Representatives, 99th Congress, Second Session, 13 March 1986.

Legislation Urging the South African Government to Engage in Meaningful Negotiations with that Country's Black Majority Hearing and Markup on House Resolution 373 before the Subcommittee on Africa of the Committee on Foreign Affairs, House of Representatives, 99th Congress, Second Session, 24 June and 6 August 1986.

United States Minerals Supply and South Africa: Issues and Options Oversight Hearing before the Subcommittee on Mining and Natural Resources of the Committee on Interior and Insular Affairs, House of Representatives, 100th Congress, First Session, 10 December 1987.

A Review of United States Policy Toward Political Negotiations in Angola Hearing before the Subcommittee on Africa of the Committee on Foreign Affairs, House of Representatives, 101st Congress, First Session, 27 September 1989.

US Policy Toward South Africa Hearings before the Committee on Foreign Relations, United States Senate, 101st Congress, First Session, 3 October 1989.

Namibian Independence: Review of the Process and Progress Hearing before the Subcommittee on Africa of the Committee on Foreign Affairs, House of Representatives, 101st Congress, First Session, 20 July 1989.

'The United States Abhors Racism', Statement by Alternative Representative Byrne to the 43rd Session of the United Nations General Assembly, 14 October 1988. Source: US Mission to the UN Press Release USUN 93-(88).

'Southern Africa: American Hopes for the Future', Statement by the Secretary of State, 4 December 1986. Source: *Department of State Bulletin,* February 1987, pp. 36–40.

'Explanation of US Abstention on UN Security Council Resolution 581', Statement by the Representative (Okun) before the UN Security Council, 13 February 1986. Source: US Mission to the UN, Press Release USUN 11-(86).

'Executive Order', Statement and Remarks by President Reagan, 9 September 1985. Source: Weekly Compilation of Presidential Documents, 16 September 1985, pp. 1048–50.

'Ending Apartheid in South Africa', Address by President Reagan to The World Affairs Council and the Foreign Policy Association, US Department of State, Bureau of Public Affairs, Washington, DC.

234

Current Policy, No. 853 (22 July 1986).

'The Democratic Future of South Africa', Secretary Shultz, US Department of State, Bureau of Public Affairs, Washington, DC. *Current Policy*, No. 1003 (29 September 1987).

'A Democratic Future: The Challenge for South Africans', Chester Crocker, US Department of State, Bureau of Public Affairs, Washington, DC. *Current Policy*, No. 1009 (1 October 1987).

'South Africa: What are America's Options?' Charles W. Freeman, US Department of State, Bureau of Public Affairs, Washington, DC. *Current Policy*, No. 1033 (9 December 1987).

South Africa's List of US Interests in Southern Africa, May 1981 (Leaked to TransAfrica – see *TransAfrica News Report*, August 1981).

Crocker, Chester 'A US Policy for the '80s', *Africa Report*, Vol. 26, No. 1 (1981).

Address by State President P. W. Botha at the Opening of the National Party Natal Congress, Durban, 15 August 1985 ('The Rubicon Speech'), The South African Consulate General, New York, August 1985.

Reagan, Ronald, 'Ending Apartheid in South Africa', Address, United States Department of State, Bureau of Public Affairs, Washington, DC, *Current Policy*, No. 853 (22 July 1986).

'Secretary Shultz's Meetings with African Foreign Ministers', Transcript of a Department of State Press Briefing, New York, 26 May 1983, in *American Foreign Policy: Current Documents Annual*, 1983, Washington, DC: GPO (1981–), Document No. 547.

Statement by the Representative at the United Nations (Kirkpatrick) before the UN Security Council, 25 May 1983, in *American Foreign Policy: Current Documents Annual*, 1983, Washington, DC: GPO (1981–), Document No. 546.

Statement by the Alternate Representative (Luce) before the UN General Assembly, 23 November 1982, US Mission to the UN, Press Release USUN 145 (82), 24 November 1982, in *American Foreign Policy: Current Documents Annual*, 1983, Washington, DC: GPO (1981–), Document No. 575.

'US Abstention in the Vote on the Security Council Resolution on Angola', Statement by Representative Lichenstein before UN Security Council, 6 January 1984, in *American Foreign Policy: Current Documents Annual*, 1984, Washington, DC: GPO (1981–), Document No. 402.

'Significance of the Angola/Namibia Agreements', Press Conference by Chester Crocker, USUN Mission HQ, New York, 21 December 1988, in *American Foreign Policy: Current Documents Annual*, 1988, Washington, DC: GPO (1981–), Document No. 395.

'Review of US Policy Toward Angola', Statement by Deputy Assistant Secretary of State for African Affairs Clark, 27 September 1989, in *American Foreign Policy: Current Documents Annual*, 1989, Washington, DC: GPO (1981–), Document No. 395.

Foreign and Commonwealth Office, *Human Rights Annual Report 2003*, Norwich: The Stationery Office, 2003.

Foreign and Commonwealth Office, *Human Rights Annual Report 2002*, Norwich: The Stationery Office, 2002.

Robin Cook, 'Human Rights – A Priority of Britain's Foreign Policy', Speech made at the FCO, London, 28 March 2001.

Robin Cook, 'Diplomacy For Democracy', Speech made at the FCO, London, 28 January 2000.

Robin Cook, 'Human Rights into a New Century' Speech made at the Locarno Suite, FCO, London, 17 July 1997.

National Archives Information

ARC Identifier: 54305, *Challenges to United States Foreign Policy: Chester Crocker Responds, 1983*. Creator: United States Information Agency (1982–) (Most Recent). Item from Record Group 306: Records of the USIA 1900–1988. Series: Motion Picture Films 1944–1999. NAIL Locator: 306.9172 Motion Picture, Sound and Video Recordings LICON, National Archives at College Park, Maryland, USA.

ARC Identifier: 54679, *President Reagan's South Africa Policy Speech, 22 July 1986*. Creator: United States Information Agency (1982–) (Most Recent). Item from Record Group 306: Records of the USIA 1900–1988. Series: Motion Picture Films 1944–1999. NAIL Locator: 306.9633 Motion Picture, Sound and Video Recordings LICON, National Archives at College Park, Maryland, USA.

ARC Identifier: 54704, *President Reagan's United Nations General Assembly Address, 1985*. Creator: United States Information Agency (1982–) (Most Recent). Date: 24 October 1985. Item from Record Group 306: Records of the USIA 1900–1988. Series: Motion Picture Films 1944–1999. NAIL Locator: 306.9659 Motion Picture, Sound and Video Recordings LICON, National Archives at College Park, Maryland, USA.

ARC Identifier: 54788, *Secretary of State George Shultz's Address to the United Nations General Assembly, 1985*. Creator: United States Information Agency (1982–) (Most Recent). Date: 27 September 1985. Item from Record Group 306: Records of the USIA 1900–1988. Series: Motion Picture Films 1944–1999. NAIL Locator: 306.9751 Motion Picture, Sound and Video Recordings LICON, National Archives at College Park, Maryland, USA.

ARC Identifier: 54794, *Secretary Shultz's Speech on South Africa, 1987*. Creator: United States Information Agency (1982–) (Most Recent). Item from Record Group 306: Records of the USIA 1900–1988. Series: Motion Picture Films 1944–1999. NAIL Locator: 306.9758 Motion Picture, Sound and Video Recordings LICON, National Archives at College Park, Maryland, USA.

ARC Identifier: 54797, *Secretary Shultz's Address on South Africa to International Management Development Institute, 1986*. Creator: United States Information Agency (1982–) (Most Recent). Item from Record Group 306: Records of the USIA 1900–1988. Series: Motion Picture Films 1944–1999. NAIL Locator: 306.9761 Motion Picture, Sound and Video Recordings LICON, National Archives at College Park, Maryland, USA.

Bibliography

ARC Identifier: 56118, *Foreign Press Center Briefing with Chester A. Crocker, 1986*. Creator: United States Information Agency (1982–) (Most Recent). Broadcast 19 December 1986. Item from Record Group 306: Records of the USIA 1900–1988. Series: Video Recordings from the 'Foreign Press' Program Series. NAIL Locator: 306-FP-34 Motion Picture, Sound and Video Recordings LICON, National Archives at College Park, Maryland, USA.

ARC Identifier: 56135, *Foreign Press Center Briefing with Dan Howard, 1987*. Creator: United States Information Agency (1982–) (Most Recent). Broadcast 4 February 1987. Item from Record Group 306: Records of the USIA 1900–1988. Series: Video Recordings from the 'Foreign Press' Program Series. NAIL Locator: 306-FP-53 Motion Picture, Sound and Video Recordings LICON, National Archives at College Park, Maryland, USA.

ARC Identifier: 56279, *Foreign Press Center Briefing with Michael Armacost, Undersecretary of State, 1985*. Creator: United States Information Agency (1982–) (Most Recent). Item from Record Group 306: Records of the USIA 1900–1988. Series: Video Recordings from the 'Foreign Press' Program Series. NAIL Locator: 306-FP-212 Motion Picture, Sound and Video Recordings LICON, National Archives at College Park, Maryland, USA.

ARC Identifier: 59701, *Role of the U.S. in Southern Africa – Crocker, 1985*. Creator: United States Information Agency (1982–) (Most Recent). Broadcast 26th June 1985. Item from Record Group 306: Records of the USIA 1900–1988. Video Recordings from the 'Worldnet Today' Program Series NAIL Locator: 306-WNET-128 Motion Picture, Sound and Video Recordings LICON, National Archives at College Park, Maryland, USA.

ARC Identifier: 59704, *US Policy Towards Africa – Wisner 1985*. Creator: United States Information Agency (1982–) (Most Recent). Broadcast 1 July 1985. Item from Record Group 306: Records of the USIA 1900–1988. Video Recordings from the 'Worldnet Today' Program Series NAIL Locator: 306-WNET-131 Motion Picture, Sound and Video Recordings LICON, National Archives at College Park, Maryland, USA.

ARC Identifier: 59633, *Status of the Peace Process in Southern Africa – Crocker, 1984*. Creator: United States Information Agency (1982–) (Most Recent). Broadcast 16 May 1984. Item from Record Group 306: Records of the USIA 1900–1988. Video Recordings from the 'Worldnet Today' Program Series NAIL Locator: 306-WNET-56 Motion Picture, Sound and Video Recordings LICON, National Archives at College Park, Maryland, USA.

ARC Identifier: 59634, *US Policy in Africa – Crocker, 1984*. Creator: United States Information Agency (1982–) (Most Recent). Broadcast 23 May 1984. Item from Record Group 306: Records of the USIA 1900–1988. Video Recordings from the 'Worldnet Today' Program Series NAIL Locator: 306-WNET-57 Motion Picture, Sound and Video Recordings LICON, National Archives at College Park, Maryland, USA.

ARC Identifier: 59713, *Political Issues – Armacost (Edited Version)*. Creator: United States Information Agency (1982–) (Most Recent). Broadcast 29 July 1985. Item from Record Group 306: Records of the USIA 1900–1988. Video Recordings from the 'Worldnet Today' Program Series NAIL Locator: 306-WNET-140 Motion Picture, Sound and Video Recordings LICON, National Archives at College Park, Maryland, USA.

ARC Identifier: 59724, *US Policy in Southern Africa – Crocker, 1985*. Creator: United States Information Agency (1982–) (Most Recent). Broadcast 26 September 1985. Item from Record Group 306: Records of the USIA 1900–1988. Video Recordings from the 'Worldnet Today' Program Series NAIL Locator: 306-WNET-152 Motion Picture, Sound and Video Recordings LICON, National Archives at College Park, Maryland, USA.

ARC Identifier: 59798, *Foreign Affairs Issues – Shultz, 1986*. Creator: United States Information Agency (1982–) (Most Recent). Broadcast 13th June 1986. Item from Record Group 306: Records of the USIA 1900–1988. Video Recordings from the 'Worldnet Today' Program Series NAIL Locator: 306-WNET-226 Motion Picture, Sound and Video Recordings LICON, National Archives at College Park, Maryland, USA.

ARC Identifier: 59926, *Current Situation in South Africa – Crocker 1987*. Creator: United States Information Agency (1982–) (Most Recent). Broadcast 27 February 1987. Item from Record Group 306: Records of the USIA 1900–1988. Video Recordings from the 'Worldnet Today' Program Series NAIL Locator: 306-WNET-356 Motion Picture, Sound and Video Recordings LICON, National Archives at College Park, Maryland, USA.

ARC Identifier: 60036, *Regional Perspectives on Southern Africa – Crocker, 1987*. Creator: United States Information Agency (1982–) (Most Recent). Broadcast 22 July 1987. Item from Record Group 306: Records of the USIA 1900–1988. Video Recordings from the 'Worldnet Today' Program Series NAIL Locator: 306-WNET-468 Motion Picture, Sound and Video Recordings LICON, National Archives at College Park, Maryland, USA.

ARC Identifier: 60161, *United States Foreign Policy With Africa – Freeman, 1987*. Creator: United States Information Agency (1982–) (Most Recent). Broadcast 15 December 1987. Item from Record Group 306: Records of the USIA 1900–1988. Video Recordings from the 'Worldnet Today' Program Series NAIL Locator: 306-WNET-594 Motion Picture, Sound and Video Recordings LICON, National Archives at College Park, Maryland, USA.

ARC Identifier: 60164, *United States – African Relations – Crocker, 1987*. Creator: United States Information Agency (1982–) (Most Recent). Broadcast 16 December 1987. Item from Record Group 306: Records of the USIA 1900–1988. Video Recordings from the 'Worldnet Today' Program Series NAIL Locator: 306-WNET-597 Motion Picture, Sound and Video Recordings LICON, National Archives at College Park, Maryland, USA.

Secondary Sources

Books

Ambrose, Stephen E. *Rise to Globalism: American Foreign Policy Since 1938*, seventh edition, New York and Harmondsworth: Penguin Books, 1993.

Attwell, Michael. *South Africa: Background to the Crisis*. London: Sidgwick and Jackson, 1986.

Baker, Pauline H. *The United States and South Africa: The Reagan Years. Update South Africa: Time Running Out*. New York: Ford Foundation and Foreign Policy Association, 1989.

Banks, Michael. 'The Foreign Policy of the United States', in F. S. Northedge (ed.), *The Foreign Policies of the Powers*, London: Faber and Faber, 1969, pp 40–68.

Barber, James and J. Barratt. *South Africa's Foreign Policy*, Cambridge: Cambridge University Press, 1990.

Barrett, David M. 'Presidential Foreign Policy', in John Dumbrell, *The Making of United States Foreign Policy*, second edition, Manchester and New York: Manchester University Press, 1997, pp. 54–87.

Bell, Coral. *The Reagan Paradox: US Foreign Policy in the 1980s*. Piscataway, NJ: Rutgers University Press 1989.

Beinart, William. *Twentieth Century South Africa*. Oxford and New York: Oxford University Press 1994.

Bissell, Richard E. *South Africa and the United States: The Erosion of an Influence Relationship*, New York: Praeger 1982.

Bloom, Jack Brian. *Black South Africa and the Disinvestment Dilemma*, Johannesburg: Jonathan Ball Publishers, 1986.

Blumenfeld, Jesmond. *Economic Interdependence in Southern Africa: From Conflict to Cooperation?* London: Pinter Press and New York: St Martin's Press for The Royal Institute of International Affairs, London, 1991.

Calvocoressi, Peter. *World Politics 1945–2000*, eighth edition, Harlow: Pearson Education Limited 2001.

Campbell, Kurt M. *Soviet Policy Towards South Africa*, Basingstoke and London: Macmillan, 1986.

Cigler, A. and B. Loomis. *American Politics*, Boston: Houghton-Mifflin, 1989.

Clemens Jnr., Walter C. 'The Superpowers and the Third World: Aborted Ideals and Wasted Assets', in C. W. Kegley Jnr. and Pat McGowan, *Foreign Policy USA/USSR*, Beverly Hills, London and New Delhi: Sage Publications, 1982, pp. 111–36.

Cohen, Herman J. *Intervening in Africa: Superpower Peacemaking in a Troubled Continent*, Basingstoke and London: Macmillan, and New York: St Martin's Press, 2000.

Coker, Christopher. 'Constructive Engagement: The United States, Southern Africa and the Use of Positive Sanctions (1969–74)', B Phil. dissertation, Wolfson College, 1981.

Coker, Christopher. *The United States and South Africa 1968–1985: Constructive Engagement and its Critics*, Durham, NC: Duke University Press, 1986.

Commonwealth Secretariat. *Racism in Southern Africa: The Commonwealth Stand*, London: The Commonwealth Secretariat, 1985.

The Commonwealth Group of Eminent Persons. *Mission to South Africa: The Commonwealth Report*, Harmondsworth: Penguin, 1986.

Cooper, Allan D. (ed.). *Allies in Apartheid Western Capitalism in Occupied Namibia*, Basingstoke and London: Macmillan, 1988.

Crockatt, Richard. *The Fifty Years War*, London and New York: Routledge 1995.

Crocker, Chester. *High Noon in Southern Africa: Making Peace in a Rough Neighborhood*, New York and London: W. W. Norton and Company, 1992.

Crocker, Chester and David A. Smock (eds). *African Conflict Resolution: The US Role in Peacemaking*, Washington, DC: US Institute of Peace Press, 1995.

Crocker, Chester (ed.). *The International Relations of Southern Africa: A Seminar Report*, Washington, DC: The Center for Strategic and International Studies, Georgetown University, 1974.

Davenport, T. R. H. *South Africa A Modern History*, fourth edition, Basingstoke and London: Macmillan, 1991.

Denenberg, R. V. *Understanding American Politics*, second edition, Bungay: Richard Clay (The Chaucer Press) Ltd. and Fontana Paperbacks, 1984.

Denoon, Donald. *Southern Africa Since 1800*, London: Longman, 1972.

Destler, I. M., Leslie H. Gelb and Anthony Lake. *Our Own Worst Enemy: The Unmaking of American Foreign Policy*, New York: Simon and Schuster, 1984.

Dobson, Alan P. and Steve Marsh. *US Foreign Policy Since 1945*. London: Routledge 2001.

Dougherty, James E. and Robert L. Pfaltzgraff, Jr. *American Foreign Policy: F.D.R. to Reagan*, New York: Harper and Row, 1986.

Doxley, Margaret. *Economic Sanctions and International Enforcement*, second edition, London: Macmillan, 1980.

Dumbrell, John. *The Making of United States Foreign Policy*, second edition, Manchester and New York: Manchester University Press, 1997.

Dunn, Keith A. 'Soviet Involvement in the Third World: Implications of US Policy Assumptions', in Robert H. Donaldson (ed.), *The Soviet Union in the Third World: Successes and Failures*, Boulder, CO: Westview Press and London: Croom Helm, 1981.

Evans, Graham and Jeffrey Newnham. *The Penguin Dictionary of International Relations*, London: Penguin Books and New York: Penguin Putnam, 1998.

Evans, Graham 'The Great Simplifier: The Cold War and South Africa 1948–1994', in Alan Dobson (ed.), *Deconstructing and Reconstructing the Cold War*, Aldershot: Ashgate Publishing Ltd., 1999, pp. 136–51.

Gaddis, John L. *The United States and the Origins of the Cold War*, New York and London: Columbia

Bibliography

University Press, 1972.

Geen, M. S. *The Making of the Union of South Africa: A Brief History 1487–1939*, London and New York: Longmans, Green and Co., 1946.

Griffith, Earnest S. *The American System of Government*, sixth edition, New York and London: Methuen 1983.

Grundy, Kenneth W. *South Africa Domestic Crisis and Global Challenge*, Boulder, CO, San Francisco and Oxford: Westview Press, 1991.

Gutteridge, William F. 'Africa', in Kurt London (ed.), *The Soviet Union in World Politics*, Boulder, CO: Westview Press and London: Croom Helm, 1980.

Hames, Tim and Nicol Rae. *Governing America*, Manchester and New York: Manchester University Press, 1996.

Harbeson, John W. and Donald Rothchild (eds). *Africa in World Politics Post-Cold War Challenges*, second edition, Boulder, CO, San Francisco and Oxford: Westview Press, 1995.

Hastedt, Glenn P. *American Foreign Policy: Past, Present, Future*, second edition, Upper Saddle River, NJ: Prentice Hall, 1991.

Henderson, Lawrence W. *Angola: Five Centuries of Conflict*, Ithaca and London: Cornell University Press, 1979.

Hero, A. O. 'The American Public and South Africa', in A. O. Hero and J. Barratt (eds), *The American People and South Africa: Publics, Elites and Policymaking Processes*, Lexington, MA: Lexington Books 1981.

Hoepli, Nancy L. *South Africa and the United States*. New York: The Foreign Policy Association, 1985.

Hough, Jerry F. *The Struggle for the Third World: Soviet Debates and American Options*, Washington, DC: The Brookings Institution, 1986.

Imishue, R. W. *South West Africa: An International Problem*, London: Pall Mall Press, 1965.

International Defence and Aid Fund for Southern Africa. *Namibia: The Facts*, London: IADF, 1980.

Irogbe, Kema. *The Roots of United States Foreign Policy Toward Apartheid South Africa 1969–1985*, Lewiston, Queenstown and Lampeter: Edwin Mellen Press, 1997.

James III, W. Martin. *A Political History of the Civil War in Angola 1974–1990*. New Brunswick, NJ and London: Transaction Publishers, 1992.

Jaster, Robert S. *South Africa in Namibia: The Botha Strategy*, Lanham, MD, New York and London: University Press of America and Center for International Affairs, Harvard University, 1985.

Jentleson, Bruce W. *American Foreign Policy: The Dynamics of Choice in the Twenty First Century*, New York and London: W. W. Norton and Company, 2000.

Joshua, Wynfred and Stephen P. Gibert. *Arms for the Third World: Soviet Military Aid Diplomacy*, Baltimore and London: Johns Hopkins University Press, 1969.

Kapp, P. H. and G. C. Oliver. *United States–South African Relations: Past, Present and Future*, Human Sciences Research Council Publication Series, No. 87, Cape Town: Tafelberg Publishers, 1987.

Katjavivi, Peter H. *A History of Resistance in Namibia*, Paris: UNESCO Press, 1988.

Kaufman, Burton I. *The Presidency of James Earl Carter*, Laurence, KS: University of Kansas Press, 1993.

Kegley C. W. and E. R. Wittkopf. *American Foreign Policy: Pattern and Process*, fourth edition, New York: St Martin's Press, 1991.

Kennedy, Paul. *The Rise and Fall of the Great Powers: Economic Change and Military Conflict from 1500 to 2000*. London: Fontana Press, 1989.

Kline, Benjamin. *Profit, Principle and Apartheid 1948–1994: The Conflict of Economic and Moral Issues in United States–South African Relations*, Studies in African Economic and Social Development, Vol. 10, Lewiston, Queenstown and Lampeter: Edwin Mellen Press, 1997.

Klinghoffer, Arthur J. 'The Soviet Union and Angola', in Robert H. Donaldson (ed.), *The Soviet Union in the Third World: Successes and Failures*, Boulder, CO: Westview Press and London: Croom Helm, 1981.

Kyvig, David E. (ed.) *Reagan and the World*, New York: Praeger, 1990. See especially Chapter 6, Robert I. Rotberg, 'The Reagan Era in Africa', pp. 119–137.

Lacour-Gayet, Robert (trans. Stephen Hardman). *A History of South Africa*, London: Cassell, 1977.

Leach, Graham. *South Africa: No Easy Path to Peace*, second edition, London: Methuen/Mandarin, 1989.

Lemon, Anthony. *Apartheid in Transition*, Aldershot: Gower, 1987.

Lugar, Richard. *Letters to the Next President*, New York: Simon and Schuster, 1988.

Manganyi, N. Chabanyi. 'The Washington–Pretoria Connection: Is There a Black Perspective?' in *The United States and South Africa: Continuity and Change*, Johannesburg: South African Institute of International Affairs, 1981.

Marquéz, Gabriel García. 'Operation Carlota' (1976) in David Deutschmann (ed.), *Angola and Namibia: Changing the History of Africa*, Melbourne: Ocean Press, 1989.

Melanson, Richard A. *American Foreign Policy Since the Vietnam War: The Search for Consensus from Nixon to Clinton*, New York and London: M. E. Sharpe, 1996.

Meredith, Martin. *In the Name of Apartheid: South Africa in the Post-War Period*, New York: Harper and Row, 1988.

McNamara, R. *In Retrospect: The Tragedy and Lessons of Vietnam*, New York: Times Books, 1995.

Mokoena, Kenneth (ed.) *South Africa and the United States: The Declassified History*, a National Security Archive documents reader, New York: The New Press, 1993.

Mutambinwa, James, *South Africa: The Sanctions Mission Report of the Eminent Church Persons Group*, Geneva: World Council of Churches and London: Zed Books, 1989.

Newsom, David D. *The Public Dimension of Foreign Policy*, Bloomington and Indianapolis: Indiana University Press 1996.

Nixon, Richard. *US Foreign Policy for the 1970s: The Emerging Structure of Peace*. A Report to the Congress by Richard Nixon, President of the United States, 2 February 1972.

Nogee, Joseph L. 'The Soviet Union in the Third World: Successes and Failures', in Robert H. Donaldson (ed.), *The Soviet Union in the Third World: Successes and Failures*, Boulder, CO: Westview Press and London: Croom Helm, 1981.

O'Callaghan, Marion. *Namibia: The Effects of Apartheid on Culture and Education*, Paris: UNESCO Press, 1977.

Ohlson, Thomas and Stephen John Stedman, with Robert Davies. *The New is Not Yet Born: Conflict Resolution in Southern Africa*, Washington, DC: The Brookings Institution, 1994.

Osgood, Robert E. *Retreat From Empire? The First Nixon Administration*, Baltimore and London: Johns Hopkins University Press, 1973.

Ovenden, K. and T. Cole. *Apartheid and International Finance: A Program for Change*. Victoria: Penguin 1989.

Papp, Daniel S. 'The Soviet Union and Southern Africa', in Robert H. Donaldson (ed.), *The Soviet Union in the Third World: Successes and Failures*, Boulder, CO: Westview Press and London: Croom Helm, 1981.

Paterson, T. G, J. G. Clifford and K. J. Hagan. *American Foreign Policy: A History Since 1900*, Lexington, MA and Toronto: D. C. Heath, 1991.

Peele, Gillian, Christopher J. Bailey and Bruce Cain. *Developments in American Politics*, Basingstoke and London: Macmillan, 1992.

Riley, Eileen. *Major Political Events in South Africa 1948–1990*, Oxford and New York: Facts on File, 1991.

Ripely, Randall B. and Grace A. Franklin. *Congress, the Bureaucracy and Public Policy*, fifth edition, Belmont, CA: Brooks/Cole, 1991.

Roskin, Michael. 'An American Metternich: Henry A. Kissinger and the Global Balance of Power', in F. J. Merli and T. A. Wilson (eds), *Makers of American Diplomacy from Theodore Roosevelt to Henry Kissinger*, New York: Scribner, 1974.

Rothchild, Donald and John Ravenhill. 'From Carter to Reagan: The Global Perspective on Africa Becomes Ascendant', in K. A. Oye, R. J. Lieber and D. Rothchild, *Eagle Defiant: United States Foreign Policy in the 1980s*, Boston, MA and Toronto: Little, Brown and Co., 1983.

Rothchild, Donald. 'US Policy Styles in Africa', in K. Oye, D. Rothchild and R. J. Lieber (eds), *Eagle Entangled: US Foreign Policy in a Complex World*, Boston, MA and Toronto: Little, Brown and Co., 1979.

Rothchild, Donald and John Ravenhill. 'Subordinating African Issues to Global Logic: Reagan Confronts Political Complexity', in K. A. Oye, R. J. Lieber and D. Rothchild (eds), *Eagle Resurgent? The Reagan Era in American Foreign Policy*, Boston, MA and Toronto: Little, Brown and Co., 1987.

Rubin, Barry. *Secrets of State: The State Department and the Struggle over United States Foreign Policy*, Oxford and New York: Oxford University Press, 1987.

Schraeder, Peter J. *United States Foreign Policy Toward Africa: Incrementalism, Crisis and Change*, Cambridge: Cambridge University Press, 1994.

Schrire, Robert. *Update: South Africa Time Running Out. Adapt or Die: The End of White Politics in South Africa*, London: Hurst, 1991.

Smith, Michael Joseph. *Realist Thought from Weber to Kissinger*, Baton Rouge and London: Louisiana State University Press, 1986.

Smith, Suzanna. *Front Line Africa: The Right to a Future*, Oxford: Oxfam, 1990.

Somerville, Keith. *Angola: Politics, Economics and Society*, London: Pinter and Boulder, CO: Lynne Rienner, 1986.

South African Embassy, London. *P. W. Botha: A Political Backgrounder*, London: South African Embassy, 1978.

South African Institute of International Affairs. *The United States and South Africa: Continuity and Change*, Johannesburg: South African Institute of International Affairs, 1981.

South African Institute of Race Relations. *Race Relations Survey*, 1985, 1986, 1987 and 1988/9 editions, Johannesburg: SAIRR.

Sparks, Alistair. *The Mind of South Africa: The Story of the Rise and Fall of Apartheid*, London: Mandarin, 1991.

Steward, Alexander. *The World, the West and Pretoria*, New York: David McKay, 1977.

SWAPO of Namibia Department of Information and Publicity. *To Be Born a Nation: The Liberation Struggle for Namibia*, London: Zed Books, 1981.

Taber, Michael (ed.). *Fidel Castro Speeches: Cuba's Internationalist Foreign Policy 1975–1980*, New York: Pathfinder Press, 1981.

Thomas, A. M. *The American Predicament: Apartheid and United States Foreign Policy*, Aldershot and Brookfield: Ashgate, 1997.

Thomas, Scott. *The Diplomacy of Liberation: The Foreign Relations of the ANC Since 1960*, London and New York: Tauris, 1996.

Thompson, Alex. *Incomplete Engagement: United States Foreign Policy towards the Republic of South Africa 1981–1988*, Aldershot and Brookfield: Avebury, 1996.

Thompson, Leonard. *A History of South Africa*. New Haven, CT and London: Yale University Press, 1990.

Thompson, Leonard and Andrew Prior. *South African Politics*, New Haven, CT and London: Yale University Press, 1982.

Vigne, Randolph. *A Dwelling Place of Our Own*, revised edition, London: International Defence and Aid Fund, 1975.

Walker, E. A. *South Africa – Oxford Pamphlets on World Affairs No. 39*, London and Oxford: Oxford University Press, 1941.

Bibliography

Williams, Basil. *Botha, Smuts and South Africa*, London: Hodder and Stoughton, 1946.

Wolpe, Harold. *Race, Class and the Apartheid State*, London: James Currey and Paris: UNESCO, 1985.

Worden, Nigel. *The Making of Modern South Africa: Conquest, Segregation and Apartheid*, Oxford and Cambridge, MA: Blackwell Publishers, 1994.

Wright, George. *The Destruction of a Nation: US Policy Toward Angola Since 1945*, London and Chicago: Pluto Press, 1997.

Journal & Newspaper Articles

America (Whole Issue) Vol. 153, No. 3 (3–10 August). Published by the Jesuits of the United States and Canada New York: America Press Inc.

Asante, S. K. B and W. W. Asombang. 'An Independent Namibia? The Future Facing SWAPO', *Third World Quarterly*, Vol. 11, No. 3 (July 1989), pp. 1–20.

Baldwin, David. 'The Power of Positive Sanctions', *World Politics*, Vol. 24, No. 1 (October 1971), pp. 19–38.

Barber, James. 'Review – *High Noon in Southern Africa: Making Peace in a Rough Neighborhood*, Chester Crocker', *International Affairs*, Vol. 70, No. 1 (1994), pp. 182–3.

Barber, Simon. 'Shadows on the Wall', *Optima*, Vol. 35, No. 2 (June 1987), pp. 68–75.

Barber, Simon. 'Creating Realities', *Optima*, Vol. 37, No. 2 (June 1989), pp. 50–7.

Bender, Gerald J. 'Angola, the Cubans and American Anxieties', *Foreign Policy*, No. 31 (Summer 1978), pp. 3–31.

Bender, Gerald J. 'Peacemaking in Southern Africa: the Luanda–Pretoria Tug-of-War', *Third World Quarterly*, Vol. 11, No. 1 (January 1989), pp. 15–30.

Bender, Gerald J. 'The Reagan Administration and Southern Africa', *Atlantic Quarterly*, Vol. 2, No. 3 (1984).

Arnold Bergstraesser Institute. 'The Namibian Peace Process: Implications and Lessons for the Future', *Review of International Conference at the Arnold Bergstraesser Institute and International Peace Academy Freiburg, Germany 1–4 July 1992*, Freiburg: Arnold Bergstraesser Institute, 1994.

Berridge, Geoff. 'Diplomacy and the Angola/Namibia Accords', *International Affairs*, Vol. 65, No. 3 (Summer 1989), pp. 463–79.

Bissell, Richard E. 'Aid to UNITA Means Peace', *Washington Post*, 8 November 1985, p. A23.

Bowen, William G. 'The Case Against Divestiture', *Princeton Alumni Weekly*, 22 May 1985.

Brittain, Victoria. 'Cuba and Southern Africa', *New Left Review*, No. 172 (November/ December 1988), pp. 117–24.

Bromley, Mark. 'Washington's Nuclear Bunker Busters', *Observer*, 28 July 2002.

'Fight Apartheid, but Don't Shut Up Shop', *Business Week*, 11 February 1985.

Christian Aid. 'Fuelling Poverty: Oil War and Corruption', text available at www.christianaid. org.uk/indepth, 25 May 2004.

Clough, Michael. 'Beyond Constructive Engagement', *Foreign Policy*, No. 61 (Winter 1985–6), pp. 3–24.

Coker, Christopher. 'Retreat into the Future: The United States, South Africa and Human Rights 1976–8', *Journal of Modern African Studies*, Vol. 18, No. 3 (1980), pp. 509–24.

Coker, Christopher. 'Collective Bargaining as an Internal Sanction: The Role of US Corporations in South Africa', *Journal of Modern African Studies*, Vol. 19, No. 4 (1981), pp. 647–65.

Crocker, Chester. 'South Africa: Strategy for Change', *Foreign Affairs*, Vol. 59, No. 2 (Winter 1980–1), pp. 323–51.

Crocker, Chester. 'Southern Africa: Eight Years Later', *Foreign Affairs*, Vol. 68, No. 4 (1989), pp.144–64.

Crocker, Chester and William H. Lewis. 'Missing Opportunities in Africa', *Foreign Policy*, No. 35 (Summer 1979), pp.142–61.

Crocker, Chester. 'Comment: Making Africa Safe for the Cubans', *Foreign Policy*, No. 31 (Summer 1978), p. 32.

Dale, Richard. 'Forces as an Instrument of South African Policy in Namibia', *Journal of Modern African Studies*, Vol. 18, No. 1 (1980), pp. 57–71.

Dale, Richard. 'Melding War and Politics in Namibia: South Africa's Counterinsurgency Campaign, 1966–1989', *Armed Forces and Society*, Vol. 20, No. 1 (Fall 1993), pp. 7–24.

De St Jorre, John. 'Africa: Crisis of Confidence', *Foreign Affairs*, Vol. 61 (1982), pp. 675–91.

Dominguez, J. I. 'Political and Military Limitations and Consequences of Cuban Policies in Africa', *Cuban Studies*, Vol. 10, No. 2 (July 1980) (Cuba in Africa Special Volume, Part Two), pp.1–35.

Elazar, Daniel J. 'Ideas for Pretoria', *Jerusalem Post*, 16 August 1985.

Faundez, Julio. 'Namibia: the Relevance of International Law', *Third World Quarterly*, Vol. 8, No. 2 (April 1986), pp. 540–58.

Flint, Julie. 'Britain Backs Ugly War for Oil', *Observer*, 16 April 2000.

Flint, Julie. 'British Firms Fan Flames of War', *Observer*, 11 March 2001.

Freeman, Charles. 'The Angola/Namibia Accords', *Foreign Affairs*, Vol. 68, No. 3, pp. 126–41.

Graebner, N. 'Cold War Origins and the Continuing Debate: A Review of the Recent Literature', *Journal of Conflict Resolution*, 13 (1969), pp. 123–32.

Green, Duncan and Claire Melamed. 'A Human Development Approach to Globalization', Christian Aid and CAFOD at www.christianaid.org.uk/indepth, June 2004.

Greenberg, Stanley B. 'Economic Growth and Political Change: The South African Case', *Journal of Modern African Studies*, Vol. 19, No. 4 (1981) pp. 667–704.

Hackland, B., Anne Murray-Hudson and Brian Wood. 'Behind the Diplomacy: Namibia 1983–5', *Third World Quarterly*, Vol. 8, No. 1 (January 1986), pp. 51–77.

Holladay, J. Douglas. 'Using Our Leverage', *Africa Report*, March–April 1986, pp. 30–3.

Ingham, Graham. 'Review of *The United States and South Africa, 1968-1985: Constructive Engagement and Its Critics*', *International Affairs*, Vol. 64, No. 2 (1986), pp. 717–18.

Jenkins, Simon. 'Looking Back on 1986', *Optima*, Vol. 34, No. 4 (December 1986), pp. 170–7.

Johnson, Loch. 'Legislative Reform of Intelligence Policy', *Polity* 17 (1985), pp. 549–73.

Kirkpatrick, Jeanne. 'Support the Contras – in Angola', *Washington Post*, 27 October 1985, p. B7.

Leys, Colin and John S. Saul. 'Liberation Without Democracy? The SWAPO Crisis of 1976', *Journal of Modern African Studies*, Vol. 20, No. 1 (March 1994), pp. 123–47.

MacAskill, Ewen. 'Analysis: Tough Love in Tripoli', *Guardian*, 11 February 2004.

MacAskill, Ewen. 'EU Ministers Strike Iran Deal', *Guardian*, 22 October 2003.

Macebuh, Stanley. 'Misreading Opportunities in Africa', *Foreign Policy*, No. 35 (Summer 1979), pp. 162–9.

Makoni, Simba. 'SADCC's New Strategy', *Africa Report*, May–June 1987, pp. 30–3.

McLean, Gareth. 'Secret Society', *Guardian*, 3 December 2003.

Milner, Mark. 'Banking on Cooperation', *Guardian*, 28 April 2003.

Nicol, Davidson. 'United States Foreign Policy in Southern Africa: Third World Perspectives', *Journal of Modern African Studies*, Vol. 24, No. 4 (1983), pp. 587–603.

Novicki, Margaret. 'Southern Africa: Behind the Scenes at the UN', *Africa Report*, Vol. 32, No. 3 (1987).

Olivier, Gerrit. 'Recent Developments in South African Foreign Policy', *Optima*, Vol. 36, No. 4 (December 1988), pp. 196–203.

Potholm, Christian P. 'After Many a Summer? The Possibilities of Political Change in South Africa', review article, *World Politics*, Vol. 24, No. 4 (July 1972), pp. 613–38.

Pridham, Helen. 'Now It's Easy to Be Green', *Observer*, 20 May 2001.

Pycroft, C. 'Review – *High Noon in Southern Africa: Making Peace in a Rough Neighborhood*, Chester Crocker', *Journal of Modern African Studies*, Vol. 32, No. 1 (1994), pp. 169–71.

Savimbi, Jonas. 'The War Against Soviet Colonialism: The Strategy and Tactics of Anti-Communist Resistance', *Policy Review*, No. 35 (Winter 1986), pp. 76–82.

Schrire, Robert. 'Russian Policy in Sub-Saharan Africa', *Optima*, Vol. 31, No. 1 (October 1982), pp. 2–17.

Sidaway, James D. and David Simon. 'Geopolitical Transition and State Formation: The Changing Political Geographies of Angola, Mozambique and Namibia', *Journal of Southern African Studies*, Vol. 19, No. 1 (March 1993), pp. 6–28.

Slavin, Terry. 'New Rules of Engagement', *Observer*, 1 September 2002.

Stockwell, John. 'The Angolans' Perennial Loser Without A Cause', *New York Times*, 22 November 1979.

The Citizen (Johannesburg). February 1985.

The Economist. 'After Sullivan', 13 June 1987, p. 71–2.

The Economist. 'Fighting Apartheid', 30 March 1985, p. 9.

The Economist. 'America and South Africa', 30 March 1985, pp. 17–34.

The Economist. 'Whatever Happened to Constructive Engagement?' 26 July 1986, pp. 29–30.

The Star (Johannesburg). February 1986.

Thompson, Alex. 'Incomplete Engagement: Reagan's South Africa Policy Revisited', *Journal of Modern African Studies*, Vol. 33, No. 1 (March 1995), pp. 83–101.

Vale, Peter and Stanford J. Ungar. 'South Africa: Why Constructive Engagement Failed', *Foreign Affairs*, Vol. 64, No. 2 (1986), pp. 234–58.

Vale, Peter. 'Crocker's Choice: Constructive Engagement and South Africa's People', review article, *South African Journal of International Affairs*, Vol. 1, No. 1 (1995), pp. 100–6.

Van Heerden, D. 'The New Nats', *Frontline*, March 1986, pp. 35–6.

Weissman, Stephen. 'Dateline South Africa: The Opposition Speaks', *Foreign Policy*, No. 58 (Spring 1985), pp. 151–70.

Windrich, Elaine. 'Review – *High Noon in Southern Africa: Making Peace in a Rough Neighborhood*, Chester Crocker', *Africa*, Vol. 65, No. 1 (1995), pp. 134–7.

Wood, Brian. 'Preventing the Vacuum: Determinants of the Namibia Settlement', *Journal of Southern African Studies*, Vol. 17, No. 4 (December 1991), pp. 742–69.

Websites

www.fco.gov.uk
www.dti.gov.uk
www.state.gov
www.bbc.co.uk
www.britishembassy.gov.uk/sudan
www.christianaid.org.uk
www.trade.uktradeinvest.gov.uk

Index

Index

Index